Managing the Margins

Managing the Margins

Gender, Citizenship, and the International Regulation of Precarious Employment

Leah F. Vosko

OXFORD

UNIVERSITY PRESS

Great Clarendon Street, Oxford OX2 6DP

Oxford University Press is a department of the University of Oxford.
It furthers the University's objective of excellence in research, scholarship,
and education by publishing worldwide in

Oxford New York

Auckland Cape Town Dar es Salaam Hong Kong Karachi
Kuala Lumpur Madrid Melbourne Mexico City Nairobi
New Delhi Shanghai Taipei Toronto

With offices in

Argentina Austria Brazil Chile Czech Republic France Greece
Guatemala Hungary Italy Japan Poland Portugal Singapore
South Korea Switzerland Thailand Turkey Ukraine Vietnam

Oxford is a registered trade mark of Oxford University Press
in the UK and in certain other countries

Published in the United States
by Oxford University Press Inc., New York

© Leah F. Vosko 2010

British Library Cataloguing in Publication Data

Data available

Library of Congress Cataloging in Publication Data

Data available

Typeset by SPI Publisher Services, Pondicherry, India
Printed in Great Britain
on acid-free paper by
MPG Books Group, Bodmin and King's Lynn

ISBN 978-0-19-957481-0
ISBN 978-0-19-957509-1 (pbk.)

3 5 7 9 10 8 6 4 2 1

For Gerald

Acknowledgements

In researching and writing this book, I benefited from the intellectual engagement of many colleagues, students, policy actors, and community activists, whose interest in this work has been sustaining.

My first debt is to the organizations providing financial support—the Canada Research Chairs Program, the Social Sciences and Humanities Research Council of Canada (standard grant no. 410–2006–2361), the Canadian Foundation for Innovation, and the Ontario Premier's Research Excellence Award program. From my home institution, York University, I am grateful to the Office of the Vice-President Research and Innovation, the Faculty of Graduate Studies, and the Atkinson Faculty for providing me with supports and precious time for research and writing.

As I wrote *Managing the Margins*, I spent time at a number of dynamic institutions. At Rutgers University (1998–9), I came to recognize the importance of gaining a grasp of the history of protective labour legislation for a study of this kind. Since then, my knowledge has been enhanced by interactions with historians Dorothy Sue Cobble and Karen Balcom and from the helpful commentary of Alice Kessler-Harris, who read a segment of the book at an important moment.

At McMaster University (1999–2001), I benefited from collaborations with the research group on Workers and Social Cohesion (Robert O'Brien, Roy Adams, Karen Bird, Belinda Leach, Wayne Lewchuk, Mark Thomas, Don Wells, and Charlotte Yates) and exchanges with Donna Baines, Robert Storey, and Robert Wilton.

Before, during, and after I took up a Visiting Research Fellowship at the Royal Melbourne Institute of Technology in the summer of 2006, Iain Campbell and Michael Rawling provided terrific feedback on Chapters 4 and 6 respectively. Both scholars also opened their networks to me, leading to connections with many fine Australian scholars whose insights further enriched this work—Marian Baird, Sarah Charlesworth, Anne Junor, Jill Murray, Anthony O'Donnell, Rosemary Owens, Barbara Pocock, Michael Quinlan, Amanda Tattersall, and Iain Watson.

Acknowledgements

Writing this book required several extended stays in Geneva, where I conducted fieldwork at the ILO, spent days in its library, and time with ILO constituents and office staff. From the ILO, I am indebted, in particular, to Enrique Marin for sharing his insights with me during long stints observing negotiations and to Anne Trebilcock for making space for me institutionally.

I completed the first full draft of *Managing the Margins* during a sabbatical at the University of Oxford (2006–7), where I was hosted by the Institute of Gender Studies, Queen Elizabeth House, and welcomed institutionally by Maria Jaschok and Barbara Harris-White. In Oxford, I was very fortunate to have two wonderful colleagues—Linda McDowell and Sue Ledwith—close at hand and eager to discuss mutual research interests. While in Britain, I also connected with other scholars from whom I received helpful feedback, particularly Colin Crouch, who read several chapters of the manuscript, as well as Neil Coe, Collette Fagan, Anne McBride, Jacqueline O'Reilly, Jill Rubery, and Kevin Ward, who invited me to share research findings at the Universities of Sussex and Manchester.

Colleagues in Canada in the academic and community sectors have also been tremendously supportive. The encouragement and feedback I received from Barbara Cameron and Joan Sangster on critical components of the manuscript was invaluable, as were the suggestions of Emily Andrew, Linda Briskin, Joseph Carens, Engin Isin, and Miriam Smith, who helped me sort out where and how to place the book. And then there are the many colleagues who consistently reminded me that this work mattered: Pat Armstrong, Hugh Armstrong, Isabella Bakker, Kate Bezanson, Wallace Clement, Deborah Clipperton, Marjorie Cohen, Tania Das Gupta, Christina Gabriel, Mary Gellatly, Wenona Giles, Marnina Gonick, Gloria Kim, Fuyuki Kurasawa, Deena Ladd, Brian Langille, Meg Luxton, Martha MacDonald, Rianne Mahon, Joanne Magee, Stacey Mayhall, Kiran Mirchandani, Ann Porter, Laurell Ritchie, Dagmar Soennecken, Neil Smith, Lynn Spink, Jim Stanford, Sandra Whitworth, Joanne Wright, and Nancy Zukewich.

As I completed the manuscript, I had the honour of overseeing a talented team of researchers in a Community-University Research Alliance on Precarious Employment in Canada. I am grateful to all alliance members for improving my understanding of the social, statistical, political, legal, and economic dimensions of precarious employment. However, I owe a particular debt to three wonderful colleagues—Cynthia Cranford, Judy Fudge, and Eric Tucker. Discussions of the legal concept of employment and alternatives for limiting precariousness among self-employed workers in Chapter 6 build respectively on a project conducted jointly with Fudge and Tucker, funded by the Law Commission of Canada, resulting initially in our report, *The Legal Concept of Employment: Marginalizing Workers* (2002), and the book *Self-Employed Workers Organize: Law, Policy, and Unions* (2005), co-authored with these colleagues and Cranford.

Since 2001, working with skilled researchers and librarians in overseeing the Gender and Work Database (GWD)-Comparative Perspectives Database (CPD) project has also been a highlight. This project helped me imagine creative approaches to comparing workers' experience of labour market insecurity across contexts. Special thanks are due to its York-based steering committee—its two successive project managers, Krista Scott-Dixon and Lisa Clark, data librarian, Walter Giesbrecht, and government documents librarian, Amanda Wakaruk.

I also gratefully acknowledge the European Commission, Eurostat, for granting me permission to use the EU Labour Force Survey 1983–2006 for the research project 'Comparative Perspectives on Precarious Employment: Developing Common Understandings across Space, Scale and Social Location', involving the development of a portrait of precarious employment as it is manifest in EU countries, using the resources of, and tables created for, the GWD-CPD. The research results and conclusions drawn from these data as presented in this book and the GWD-CPD are my responsibility rather than that of the Eurostat. For the use of unit record data from the Household, Income and Labour Dynamics in Australia (HILDA) Survey, I am similarly appreciative of the HILDA Project, initiated and funded by the Australian Government Department of Families, Housing, Community Services and Indigenous Affairs (FaHCSIA) and managed by the Melbourne Institute of Applied Economic and Social Research (MIAESR). The findings and views reported in the book, however, are those of the author and should not be attributed to either FaHCSIA or the MIAESR.

My sincere gratitude goes to the workers and employers, representatives of national, supranational, and international unions and union confederations and employers' associations and confederations, as well as policy-makers with whom I conducted the interviews listed in Appendix C. These individuals gave generously of their time, and their insights were critical in developing the analysis. I also thank the Canadian government for permitting me to sit as an observer with its delegation to the International Labour Conference during its 85th, 90th, 91st, and 94th sessions.

The graduate students from whom I have learned over the years have been a source of inspiration. I thank Susan Braedley, Jeff Butler, John Grundy, Heather Krause, Genevieve Le Baron, Beth O'Connor, and

Acknowledgements

especially Sandra Ignagni and Kim McIntyre, who participated in this project by providing vital research assistance.

During the time in which I completed this book, I had the privilege of working with several outstanding post-doctoral fellows. These individuals brought me into their intellectual worlds at this vital stage of their careers and their ongoing engagement is a gift: Enda Brophy, Cynthia Cranford, Deborah Cowen, Sylvia Fuller, Jacqueline Krikorian, Deepa Rajkumar, Justyna Sempruch, and Bonnie Slade.

In Anastasia Mandziuk, and her predecessor Adinne Schwartz, I had the pleasure of working with two outstanding research administrators. At a time when the manuscript was far too long and detailed for any press to accept, Jane Springer's patient and incisive editorial assistance helped me move *Managing the Margins* forward. After that, David Musson at Oxford University Press deftly guided the manuscript through the review process—I am grateful to David for his dedication to the project, to the three anonymous reviewers for their helpful comments on the penultimate draft, and to the staff at the Press, particularly Abigail Coulson, Matthew Derbyshire, Emma Lambert, and Virginia Williams for seeing the book to completion. I am indebted as well to Susana Reisman for allowing her magnificent photographic study to appear on the cover.

An earlier version of a portion of Chapter 4 appeared as 'Precarious Part-Time Work in Australia and in Transnational Labor Regulation: The Gendered Limits of SER-Centrism' in *Labour and Industry* 17, 3 (April 2007): 99–125. I also first developed parts of the analysis for Chapter 5 in 'Temporary Work in Transnational Labour Regulation: SER-Centrism and the Risk of Exacerbating Gendered Precariousness', *Social Indicators Research* 88, 1 (August 2008): 131–45 and 'Less than Adequate: Regulating Temporary Agency Work in the EU in the Face of an Internal Market in Services', *Cambridge Journal of Regions, Economy, and Society* (April 2009): 1–17.

When I count my blessings, my family (especially my mother, the transatlantic Vosko-Marriott cheering team, and the Kernerman family) and friends come to mind first—they never failed to support me as I wrote this book.

My partner in life, Gerald Kernerman, is my best friend and also my greatest critic. Gerald carefully read and discussed the manuscript with me, lovingly cheered me on at each and every stage, and never let me lose faith in my ability to finish it. I dedicate the book to him.

L.F.V.
May 2009

Contents

Contents

Contents

Contents

List of Figures

List of Tables

List of Abbreviations

AIRC	Australian Industrial Relations Commission
ALP	Australian Labor Party
CEDAW	Convention on the Elimination of All Forms of Discrimination Against Women
CEU	Council of the European Union
CIETT	International Confederation of Private Employment Agencies
EC	European Commission
ECJ	European Court of Justice
EES	European Employment Strategy
EP	European Parliament
ETUC	European Trade Union Confederation
EUROCIETT	European Confederation of Private Employment Agencies
IALL	International Association of Labour Legislation
ILO	International Labour Organization
IMEC	Industrialized Market Economy Countries
NSWIRC	New South Wales Industrial Relations Commission
OECD	Organisation for Economic Cooperation and Development
OMC	Open Method of Coordination
PIACT	International Programme for the Improvement of Working Conditions and the Environment
SAIRC	South Australian Industrial Relations Commission
SER	Standard Employment Relationship
UNICE	Union of Industrial and Employers' Confederations of Europe
WRA	Workplace Relations Act

Introduction

This book seeks to understand the precarious margins of late-capitalist labour markets by analysing the interplay of employment norms, gender relations, and citizenship boundaries.

My point of departure is the prevailing view that the full-time continuous job is being eclipsed by part-time and temporary paid employment and self-employment. Is such a shift taking place? If so, what are its precise characteristics and what are its implications for the nature and prevalence of precarious employment and those struggling against it?

In these pages, I approach these questions through a broad historical compass, examining the construction, consolidation, and contraction of the 'standard employment relationship' (SER) defined by a full-time continuous employment relationship, where the worker has one employer, works on the employer's premises under direct supervision, and has access to comprehensive benefits and entitlements. The SER was never universal, of course. Even at its peak, it was not accessible to all workers. Nor was it ever meant to be. Indeed, the SER cannot be understood apart from its exclusions. It rests on them. For this reason, I analyse the historical and contemporary management of the SER *at its margins*.

This inquiry takes as its focus the contested emergence at multiple scales (i.e. within, amongst, and across different nation states) of regulations focusing on 'non-standard' forms of employment (e.g. part-time work, fixed-term work, temporary agency work, homework, and self-employed or 'economically dependent' work). Despite their considerable variation across contexts, implicit in these regulations is the assumption that these forms of employment are more likely to be precarious because they deviate from the SER, and thus to require intervention. The difficulty is that while there is truth in this assumption, it can also lead us astray because it frames the SER itself—or close proximity to it—as the logical solution. As I shall argue, the resulting regulatory frameworks do little more than *manage* the precarious margins of late-capitalist labour markets. The task of their elimination remains.

Precarious Employment

References to 'precarious employment', or related terms such as 'contingent work' and 'atypical employment', are increasingly common in popular and scholarly discourse. Such terms are often used interchangeably and so a more precise definition is in order. I define precarious employment as work for remuneration characterized by uncertainty, low income, and limited social benefits and statutory entitlements. Precarious employment is shaped by the relationship between *employment status* (i.e. self- or paid employment), *form of employment* (e.g. temporary or permanent, part-time or full-time), and *dimensions of labour market insecurity*, as well as *social context* (e.g. occupation, industry, and geography) and *social location* (or the interaction between social relations, such as gender, and legal and political categories, such as citizenship).

The notion of dimensions of labour market insecurity integral to this conception builds on the formative interventions of Rodgers (1989) who identifies four dimensions applicable to paid workers,[1] each of which I expand upon while also incorporating the situation of self-employed workers (see also Vosko 2006a). The result is a modified set of dimensions including: *degree of certainty of continuing employment*, referring not only to whether a job is permanent or temporary but to job tenure in multiple jobs and work relationships involving multiple parties and/or work outside an employment relationship; *degree of regulatory effectiveness*, concerning not only the existence of formal protections but their design, application, and enforcement (see also Bernstein et al. 2006); *control over the labour process* (i.e. working conditions, wages, and work intensity), encompassing both union membership and/or coverage under a collective agreement and equivalent mechanisms for self-employed workers; and, the *adequacy of the income package*, covering not only workers' income from employment but also government transfers (direct and indirect), and statutory and employer-sponsored benefits.

To return to the vexed relationship between precarious and non-standard employment, even as these two terms are *not* synonymous, there is clearly a relationship between them: part-time employment rarely provides workers with income supports sufficient to maintain themselves and dependants;

temporary employment is, by definition, uncertain; and a central characteristic of most self-employment is the absence of labour protections. This connection is, however, far from straightforward. Some non-standard employment is relatively secure and some full-time permanent employment is precarious. Precariousness can cut across all kinds of work for remuneration. When we conflate precarious employment and non-standard employment we risk obscuring and reinforcing the very problems that need to be addressed.

Contemporary regulatory responses to precarious employment are prone to making this very mistake. They 'see' the problem of precarious employment in 'non-standard' (in deviation from the SER), which leads them to seek solutions that minimize the deviations. Even as full-time permanent employment is declining in significance and as more work for remuneration falls outside this pattern, most contemporary approaches to dealing with precarious employment continue to take the SER as a guide. In this inquiry, I label such approaches 'SER-centric' and I illustrate how they leave intact the precarious margins of the labour market.

An Integrated Analysis

In the tradition of feminist political economy, this book pursues an integrated analysis of precarious employment that reaches beyond familiar questions about the employment levels of women and immigrant workers (as important as such questions remain) to explore the relationship between production for the market and social reproduction. The resulting framework employs three conceptual lenses—the normative model of employment, the gender contract, and citizenship boundaries—as windows into the dynamics of precarious employment in late-capitalist labour markets.

The Normative Model of Employment

The normative model of employment reflects the interplay between social customs and conventions and governance mechanisms that link work organization and the labour supply (Deakin 2002: 179). The SER[2] became normative in industrialized capitalist countries in the post-World War II era, with the rise and consolidation of Fordism, the international state system, and the Keynesian welfare state.[3] It described and constructed a particular labour market reality and served as a model around which policies and practices were based, especially in high income countries.

The SER was at first extended primarily to male blue-collar workers and subsequently to white-collar workers. It engendered and sustained social norms and regulatory mechanisms organized around employee status, full-time hours, permanency, and the performance of work at the employer's worksite. Rather than engaging in day labour or working on a project basis, for the first time a significant subset of workers received a wage accounting for periods of rest, leisure, and unpaid work for times in which they were not engaged directly in work for remuneration (Harvey 1999; Clarke 2000; Bosch 2004). Instead of working unpredictable or indeterminate hours, a regular working day and a working week were established. Furthermore, protections against unfair dismissal made ad hoc personnel decisions expensive for firms, leading them to plan how to deploy their workforces more carefully (Bosch 2004: 620). As Marsden (2004) illustrates, firms also used this constellation of rules to contain conflict and limit arbitrary decision-making; the SER enabled employers to secure cooperation and surplus product (see also Nolan 1983: 301–3). In turn, workers in employment situations characterized by these core features could expect 'a degree of durability and regularity in employment relationships' (Rodgers 1989: 1), protection from the ills of unemployment, and a social wage or a bundle of social benefits and entitlements beyond earnings enabling them to reproduce themselves and support their households.

At its height in the late 1960s and early 1970s, when 'advanced Fordism'—characterized by bounded national labour markets, protected markets for products and services, and growth based on internal and external expansion and planned obsolescence (Teeple 1995: 18–19)—and the full slate of Keynesian welfare state policies were in place, the SER constituted an ideal type around which policy-makers crafted labour and social regulations. The social wage model integral to this norm assumed that statutory benefits and entitlements, as well as employer-sponsored extended benefits, are best distributed to workers, assumed to hold citizenship in the countries in which they are employed, and their dependants, assumed to reside within one dwelling, via a single earner. In this way, the SER shaped labour force and migration patterns as well as familial obligations, household forms, and firm-level strategies.

Alluding to the normative character of the SER, Bosch (2004: 618) distinguishes between its function and its form. This distinction is instructive, especially in probing the relationship between, on the one hand, the general logic of SER-centrism and, on the other hand, variations in the way the SER manifests itself. At its apogee, the SER functioned to provide access to training, regulatory protections and social benefits, decent wages, and a social wage sufficient to support a man and his family (see e.g. Rodgers 1989; Bütchtemann and Quack 1990; Fudge 1997; Vosko 2000). It did so on the basis of various historically contingent and socially mediated circumstances, chiefly the series of social, economic, and political compromises associated with the end of World War II and the balance of power between workers and employers coming in its trail, marked by sustained worker resistance to employer control (e.g. workers' struggles to reduce working hours) (see e.g. Nolan 1983; Deakin 1998; Fudge and Vosko 2001a, 2001b; Bosch 2004). In practice, the SER fulfilled such functions partly through a 'psychological contract' premised upon shared beliefs among employers and employees about the nature of the employment relationship and mutual obligation (Rousseau 1995; see also Stone 2001) and risk-sharing, through which employers provided workers with long-term incentives, not only offering continuity and stability but deferred pay and career opportunities, in exchange for loyalty and productivity (Marsden 2004). These crucial ingredients in the SER's success were buoyed by a legal regime governing labour relations built on what Langille (2002) calls the 'platform' of the employment contract, through which workers had to establish that they were employees in order to benefit fully from labour protection (Fudge et al. 2002; Cranford et al. 2005; Vallée 2005).

The series of psychological, economic, legal, political, and social compromises underpinning the SER consolidated three of what I shall label its central 'pillars', related to working time, continuous employment, and employee status. They contributed to the restructuring of working time, which led 'measured time' (Thompson 1967) to become a means both of achieving subordination, or allowing employers to 'value what labour is worth' (Supiot 2001: 60), and of limiting employer control. Time-related boundaries around the relationship between the wage package and the labour required of workers on a daily, weekly, or yearly basis to secure a decent standard of living were a hallmark of this employment norm (Clarke 1991; Harvey 1999). So, too, were the checks on employer power, and the solidarities cultivated amongst workers produced by working-hours regulation. In addition to the pillar of standardized working time, these compromises also cultivated the pillars of employee status and continuous employment, which served together as a means of achieving subordination, largely through direct supervision at a given workplace (i.e. the employer's premises), and securing employer support for on-the-job training, job progression, and measures designed to sustain the health and vitality of the worker over a lifetime, such as holidays with pay and various social wage benefits. Indeed, the institutionalization of continuous employment relationships involving full-time hours limited the means by which employers could increase work intensity, especially over the long term.

Although the SER was normative across late capitalist labour markets, its pillars took on, and continue to have, different manifestations in different contexts.[4] For example, under many labour and social policies the standard for full-time weekly working hours is 40 in the United States but 35 in Canada and France. Similarly, in the United States permanency is often equated with 'ongoing' employment and associated with all wage and salary workers who expect their job to last, whereas it relates to unfair dismissal protections, often pegged to duration of employment, in many countries belonging to the EU (Polivka 1996; OECD 2002). In the former, in the absence of provisions by collective agreement, an employee may be dismissed at will, while employment protection legislation has been a mainstay of legal and policy regimes governing labour relations in the latter. Another notable distinction concerns the platform of the contract of employment: it encompasses 'dependent contractors' in certain jurisdictions in Canada, who typically have a limited number of clients or customers and are 'legally contractors but economically dependent' (Arthurs 1965: 89; see also Bendel 1982: 374–6; Clement 1986; MacPherson 1999; Fudge et al. 2002), and to a significant extent 'workers' in the United Kingdom, a group including the 'dependent self-employed' (e.g. freelance workers, sole traders, home workers, and casual workers) (Barnard 2004: 134; see also Freedland 1999; Davies and Freedland 2000a, 2000b; Davidov 2004). This platform is, however, narrower in the United States, where very few jurisdictions take the economic realities of these types of workers into consideration (Hyde 2000; Commission for Labour Cooperation 2003; Stone 2004), and in Australia, where many such workers are excluded from labour protection (see e.g. Clayton and Mitchell 1999).

The Gender Contract

The SER is best understood as intertwined historically with a particular gender contract. Distinct from concepts such as 'gender system' (Pfau-Effinger 1999) and 'gender order' (Connell 1987), which refer to broader patterns of relationships between men and women, the 'gender contract' is the normative and material basis around which sex/gender divisions of paid and unpaid labour operate in a given society (Rubery 1998b: 23; see also Fraser 1997). The concept aims to capture social, legal, and political norms surrounding the exchange between breadwinning and caregiving, protection and freedom, and public and private responsibilities.

O'Reilly and Spee (1998: 259) define the gender contract with reference to the notion of the social contract central to liberal democratic theory, linked to citizenship and conceived as the rights and obligations arising from the relationship between individuals and the state. Drawing from scholarship in industrial relations and comparative political economy on systems of employment regulation adopted after World War II (see e.g. Crouch 1993; Supiot et al. 1999b), they also helpfully link this concept to the notion of a compact or settlement between organized labour and capital. Furthermore, as such syntheses suggest, the gender contract concept owes a debt to feminist scholarship developing the idea of a sexual contract regulating men's and women's relations in marriage, paid work, and 'the family' (Pateman 1988) and notions of gendered social policy regimes used to analyse and distinguish between the treatment of women as paid workers, mothers, and wives, particularly Lewis's (1992) 'breadwinner regimes' (see also Ostner and Lewis 1995; Sainsbury 1996). It also grew out of literature on the sociology of work advancing a 'gendered employment systems' approach that links 'economic production (firms), social reproduction (households), and the regulation of industrial relations (the State)' (O'Reilly and Spee 1998: 263; see also O'Reilly 1994; Rubery and Fagan 1994; O'Reilly and Fagan, eds., 1998). The merits of this cluster of scholarship are its integrated character, the possibilities it offers for comparing different types of regulations and policies and their impact on its three spheres of concern, and its attentiveness to common economic pressures as well as the specific circumstances of different actors.

This last set of literature is a reference point for the conception of the gender contract employed in this book, which is also indebted to scholarship in feminist political economy long concerned with linking the 'supply' and 'demand' sides of the labour market (and specifically the organization of unpaid and paid work) and situating these processes historically (see especially Picchio 1981; Armstrong and Armstrong 1983; Humphries and Rubery 1984; Luxton 1990), and more recent interventions developing the concept of 'social reproduction' (see especially Picchio 1992). In feminist political economy scholarship, social reproduction refers broadly to daily and intergenerational reproduction or, according to Clarke (2000: 137), 'on the one hand, training and the development of skills and the continued well being of the worker for the labour process and, on the other hand, the general standard of living, education and health sustained in society'. For Picchio (1981: 194), social reproduction is 'central to labour market analysis' because it 'determines the position of individuals within the labour market, provides the basis for standards of living (and is thus the reference point for wage bargaining), [and] structures inter- and intra-class relations and the distribution of the product'. Institutions connected to social reproduction identified in contemporary accounts include the state, the education system, the public sector, the family/household, firms, and trade unions. In capitalist labour markets, social reproduction thus occurs at multiple levels, including at the interstate level via processes such as immigration (Sassen-Koob 1981; see also Arat-Koc 2006).

The gender contract that helped lay the basis for the SER had its origins in the late 19th century but reached its height in the post-World War II era. On the one hand, this contract assumed a male breadwinner pursuing his occupation and employment freely in the public sphere, with access to a full-time continuous employment relationship with a single employer and in receipt of a family wage. On the other hand, it assumed a female caregiver performing unpaid work necessary for social reproduction, prin-cipally in the context of a heterosexual household (Wittig 1980), possibly earning a 'secondary wage', and receiving supports such as social insurance via her spouse (on the related concept of the male breadwinner model, see Lewis 1992: 161). In a wide range of contexts, early variants of this gender contract contributed to the introduction of protective legislation at the end of the 19th and the beginning of the 20th centuries (e.g. the prohibi-tion of night work), although not without contestation.

The male breadwinner / female caregiver contract pivoted on a dichotomous conception of time in which 'time allocated to the employer in exchange for a wage' was defined as 'time spent at work', whereas 'time spent in the private sphere', including responsibilities attached to biological and social reproduc-tion, was supposedly 'free' (Everingham 2002: 338). One side of this dualism reflected the measured time of the male employment norm, while the other side mirrored limitless 'female time', grouping 'unpaid work' together with 'rest' and 'consumption' (Supiot 2001: 68; see also Kristeva 1981). This contract pivoted on a male lifecycle assuming ongoing labour force attachment throughout adulthood, typified by a permanent and ongoing employment relationship between a worker and an employer, lasting from the completion of formal education until retirement, and the absence of responsibility for activities integral to social reproduction. It assumed that the daily and inter-generational maintenance of workers takes place outside of the labour force—Esping-Andersen's (2002) 'masculine life-course' par excellence.

This last feature of the gender contract associated with the SER was made possible by the centrality of the institution of the family as the principal site of social reproduction characterized by unequal sex/ gender divisions of unpaid labour (Armstrong and Armstrong 1983; Luxton 1990; Picchio 1992; Elson 1995). It rested on the supposed natural role of women in producing and sustaining workers and on the notion that households, composed of a single male breadwinner and his dependants, are primary sites of relations of distribution or 'sequences of linked actions through which people share the necessities of survival' (Acker 1988: 478). The male breadwinner / female caregiver gender contract largely had the endorsement of working-class men, and their unions, which is not to suggest that this contract went totally without women's support. As Lewis (1986b: 17–18; see also McLaughlin 1995: 294) argues in describing the situation of many working-class and middle-class British women between 1850 and 1940, 'the sexual division of labour between male breadwinner and female household manager' was, in crucial ways, a 'shared ideal, largely because it made sense when the burden of women's household labour and frequent pregnancies was so large. This is not to deny that the male breadwinner family model discriminated against women as workers and privileged men within the home'. Such insights underscore the complex pragmatic issues influencing the politics and organization of exchanges surrounding breadwinning and caregiving between men and women, and their respective public and private responsibilities.

There were always national variations on the form of the male breadwinner / female caregiver contract and thus the gendered character of the SER. For example, part-time work has long been common among women in Australia (Probert 1997; Junor 1998; Pocock et al. 2004). Studies date employers' recruitment of women as temporary workers, especially in the clerical sector, back to the 1920s and 1930s in Canada, the United States, and Nordic countries such as Sweden (ILO 1966; Lowe 1980; Krasas-Rogers 2000; Vosko 2000). Furthermore, numerous scholars demonstrate that state policies cultivating dual breadwinning emerged earlier in some places, such as Denmark and Sweden, than in others, such as the United Kingdom (Ravn 1990; Lewis and Astrom 1992; Conaghan 2002). Historical differences in the nature of and the time allocated to unpaid work by women and men in different places also attest to variation in patterns of caregiving (Picchio 1998; Anxo 2002).

Citizenship Boundaries

An integrated analysis also requires making connections between employment norms, gender relations, and citizenship boundaries, which are too often overlooked. Indeed, looking through the lens of citizenship shows that in addition to being sustained by a particular gender contract, the emergence of the SER rested on a particular conception of membership in a community and the rights and obligations attached to this membership (see for example Lister 1997: 14; Stasiulis and Bakan 2005: 1–2). The community membership identified with modern citizenship is tied to the emergence of the nation-state system, stemming from the idea of national sovereignty defining populations that could make claims on the state in contrast to those, within and outside a given national territory, who could not (Hall and Held 1990: 176; Brodie 2002: 44; Stasiulis and Bakan 2005: 16).

The identification of citizenship with the nation state contributes to two broad emphases of contemporary scholarly investigation—one focused on inclusions and exclusions *within* a nation state and another on those *surrounding* nation states. Evincing a methodological nationalism (Wimmer and Schiller 2002), much scholarship in industrial relations and comparative public policy reflects the first emphasis. It takes the nation state as a given and examines citizenship's boundaries from within, largely without questioning the territorial limits of labour and employment regulation.[5] A significant body of scholarship on migration, in contrast, focuses on the exclusive character of national citizenship. Much of this literature reveals how, as Brubaker (1994: 230) puts it, 'the institution of citizenship, tying particular persons to particular states...serves as a powerful instrument of social closure'.[6] As an alternative to this either/or focus, in their book *Negotiating Citizenship: Migrant Women in Canada and the Global System*, Stasiulis and Bakan (2005: 16) describe citizenship as a type of nation-state membership combining universalistic and particularistic elements and assert that 'these criteria, which appear to be contradictory to one another, actually are complementary and interdependent in the citizenship matrix'. This conception guides this inquiry.

Premised on the congruence between membership and territory, the spatial container for the SER was the nation state. The rights and obligations associated with this conception of citizenship emanated from a common nationality, defined typically on the basis of birth, lineage, and/or residence (Sainsbury 2006: 231), and they were presumed to be universal among those holding membership. In T. H. Marshall's (1963: 87) influential formulation, 'citizenship is a status bestowed on those who are full members of a community. All who possess the status are equal with respect to the rights and duties with which the status is endowed'. As the SER ascended as a norm, nationality was central to community membership and its legitimacy; it was a primary basis for determining who was to be accorded formal civil, political, and social rights (Soysal 1994).

The system of nation states within which the SER took shape is frequently assumed but rarely acknowledged. Bringing it into sharper focus is key to identifying how adult male citizens came to be the subjects of this employment norm as well as to how certain groups of workers came to be excluded from it. Workers lacking citizenship in the nation states in which they worked were excluded from the SER through both immigration policies differentiating immigrants by their entry category and policies directed explicitly at migrant workers.[7] The former included policies advancing a hierarchy of rights tied to form of immigration and limiting migrant workers' access to features of the SER, such as permanency, while the latter included policies excluding migrant workers from certain employment rights and protections by design, application, or enforcement.

The nation-state-centred conception of citizenship associated with the SER was premised on the fusion of continuity of employment and territorial belonging. This meant providing for open-ended employment relationships for workers holding national citizenship, while simultaneously limiting non-nationals to temporary engagements. In this way, it reinforced the masculine biography associated with the male breadwinner / female caregiver gender contract presuming men's labour force attachment from the onset of adulthood until retirement. At the same time, the effective requirement that workers be permanent residents or citizens to gain access to the SER served as a mechanism for limiting migrant workers' access to this normative life course.

National citizenship enabled host states to perpetuate the distinct role of migrant labour as a component of the labour supply defined by the institutional differentiation of its processes of reproduction and maintenance and migrant workers' specific form of powerlessness. As Sassen-Koob (1981: 70) illustrates, in the case of migrant labour, intergenerational reproduction occurs in the sending country, facilitated by its institutions, and daily maintenance takes place only partly in the host country. Host states, and employers within them, externalize the costs of renewal in various ways (Buroway 1976; Sassen-Koob 1978). They have at their disposal the possibility of repatriation. Short-term 'savings' flowing from this possibility include limiting costs associated with unemployment, disability, or medical care, while long-term cost reductions relate to 'exempting the [host] economy from the need to build the kinds of infrastructure and service organizations that would be required by an equal number of national workers' (Sassen-Koob 1981: 71). Employers, in turn, use migrant labour to reduce labour costs directly though the provision of lower wages or indirectly through 'organizational flexibility' (e.g. the ease of hiring and firing).[8] Because of these features, 'the same conditions that make international migration one of the most important labour supply systems also promote the development of nation states as the basic political unit of world capitalism' (Sassen-Koob 1981: 65).

These distinct features of migrant work are historically contingent and nationally variable, depending, for example, upon relations between the sending and receiving states. However, the particular form of powerlessness experienced by migrant workers without prospects for attaining national citizenship—especially workers of colour from the global South for whom immigration policies in many high-income countries have actively discouraged permanent settlement—highlights the linkages between women's socially assigned role of reproducing the labour force on the basis of unpaid work under the male breadwinner / female caregiver gender contract associated with the SER and its nation-centred conception of citizenship.

Once inside host states, migrant workers lacking national citizenship gained only limited access to civil, political, and social citizenship rights (see e.g. Arat-Koc 1990; Soysal 1994; Lister 1997; Abu-Laban and Gabriel 2002).[9] The tendency for states to extend minimal rights to migrants has prompted scholars to speak of the 'negotiated citizenship' (Stasiulis and Bakan 2005) of migrant workers, 'partial citizenship' (Lister 1997), and the 'citizenship of alienage' (Bosniak 2002).

The gradual and selective extension of partial citizenship to migrants was interwoven with the experiences and struggles of women, people of colour, and Aboriginal people residing permanently *within* the societies hosting migrant workers. In many liberal democracies, partial citizenship acted together with a gender contract entailing bars or limits to women's labour force participation upon marriage or pregnancy,[10] limited or conditional rights to social wage and social security benefits attached to the SER, such as unemployment insurance,[11] and delayed or qualified access to civil and political rights as well as other social rights.[12] Partial citizenship was also racialized.[13] In these ways, the internal inclusions and exclusions of national citizenship and the male breadwinner / female caregiver contract were intertwined under the SER. The key link between them: their contributions to the daily and intergenerational reproduction of workers in the societies in which this employment norm arose.

Regulations at Different Scales

In exploring how the interaction of employment norms, gender relations, and citizenship boundaries shapes contemporary responses to precarious employment, this book analyses regulations operating at different scales from the late 1800s, when national and international measures prefiguring the construction of the SER took shape, to the present, with the construction of a package of international regulations directed at non-standard employment. It analyses the contested development of such regulations in parts of Western Europe as well as in Australia, Canada, and the United States and in what is often called the International Labour Code—or the compendium of labour standards of the International Labour Organization (ILO) plus those of other supra-state organizations (e.g. the European Union (EU) and the United Nations (UN)) (for a table of international labour regulations discussed, see Appendix A).

International labour regulations emerge from the interaction between laws, policies, and practices operating at multiple levels. They include conventions, recommendations, and resolutions devised and adopted by member states of the ILO in conjunction with representatives of workers and employers in tripartite forums and conventions adopted by the UN. Conventions are the 'hard laws' of the International Labour Code—once ratified by a nation state, they have the status of treaties—whereas recommendations, which often supplement conventions, and resolutions are 'soft laws' or non-binding instruments (on the distinction between hard and soft laws, see contributions to Kirton and Trebilcock 2004). International labour regulations also include supranational agreements, such as treaty-provisions emerging at the European level through the European Economic Community (EEC) Treaty and EU Directives, which may be formulated directly by the European Commission or brought to the European Commission by the social partners through framework agreements.[14] They are not stand-alone instruments, but rather are constructed through cumulative processes of exchange between interconnected sources of regulation. This conception builds on scholarship illustrating that ILO standards 'exist prior to and independent of national ratification' and that their role is to provide frameworks for adaptation in multiple contexts (Murray 2001b: 6; see also Hepple 1994; Sengenberger 1994, 2002; Swepston 1997; Cooney 1999; Murray 2001c; for historical insights, see Mahaim 1921; Thomas 1921; Alcock 1971). International labour regulations contribute to wider outcomes related to labour and social conditions and they can express social aspirations as well as advance fundamental human rights key to the labour field, which may or may not be addressed elsewhere (Sengenberger 2002: 93; see also Murray 2001d).

International labour regulations can take the form of procedural regulation, which include what Hepple (1997: 357; see also Mückenberger and Deakin 1989: 157) labels 'pro-collective' regulations, such as those promoting freedom of association and the right to organize and bargain collectively, as well as non-discrimination, and which contribute to establishing 'norms governing the process of bargaining' (Deakin and Wilkinson 1994: 291; see also Freedland 1995). They can also be promotional or advance standards shaping national or supranational macroeconomic goals (Murray 2001b: 12). Those devised to respond to precarious employment are, however, strongly substantive in so far as they promote the insertion of minimum protection into the employment relationship (Deakin and Wilkinson 1994: 290). These substantive regulations also seek harmonization, as opposed to the establishment of uniform rules for certain rights, which is the goal of pre-emptive legislation (Stone 1995: 999).[15] Harmonization, it should be emphasized, does not necessarily encourage a loss of regulatory diversity, either in the case of EU directives or in ILO conventions and recommendations.[16] Rather, it promotes conformity in results over the long term; the emphasis on harmonization of this sort in international labour regulations makes them an instructive entry point for investigating efforts to deal with precarious employment at multiple scales.

These international labour regulations are also a point of departure because examining their development helps place an 'integrated political economy' (Gill and Law 1988, p. xxiii) at the centre of the analysis. Processes shaping their design and implementation transcend conventional divides between state and non-state actors, as well as between domestic and international politics, since ILO and EU regulations are crafted by states and organizations of states in conjunction with unions and employers, and increasingly with the input of other segments of civil society, which also play central roles in the UN system. Although it is informed by scholarship analysing regulations of the ILO, the UN, and the EU in the context of international law and politics (see especially Charnowitz 1987, 1995; Langille 1997; Murray 2001c; and Alston 2005) and studies of the role of international organizations (e.g. the ILO) in the global political economy (see e.g. Cox 1973, 1977), this book is not a study of international labour regulations per se. Instead, it uses the contestation surrounding these (as well as national) regulations as a means for understanding the logic of SER-centrism.

International labour regulations adopted in response to precarious employment in the post-1990 period focus principally on part-time and temporary employment, and the employment relationship. This investigation explores the logic of such regulations, focusing on the ILO Convention on Part-Time Work (1994), the EU Directive on Fixed-Term Work (1999), the EU Directive on Temporary Agency Work (2008), and the ILO Recommendation on the Employment Relationship (2006). It does so partly through detailed examinations of approaches to regulating part-time and temporary paid employment where they are well-developed and self-employment, where the rise of paid employment waned in the post-1980 period and forms of work for remuneration falling outside the strictures of the employment relationship became more widespread.

A Multi-Method Approach

In pursuit of an integrated analysis, this book takes an interdisciplinary approach drawing from and making connections between the disciplines of political science, law, sociology, history, labour studies and industrial relations, women's/gender studies, and citizenship/migration studies. It also employs multiple methods, incorporating textual analysis of historical and contemporary documents, observation, interviews, and statistical analysis. Brief discussions of each of these methods follow and the appendices contain further elaboration as indicated.

The historical research involved examining developments prefiguring the adoption of the earliest international labour regulations, as well as early national and supranational labour regulations. To develop the international dimension, I conducted archival research at the ILO, where I examined texts dating to well before the organization's inception and its extensive collection of national and regional legislation and I gathered parallel documentation at the Commission of the EU. To chart historical developments in the national contexts of Australia, Canada, and the United States, as well as among the EU 15, I surveyed laws, legislation, regulations, and policies addressing precarious employment, as well as debates surrounding their enactment. My concern in examining these primary texts was to track regulatory developments at different scales contributing to the emergence and development of the SER as a normative model of employment.

To understand the contemporary motivations and strategies of international organizations, states, unions, and employers, between 1997 and

2006 I attended key sessions of the ILO's annual International Labour Conference, which takes place in Geneva for approximately three weeks each June. I did so as an academic observer (i.e. a non-participant) sitting with the Canadian government delegation to these meetings in daily tri-partite sessions and parallel government meetings of all member states and of the Industrialized Marked Economy Countries (IMEC) group of the ILO (for a list of sessions observed, see Appendix B).

To complement such observation, I conducted interviews with representatives of workers and employers engaged in the negotiation of ILO regulations and with ILO officials involved in drafting texts for debate and implementation, as well as with representatives of workers, employers, and EU parliamentarians who were central in formulating EU-level framework agreements and directives and officials of the European Commission involved in monitoring their transposition by member states and in developing new policy frameworks.

In studying the illustrative cases of part-time employment, temporary employment, and self-employment, I also interviewed workers and representatives of their organizations and other relevant actors. In Australia, for example, I interviewed workers and union leaders centrally involved in two key cases challenging the precarious character of much part-time employment—at a federal level, the Family Provisions Test Case, and in the state of New South Wales, the Secure Employment Test Case. In the EU, I interviewed representatives of union and employer confederations in the temporary agency sector at the supranational level (UNIEUROPA and EUROCIETT) and their national counterparts. Through such interviews, I attempted to uncover both strategies underlying different actors' positions, including intra-employer and intra-union divisions, on regulations under development and those already in effect, as well as to gain insight into the interpretations of specific aspects of in-progress and prevailing regulations and their effects (for a full list of interviews conducted, see Appendix C).

Finally, to chart forms and dimensions of precarious employment in the post-1980 period, I developed a statistical portrait, drawing on primary data collected by national and international agencies. Developing this portrait was challenging because approaches to conceptualization and measurement employed in national and international data sources reflect, and often reinforce, the tendency to conflate precarious and non-standard employment—that is, statistical categories tend to mirror social norms, making it difficult to measure the 'abnormal'. For example, the ways in which surveys are formulated often contribute to grouping a multiplicity of forms of employment into a single catchall (i.e. non-standard employment) or make it difficult for analysts to look in-depth at a given type of employment, such as part-time employment, to analyse part-time paid employment versus part-time self-employment or part-time temporary versus part-time permanent paid employment. Definitions of forms of employment also vary, according to different institutional, legal, political, and social arrangements, as do indicators that capture dimensions of labour market insecurity. To meet these challenges, the statistical portrait developed across Chapters 3 to 6 attempts to use indicators of forms of employment in a manner sensitive to context (e.g. it is attentive to institutional variation in the SER across late capitalist labour markets), as well as to gender relations and citizenship boundaries. In addition to providing a full list of data sources and explanatory notes for statistical tables and figures, Appendix D also includes extended commentaries on my approach to specific data issues.

The Book in Brief

In Chapters 1 and 2, I trace the history of the SER through an analysis of regulations emerging at different scales from the late 19th century to the contemporary period. Feminist scholarship on the SER has long documented its gendered character and, in particular, how this employment norm is sustained by norms of female caregiving. Close scrutiny of the roots of international labour regulations makes it possible to develop such insights further: Chapter 1 shows that the first successful efforts to forge minimum international humanitarian labour standards in the 19th century centred on women and children. They were pursued in the name of 'protecting the weak', and were made possible partly by the assumption that rights associated with citizenship should be geared to adult men. With the emergence of the International Labour Code, national governments, trade union federations, and employers' associations cultivated notions of women as 'the weaker sex' and 'mothers of the nation' through sex-specific regulations addressing maternity and night work, which reinforced norms of unpaid caregiving among women and, like the national regulations emerging around that time, bolstered the freedom of contract among newly enfranchised men. Only subsequently did they extend similar standards for labour protection to adult male citizens.

Having established the centrality of the evolving male breadwinner / female caregiver gender contract to its emergence, Chapter 2 charts the SER's construction and consolidation in international labour regulation in the interwar and post-World War II periods. This aspect of the analysis is organized according to the three central pillars of employee status (i.e. the bilateral employment relationship), standardized working time (normal daily, weekly, and annual hours), and continuous employment (permanency). It also highlights the significance of exclusions and qualified inclusions in the creation and persistence of this employment norm, demonstrating how regulations on such subjects as hours of work and unemployment relied upon and reinforced the male breadwinner / female caregiver contract by limiting their terms principally to wage-earners in industry and exempting 'special' classes of workers (e.g. casual workers and homeworkers and workers employed in family businesses). Notably, regulations adopted subsequently in response to a crumbling male breadwinner / female caregiver contract sought to strip the SER of its formal exclusions. With the chief exception of exclusions based on nationality, formal equality was pursued in many regulations adopted, starting in the 1950s, including those on equal remuneration and non-discrimination. However, by neglecting processes of social reproduction, such regulations could only begin to challenge an employment norm geared to adult male citizens.

Chapter 3 initiates the book's statistical portrait of contemporary employment trends in industrialized contexts. Addressing one of the questions raised at the outset, it illustrates the slow decline of the SER in the neoliberal era in a range of countries where it had reached ascendancy by the late 1970s. It reveals further that full-time permanent employment and non-standard employment remain gendered and shaped by citizenship status to the present. The chapter also lays the foundation for the book's discussion of post-1990 international labour regulations directed at non-standard employment.

Chapters 4, 5, and 6 analyse in greater detail the SER-centric logic and effects of these international labour regulations alongside concurrent approaches within and among nation states. International labour regulations developed to respond to precarious employment focus on bringing those forms falling just outside the SER within its range. They address divergence from the SER on the basis, among other things, of working time, continuity, and employment status. The chapters comprising the body of this book are organized accordingly—each explores the interface between the normative model of employment, the gender contract, and citizenship boundaries and a particular instrument or grouping of instruments of international labour regulation, and each uses a detailed illustration to develop the analysis.

Chapter 4 evaluates regulatory responses to challenges to the temporal boundaries of the SER and the precariousness with which they are associated, beginning with the ILO Convention on Part-Time Work (1994) and its framework for fostering equal treatment on the basis of form of employment. To analyse the logic of this regulation, the chapter considers the nature and significance of part-time employment in Australia, where it is widespread and also deeply gendered. However, it is the composition of part-time employment that most distinguishes Australia from other industrialized countries. In Australia, a relatively small proportion of part-time workers are permanent employees. Instead, many part-time workers are either employed on a casual and/or a fixed-term basis or are self-employed. Even among all part-time employees, most are casual, a disproportionate percentage of whom are women. Despite sustained attempts on the part of workers and their unions to curtail the spread of part-time casual employment, a sizeable subset of part-time employment in Australia is defined not only by shorter than 'normal' working hours but by a lack of certainty indicated typically by an indefinite contract of employment. Compounding this uncertainty, casual workers lack access to paid vacation, paid sick leave, paid public holidays, notice of termination, and redundancy pay. SER-centric approaches to responding to precariousness amongst part-time workers chiefly address the situation of permanent part-time wage-earners—they typically exclude the self-employed and those engaged on temporary or casual bases. The Australian case illustrates the implications of these exclusions and the logic that they reflect.

Chapter 5 considers responses to the erosion of continuity of employment, denoted by an open-ended employment relationship between a worker and an employer where the worker works on the employer's premises under direct supervision, cultivating certainty in employment. It considers the EU Directive on Fixed-Term Work (1999), which subscribes to equal treatment, the EU Directive on Temporary Agency Work (2008), which qualifies equal treatment, as well as efforts to regulate both types of temporary employment in the EU 15. The analysis shows that while SER-centric approaches extend some protections and benefits to fixed-term workers, lesser protections apply to temporary agency workers. In the EU 15, both fixed-term and temporary agency workers confront uncertainty and limited access to social benefits and statutory entitlements due to the tenure of employment. Temporary agency work is, however, especially likely to be precarious. Temporary agency workers encounter difficulties securing protections requiring the identification of a single employer, such as wage protections in the case of insolvency or default on the part of the agency, and they have lower average hourly wages than workers in other forms of employment. These insecurities are magnified among workers lacking national citizenship in the countries in which they are employed. They are also amplified among women workers because of their partial citizenships within national labour markets and the still prevalent assumptions that they do not require wages sufficient to cover themselves and dependants. Examining the case of temporary agency work in the EU 15 in relation to fixed-term work is thus instructive in understanding the tiered effects of SER-centrism.

Chapter 6 focuses on legislative responses to ambiguity and instability in the employment relationship at the crux of the SER. The international labour regulation of principal interest is the ILO Recommendation on the Employment Relationship (2006), which denotes the limit of SER-centrism by shifting the emphasis from equal treatment to effective protection. The empirical focus is on several industrialized market economy countries belonging to the ILO experiencing a rise of self-employment resembling paid employment and exhibiting dimensions of labour market insecurity, starting in the late 20th century. The chapter places an accent on two distinct approaches to regulating self-employment. One approach is exemplified by change at the federal level in Australia, where in the 1990s and early 2000s the government withdrew protections designed for workers in precarious employment situations falling outside the employment relationship. The other approach is typified by developments in several EU member states as well as at the EU level, where over the same period, new policies supporting entrepreneurship aimed to respond to the insecurities confronting many self-employed people. Both approaches to self-employment attempt, at a minimum, to limit so-called disguised employment relationships. Yet even the most extensive policy proposals advanced at the EU level in the early 2000s, which called for extending some supports to a subset of the self-employed known as 'economically dependent workers', drew the line. They refused to extend labour protection to those engaged in forms of work for remuneration falling outside the strictures of the employment relationship, including workers most in need of it.

Taken together, Chapters 4 to 6 demonstrate that approaches to regulation taking the SER as a baseline mainly extend labour protection to forms of employment falling just beyond its range. Those employment situations deviating sharply from the SER are least likely to be improved.

Given this verdict, Chapter 7 assesses three alternative approaches to regulation: the 'tiered' SER examined in Chapters 4 to 6; the 'flexible SER' (Bosch 2004); and 'beyond employment' (Supiot et al. 1999b; and Supiot 2001). Among these approaches, beyond employment holds most promise. As an alternative basis for labour and social protection, it attempts to de-link employment status and form of employment from dimensions of labour market insecurity, while simultaneously addressing the relationship between employment norms and gender relations and extending citizenship's boundaries. Even this approach has limitations, however. In response to the menu of available possibilities, the book concludes by calling for an alternative imaginary building towards transformative visions of caregiving and community membership.

Notes

1. Rodgers's (1989: 3–5) four dimensions are: degree of certainty of continuing paid employment related to whether a job is permanent or temporary; degree of regulatory protection or the worker's level of access to protection through union representation or the law; control over the labour process linked to the presence or absence of a trade union; and income level (see also Bettio and Villa 1989; Mückenberger 1989; Rubery 1989; Bütchtemann and Quack 1990; and Standing 1992; on dimensions of employment security, see Standing's later work: 1997, 1999a, and 1999b).
2. There is a large body of scholarship on the SER. In writing this book, and in some of my previous work (Vosko 1997 and 2000), including collaborative work (Fudge and Vosko 2001a and 2001b), I have been influenced particularly by Mückenberger (1989) and Bütchtemann and Quack (1990) as well as by Leighton (1986), Rodgers (1989), Tilly (1996), Fudge (1997), and, more recently, by Bosch (2004).
3. By Fordism, I mean the mode of production first prevailing in the industrial world after World War I: namely, a system of mass production involving partially automated assembly lines and cultivating expanding markets, first domestic markets and subsequently external markets, for inexpensive consumer goods— that is, mass consumption. For in-depth discussions of its phases and its varieties, see for example Harvey (1989) and Jessop (1993).

   Connected to Fordism, the Keynesian welfare state refers to the modern welfare state emerging in rapidly advancing capitalist countries after World War II, identified with Keynes's contention that states can intervene productively to shape levels of investment and domestic income and thus regulate unemployment through policies of 'demand management'. Such policies serve to partially socialize both the costs of production (e.g. through tax credits and various state concessions) and workers' reproduction (e.g. through various forms of income support as well as public works) (Teeple 1995: 17). Their introduction is rooted historically in an entente between workers and employers to constrain the business cycle to avoid the unrest characterizing the 1930s as well as a deal between capitalist states to finance the reconstruction of Western European economies destroyed by World War II in order to moderate the postwar attraction to socialism, on the one hand, and facilitate reforms to laissez-faire economics, on the other hand.

4. For studies providing insight into the different features of the SER in different contexts, see for example, on the United Kingdom, Benyon et al. (2002) and Deakin (2002); on Sweden and France, Anxo et al. (2001); on Germany, Mückenberger (1989) and Bosch (2004); on the Netherlands, Burri (2005); on Canada, Vosko (2000) and Fudge and Vosko (2001a); on the United States, Hyde (2000), Appelbaum (2002a and 2002b), and Piore (2002); and, on Australia, Burgess and Campbell (1998).

5. I include some of my own previous work, including collaborative work, in this category (see e.g. Vosko 1996; Fudge and Vosko 2001a and 2001b); for other examples from the industrial relations, public policy, and legal studies literatures, see Deakin 2002; Langille 2002; Bosch 2004.

   As Bosniak (2002: 29) suggests, this tendency is also evident in analyses of universal citizenship, or what she labels the 'tale of progressive incorporation', which she identifies principally with democratic theory, particularly the work of Karst, Young, and Walzer.

   Bosniak (2002, see especially chapter 5) and Williams (1995) also illustrate that much scholarship exploring axes of racialized and gendered differentiation also presumes rather than questions national citizenship boundaries. (Focusing on the American case, Bosniak cites work by Kessler-Harris and Smith, but one might also cite others, such as Pateman 1988; Gordon 1990; and Orloff 1993.)

6. In her discussion of citizenship's subjects, Bosniak (2002: 31), for example, develops the helpful notion of 'bounded citizenship' to refer to 'the way in which the community's membership and boundaries are constituted in the first instance' or the 'threshold' of the political community, which, 'in most versions . . . is that of the nation state'.

   This book is influenced by this conception. However, references to citizenship's external boundaries are also informed by Hindess's (2000) idea of the international management of populations covered by the nation state system. As Hindess argues, it is helpful to see citizenship as marking out or identifying populations partly to 'advis[e] state and non state agencies of the particular state to which an individual belongs' (1495). Drawing out Hindess's insights further, Walters (2002: 267) suggests that 'the remarkable thing about citizenship is that it represents a regime that regulates "the division of humanity into distinct national populations" and operates "as a dispersed regime of governance of the larger human population"'. This interlinked process, along with the constitution of community membership by individual nation states identified by Bosniak (2002), contributes to producing bounded citizenships and citizenship's boundaries.

7. As it is used here, the term 'migrant work' refers to work performed by workers lacking national citizenship in the states in which they are employed and the corresponding term 'migrant worker' refers to workers engaged in migrant work. In contrast, the term 'immigrant worker' refers to workers who are foreign born but hold citizenship or permanent residency in the countries in which they are employed.

   Immigration laws, policies, and regulations address and often distinguish between migrants and immigrants. As Sainsbury (2006; 239) illustrates, in receiving countries such as Australia, Canada, and the United States, as well as various countries in Western and Northern Europe, 'the social rights of immigrants are differentiated by entry categories associated with the form of immigration'.

8. The externalization of costs at both these levels may be aided by migrant workers' lack of knowledge or familiarity with laws, policies, and politics, including union politics, and the hostile treatment many receive from national citizens threatened by their presence. In the labour process, the powerlessness experienced by migrant workers stems partly from the direct and partly from the structural control to which they are subject. Direct control, according to Sassen-Koob (1981: 79, 81), cultivates the tendency to treat migrants as commodities or production factors.

9. As Soysal (1994: 120) illustrates, however, based on an examination of guest workers' incorporation in Western European countries in the post-World War II period, the order in which migrant workers typically attained partial citizenship rights in host countries 'reverses T.H. Marshall's way of organizing rights historically [i.e. civil, political, social]'.

10. On Australia, see for example Hunter 1988; see also Shaver 1992 and Cass 1994; on Canada, see for example Archibald 1970; Hodgetts et al. 1972; and, on the United States, see for example Kessler-Harris 1982.

11. On Australia, see for example O'Connor et al. 1999; on Canada, see for example Pierson 1990; Porter 1993; Vosko 1996, 2003; and, on the United States, see for example Pearce 1990; Fraser and Gordon 1994.

12. Even Marshall (1963: 79, emphasis added), much criticized for his lack of gender analysis (see e.g. Fraser 1994, 1997; Lister 1997, 2001), briefly acknowledges women's partial citizenship in these nation states by noting that 'the story of civil rights in their formative period is one of the gradual addition of new rights to a status that already existed and was held to appertain to all adult members of the community—or perhaps one should say to all male members, since *the status of women, or at least of married women, was in some important respects peculiar*'.

23

13. The lack of civil rights among people of colour until the mid-20th century in the United States is one example (Shklar 1991; Glenn 2002). Another is the late extension of political rights to racialized groups in Canada, such as people of Japanese descent, and to Aboriginal people, who were not granted the right to vote until 1949 and 1960, respectively. In many contexts, the extension of political rights to such groups was further differentiated by gender—in Australia, for example, it took until 1967 for Aboriginal women to attain voting rights.

14. Other mechanisms encourage greater conformity in labour protection at the EU level and thereby support directives. The foremost is the Open Method of Coordination (OMC) fostered by the European Employment Strategy (EES), described in Chapter 5.

15. According to Stone (1995: 999), regulations fostering harmonization involve 'structured incentives and pressures . . .' aiming to induce states 'to bring their labor laws [and policies] into conformity'. A good example is the EU Directive because member states are required to implement it by transposing its terms to their own employment and labour policy regimes, although ILO and UN conventions also foster harmonization.

    In contrast, rules flowing from pre-emptive legislation take effect through national courts and tribunals of minimum labour standards and participative frameworks which are agreed to on an international basis (Hepple 1997: 362). They may be advanced through procedural or (compulsory) substantive regulation. Some argue that EEC Treaty provisions fall into this category. However, there is a debate over the extent to which these provisions actually advance 'core' labour rights (Stone 1995: 999–1000; Hepple 1997: 362–3).

16. As Deakin and Wilkinson (1994: 292) contend in discussing EU regulations:

    > harmonization of standards—as norms—does not necessarily imply the achievement of uniformity of standards . . . that is the actual level of protection achieved in a particular country; nor does it imply that the same system of labour law will necessarily be adopted in each member state, since the mechanisms by which norms are set and implemented at a national level may continue to be sensitive to the traditions and history of different systems.

    These authors' analysis is supported by the finding that while harmonization is taking place in the EU, member states are not translating supranational regulations at the national level in a literal or uniform way (see e.g. Kilpatrick and Freedland 2004).

    In assessing the meaning of harmonization in the case of ILO standards, Sengenberger (1994) helpfully distinguishes between 'fundamental' ILO conventions and the remaining ILO conventions and recommendations. Deemed universal, the former are attached to the principles in the Declaration on Fundamental Principles and Rights at Work (1998) and tied to the ILO Constitution; they do not have regard for the different capabilities of member states to ratify and implement the international norms. The latter, in contrast, take account of 'local diversity of economic and social conditions'; more in line with EU directives, they do not countenance setting differential standards for different countries but aim at equivalence (Sengenberger 1994: 41). Many also provide for exemptions and qualified inclusions or permit conformity to occur gradually.

1

Forging a Gender Contract in Early National and International Labour Regulation

> The protection of the weak, and therefore of women as well as of children and young persons, is one of the fundamental principles underlying the movement which led to the creation of the International Labour Organization.
>
> ILO (1921a) The International Protection of Women Workers, *Studies and Reports, Series I, No.1*: 1.

Feminist scholarship on the SER has long demonstrated its gendered character. This chapter aims to further this appraisal by examining developments contributing to its rise at both the national level and in the International Labour Code.

A large body of feminist scholarship has shown how the earliest attempts to establish minimum conditions of work and employment in Europe, North America, and other industrializing contexts centred on 'protecting women' (see especially contributions to Wikander et al., eds., 1995). In the 19th century, with the rapid growth of industrial capitalism and the enfranchisement of working-class men, and their newly achieved civil right to contract freely with employers, national labour legislation set limitations on women's working hours and night work, prohibited women from working with dangerous substances, fixed minimum wages in female-dominated industries, and established maternity protections. Similarly, prohibitions against women's night work in industry and the use of white phosphorous in match production were the first subjects of international labour regulation beginning in 1906 and such subjects, as well as maternity protection and lead poisoning, were also addressed at the inaugural conference of the ILO in 1919. This congruence was not accidental. Indeed, only once the contours of the male breadwinner / female caregiver gender contract were established could the SER emerge as the normative model of employment.

At the same time, the selection of early subjects for international labour regulation was not without contestation. There were struggles over the merits and shortcomings of protective labour legislation for women between and amongst trade unionists, working-class and liberal feminists, women social reformers, and philanthropists. Debates pivoted on whether to pursue 'equal protection' for men and women or protection for women exclusively. On the one hand, liberal feminists and social democrats cast protective labour legislation as discriminatory, a position tied to their pursuit of equal civil and political citizenship rights for women. On the other hand, large segments of the male trade union movements and some working-class women viewed protective labour legislation as a pragmatic strategy in the struggle against women's subordination in free labour markets and, ultimately, against the exploitation of the working class as a whole; this diverse group often found itself in strategic alignment with national governments and their representatives at the international level. The outcome of these debates was that the patchwork of protective labour legislation in rapidly industrializing countries was gradually solidified in international labour regulations.

The ensuing discussion traces the gendered foundations of the SER as the normative model of employment in industrializing capitalist labour markets by sketching the development of select national regulations and the creation of the initial body of standards of the International Association of Labour Legislation (IALL) in 1906 and the ILO in 1919. After synthesizing scholarship by feminist historians documenting the evolution of protective legislation in various parts of Europe and North America as well as in Australia and charting debates surrounding the adoption of international labour regulations, the chapter shows how by cultivating a male breadwinner / female caregiver gender contract, early labour regulations adopted nationally as well as internationally helped lay the foundation for the SER.

Select National Developments, 1830s–1930s

The timing of the introduction of protective legislation varied nationally, yet regulations governing hours of work and night work, wages, the use of dangerous substances, and maternity shared several features. Most early laws targeted children and subsequently sought to limit the extent or alter the character of women's paid work, especially in industry, in order to encourage them to fulfil caregiving duties as well as to inhibit competition between women and men (Kessler-Harris et al. 1995: 4). This pattern gives credence to T. H. Marshall's (1963: 84) observation that early Factory Acts 'meticulously refrained from giving this protection directly to the adult male...out of respect for his status as a citizen, on the grounds that enforced protective measures curtailed the civil right to conclude a free contract'. Protective legislation set limits on women's labour force participation through such measures as compulsory confinement for pregnant women and new mothers and occupational prohibitions. Protection was pursued primarily by the state and supported by humanitarian capitalists, many male trade unionists, and women social reformers. Their arguments emphasized motherly duties to protect the unborn and to fulfil domestic obligations, the 'preservation of the nation', and women's supposed lesser physical and moral fitness to engage in certain forms of employment and occupations. In many cases, protections did not apply to categories of work deemed acceptable for women, perceived either to be intermittent, performed in the domestic sphere, or tied to caregiving, such as household servants, agricultural workers, casual workers, family workers, and workers in small workshops, as well as waitresses and nurses (see e.g. Hutchins 1907; McCallum 1986; Fredman 1997). Furthermore, seldom discussed were issues of whether men should engage in paid work (Fredman 1997), whether men's work in certain occupations or industries endangered the unborn (Whitworth 1994), or whether men had domestic obligations.

Hours and Night Work

In Britain, where sex-specific legislation governing hours of work was pioneered, workers' efforts to reduce their hours began with gender-neutral calls for limits on the working day. While many such efforts, dating to the early 1800s, were ignored, the British Factory Act of 1833, responding partly to the ten-hours movement seeking a reduction in children's hours, barred children under 9 years of age from working in textile factories and reduced the working day to 12 hours for 13–18-year-olds. In 1844, women were included under such legislation, which characterized them 'to be, like children, "unfree agents" in the labour market' (Lewis and Rose 1995: 99).

According to Lewis and Rose (1995: 92), British working men, such as those working in textile factories where everyone's work was interdependent, did not want to undermine their newly won freedom of contract, and so they supported legislation affecting women and children, presuming that ultimately men's hours would be shortened. But, while early Factory Acts are often cited as the first formal limit on women's paid work in Britain, inattention to men's situation is equally notable (Fredman 1997). Only in the late 1800s did trade unions begin to push, once again, for a general eight-hour day and to argue that, as one union leader (quoted by Lewis and Rose 1995: 108) put it, 'the veil must be lifted...Women and children must no longer be made the pretext for securing a reduction of working hours for men'. Henceforth, Britain began to set limits on working hours, and factory work more generally. Still, as Fredman shows (1997: 72–3), limits to working hours were most comprehensive in industrial settings, especially in large textile factories, where the presence of wage-earning women often threatened their male counterparts; in 'small workplaces, home workers and family workers were protected only sporadically... Yet some of the worst abuses of sweated labour took place in these workshops.'

In Australia, some male workers gained a shorter work day through industrial action in the mid-19th century (e.g. stonemasons won an eight-hour day in 1856 in Sydney and Melbourne) (Buckley and Wheelwright 1988: 166 and 168). However, early government policies regulated the working hours of women and children. Victoria's Supervision of Workrooms Factories Act (1873), the first legislation of its kind in the country, resembled its British counterpart. A model for subsequent legislation in other Australian states, this Act, and later amendments, set up factory inspectors, established health and safety conditions, and limited hours of work for women and children (Howe 1995: 320). Early laws initially defined factories as establishments employing no fewer than ten people, leaving aside small establishments, and thereby neglecting the long hours associated with outwork, family work, or home-based workshops, which did not threaten male-breadwinning (Frances et al. 1996: 62; see also Howe 1995; 320).[1]

Developments in Canada also followed those in Britain in so far as workers' demands for a shorter work day were cast initially as universal, while state interventions, supported by many male workers, limited the working hours of women and children through Factory Acts. Against the backdrop of, for example, cross-occupational alliances such as the Nine Hours Leagues of 1872, many argued that shorter working hours would allow workers to 'become better citizens and family men with more time away from the job' (Heron 1989: 15). Early factory laws were enacted by provincial governments, first in Ontario (1884), followed by Quebec (1885), and later Western Canada and the Maritimes. Before the introduction of these Acts, as Ursel (1992: 85) illustrates, very few laws contained clauses protecting workers' interests and/or rights, but Ontario's Factory Act changed this by providing for health and safety regulations for all workers and restricting daily working hours to ten for women and children (Ontario 1884: chapter 39, s. 6.3; see also Guest 1985: 40). Such legislation 'rested on the assumption that female workers needed greater protection than male workers because of their presumed physical frailty and moral vulnerability' (Frager and Patrias 2005: 105).

Shifting to the French case, here legislators restricted hours of work in industry first for children in 1841, followed by a successful movement in 1848 to limit hours of work for all workers in large-scale industry to 12 per day (ILO 1932: 95). Further limitations to daily hours of work in 1874 addressed children only, and made Sunday rest compulsory for girls below 21 years of age, before legislators began regulating hours of work for women of all ages. By the 1890s, French legislation was so complex that it entailed four distinct subsystems, regulating hours for children under 16 (10 hours a day), girls between 16 and 18 (60 hours a week), women over 18 (11 hours a day and 60 hours a week), and men (12 hours a day) (ILO 1932: 96). In an effort to simplify regulation in 1900, French legislators reduced the maximum hours of work for women of any age to that of children (10 hours), and a few years later, they reduced the hours of men working in the same workplaces as women and children to equivalent levels (Boxer 1986: 46–7).

France is also well-known, though not unique, for having actively regulated women's industrial employment at night, through legislation such as the Millerand-Colliard Law (1892), in an attempt to limit evening work, then prevalent among dressmakers as well as among workers in other luxury industries common in large urban centres (Delevingne 1934: 34). Legislators proceeded over the objections of women textile workers, large groups of whom struck to defend their piece rates against the probable loss of wages due to hours-restrictions (Hilden 1986: 817). They also acted against the wishes of many employers concerned about the prospects of lower productivity and rates of profit and the fears of many male workers, especially in the same firms, that reducing women's hours would contribute to a reduction for them. These objections led to a series of 'tolerances' or exemptions that, as Stewart (1989: 121) shows, cultivated a 'pattern of inclusion and exclusion in the ban fortif[ying] a decaying barrier in the labour market by reserving higher paying night work for men and as well as by facilitating lower paying night work for women'.

In the United States, early hours-regulation was not limited to women and children, as it had been in most parts of Britain, Australia, and Canada.

For example, a ten-hour day was established for federal employees in 1840, and worker-led struggles for hours-legislation multiplied in the mid-1840s (Kessler-Harris 1982: 182). Shortly thereafter, some states also responded to the problem of long working hours by enacting gender-neutral maximum hours legislation. In one early case, in 1847, New Hampshire passed a law establishing ten hours a day as the general standard 'in the absence of an express contract requiring greater time' and other states followed suit (Klem et al. 1950: 49). However, where they existed in the late 19th century, according to Roediger and Foner (1989: 101; see also Kessler-Harris 1982: 183), state laws 'either lacked provisions for enforcement, contained loopholes, or became objects of conflicting interpretation'. This is where gendered patterns emerged as the earliest *enforceable* hours laws applied only to women.[2]

As struggles over hours of work regulations played out in the United States, so did debates over prohibiting women's work at night. The impetus for sex-specific legislation came from high court rulings preventing across-the-board, and thereby gender-neutral, limitations on maximum hours (e.g. the United States Supreme Court Ruling in *Lochner v. New York* of 1905). When American courts intervened to prevent states from restricting maximum hours for the sake of (male) workers' liberty, as the work of Kessler-Harris shows, in particular, social reformers stepped up their efforts in pursuit of sex-specific limitations. They focused on prohibiting night work for women because it was a practical means of limiting employer avoidance of maximum daily hours for women through the use of split shifts and of preventing women from holding two jobs. Social reformers, such as those connected to the National Consumers' League, used the courts' actions to 'exaggerat[e] gender differences and plac[e] the qualities of women, not social justice for workers, in the forefront of debate' (Kessler-Harris 1995: 341). Their actions shaped both subsequent court rulings and legislative action. They offered the courts a rationale for allowing legislators to protect women in the national interest (i.e. to preserve maternal health), permission granted by the United States Supreme Court in a 1908 decision (*Muller v. Oregon*). Such pronouncements, in turn, led 12 states to adopt laws restricting women's work at night between 1908 and 1918 and enabled 42 states to uphold sex-specific maximum hours laws existing by that time (Kessler-Harris 1995: 355).

Wages

Like those governing maximum working hours and night work, many early wage regulations were formulated to respond to the prevalence of sweating (i.e. exploitative working conditions) among women, although concerns about male breadwinners' wages often lay behind these interventions.

The Australian state of Victoria, where women comprised about half of the workforce in the late 19th century, offers a window into the nature of early minimum wage-setting. While the setting of a minimum wage was by no means unique to Victoria, its Factories and Shops Act of 1896 was early in instituting enforceable minimum wages and overtime rates for Australian women and men in sweated trades. Such measures took effect through the creation of wages boards with enforcement powers, appointed to set wages and piece rates for factory workers and outworkers in six named trades (Hutchins 1906; Howe 1995: 322). The boards were introduced by parliamentarians to 'protect women and children "who cannot help themselves," compared to men who are "able to organize and unite"' (Rickard, quoted in Howe 1995: 321). Yet the 1896 legislation also applied to men in the named trades because of a successful Labor Party amendment.

As Howe (1995) illustrates, these early forays into wage regulation cultivated a series of gendered ironies. Minimum wage-setting had a positive impact on women employed in clothing and textile industries, whose wages rose. However, the actions of boards did little to limit wage differentials between men and women as they typically set women's wage rates at least 50% below men's. This early wage-gap was justified by women's and men's presumed different needs and requirements for subsistence tied to growing efforts to normalize a 'family wage'. The boards' prescriptions took seriously the concern that 'factory employment should not be attractive enough to entice married women away from the home', expressed by a Royal Commission on Female and Juvenile Labour in Factories and Shops in the state of New South Wales (1911–12) (quoted in Howe 1995: 328). Although women in industries regulated by the wage boards did better than those in industries outside their purview, these women's wage rates hovered around subsistence levels, defined in accordance with increasingly prevalent norms of female caregiving.[3] Boards also helped preserve sex segregation in trades such as clothing, where cutting and pressing were the dominion of men (Lee 1987).

At the end of the 1800s and in the early 1900s, low pay was also a characteristic feature of women's paid work in Britain, where the sex-segregated nature of the evolving labour market facilitated this situation. Initially, rationales casting women as naturally less efficient than men and having lower subsistence needs worked to delay state intervention into pay levels. However, in the early 1900s, Britain began to regulate minimum wages in response to sweating, moral fears about prostitution, eugenicist fears over the health of the English race, and suggestions that low-priced labour could hinder economic progress (Lewis 1984: 200–1; Fredman 1997: 75). Here, too, the strategy involved introducing minimum wages in trades that were predominantly female, where sweating was common (Lewis and Rose 1995: 94). Consequently, in 1909, Britain passed the first Trades Boards Act, which created wage-setting machinery for application in such trades as tailoring, paper and cardboard box-making, chain-making, and lace mending and finishing (ibid. 114).[4]

Even with the introduction of trade boards (first called wage councils) in Britain, Lewis (1986b: 10) shows that the average wage of women in regulated industries hovered around subsistence levels in this period, and that the regulations of the boards applied to just one-sixth of all women workers, excluding casuals. While trade boards increased women's wages in the trades covered, as Fredman (1997: 77) shows, they reinforced the assumption that low wages were intrinsic to women's work by permitting sex-based differentials, even in cases where men and women were performing the same work. The boards' approach to wage regulation reinforced inequality between women and men, improving women's wages while simultaneously upholding their broader dependence on men and hence their responsibility for caregiving.

In the United States, the earliest minimum wage legislation covered only women and children (Waltman 2000: 28–9). Some scholars contend that American laws were weak since efforts to enforce them tended to weigh the health of women workers against the health of industry in general and employers' capacity to pay adequate wages (Levin-Waldman 2001: 54). Nevertheless, 15 states, the District of Columbia and Puerto Rico enacted minimum wage legislation for women between 1912 and 1923, and wage minima were set by boards for certain occupations within industries (Mutari and Figart 2004: 29). As with legislation on maximum hours and night work legislation, the American courts played a central role in defining the gendered character of early minimum wage legislation, especially the Supreme Court Ruling of 1908 finding that preserving women's reproductive capacities took precedence over their freedom of contract. Yet, by 1923, the Supreme Court, in *Adkins v. Children's Hospital*, had voided federal minimum wage legislation on the grounds that it dangerously extended the police power of the state, a decision that made remaining state minimum wage laws effectively unenforceable (Waltman 2000: 29–30; Mutari and Figart 2004: 30).

As Frances et al. (1996) illustrate, the absence of significant state intervention in the area of wage regulations stands out most in Canada. Women's organizations, such as the National Council of Women of Canada, vocalized concerns about women's low wages as early as the 1890s, but Canada and the provinces did not intervene for some years (Guest 1985: 73; McCallum 1986: 31, 33). In 1900, the federal government made a modest attempt at wage regulation by issuing a policy to 'ensure the payment of "fair wages" to persons employed on all public works and Government contracts', although there was a sharp distinction between this type of policy and minimum wage legislation, which emerged later and targeted women and girls (Lorentsen and Woolner 1950: 104).

Canadian provincial legislation covering minimum wages only emerged in the late 1910s. By the early 1920s, most provinces had legislation 'providing for a three- or five-person minimum wage board to set wage rates for female wage-earners on an industry-by-industry basis after consultation with representative employers and employees' and provided for the typical exclusions (e.g. domestics, farm workers) (McCallum 1986: 31); furthermore, as Frager and Patrias (2005: 107–8) emphasize, 'employers wishing to observe the letter of the law could rely on an ever-changing workforce of "learners" and on part-time workers who could be paid less than the standard minimum'.

Dangerous Substances and Occupations

Among the various forms of protective legislation taking shape in the late 19th and early 20th centuries, those centring on dangerous substances and occupations were forged most tightly around assumptions about biological difference, and especially the sanctity of motherhood. In Britain, as well as in Canada, the United States, and France, there was considerable consensus among legislators and social reformers in support of sex-specific regulations in this area. Underground work and the manufacture of pottery and white lead were believed to endanger women's reproductive health and certain types of work (e.g. mining) were perceived to limit their ability to fulfil their domestic responsibilities (see for example Humphries 1981: 16–20; Kessler-Harris 1982: 185; Lewis and Rose 1995: 98).

Beginning with prohibiting women from working underground in the Mines and Collieries Act (1842), Britain adopted some of the earliest protective measures governing work involving dangerous substances and occupations. As Lewis and Rose show (1995), speeches by British parliamentarians favouring the adoption of this Act focused on the harmful effects of underground work on pregnancy and the consequences of dirty and dangerous work for the family, including the immoral behaviour that underground work among 'disorderly' women supposedly encouraged. Indeed, 'the sensationalism of the issue of immorality silenced those who were concerned with the principles of political economy and the state regulation of industry' (ibid. 98). Consequently, prohibition was the standard response in Britain. France also prohibited women and children from underground work, beginning in 1874 (Hutchins 1907: 2). In the United States, many states also limited women's work underground, although, as Kessler-Harris (1982: 185) suggests, such action had little more than symbolic power since work in underground mines was never prevalent: restrictions, rather, reinforced political discourses asserting women's weakness as well as justified prohibiting altogether, the work of women in certain occupations'.

Sex-specific prohibitions also extended to other areas. In Britain, for example, the Factory and Workshop Act (1891) was amended in 1895 to empower the British home secretary to prohibit women and children from particular trades or occupations (Malone 1998: 178). Initially, the government exercised these powers in the white lead and pottery trades, effectively banning women from working in the most dangerous (and high-paying) jobs in these trades. The effects of toxic substances on men's reproductive capacities were not addressed: as Malone (1998: 187) reports in her study of gendered discourses on danger and protective legislation in Britain in the late 1800s, scientific theories of biological differences between men and women 'infused with prejudices of their creators' assisted employers in replacing women with men in dangerous trades while substantiating the 'prevalent separate-spheres ideology'.

Legislation enacted in the 1880s in France also forbade women and children from working in almost all dangerous processes in various lead trades, permitting special rules for specific trades. But the use of certain substances (e.g. white phosphorous) was forbidden in all industrial processes by 1898 and, by 1907, legislators had passed a general law requiring precautionary measures in all unhealthy industries (Hutchins 1907: 6). These measures were gender-neutral, suggestive of the different assumptions about women's roles in labour markets in continental Europe than in the United States or Britain. Jenson (1989) observes that, together with the emphasis on women's civil rights, the form of protective legislation reflected both the premise that women would always engage in employment *and* the centrality of the family to the future of the French Republic, whereas, in the United States, the notion, hegemonic at that time, was that women were either mothers *or* workers. In contrast, in Britain, the idea was 'that the "working woman" and later the "working mother" were contradictory terms' (Lewis and Rose 1995). These distinct conceptions of women's social roles also shaped early protective legislation linked to maternity.

Maternity Protection

In the early 20th century, some governments sought to restrict women's labour force participation after and, in some instances, before the birth of their children. Others attempted to confine their labour force participation to certain spheres, occupations, and categories of employment.

The British approach to maternity regulation was typical of the first group. Under the Factory and Workshop Act (1891), it barred women from returning to work for four weeks after childbirth and in the subsequent Act in that name (Factory and Workshop Act 1901), it enacted provisions punishing employers for knowingly employing a woman within four weeks of the birth of her child.[5] The United States also used maternity protection to deter mothers' labour force participation by leaving unprotected women's jobs during such necessary absences. Instead of state-supported maternity leave, American states, backed by social reformers, combined restrictions on the employment of pregnant women and new mothers with strategies for limiting infant mortality, including the provision of pure or sterilized milk through municipal milk stations operating during daily working hours only (Jenson 1989: 244). Consequently, although maternity protections were ultimately introduced in some states, such as in New York in 1919, when the American Association for Labor Legislation called in 1916 for a federal maternity benefit akin to those available in Nordic countries, the proposal failed; as Kessler-Harris et al. (1995: 12) demonstrate, 'convinced that women should simply quit work when they married or became pregnant, reformers who led the campaign to restrict women's work paid no attention at all to maternity leave. The resulting hardships for wage-earning women strengthened arguments for a family wage for male breadwinners.'

Among the second group, which included several countries with relatively weak women's movements, some provided leave benefits as part of a package of maternity protection.[6] This is true of Germany, the first state to extend public compensation to mothers for lost earnings during mandatory maternity leaves in 1883, which did so as part of health insurance because many women were evading prohibitions in order to subsist (Berkovitch 1999: 48, 135). France took a somewhat different approach, viewing maternity protection as both an aid to women's continued labour force participation and a means of securing the growth of the population. Confronted with high rates of infant mortality and declining fertility rates, and concerned with depopulation, in 1913 it introduced prenatal and compulsory postnatal leave for women working in industrial and commercial establishments (Jenson 1989: 241; Koven and Michel 1990: 1088; see also Klaus 1993; Pedersen 1993). France also passed legislation guaranteeing a daily maternity allowance to make up for lost wages during the eight weeks before and after childbirth, and provided for a nursing bonus (McDougall 1983; see also Koven and Michel 1990: 1105). To ensure that women could fulfil their maternal roles upon return to the labour force, women effectively lobbied for nursing rooms in factories and daycares in local communities. The French state, building on a consensus between workers' organizations, nationalists, and social Catholics, as well as early feminists, adopted this package of maternity protections to provide greater space for family life in French society. The goal was to reinforce what Jenson (1989: 250) characterizes as the identity of the 'citizen-producer' through building a society on the basis of solidarism, in which the family is the basic unit.[7]

By the time that international labour regulations began to take shape in the early 1900s, protective labour legislation in Europe and North America had established the basis for the emerging male breadwinner / female caregiver gender contract. National measures varied, but legislation on hours of work and night work, wages, and dangerous substances and occupations, while excluding categories of work deemed acceptable for women, were largely rationalized on the basis of women's supposed weakness and their role in reproducing and maintaining the population, the need to establish an industrial worker norm among men, and, along with maternity protections, the desire to normalize the nuclear family household. International labour regulations followed a similar course.

International Developments, 1870s–1919

The establishment of international labour regulation was driven initially by concerns to limit unfair competition between countries. As early as the mid-19th century, prominent figures such as Robert Owen and Daniel Le Grand argued that certain humanitarian requirements, such as safe working conditions, should be removed from the sphere of international competition (ILO 1921a: 1, 2001: 23). By 1906, when the first international labour conventions and recommendations were adopted, there was a formal recognition on the part of legislators in many industrializing countries that competition in industry between different countries represented an obstacle in the development of national legislation (Mahaim 1934: 4). On the basis of these acknowledgements, national governments worked with representatives of trade unions and employers' associations to pursue international labour regulations, and an early focus was 'the protection of the weak', and thereby women and children. The decision to focus first on protecting women and children met with resistance from some quarters, especially from feminists calling for 'equal protection' as a means of advancing women's civil and political rights. Yet in the early stages of their development, philosophical and strategic disagreements over whether to focus energy on suffrage or the rejection of sex-specific protective legislation between and amongst working-class and liberal feminists, as well as women involved in socialist and social democratic movements who did not identify with feminism, hindered coordinated action.

Consensus and Contestation around Protecting Women, 1878–1913[8]

The early stages in the evolution of international labour regulation were characterized by sharp divisions over protective measures and to whom they should apply, evident especially in the meetings of socialist and women's congresses, both broad women's congresses and meetings of socialist and social democratic women. In 1878, for example, the first general international women's congress was held in Paris and a central issue—over which there was no agreement—was whether to support prohibiting women from working at night. In the ten women's congresses held across Europe and the United States before 1900, women remained divided. Some self-proclaimed 'feminists' opposed protective measures, including many French women who argued against them from the standpoint of equal rights and liberty, whereas a diverse group of women, including middle-class women social reformers and working-class women, supported such measures as prohibitions on night work (Wikander 1992: 12–13; see also Hilden 1986). The divisions were exacerbated by the 1888 formation of the International Council of Women, whose initial radical and internationalist goals were quelled by the broad coalition of women's groups that attended its first meeting in Washington (Wikander 1992: 16, 1995: 46; Rupp 1997; see also Anderson and Winslow 1951).[9]

Protective legislation was also high on the agenda of the male-dominated socialist congresses. Indeed, the Socialist International Labour Congress held in Paris in 1889—the inaugural meeting of the Second International—passed a resolution on general labour legislation, which highlighted the importance of the eight-hour day for all workers. Yet consistent with a resolution opposing the employment of women at night passed at the first Socialist International two decades earlier (ILO 2001: 24), two other resolutions addressed women exclusively: one focused on prohibiting women from industrial jobs that could damage female organs and the other on prohibiting women and children from working at night. Although both resolutions passed, there were dissenting voices, such as Clara Zetkin, who famously objected to limits on women's paid employment by arguing that 'if we wish women to be free human beings, to have the same rights as men in our society, women's work must be neither abolished nor limited except in certain quite isolated cases' (Zetkin, as cited by Bell and Offen, eds., 1983: 87; see also Wikander 1995: 34; see also DuBois 1998: 261; Bryson 2003: 108–10 and 111–12).

The first international congress on general protective legislation convened by German Emperor Wilhelm II in Berlin in 1890, which would eventually become the IALL, itself the precursor to the ILO, aimed to induce cooperation between countries on competition and trade. According to Mahaim (1934: 16), 'the ultimate purpose of international labor legislation would, of course, be achieved if all national legislation became identical. This, however, [was] not a practical possibility...'. Thus the aim was 'not absolute equality [i.e. identical legislation] but rather equivalence'. The 'social question' was another common concern, as delegates debated a day's rest for all, as well as reductions in working hours for women and children (Wikander 1992: 20–1). Although this congress failed to produce any binding measures, delegates recommended that women not be allowed to work at night or on Sundays, that their workday not exceed 11 hours, that they receive daily breaks, and that they be prohibited from work for four weeks after giving birth (Wikander 1995: 35–6; ILO 2001: 24). In this way, by 1890, the contours of the gender contract were beginning to take shape at the international level.

In the ensuing years, several general women's congresses met in Europe, and delegates to one in 1892, the Congrès Général des Sociétés Féministes, demanded a night work prohibition for all workers, as well as suffrage for women, partly in response to France's initial ban on night work for women that year; the resolutions of a subsequent congress of the same group in 1896 similarly called for no restrictions for women that did not also apply to men, an eight-hour day for all, and equal pay for equal work. Moreover, deliberations at another women's congress held in Brussels a year later took a similar position to the French Congress (Wikander 1995: 44–5).

In this period, however, some male trade unionists expressed hostility towards the 'bourgeois feminists (or "women's righters" as they were [also] often called)' (Bryson 2003: 108, 109), and, at the third congress of the Second International in 1893, women's equality was debated, and key actors shifted their views (Wikander 1995: 36). For instance, in the interest of making the institution of the family more central in workers' collective struggles, Clara Zetkin had changed her position to support protective legislation for women, noting that:

it is out of the question that the task of socialist women's activity should be to alienate proletarian women from their duties as wives and mothers . . . the better relations are in the family and the more efficiently work is done in the home, so much the more effective is the family in the struggle. (Zetkin, as cited by Draper and Lipow 1976: 199–200; see also Honeycutt 1976: 136; Bryson 2003: 111–12)

According to Wikander (1995: 36–7), Zetkin followed Louise Kautsky, of Austria, who presented a resolution to the congress calling for special protection for women. The resolution—for an eight-hour day, prohibition of night work, and prohibition from paid work two weeks before and four weeks after childbirth—generated considerable discord, and a number of women opposed it on the grounds of women's equality. Consequently, delegates successfully proposed adding a clause on equal pay to temper the effects of the resolution. For Wikander (1995: 37), henceforth the 'combination of special protection for women plus the demand for equal pay was to become the standard position of the Second International on these issues' (see also Cole 1963). And it would have a broader influence too.

After the 1890s, a decade in which attention to equal protection diminished in many women's congresses, marking a new more official phase in the evolution of international labour regulation, there were further victories for proponents of protective measures. Between around 1900 and 1913, according to Wikander (1992: 13), a split persisted between European socialist feminists, who opposed protective legislation, and North American liberal feminists, some of whom favoured it and many of whom preferred to devote their energy to women's suffrage, although this split was not always clear cut since some older American women allied themselves with the feminist stance and some European women, especially German women, sided with the North Americans. Nevertheless, in the United States, many women argued that social and labour protections could bolster the case for women's suffrage (Spruill-Wheeler 1995). Although efforts to establish suffrage for women began in the 19th century, in most countries the first international labour legislation emerged before formal political rights were extended to women, with a few notable exceptions such as New Zealand and Australia, which granted women the vote in 1893 and 1902, respectively.

At the first official congress of the IALL in 1901 after its founding in Paris in 1900, delegates discussed the regulation of night work for women and the regulation of industries injurious to (especially women) workers' health. They instructed the International Labour Office to undertake further study and formed a committee to draw up proposals justifying regulations on such topics. This set the stage for two successive congresses of the IALL in Berne (ILO 1921a; see also League of Nations 1919c): the first, in 1905, was a technical meeting at which delegates discussed the potential function of an international labour convention and decided that it would have to be ratified by national parliaments and converted into national law in order to become legally binding. Around the same time, countries began to negotiate bilateral treaties related to workers' protection.[10] The second, in 1906, inaugurated the age of international labour regulation, as participants adopted the first two international labour conventions—one convention prohibited the use of white phosphorous in the match production industry and the other prohibited women's night work in industry (see Appendix A).

Oft labelled the 'first article of the International Labour Code' (ILO 2001: 27), and known simply as the Berne Convention, the convention on night work resembled national measures in many respects. It only covered employed women in industry, prohibiting them from working between 10 p.m. and 5 a.m. It did not extend to women working in small workshops, homes, agriculture, or commerce. Nor did it cover industrial undertakings in which only family members were employed, suggesting that the family had independent protective interests and capacities akin to the state. However, the convention did cover mines and quarries, and manufacturing industries, important domains of employment for men. Later in 1906, the IALL adopted a resolution limiting women's workday to ten hours, choosing this softer form of standard-setting to accommodate the patchwork of national measures emerging around that time.

After several years of relative inactivity on questions surrounding the regulation of women's work for pay, given the growing focus on suffrage, debates at various congresses were renewed; for example, in 1910, at the second women's 'shadow international' in Copenhagen (the pre-congress responsible for establishing 8 March as International Women's Day) (Kaplan 1985), a group of women from Scandinavia argued against special legislation and for equal protection for all workers in opposition to their German-led socialist sisters (Wikander 1995: 52). However, the hiatus ended in 1911, when a new general women's organization—International Correspondence—formed briefly with the specific aim of rejecting labour legislation for women only (Wikander 1992: 31). Its central goal of annulling the Berne Convention's prohibition on night work for women galvanized feminists who were against protective legislation, and, according to Wikander (1995: 53–4), its efforts contributed to participants' double demand for equal pay and protection, at a general women's congress in Paris in 1913, held under the auspices of the conservative International Council of Women.

Despite such developments, the IALL largely continued to support sex-specific protective measures. Indeed, in 1913, the IALL proceeded along its previous course as delegates adopted the principle of a ten-hour day for women; there was some debate about setting a fixed standard on the grounds that maximum hours varied nationally, but the compromise reached 'allowed considerable latitude in the methods of its application' (ILO 1921a: 3–4). Notable at its 1913 forum, however, was the vocal opposition of a Norwegian delegate who, emphasizing the importance of protective labour legislation for all workers, objected to both measures on the basis of a 'strong trend of opinion in opposition to all special protection for women . . . [and] demanded equal legislation for men and women workers' (ILO 1921a: 4). Although feminist historians have shown that such principles were expressed at earlier meetings, from the subsequent official perspective of the ILO, formed just eight years later:

This was the *first appearance of this essentially feminist principle* in an international labour conference. *Up till that time the desirability of special protection for the weaker members of the working community had never been questioned.* Since that time there has always been one section of opinion which lays particular stress on the equal competition of men and women, and which does not wish to destroy this equality by placing women in an inferior economic position . . . (ILO 1921a: 4, emphasis added)

The Consolidation of Female Caregiving and the Birth of the ILO, 1919

With the end of World War I and the Treaty of Versailles, discussion of international labour regulation accelerated. The Labour Charter of 1919 (Part XIII) entrenched seven core principles: the right of association, payment of adequate wages to maintain a reasonable standard of living, equal pay for equal work, an eight-hour day or 48-hour week, a weekly rest of at least 24 hours, the abolition of child labour, equitable economic treatment of all workers in a country, an inspection system to ensure the enforcement of laws and worker protections, and the principle that 'labour should not be regarded as a merely a commodity or article of commerce' (League of Nations 1919b: Art. 427; ILO 1921a: 4; Lee 1997; Vosko 2000). These principles framed the subsequent creation of international labour regulations by the Commission on International Labour Legislation, established in Paris in March 1919, which gave birth to the ILO.

Replacing the IALL, the ILO was to be a tripartite body involving representatives of workers, employers, and governments with the power to adopt conventions (and make recommendations) at its annual international labour conference, which would then be submitted to member states for ratification. From its inception, the ILO's emphasis (and voting) was weighted towards governments, with two government representatives per country, and one representative each for workers and employers per country. The structure of the ILO was accepted by governments both because of this weighting and because the compromise formula for adopting conventions meant that member states were not to be bound by standards; rather, the International Labour Code would gain legitimacy through norm-setting. The creation of the ILO was not without contestation, however, as the United States opposed the inclusion of the word 'class' in its mandate. The draft mandate indicated that the League of Nations aimed to establish universal peace and stated that 'such a peace can be established only if it is based upon the prosperity and contentment of all *classes* in all nations'. To address American opposition, the last clause was replaced with 'lasting peace through *social justice*', representing a compromise that would shape fundamentally the politics of the ILO (Alcock 1971: 27, emphasis added; see also Morse 1969: 9). In forming the ILO, member countries thus aimed to foster mechanisms through which trade unions could participate in making social reforms within the confines of capitalism rather than outside of them (Cox 1977).

The movement toward the adoption of international labour standards began with deliberations at the Paris Conference itself, prior to the formation of the ILO, when the Commission on International Labour Legislation that prepared the labour clauses heard from, among others, women's organizations, beginning with a general delegation of women's associations. The delegation was led by Gabrielle Duchêne of the Women's International League of Peace and Freedom, a leading feminist, pacifist, and anti-fascist (Carle 2004). After asserting that 'special legislation concerning women only serves, most often, to limit their scope of work and to exclude them from certain industries, while leaving them free nevertheless to engage in work which is not prohibited but which is prejudicial to their health', Duchêne called for establishing all protective labour legislation 'on a basis of absolute equality for all adult workers without distinction of sex', along with changes to work processes, to make them safer, instead of prohibitions on women participating in them; she also argued that women prohibited from working while pregnant or nursing should be provided 'a living compensatory indemnity in view of the forfeited salary' (ILO 1921a: 4, 5).

Taking a position distinct from Duchêne's, in a memorandum submitted on behalf of the International Council of Women, Avril de Ste Croix (ILO 1921a: 5, 6) wrote against 'the continuance of inequality of treatment between the workers of the two sexes' and in favour of equal pay for equal work, but also argued that night work among women 'is injurious and detrimental to family life', asserting that 'whenever it may be possible without creating a situation unfavourable to women, night work should be suppressed'. Ste Croix additionally called for exceptional measures in the case of maternity and supported the establishment of women's labour commissions. The Allied Women's Suffragists, represented by Mrs Brunschevig, concurred on the latter proposal. Taking a middle ground, they argued that women should 'not be employed in work known to be really dangerous for them in the event of maternity'; still, they stressed the importance of changing women's conditions of work and called for a state-provided allowance during the six weeks before and after childbirth 'for every woman, whether a wage-earner or not' in the name of women's economic independence (ILO 1921a: 6–7). This support for women's economic independence, as well as equal wages, was reinforced by the representation of another woman speaking on behalf of the organization, a Miss van den Plas (ILO 1921a: 6), who requested that the question of 'half-time work for married women' be added to the agenda of the initial International Labour Conference on the basis that 'under such an arrangement a married woman would be able to work without abandoning her household and her children, and without, on the other hand, being subjected to the low wages which were given to her on the pretext that she only needed a nominal wage'.

Such groups influenced the drafting of Part XIII of the Peace Treaty, particularly its emphasis on the protection of children and young persons; the inclusion of the principle of equal remuneration for work of equal value; and the call for labour inspection. However, the demand for equal protection was largely ignored by the Commission on International Labour Legislation, which chose instead to place women's employment during the night and dangerous work and dangerous work processes on the agenda of the first international labour conference in Washington in 1919, along with women's employment before and after childbirth (ILO 1921a: 7).

This inaugural conference of the ILO took place in parallel to an International Congress of Working Women, where delegates came together to protest the underrepresentation of women in the forming of the ILO, to develop a platform for women to be heard, and to debate strategy (ILO 1921a: 7; Lubin and Winslow 1990: 28–31; see also Anderson and Winslow 1951). Delegates to the International Congress of Working Women agreed on the need to improve representation among women. They also adopted a number of recommendations on the maternity question, including that no woman should be employed for six weeks before or after childbirth; that every woman, whether wage-earning or 'the wife of a wage-earner', should be entitled to free medical care and a monetary allowance 'adequate for the full and healthy maintenance of mother and child' during maternity; that each country should create government commissions to study ideal methods of maternity and infant care; and, that the Labour Office of the League of Nations establish a bureau addressing maternity and infant care (ILO 1921a: 7–8). Yet the resolution advanced by a minority of participants for an indemnity for mothers based on the living wage in a given district was rejected. They also called for the maintenance of the Berne Convention, while 'urg[ing] that night work for men . . . be prohibited as far as possible' (ILO 1921a: 8). These outcomes amounted to tepid support for equal protection, qualified by special maternity protections.

At the meeting of the ILO itself, prohibiting night work for women in industry and extending maternity protections was also subject to some debate. Prior to the meeting, a preparatory report by the Organizing Committee for the International Labour Conference (League of Nations 1919c: 16) on the Employment of Women and Children and the Berne Conventions of 1906 recommended that the Berne provisions on night work simply be extended, but during the proceedings of the Commission on the Employment of Women at the Washington conference, some delegates spoke in favour of further restricting night work among women, called for longer periods of night-time rest, and raised concerns about the potentially abusive use of shift work to eliminate rest periods. In contrast, others, such as a delegate from Norway, opposed special protective laws for women, arguing that the goal should be to work towards the prohibition of absolutely all unnecessary night work (ILO 1919j: 103). Familiar tensions among women over whether to support sex-specific measures or protective legislation for all workers persisted in this forum. The conference followed the recommendation of the official organizing committee's preparatory report, but opted to supplement the Berne Convention with a distinct ILO Convention on Night Work (Women) (1919). The key differences between this ILO convention and its IALL precursor were that it applied to all industrial undertakings (rather than those where a minimum number were employed) and defined the term 'industry' more broadly, enabling signatories to delineate the division between industry, commerce, and agriculture (ILO 1919a: Arts. 1.1 and 1.2). There were similarities as well, including the familiar exception for women employed in undertakings where only members of the same family are employed (ILO 1919a: Art. 3). The presence of family members was, once again, presumed to accord women equivalent protection to the private sphere during the night.

The Commission on the Employment of Women also proposed that the conference endorse the protection of women after childbirth for a period of four weeks, in contrast to the resolution adopted by the International Congress of Working Women, which called for limiting women's labour force participation six weeks preceding and six weeks following birth. This commission 'did not feel impelled completely to prohibit the employment of women during the period preceding childbirth, but only to authorize pregnant women to stop work upon the production of a medical certificate' (ILO 1921a: 9). It also proposed free medical treatment and a benefit sufficient for the maintenance of the mother and the child under healthy conditions. The outcome was the adoption of an ILO Convention on Maternity (1919) that built on the Berne Convention by protecting women from terms and conditions of work interfering with their capacity to bear children and fulfil their domestic responsibilities. As an ILO report on *Women's Work under Labour Law: A Survey of Protective Legislation* (1932: 18, emphasis added) later confirmed:

It is clear that the aim of most of the legislative measures concerning the employ-ment of women will be maternity protection. Their purpose is to maintain intact the vitality of the woman worker so as to enable her to fulfil this function normally, and to help her carry out the tasks resulting from maternity in succeeding years, such as the care of her children, their education, etc. By strictly limiting the hours of work for women, by sparing them night work, which is so exhausting and trying, and by preventing their physical organs from being deformed by carry-ing too heavy weights or poisoned by dangerous substances, *the legislator is really endeavouring to preserve the maternal function and to ensure the well-being of future generations.*

The Convention on Maternity (1919) made exclusion from the labour force compulsory for women for six weeks following childbirth whether they were employed in public or private industrial or commercial undertakings, with the exception of family-run businesses, during which period they were to 'be paid benefits sufficient for the full and healthy maintenance of herself and her child' (ILO 1919b: Art. 3). These terms contrasted with the social wage entitlements beginning to be attached to the emergent normative model of employment, and identified subsequently with social citizenship, which were to be sufficient to cover a 'man and his family'. As envisioned by delegates to the first conference of the ILO, maternity benefits were not designed to encourage women's labour force participa-tion, yet women were to gain access to these benefits on this basis. Absent were provisions preserving the job a woman held prior to the period of compulsory leave; the primary gestures towards labour force reintegration were protections against dismissal during maternity leave or due to illness after giving birth and provision for nursing mothers to have 'half an hour twice a day during her working hours for this purpose' (ILO 1919b: Art. 3d).

Alongside the adoption of these two sex-specific conventions, the inter-national labour conference also devised several recommendations on 'unhealthy industries'. Delegates agreed, for example, to a Recommenda-tion on Lead Poisoning (Women and Children) (1919) that called for excluding women and young persons under the age of 18 from various processes involving lead, on the basis that it involves dangers 'to the function of maternity and to the physical development of children' (ILO 1919c: Art.1). They chose a recommendation rather than a convention, due to the lack of adequate medical statistics on the relative susceptibility of women and men in the majority of industries involving the use of lead (ILO 1921a). However, the calls of women advocating for the elimination of hazardous working processes in industry for all workers may have had some effect on the form of the instrument as delegates endorsed a gender-neutral recommendation on the Prohibition of the Use of White Phosphorus in the Manufacture of Matches (1919).

Preparing the Ground for the SER

The earliest international labour standards also included two conventions central to establishing the pillars of the SER—on hours of work in industry and unemployment—that are analysed in Chapter 2. The era beginning in 1919 is thus characterized typically as one in which proponents of international labour regulation moved to extend protection to all workers and to provide equal protection for adult men and women (Alcock 1971). Accordingly, casting attention to this perceived shift, on the eve of the 1921 International Labour Conference, the International Labour Office reported that:

the principal importance of the Conference which is about to be held lies...not in the special measures that it may adopt for the protection of women workers, so much as in the proposal to put men and women on a footing of almost complete equality in all protective measures contemplated. It is in this direction that women desire to see the development of protection for women workers. They no longer ask for privileges—they demand absolute equality. (ILO 1921a: 11)

There are, however, other possible interpretations of the nature of the package of international labour regulations that grew up immediately following the creation of the ILO, against a backdrop of national and international measures by then well-established. As Chapter 2 will argue, they could also be identified with the birth of a package of international labour regulations installing the SER as a normative model of employment geared to adult male citizens, and preparing the ground for ongoing exclusions on the basis of gender and citizenship status.

Notes

1. The Australian Factory and Shops Acts of 1885 and 1896 tried to limit the exclusion of small workshops by altering the definition of a factory first from a minimum of ten people to a minimum of six and subsequently a minimum of four, although this did not address problems associated with outwork, family work, and home-based workshops (Hutchins 1906: 2; see also Frances et al. 1996: 62).

2. According to Klem et al. (1950: 51), the first enforceable law was enacted in Massachusetts in 1874 (and strengthened in 1879 by deleting a wilful violation requirement). It set limits on working hours for women at 10 per day and 60 over the week, without the nullifying clause exempting those under contract.

3. As Hutchins (1906: 5) suggests, this situation stood in stark contrast to employers' key 'causes of complaint' surrounding the introduction of wage boards: the possibility that they would 'fix "fancy" wages on an unpractical basis'. To pre-empt such concerns, boards erred in the opposite direction: an amendment to the Act in 1903 required that the Board ascertain 'average wage rates paid by reputable employers to employees of average capacity, and that the lowest rates fixed by the determination shall in no case exceed the average rates so ascertained', unless the Board viewed the average wage to be 'unreasonably low'.

4. This Act, too, was constructed to limit the degree of state intervention—the scheme applied only where women's wages in a particular trade were extremely low relative to other wages (hence its limit to four industries) (Fredman 1997: 76).

5. From 1891 until 1911, Britain prohibited postnatal employment and according to Koven and Michel (1990: 1105), only in 1911, under the National Insurance Act, were 'the wives of insured workers and women finally granted a lump sum payment, usually 30 shillings at confinement, to address this hardship. Initially, the benefit was paid to the husband, but after strenuous lobbying by groups including the largely working-class Women's Cooperative Guild, mothers gained direct control over these funds'. Costs of the maternity benefit were shared by workers, employers, and the state, and it was available to workers earning less than £160 a year.

6. In this way, Koven and Michel's (1990) assessment of the inverse relationship between the power of women's social action movements and the range and generosity of state welfare benefits for women and children in Germany, the United States, the United Kingdom, and France complements other research on protective legislation by women's labour historians. Particularly complementary are their claims that, on the one hand, 'the United States, with the most politically powerful and broadly based female reform movements and the weakest state, yielded the least extensive and least generous maternal and child welfare benefits to women' (and that a similar but weaker pattern prevailed in Britain), while, on the other hand, 'Germany, with the strongest state,' yet 'politically ineffective women's movements offered the most comprehensive programs for women and children' (1080).

7. Jenson (1989: 257) argues that French feminists did not pursue suffrage with the same vigour as their American counterparts. The vote was a tool for reform in the United States, 'whereas in France the left feared female suffrage as a buttress for the church while Solidarists saw it as unnecessary in a society of families whose male head could represent the whole'.

8. With the primary exception of work by Anderson and Winslow (1951), Lubin and Winslow (1990), Wikander (1992, 1995), Whitworth (1994), Rupp (1997),

and Bryson (2003), there is a dearth of scholarship documenting international debates pertinent to protective legislation in women's congresses and related forums during the period covered in this subsection. The discussion is therefore influenced greatly by the insights of these scholars, especially Wikander's two investigations (published in English), both the chronology of events they present and their description of debates taking place at different congresses.

9. According to Rupp (1997: 20), the International Council of Women became a United States-sponsored organization that primarily included representatives from North America and Western Europe and espoused conservative and Euro-centric views. Led by Lady Aberdeen of Scotland for 40 years, the Council characterized women's 'first mission' as 'her home'.

10. Indeed, that same year, France and Italy negotiated a workers' protection treaty.

2

Constructing and Consolidating the Standard Employment Relationship in International Labour Regulation

[M]ost important... is the recommendation that national policies be prepared on a tripartite basis within each nation, to lead towards full employment, social security, and rising standards of living.... It is up to us to remove the cruelty of exploitation. It is up to us to help create opportunity for men to live and work as self-respecting individuals.

ILO (1944c) Mr. Robert J. Watt, Workers' delegate of the United States of America, *'A New Era': The Philadelphia Conference and the Future of the ILO*, Montreal: 18.

Along with the emergence of Fordism and the Keynesian welfare state, the package of international labour regulations crafted in the interwar years and the post-World War II era centred on establishing the SER as a normative model of employment geared to adult male citizens. The SER was never universal of course—many women and migrant workers were excluded from its central pillars and lacked access to its associated benefits and entitlements. Yet even as the SER materialized for many working-class male citizens, the gender contract with which it was intertwined began to unravel.

This chapter traces the evolution of the SER as the baseline of international labour regulation in the interwar and postwar periods. Between 1919 and the immediate post-World War II era, a regulatory architecture built upon employee status (i.e. the bilateral employment relationship), standardized working time (normal daily, weekly, and annual hours), and continuous employment (permanency) emerged in international labour regulations. Through these pillars, the SER came to serve as a baseline for the extension of labour protections and social benefits, sufficient wages, and a social wage designed to support adult male citizens and their dependants. Alongside the consolidation of the SER in the 1950s and the 1960s, its associated gender contract began to crumble. In these decades, international labour regulations were adjusted to reflect and reinforce challenges to norms of male breadwinning and female caregiving and to sustain national citizenship boundaries, while extending select protections to migrant workers. At the same time, despite the embrace of mechanisms fostering formal equality, there remained regulations preserving sex-specific measures and continued exclusions from the SER's central pillars on the basis of nationality.

Constructing the Pillars of the SER: The Interwar and Immediate Postwar Years

The origins of the SER in international labour regulation rest in a constellation of conventions, recommendations, and resolutions adopted by the ILO beginning in 1919, contributing to what this book labels its central pillars. In this chapter, these pillars serve as a heuristic device in organizing the many debates and discussions surrounding the adoption of early regulations of the International Labour Code. For this reason, the ensuing discussion refers only to select regulations. Rather than follow a strictly chronological order, it proceeds by discussing employee status (i.e. the bilateral employment relationship), standardized working time, and continuous employment, addressing overlap both between the pillars and the regulations identified with them (for a table of international labour regulations presented in the chapter, see Appendix A).[1]

The Bilateral Employment Relationship

The employment relationship,[2] identified typically with a contract of employment between an employee and an employer, is the foremost pillar of the SER. As a legal concept, employment is central to determining the labour protections attached to different forms of paid work (Fudge et al. 2002: 1); it marks the dividing line between the sphere of commerce, a universe assumed to be populated by business enterprises, and that of the labour market, populated by workers (see also England et al. 1998: 1–2; Engblom 2001: 220; Perulli 2003: 6–7).[3] One side of this distinction is governed by laws, policies, and contractual relations promoting competition. The other side removes workers and their organizations from the bounds of commercial regulation in recognition that capitalist labour markets require not only the circulation of labour power but the production of labourers (the embodiment of labour power), which differs from the production of all other commodities in that it requires constraints on the market circulation of labour power (Vosko 2000: chapter 1).

Over the course of the 20th century, employee status became a prerequisite for workers' access to labour protections ranging from those governing maximum hours, minimum wages, and the right to refuse dangerous work, to statutory holidays and to maternity leave, as well as to forms of social insurance, such as unemployment insurance and pensions, and in many cases collective bargaining. In contrast, workers who depended on their capacity to sell their labour power but fell outside the strictures of the employment relationship, especially 'self-employed workers' (Cranford et al. 2005), were often treated as independent business entrepreneurs not requiring labour protection (Fudge et al. 2002), alongside, in some instances, workers in triangular relationships, such as temporary agency workers (Vosko 2000; Davidov 2004).

Employee status played a pivotal role in standardizing contracts for the performance of work under Fordism, as well as in shaping social insurance provision in the world of welfare capitalism. More than any other feature of the SER, it facilitated the combination of a high level of subordination on the part of the worker to the employer and long-term stability. In so doing, it set boundaries around the activities of the firm. As Engblom (2001: 221) observes, the rise of the employment relationship as the principal basis for labour protection helped confine the production of goods and services to individual firms, which engaged workers through contracts of employment for which 'labour law set the rules', while cultivating the use of commercial contracts 'for the acquisition of goods and services outside the firm'.

Given the significance of the employment relationship to the SER, it is not surprising that the 'first principle' of international labour regulation, expressed in the Labour Charter (League of Nations 1919b: Part XIII, Annex, Art. 427), was quite literally that 'labour should not be regarded merely as a commodity or article of commerce'. Advancing this sentiment, the employment relationship was institutionalized in many early ILO conventions, most concretely in the Convention on Unemployment (1919). This convention encouraged states to support the formation of the modern (i.e. free) labour market by introducing mechanisms distinguishing it from other commodity markets. One of its central aims was to cultivate national systems of free public employment agencies to match workers with employers (ILO 1919g: Art. 2). Reflecting the maxim endorsed as a general tenet in the subsequent Philadelphia Declaration (1944), 'labour is not a commodity' (specifically, that workers should not have to pay for work), the Recommendation on Unemployment (1919) called for states to 'prohibit the establishment of employment agencies which charge fees or which carry out their business for profit' (ILO 1919h: 1–2). This provision also followed from the ILO's mandate to protect 'the interests of workers when employed in countries other than their own' and its growing concern with the unscrupulous activities of for-profit private employment agents placing migrant workers (League of Nations 1919b: s. 1).

It took until 1932 for delegates to an International Labour Conference to draft a convention on fee-charging employment agencies, at which time they decided to include all commercial establishments, including those charging fees to employers, on account partly of their desire to regulate private employment agencies carrying on recruitment and placement activities between nations (Vosko 2000: 68–9). Shortly thereafter, a Convention on Fee-Charging Employment Agencies (1933) was adopted, which provided for their prohibition. This move amounted to the rejection of triangular relationships between workers, employers, and private employment agencies, and it installed the bilateral employment relationship as the legitimate basis for labour regulation (ILO 1933a and 1933b; Vosko 2000: chapters 1 and 2). Eventually, the prohibition was relaxed somewhat, as strict regulation of private employment agencies became an option with the Convention on Fee-Charging Employment Agencies (Revised) (1949). However, just prior to its adoption, two new regulations offering a framework for the creation and coordination of national public employment services— the Convention and Recommendation on the Organization of the Employment Service (1948)—augmented the notion that workers should be entitled to free public assistance in obtaining employment, 'obviat[ing] the need for private employment agencies' (ILO 1948g: para. 26).

Standardized Working Time

The sale of labour power to an employer over a specified period of time represents a second pillar of the SER. The main benefits to employers of this exchange are exclusivity and direct control. As the SER emerged, these features enabled firms to monitor workers' efforts, to ensure that they were in sync with technological change and developments in work organization, and to alter their tasks without the necessity of re-contracting (Bosch 2006: 44; Rubery et al. 2006: 124; see also Marsden 1999). The period of recuperation from paid employment produced by this arrangement also generated improvements in workers' health, leading to greater efficiency, as well as increased profitability for employers (Ford 1926). In exchange, workers gained predictability from the commitment to minimum periods of engagement as well as guaranteed earnings (Clarke 1992: 2000). They also benefited from rules governing the utilization of their labour power under the employment contract. Standardized working time served as a means of brokering employers' aim to extract surplus value and workers' demands for greater control over the labour process and their lives outside the labour force.

One outcome of this bargain was the establishment of a conception of 'standardized time', characterized by a uniform and synchronized paid working day (typically eight hours), working week (approximately 40 hours), and working year (with statutory holidays and leave provisions) (Supiot 2001: 63; Boulin 2006: 197; see also Mückenberger 1989; Bosch 2004, 2006). Another result was the presumed segmentation of workers' lives into three distinct sequences: education, market work, and retirement (Anxo et al. 2006a: 93).

The 'homogeneous' (Supiot 2001: 63) conception of time characterizing the 'market work' sequence of the life-course assumed remuneration for all the time when the employee is at the employer's disposal (Rubery et al. 2006: 125). Pay for job inactivity enabled employers to develop and retain a regular workforce, willing to adjust its output to match changes in demand, even as they continually tested its limits through layoffs and minimal notice provisions (Jacoby 1985; see also Bosch 2006).

The notion of standard working time, and the normative life-course it assumed, was always deeply gendered. In addition to segmenting sequences of the life-course to conform with a 'male' pattern, it cast the unpaid work of daily and intergenerational reproduction as 'non-work' or 'free time' (Everingham 2002: 336; see also Supiot 2001: chapter 3). At its height, standardized working time also reconfigured, as consumption, elements of this supposed non-work (Aglietta 1979). In these ways, it supported the dualistic conception of time integral to the male breadwinner / female caregiver contract. One side of this conception reflected the uniform and measurable time associated with the employment norm, what Supiot (2001: 68) calls 'male time', while the other side reflected 'unlimited time, female time, a space populated by retired workers, women and children'. Together, both sides upheld the unequal sex/gender divisions of labour (paid and unpaid) intrinsic to this gender contract.

As Chapter 1 demonstrated, growing out of protective labour legislation targeting women's work at night and setting sex- and age-specific maximum daily and weekly hours, the standard work day and work week, including periods of rest and holidays, were codified in the early 20th century in Australia, Canada, the United States, and various countries of Western Europe. Although their lineage may be traced to the 1906 Berne Convention, international labour regulations establishing regular working hours date to 1919 and the adoption of the ILO's first convention—the Convention on Hours of Work (Industry)—introducing the eight-hour day and the 48-hour week. This convention covered wage workers only and exclusively those in industry, a designation which many wage-earning women lacked due to narrow conceptions of industrial employment (ILO 1919d: Art. 2). The assumed norm for women was caregiving and for their male counterparts, breadwinning. Accordingly, in debates addressing to whom the convention would apply, a delegate from Panama stated: 'with regard to production, assurance can well be given that if the men performed productive labour.... we could very well produce all that is necessary to meet the requirements of consumption, without having to commit the cowardice of making mothers... and children work' (ILO 1919j: 68).

The convention also permitted countries to exclude 'certain classes of workers whose work is essentially intermittent', such as casual workers, as well as workers in undertakings 'in which only members of the same family are employed' (ILO 1919d: Arts. 2 and 6). The effect was to characterize women and children, for whom casual work and work in family-run enterprises was especially common, as falling outside the realm where hours protections were necessary (ILO 1919d: Art. 6). During the negotiation process, workers' delegates had attempted to clarify that the exclusion of workers in family-run enterprises did not cover homeworkers. Their amendment was defeated because, in the words of a government delegate, it is 'impossible to regulate this work, as it would require an immense system of inspection, and the efforts of the ILO ought to be directed towards suppressing home work rather than towards regulating it' (ILO 1919f: 10). Furthermore, in the view of an employers' delegate, such an amendment would 'give the State too large a control over private life' (ILO 1919f: 10).[4]

The hours-pillar of the SER was subsequently elaborated and solidified by regulations on weekly rest, leisure time, women's work at night, and weekly working hours. The first set, on weekly rest, recognized workers' entitlement to 'time for recreation, for education, and for the discharge of social and family duties' (ILO 1921e: 33). In 1921, delegates to the International Labour Conference adopted a Convention on Weekly Rest, applicable to industry, and advanced a recommendation, geared to commerce, stipulating an uninterrupted day of rest per week. These instruments also introduced the notion of 'community time', suggesting that the rest period be 'granted simultaneously to the whole of the staff of each undertaking' on the day coinciding with that 'established by the traditions or customs of the country or district' (ILO 1921c: Arts. 2.2 and 2.3, see also 1921d). Notably, the records of debates indicate that no explicit provision for domestics and house servants was deemed necessary, 'since domestic work is distinct from work in industry and commerce' (ILO 1921e: 122–3). The hours-pillar was limited to workplaces in the public sphere with implications for the configuration of gendered class relations.

The Recommendation on the Utilization of Spare Time (1924) set limits on the working day in order to make possible relaxation time for workers engaged in 'ordinary work', a notion bolstering the emergent ideal of normal (i.e. full-time) work and prefiguring the related notion of continuous employment. As repeated references to the gender non-neutral in the preamble (e.g. 'his productive capacity') attest, the male wage-earner in this ordinary situation was the presumed subject (ILO 1924). Furthermore, as Murray (2001a: 27) observes in her important study of maternity regulation, the notion of leisure time for men 'reflected a complete sexual division of labour, as the archetypal male was not conceived as the person who engaged in unpaid domestic labour in the private sphere of the home'. Specifically, the recommendation aimed to improve 'social hygiene' by promoting sports, gardening, and intellectual pursuits among men who were assumed to be employed on an ongoing basis. It also addressed leisure, relating it to the 'full and harmonious development' of the individual, family, and community, while neglecting domestic work entirely (ILO 1924: Part IV).

With the Great Depression came a revised Convention on Night Work (Women) (1934), which relaxed earlier provisions by permitting women holding 'responsible' positions to work at night. As one government spokesperson noted in the lead-up to its adoption: 'we consider that the distinction between the ordinary woman worker and the woman who occupies a post of management involving responsibilities is a just one' (ILO 1934c: 194).[5] Delegates did not arrive at this position without debate, however. A spokesperson for British workers, for example, registered strong opposition to this change:

We are opposed to night work for women, and we maintain that this alteration will open the door very much more widely for the employment of women at night. I have yet to be convinced that employers will employ women in these higher posts which are usually reserved for the men, and if we give permission for women to be employed in this way it will mean that various excuses will be made to open the door more widely for the employment of women at night. (ILO 1934c: 193)

From a different standpoint, the spokesperson for Belgian workers argued that 'at a time when the whole working class is crying for reduced hours of work, it is inopportune to demand any modification of a Convention which may imply longer working hours' (ILO 1934c: 201). His position reflected a broader strategy, regaining momentum at the time, that retaining limitations on night work for women offered an entrée into limiting it for all workers. The provision allowing women managers to work at night nevertheless passed by a majority vote, as did one allowing women 'not ordinarily engaged in manual work' to do the same, thereby preserving gender norms for industrial workers (ILO 1934a: Art. 8). In loosening provisions for managers while retaining wider limitations, the balance sought was well expressed by the government representative of Spain, who noted 'it is a question of retaining the principle of freedom for women at the same time as assuring them the protection, which is their right' (ILO 1934c: 194). This delegate went on to stress the problems facing unattached women, in particular:

[I]n many countries where women cannot get to work at 5am, it is impossible for them to work on the second shift and that amounts to an absolute prohibition of work by women...That may be desirable from the male point of view, because it may mean a fall in male unemployment; but the loss suffered by the household where the woman is the breadwinner can never be made up in many of these cases. We must remember that it is our legal duty to legislate socially, but to make that legislation conform to the actual conditions which prevail. (199)

A year later, consistent with this concern to 'legislate socially', the Convention on the Forty-Hour Week (1935) responded to widespread unemployment and the 'many millions of workers throughout the world suffering hardship and privation for which they are not themselves responsible and from which they are justly entitled to be relieved' by aiming at a reduction in paid working hours (ILO 1935a: Preamble).

Continuous Employment

Continuous employment is a third pillar of the SER. Since social relations distinguish the exchange of labour power from all other forms of exchange, ownership and control of the means of production is not, in itself, a guarantee of employers' ability to extract profit from the production process; workers' cooperation is essential. Employers thus cultivate forms of labour control aimed at maximizing profit, while minimizing tensions and conflicts inherent in the labour relationship (Buroway 1979; Edwards 1979; Nolan 1983: 303). In the early 20th century, with the decline of forms of labour contracting, such as the drive-system, and the transformation of the firm from a coordinator of contracts into an 'employing organization', continuous (or open-ended) employment facilitated this process of mediation (Deakin 2002; Marsden 2004: 663).

The open-ended employment relationship at a common workplace materialized later than the bilateral employment relationship itself; emerging initially in large firms, it was also associated with internal labour markets (Doeringer and Piore 1971). It allowed employers to develop highly skilled, reliable workforces that could be assigned new tasks within the firm without renegotiating contracts. In return for their loyalty and willingness to learn, workers gained continuity. Under the open-ended employment relationship, workers represented an investment for employers that required ongoing care to ensure retention over the long term. At the same time, the promise of permanency gave workers stability. Mechanisms integral to the open-ended employment relationship included limited and selective recruitment strategies, typically through the identification of pre-specified ports of entry, firm-specific job ladders, investments in on-the-job training, clear and enforceable terms and conditions of employment, as well as work rules establishing the obligations of both the parties and protecting against opportunistic behaviour, while providing predictable wages, and deferred benefits (Nolan 1983: 304; Bosch 2004: 619; Marsden 2004: 663; Stone 2004: 53). The success of this constellation of features, for both workers and employers, pivoted on the presumed indefinite duration of the employment relationship. Career pay systems were, for example, premised on the theory that employees would initially receive wages and benefits exceeding their productivity, while their outputs mid-career would surpass their level of remuneration, providing both for investment in the firm and for sustaining workers' wage levels late-career in the face of predicted lower productivity. They meant, as Marsden (2004: 667) observes, that 'the longer the anticipated period of enhanced earnings, the greater the employee's corresponding loss if dismissed for poor performance—and also, arguably, the greater the quasi gift-exchange to encourage above average performance'.

The open-ended employment relationship secured the risk-sharing integral to the psychological contract upholding the SER. At the same time, it fostered a gender contract assuming male providers and female caregivers: the notion of a continuous employment relationship, predicated on dividing individuals' lives into 'water-tight' stages of education, ongoing employment, and retirement (Anxo et al. 2006b), prescribed loyalty and mutuality in the limited sphere of the labour force and especially in individual firms. Instead of inspiring these values at a community level, the open-ended employment relationship relied on sex/gender divisions of labour, especially the unpaid domestic labour contributing to workers' daily and generational reproduction. For the (mainly male) workers with such relationships, there was some room for leisure in the employment phase of life, but little space for sharing unpaid caregiving.

In international labour regulation, the pillar of continuous employment began to form with early ILO regulations on unemployment encouraging government-administered unemployment insurance. In 1919, the Recommendation on Unemployment called for establishing 'effective system[s] of unemployment insurance' at the national level (ILO 1919h: para. III). Such systems were deemed necessary to accumulate supports for wage-earners normally employed on a continual basis experiencing bouts of unemployment. Under the recommendation's terms, the typical unemployed person was assumed to be an adult male employed formerly in industry. Yet preparatory reports also highlight delegates' concern for male workers routinely employed seasonally, such as construction workers, dock and wharf workers, porters, and those on the 'fringe in large industries' facing bouts of unemployment (ILO 1919k: 6).

In its support for sustainable systems of unemployment insurance accessible to workers formerly employed on a continual basis, the Convention on Unemployment also obliged ratifying countries with such systems to make arrangements to provide the same rates of unemployment benefits to migrant workers as national citizens (Art. 3). Article 3 of the Convention was motivated by concerns about unfair competition within nations, specifically that the limited duration of many migrant workers' stay would undermine the sustainability of social security provision for worker-citizens (ILO 1921b: 551–2). According to Hasenau (1991: 690), 'concern about the competitive repercussions of advanced social security schemes' influenced early ILO regulations encouraging countries to negotiate bilateral agreements to provide select provisions for equality of treatment between national and migrant workers.

Several conventions and recommendations adopted starting in the 1930s advanced the norm of the open-ended employment relationship further. In 1934, the Convention on Unemployment Provision made an explicit link between access to unemployment benefits and continuous employment relationships. It prescribed that unemployment insurance be available to 'persons habitually employed for wages or salary' (ILO 1934b: Art. 2.1). In the process, it defined habitual employment narrowly by excluding persons engaged only occasionally and persons employed in a family business (ILO 1934b: Art. 2.2). This convention also permitted the exclusion of young workers, domestic workers, and homeworkers, regardless of the nature of their employment relationship or its duration. In this way, it provided for excluding workers working in the private sphere or in worksites outside the employer's premises from unemployment provision. Even for those workers deemed to be 'habitually employed', the convention made the receipt of benefits 'conditional on the need of the claimant', conveying the message that social wage entitlements properly flow through a single wage-earner (ILO 1934b: Art. 12.2).[6]

Also addressed to workers engaged in continuous employment relationships, the Convention on Holidays with Pay (1936) prescribed paid vacations for all employed persons in industry and commerce, with the exception of persons employed in family businesses (ILO 1936a: Art 1.3a). The motivation for employers: 'employees fresh and eager for work' (ILO 1935b: 82). As the record of proceedings of the 1935 session notes, 'it would undoubtedly be a fallacy even from a purely economic point of view, to regard paid holidays as a burden on the employer for which he receives no return' (82). With the growing assumption that open-ended employment relationships were a sound investment for both parties, employers were motivated to provide workers with long-term incentives to preserve their health and thereby their efficiency.[7]

Reinforcing the Pillars: Freedom of Association and Collective Bargaining

By mid-century, the central pillars of the SER had formed in international labour regulation: essentially, this meant full-time continuous wage or salaried employment performed by an adult male citizen for a single employer. Consolidating the post-World War II compromise, at this juncture the emphasis shifted to codifying rights to freedom of association and collective bargaining—the primary governance mechanisms linking work organization and the labour supply under the SER. The ILO Constitution had affirmed the principle of freedom of association in 1919 and in 1944 the Declaration of Philadelphia reaffirmed this principle, as well as recognized the right to collective bargaining. However, due to the depth of disagreement between workers, employers, and their governments at the time, efforts to craft a single convention on freedom of association and the right to collective bargaining failed. The reasons provided for this failure include: splits over whether freedom of association should be extended for 'lawful purposes' only; tensions over which body—the ILO or the new UN Economic and Social Council—should be responsible for overseeing these rights; and, whether the right of association should extend to workers only or to both workers and employers. The compromise, reached following the end of World War II, was to adopt two conventions—one on freedom of association covering all workers and employers and another setting general parameters for collective bargaining.

The Convention on Freedom of Association and the Right to Organise (1948) extended to 'workers without distinction whatsoever'. At that time, delegates to the International Labour Conference chose between adopting the wording 'workers without distinction' or enumerating typical grounds of discrimination. They selected the former because it offered a 'more comprehensive...formula' than one enumerating different kinds of discrimination, 'which always entails the risk of certain types being omitted' (ILO 1948b: 86–7). Thus the self-employed fell within the scope of the convention, as did migrant workers. The Convention on the Right to Organise and Collective Bargaining (1949), in turn, provided a framework for regulating conditions of employment through collective agreements governing 'relations between employers and workers' (ILO 1948c: 182–3). It also contributed to a particular worksite norm; although the convention recognized various forms of collective bargaining, including industry- or sector-wide and enterprise-level bargaining, the wage-earners of principal focus in discussions leading to its adoption were 'workpeople in an undertaking' (ILO 1947: 64–5, 66).

Migrant Work

Migrant work was a central item on the ILO agenda from its inception—recall, for example, that the unscrupulous actions of fee-charging agencies engaged in recruiting and placing migrant workers spurred calls for their prohibition in the 1919 Recommendation on Unemployment. Recall too the provision for extending the same rates of unemployment benefits to migrant workers and national citizens in the Convention on Unemployment. The first international labour regulation addressed exclusively to the situation of migrant workers was the Recommendation on the Reciprocity of Treatment of Foreign Workers (1919), which called for equality of treatment, on the condition of reciprocity, between citizen and migrant workers regarding a broader set of social protections that included unemployment relief as well as freedom of association. Together with the Recommendation on Unemployment, it worked to shape the subsequent Convention on Equality of Treatment (Accident Compensation) (1925). Significantly, this convention provided for extending to migrant workers and their families equality of treatment in terms of workers' compensation subject neither to reciprocity nor to any condition of residence. Yet, as future developments would show, accident compensation was for decades to remain the main area in which no such conditions were to apply (see Creutz 1968).

In the 1920s, building on concerns raised in discussions towards the first ILO Convention on Unemployment, there were also numerous efforts to understand and quantify migrant work, including key conferences in Geneva, Rome, and Havana. These conferences established formative committees, such as the International Emigration Committee, and focused on how best to undertake the collection of migration statistics. Their emphasis was, however, extra-regulatory activity, because countries with restrictive immigration policies were reluctant to elaborate all but a few binding international labour standards on migration.[8] At the same time, delegates articulated the need to protect migrant workers—and they did so along gendered lines. As the record of proceedings of the 1927 ILO Conference on Migration in its Various Forms (ILO 1927: 14) noted:

the overseas emigration of males has, both for the countries from which they emigrate and those to which they immigrate, a different significance from that of females. In the first instance the emigrants are generally productive workers, whereas in the second case they are usually persons connected with the male emigrants and do not directly participate in the economic production of the country.

The proceedings of this conference stressed the need to extend protection to male migrant workers not destined for permanent settlement, noting that 'the expenses and inconveniences arising from the maintenance of two households, such as occurs when married men emigrate, leaving families in their own country, should also be taken into consideration from the economic and moral standpoint' (ILO 1927: 14). Nevertheless delegates made no concrete proposals for regulations extending such protections.

It was only in 1939 that the ILO adopted a Convention on Migration for Employment, focusing on limiting abuses, such as misleading propaganda, and on the supply of information and the provision of services to migrant workers. Like its forerunners, this convention had called for agreements between countries, setting out terms for recruitment, placement, and conditions of employment. In addition, it provided a framework for applying 'to foreigners treatment no less favourable than that which it applies to its own nationals', with respect to remuneration, the right to belong to a trade union, employment taxes, dues or contributions, and legal proceedings related to contracts of employment, provisions that could be made subject to reciprocity (ILO 1939: Arts. 6.1 and 6.2). However, the 1939 convention never came into force because it did not achieve a sufficient level of ratification: indicative of states' concern to retain control over labour and employment regulation within their national borders, governments' objections to the provision for equal treatment, even highly qualified, between national citizens and migrant workers thwarted its introduction.

A decade later, a Convention on Migration for Employment (1949) was finally adopted, and quickly came into force. It required any state that ratified it to give 'immigrants lawfully within its territory treatment no less favourable than that which it applies to its own nationals' on matters relating to remuneration, family allowances, and, where applicable, hours of work, overtime arrangements, holidays with pay, membership of trade unions, and the benefits of collective bargaining and social security (ILO 1949b: Art. 6.1). Yet, in these and other areas, the notion of treatment no less favourable than nationals was qualified considerably. For example, social security provision was subject to arrangements, set out by receiving countries, for the acquisition of rights; the convention also permitted receiving countries to 'prescribe special arrangements concerning benefits or portions of benefits which are payable wholly out of public funds' (ILO 1949b: Art. 6.1b.i–ii). Although its provisions were to apply 'without discrimination in respect of nationality, race, religion or sex', the terms of the convention extended most fully to workers entering with authorization to settle permanently and ultimately to obtain citizenship in a receiving country (ILO 1949b: Art 6.1). To advance this end, a Model Agreement on Temporary and Permanent Migration for Employment appended to the associated recommendation included a provision calling on authorities in the country of immigration to 'facilitate the procedure of naturalisation' for those destined for permanent migration (ILO 1949c: Annex Art. 14). The convention's provision for preferential treatment of immigrants took particular expression in Article 11.1, permitting exclusions from the definition of 'migrant for employment', including 'short-term entry of members of liberal professions and artists'. To facilitate ratification, the convention also included a section of universally applicable general provisions, as well as three optional annexes, which governments could include or exclude in any combination.

This formulation, as well as provisions permitting preferential treatment for immigrants, inaugurated yet another fundamental distinction tied to national citizenship that would later become entrenched in ILO and UN regulations—the division between migrant workers authorized to reside on a temporary basis and immigrants destined for permanent residency. Only immigrants were to benefit, as far as possible, from the rights and entitlements attached to the SER. In this way, early ILO standards on migration provided for inferior rights and entitlements for employed workers lacking national citizenship in the countries in which they worked.

Stripping the SER of its Exclusions: The Era of Formal Equality

Even as the SER was materializing among many adult male citizens, the gender contract which helped make it possible began to crumble. This story is familiar, having been told from a variety of perspectives and with different emphases across contexts in which the SER rose to ascendancy (see for example on Australia, Pocock 2006; on Britain, Crompton 1999 and Lewis 2001; on Canada, Armstrong and Armstrong 1994; Vosko 2002b; and, on the United States, Appelbaum et al. 2002 and Grunow et al. 2006). While the decline of the male breadwinner / female caregiver contract was uneven, there were common themes: no longer was breadwinning assumed to be the domain of men. Women's employment was not discouraged to the degree it had been; accordingly, women's labour force participation rates rose dramatically in industrialized countries in the latter decades of the 20th century (see for example Standing 1989 and 1999b). International labour regulations adopted as early as the 1950s reflected and reinforced such shifts. Their emphasis: removing explicit exclusions from the SER, especially those targeting women, as well as, albeit to a lesser extent, other socially disadvantaged groups, such as migrant workers.

Equal Remuneration, Maternity, and Social Security

The Convention on Equal Remuneration (1951) was the first in a series of regulations attempting to 'de-gender' the SER. This convention advanced a framework for equal pay for men and women workers for work of equal value. It targeted principally workers in employment relationships, defining 'remuneration' to include 'the ordinary, basic or minimum wage or salary and any additional emoluments whatsoever payable directly or indirectly by the employer to the worker' (ILO 1951: Art. 1a). Under the convention's terms, 'equal remuneration...for work of equal value'

65

referred to rates of pay established without discrimination based on sex (ILO 1951: Art. 1b). To give this principle effect, the convention called for 'objective appraisal of jobs' to be determined by state authorities or collective agreement (ILO 1951: Arts. 3.1–3.2). The reference to 'value' represented a move beyond 'equal pay for equal work', which, as Chapter 1 showed, some advocates of protective legislation supported in the early 20th century as a means of preserving men's jobs. At the same time, Article 3 of the convention permitted 'differential rates between workers, which correspond, without regard to sex, to differences, as determined by objective appraisal, in the work to be performed', leaving room for assigning work in occupations and industries long identified with the SER greater value than those traditionally falling outside its ambit. Women and men in jobs conforming to the pillars of the SER were to be compensated equally for work whose value was determined to be the same.

Following the Convention on Equal Remuneration, the approach to maternity protection changed as well. The 1952 Convention on Maternity (Revised) strengthened and affirmed women's caregiving role, maintaining a strong protective orientation. However, it also provided for several improvements for women seeking to remain in the labour force after childbirth: employers were barred from dismissing women on maternity leave and nursing periods were to count as part of the working day. Simultaneously, in a move acknowledging women's entitlements as breadwinners, provisions relating to cash benefits were modified to refer to 'a suitable standard of living' for a woman and her child, altering somewhat the tacit acceptance of lower than subsistence level benefits in the previous instrument (ILO 1952c: Art. 4.6). Even as the presumption of their primary role as mothers remained, the revised Maternity Convention recognized women's growing dual roles. During the lead-up to its revision, a delegate from the United States noted accordingly that 'the Convention is of more than ordinary significance because, in addition to safeguarding the health of women who carry the double burden of paid employment and motherhood, it directly affects the right of children to be well born and promotes the welfare of the race' (ILO 1952d: 13–14).[9]

At the same time, the revised convention effectively extended access to the SER to women workers taking leave to care for their infants. It did so by providing for the extension of cash and medical benefits to new mothers, advancing a model of what feminist scholars have come to label 'public patriarchy' (see for example Gordon 1990), whereby the state, rather than employers, is centrally responsible for ensuring the daily and intergenerational reproduction of the labour force. Cash benefits were, however, to be pegged only at 'a rate of not less than two-thirds of the women's previous earnings', and thereby poised to compensate only partially for women's already low earnings (ILO 1952c: Art. 4.6). Furthermore, Article 4.5 of the convention provided that 'in no case shall the employer be individually liable for the cost of such benefits due to women employed by him'. This provision, which aimed explicitly to prevent employers from using the excuse that women of childbearing age were too costly to employ, at the same time symbolized delegates' efforts to cushion employers from an expanded SER that no longer excluded women.

Indicative of the still male baseline of international labour regulation, another convention adopted the same year enlarged the social wage function of the SER without quite overturning the gendered assumptions about breadwinning and caregiving at its root. The Convention on Social Security (Minimum Standards) (1952) advanced minimum standards in areas such as medical care, sickness, and unemployment. It introduced guidelines for extending social security benefits and entitlements on the basis of employee status and continuity of service as well as place of work (ILO 1952a); reflecting these pillars of the SER, the subsection on unemployment benefits, for example, retained the large industrial workplace as a norm by prescribing minimum standards for 'employees, constituting not less than 50 per cent of all employees in industrial workplaces employing 20 persons or more' (ILO 1952a: Part XI, Art. 21). At the same time, it cast 'the ordinary' beneficiary of social insurance as an adult male labourer with a wife and children engaged in work for wages on an ongoing basis, and defined 'a wife' as someone 'who is maintained by her husband' (ILO 1952a: Schedule to Part XI, Art. 1(c), see also Art. 66 and ILO 1952b: 138–9).

Non-Discrimination

Deepening efforts to limit exclusions from the SER, the Convention on Discrimination (Employment and Occupation) was adopted in 1958 with the aim of eliminating discrimination so that 'all human beings . . . have the right to pursue both their material well-being and their spiritual development in conditions of freedom and dignity, of economic security and equal opportunity' (ILO 1958a: Preamble, see also Art. 2). The Convention emerged in response to collective struggles for political, social, and economic rights among socially disadvantaged groups (ILO 1956 and 1957). Following UN anti-discrimination policy, especially Article 1 of its founding Charter and Article 2 of the Universal Declaration of Human Rights, the grounds for non-discrimination included not only sex, but race, colour, religion, political opinion, and national extraction. However, they did not include nationality, despite sustained opposition (ILO 1958c). Indeed, negotiations towards the convention pronounced that restrictions on employment based on nationality are 'expected, non-discriminatory and a natural outcome of the migration contract', an interpretation prevailing through to the end of the 20th century (ILO 1956: 17–18).[10]

For the prohibited grounds falling within its scope, the convention defined discrimination as any distinction, exclusion, or preference that impairs equal opportunity or treatment (ILO 1958a: Art. 1.1). Yet it still included several qualifications permitting sex-specific measures. Rather than acting retroactively to make pre-existing conventions conform with its core principles, it deferred to them by permitting 'special measures of protection or assistance provided for in other [ILO] Conventions or Recommendations' (ILO 1958a: Art. 5); for example, it upheld the terms of the revised Maternity Convention as well as others addressed to women, such as those on night work. It also deemed 'any distinction, exclusion or preference in respect of a particular job based on the inherent requirements' not to be discrimination (ILO 1958a: Art. 1.2). These qualifiers provided for the coexistence of policies promoting a gender-neutral SER and protective measures for women.

Debates preceding the adoption of the Convention on Discrimination attest to some delegates' efforts to retain a normative model of employment geared to adult male citizens. In discussing continuity of employment, for example, a number of government representatives proposed preserving the ability of employers to give 'greater security of tenure on social grounds to certain categories (for instance family breadwinners)' (ILO 1957: 108). Some representatives also expressed support for wider provisions permitting governments to favour male breadwinners: to this end, the delegate from Ireland suggested that the term 'sex' be subject to certain limitations in the interests of protecting family (ILO 1957: 101). These sorts of proposals did not materialize in either the Convention or the Recommendation on Discrimination but they were indicative of lingering support for the continuation of an explicitly male standard.

A male standard also guided subsequent ILO regulations centring on the relationship between breadwinning and caregiving. For instance, the 1965 Recommendation on Employment (Women with Family Responsibilities) aimed to help remedy the 'special problems faced by women' with caregiving responsibilities that are also an 'integral and essential part of the labour force' (ILO 1965: Preamble, paras. 2, 4). Subscribing to tenets of the Convention on Discrimination, it acknowledged that many of the 'problems faced by women are not problems peculiar to women workers but are problems of the family and society as a whole' that could, for example, be remedied through the reduction of daily and weekly hours of paid work for all. Still, it rested on the assumption that *women* 'need to reconcile their dual family and work responsibilities'; in this way, it endorsed the qualifiers (permitting 'special measures') under its non-discrimination forerunner (ILO 1965: Preamble, paras. 3, 4, 5). The framework of the recommendation provided greater opportunity for breadwinning among women, while retaining the notion that women are suited to holding the dual roles of 'primary' caregivers and 'secondary' breadwinners (ILO 1965: Part I, 1a). Women were to be integrated into the labour force on an equal basis, but, at the same time, certain measures were deemed necessary to enable them to continue their unpaid caregiving work, such as reduced hours of 'normal' paid work (ILO 1965: Part II, 2, and Part III, 2, 4). A report issued prior to the adoption of the recommendation acknowledged, for example, the extreme fatigue experienced by women workers with family responsibilities, observing that 'the two day weekend is of course of particular importance to women workers, facilitating the accomplishment of household tasks and the enjoyment of rest' (ILO 1963: 44).

During this period, there were a number of other efforts to eliminate discrimination against women. For example, in 1976 the Council of the European Communities adopted a Directive on the Implementation of the Principle of Equal Treatment for Men and Women as Regards Access to Employment, Vocational Training and Promotion, and Working Conditions (the Equal Treatment Directive) to ensure women's right to engage in paid work (Luckhaus 2000).[11] The stated purpose of this directive was to achieve 'equality between men and women as regards to access to employment and vocational training and promotion and as regards to working conditions, including pay' (CEU 1976: Preamble, para. 5). By foregrounding equality as an end goal, especially by emphasizing access to employment, the potential outcomes of the Equal Treatment Directive were broader than its ILO precursor.[12]

Shortly thereafter, the UN adopted a Convention on the Elimination of All Forms of Discrimination against Women (1979) (CEDAW), which stretched beyond its earlier efforts to de-gender employment norms through formal equality measures. Mandating 'positive action' on discrimination, CEDAW suggested that the principle of equality requires governments to take 'all appropriate measures, including legislation, to ensure the full development and advancement of women, for the purpose of guaranteeing them the exercise and enjoyment of human rights and fundamental freedoms on the basis of equality with men' (UN 1979: Art. 3).

Despite their attempts to move beyond formal equality, evident to greater degrees in the CEDAW and the EU Equal Treatment Directive than the earlier ILO Convention on Discrimination, each was premised on an adult male employed worker subject.[13] Following along the path delineated by the UN's founding Charter and subsequent Universal Declaration of Human Rights, as Procacci and Rossilli (2003: 505) contend in assessing such UN instruments, they 'assimilat[ed] woman into the category of an abstract universal subject' and treated her largely as gender neutral. Several further deficiencies arose from the largely procedural approach underlying these international labour regulations. It was capable only of remedying limited forms of inequality. It focused on addressing differences between 'similarly situated' individuals and on promoting consistency between them; thus, even though the approach recognized group-based inequalities, it was limited in responding to them (Scott 1988; Hepple 1994; Hirshmann 1999; Bartlett et al. 2002). This limitation stemmed in part from the neglect of who should bear the responsibility for workers' social reproduction. Yet as Chapter 1 illustrated, the fact that unpaid caregiving was assigned to women was vital to the development of early sex-specific protective labour legislation at both the national and international levels. Furthermore, as the preceding discussion has shown, the fact that receiving states could externalize costs associated with immigrants' social reproduction shaped early limitations on their access to protection, especially those of migrant workers only permitted to reside for specified periods.

The Resilience of the Baseline

In international labour regulation, attempts to strip longstanding exclusions from the SER through formal equality were uneven and contradictory. They acknowledged and sought to mediate tensions in the gender contract and sought to extend some protections to migrant workers, while maintaining exclusions from the SER's central pillars on the basis of nationality. However, by neglecting processes of social reproduction, they upheld this employment norm, geared initially to adult male citizens, as a baseline. As a prelude to outlining contemporary efforts to manage the margins of the labour market in international labour regulation, Chapter 3 charts the trajectory of the SER statistically in the post-1980 period in several industrialized countries where it reached ascendancy. It also explores both the parallel expansion of non-standard employment, and patterns and tendencies in sex/gender divisions of paid and unpaid work.

Notes

1. For the sake of presentation, the Table of Selected International Labour Regulations, 1906–2008 presented in Appendix A is organized chronologically, listing regulations only once and identifying them with the 'pillar' with which they are discussed initially.

2. My discussion of the employment relationship draws on research on the legal concept of employment conducted jointly with Fudge and Tucker (especially Fudge et al. 2002 and 2003a).

3. As Davies (1999: 166) demonstrates, the concept of employment also 'transcend[s] rather than conform[s] to the boundaries between common and civil law systems'. This is so because the common-law test for employment (i.e. whether the employer has the right to control) is similar to the traditional continental European test of subordination.

4. Many of the terms of the Convention on Hours of Work Industry (1919) were replicated for white-collar workers in the Convention on Hours of Work (Commerce and Offices) in 1930, although the latter permitted hours-averaging over a three-week period and a ten-hour daily maximum to reflect the distinct rhythms of commercial and office work (ILO 1930: Arts. 3 and 4).

5. Regulations were further relaxed with the Convention on Night Work (Women) (Revised) 1948, through which professionals and health care workers joined managers as groups of women workers exempt from the ban. Responding to employer pressure to facilitate expanded production processes, the term 'night' was also redefined to cover a shorter period (from 10 p.m. to 5 a.m.) and provisions were introduced to permit a half day of work on Saturdays as well as shift work, including swing-shifts, a modification defended partly on the basis of growing acceptance of some women's double work day (ILO 1948e).

6. In this way, the convention ultimately adopted carried forward concerns expressed by government representatives at the 1919 International Labour Conference, who emphasized that unemployment 'is best understood by reference to the social consequences—disease, premature death and incompetent citizenship—which affect unemployed persons [and] their dependents' (ILO 1919k: 9–10).

7. The Recommendation on Holidays with Pay (1954), building on such tenets and advancing a framework for leave entitlements, also reflected this view, and it too was premised on a norm of full-time continuous employment (ILO 1954a: para. 4.1). It nevertheless took until 1970 for a more binding Convention on Holidays with Pay (Revised) (1970) to extend such terms to all employed persons, except seafarers.

8. For example, Canadian and British officials argued that international labour standards on migration would undermine state sovereignty and advocated a purely information-gathering role for the ILO in the area of migration (see for example ILO 1929: chapter III).

9. The revised convention defined 'woman' as 'any female person, irrespective of age, nationality, race or creed, whether married or unmarried' (Art. 2), a definition which subsequently prompted some analysts to contend that its terms also applied to female migrant workers (see Creutz 1968: 354). When it was adopted, however, there were already separate regulations delineating standards for the provision of social security for migrant workers, standards that had begun to distinguish between workers migrating under different entry categories.

10. When asked to clarify if nationality falls within the definition of national extraction, the ILO Committee of Experts' General Survey on Equality in Employment and Occupation repeatedly found that 'national extraction' encompasses exclusively distinctions between citizens of a single country based on place of birth or ancestry, not those between citizens of different countries (ILO 1996c).

11. The full title for this instrument is the Directive on the Implementation of the Principle of Equal Treatment for Men and Women as Regards Access to Employment, Vocational Training and Promotion, and Working Conditions.

12. The emphasis on 'achieving' equality in the directive is believed by some (e.g. Ellis 2005: 220) to have contributed to the European Court of Justice's (ECJ) broad interpretations of access to employment to include, for example, environmental 'factors which influence a person's decision as to whether or not to accept a job' and, equally critically, to the ECJ's rulings that working conditions extend beyond the specific terms of the contract of employment.

13. The subject of ILO and EU regulations was, in addition, presumed to be a citizen, although this term was associated with the national in the former and both the national and supranational in the latter, depending upon the instrument in question.

3

The Partial Eclipse of the SER and the Dynamics of SER-Centrism in International Labour Regulations

> A tendency which appears to be a common denominator in recent changes in employment relationships, irrespective of the specific factors at their origin, is a general increase in the precarious nature of employment and the decline of workers' protection.
>
> > ILO (2000c) *Meeting of Experts on Workers in Situations Needing Protection (The Scope of the Employment Relationship)*. Basic Technical Document: para. 104.

As an SER stripped of formal exclusions came to orient international labour regulations, as well as labour regulations at other levels, fundamental structural changes occurred in the global economy, fuelled, beginning in the 1970s, by the world property crash, OPEC's decision to raise oil prices, and oil embargos on the West and associated with high unemployment and stagflation (Gill and Law 1988: 171–4; Lee 1997: 482; Boulin et al. 2006: 14–15)—all contributing to a period of competitive austerity (Albo 1994). In industrialized contexts, these developments marked the transition from advanced Fordism to flexible accumulation,[1] from nationally based economic development to a global economy, and from the Keynesian welfare state to the neoliberal state. With this neoliberal era[2] came significant challenges to the SER, denoted by the declining significance of full-time permanent employment and the expansion of forms of employment then labelled 'non-standard' or 'atypical', and in some instances 'contingent', by policy actors in various contexts and at different scales (see for example Cordova 1986; Australian Bureau of Statistics (ABS) 1988; Belous 1989; Polivka and Nardone 1989; Economic Council of Canada 1990). At the level of international labour regulation, concern about the spread of precarious employment accompanied this shift, contributing to a series of SER-centric regulations directed at the margins of the labour market.

This chapter initiates this book's contemporary investigation of this logic. It begins by charting patterns and trends in full-time permanent employment and non-standard employment in several countries where the SER had become normative. Addressing one of the questions raised at the outset of the book, this profile illustrates the partial eclipse of the SER in the post-1980 period. It also shows that full-time permanent employment and non-standard employment remain gendered and citizenship-coded in the early 21st century. As a prelude to Chapters 4 to 6, the chapter then shifts to describe the SER-centric logic and effects of international labour regulations adopted between 1990 and 2008, responding to concerns about labour market insecurity, organized along the pillars of working time, continuity, and employment status.

A Portrait of the SER in Australia, Canada, the EU 15, and the United States, 1980s–2006

Mounting concerns over the decline of the full-time permanent job characterized the post-1980 period. Consistent with scholarly accounts, the statistical data suggest that such concerns are justified, although the eclipse of the SER was nowhere more than partial, and not in equal evidence everywhere (on the instability of full-time permanent employment in Australia, various parts of Europe, the United States, and Canada, see for example Burgess and Campbell 1998; Standing 1999a; Supiot 2001; Vosko 2002b; Bosch 2004; Marsden 2004; and Stone 2004).

The Declining Significance of Full-Time Permanent Employment

Before reviewing the data, it is important to underscore the challenges of charting the decline of the full-time permanent job statistically. In addition to documenting the statistical sources, Appendix D contains several extended discussions of these challenges and my approach to meeting them.[3] Simply put, strictly comparable data available for tracking the evolution of the SER in Australia, Canada, the United States, and the EU 15 allow principally for the consideration of full-time hours and employee status (as they are defined nationally)—a reasonable approximation of the SER, albeit one that does not include all of its 'pillars'. Figure 3.1 depicts full-time paid employment as a percentage of total employment in Australia, Canada, the EU 15, and the United States between the early 1980s and 2006. In these

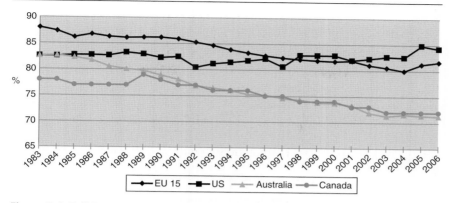

Figure 3.1 Full-Time Paid Employment as a Percentage of Total Employment, Australia, Canada, the EU 15, and the United States, 1983–2006

years, full-time paid employment slipped from 83% to 71% of total employment in Australia, 78% to 72% of total employment in Canada, and 88% to 82% of total employment in the EU 15. After experiencing a modest decline in full-time paid employment in the 1970s (from 86% to 82% of total employment between 1968 and 1982), levels stabilized in the United States in the 1980s and 1990s—such that it stood at 84% percent of total employment in 2006.

Time series data are not as readily available for another of the SER's central pillars—continuity or permanency identified with an open-ended employment relationship. Figure 3.2 exhibits trends in full-time permanent employment as a percentage of total employment between the earliest year in the 1980s for which data are available and 2006 for Australia, Canada, and the EU 15. It shows a decrease in full-time permanent employment in Canada (from 67% to 63% of total employment between 1989 and 2006), a steeper decline in the EU 15 (from 67% to 60% of total employment between 1983 and 2006), and a still steeper decline in Australia (from 64% to 52% of total employment between 1984 and 2006).

There are no equivalent figures available for the United States, since permanence of employment is not an applicable statistical category. Instead, 'employment at will' prevails in this context—that is, any employee, whether their employment is characterized as ongoing or temporary, could be discharged legally at any time 'without notice for good reason, bad reason or no reason' (Commission for Labor Cooperation 2003: 26). This feature of the American case means that in the United States the decline of the SER may be gauged more in the eroding quality and security of full-time ongoing employment than in its quantitative decline. The absence of broad

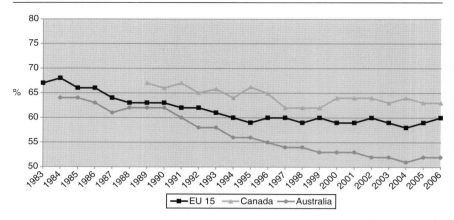

Figure 3.2 Full-Time Permanent Employment as a Percentage of Total Employment, Australia, Canada, and the EU 15, 1980s*–2006

* Data on permanence of employment only became available for the EU 15 in 1983, Australia in 1984, and Canada in 1989.

legislative protections against unfair dismissal in the United States is long-standing, but its consequences grew acute with falling rates of unionization in the 1980s, because collective agreements provided for such protection at the height of the SER.[4]

The decline of full-time permanent employment was slightly greater for men than for women in Canada and the EU 15 and approximately the same for both sexes in Australia in the post-1980 period.[5] However, gendered patterns remained sharp, as reflected in men's and women's shares of full-time permanent employment: in 2006, 63%, 61%, and 60% of workers with full-time permanent employment were men in Australia, Canada, and the EU 15 respectively. The same year, 58% of workers with full-time employment in the United States were men.

Gendered patterns characterizing full-time permanent employment at the height of the SER persisted through to the early 21st century. Perhaps this should not be surprising given the preceding critique of efforts to de-gender the SER through formal equality. Indeed, as Chapter 2 showed, a procedural approach to equality does not contribute to altering fundamentally women's socially assigned responsibility for unpaid caregiving, as substantiated by the large body of research documenting continued sex/gendered divisions of unpaid work alongside women's rising and/or high rates of labour force participation (see for example on Canada, Armstrong and Armstrong 1994 and MacDonald et al. 2005; on Australia, Bittman 1999,

Baxter 2002, and Baxter et al. 2005; on the United States, Hochschild 1997, Bittman et al. 2003, Sayer 2005; and on France and Sweden, Anxo 2002). One means of linking these trends involves examining patterns in men's and women's 'total work', or all economic activities falling inside and outside of national account systems (Picchio 2000: 207–8). In Canada, the United States, and in many of the EU 15, by the early 2000s there was near parity in men's and women's total work, whereas women performed more total work than men in Australia.[6] At the same time, as Figure 3.3 illustrates, when men's and women's total work was broken down by paid and unpaid, the gender differences were sharp: in Australia, Canada, and most of the EU 15, as well as in the United States, women performed roughly two-thirds of unpaid work and men performed a greater proportion of paid work in the latest year for which data are available.

Even amongst those with children, there were marked differences in the composition of men's and women's total work, with women performing a greater share of unpaid work than men across contexts.[7] These gendered patterns in the performance of unpaid housework and childcare held in households where both parents engaged in paid work.[8]

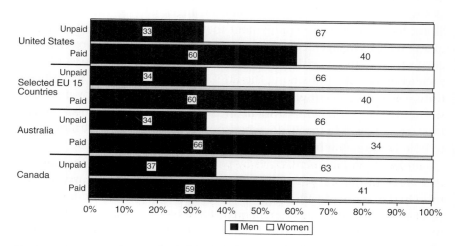

Figure 3.3 Men's and Women's Shares of Total Paid and Unpaid Work, Australia (2006), Canada (2005), Selected EU 15 Countries (1998–2002),* and the United States (2006)

* Selected EU 15 countries include Belgium, Finland, France, Germany, Italy, Spain, Sweden, and the United Kingdom. For further information on data sources and years, see notes to Figure 3.3 in Appendix D.

The Expansion of Non-Standard Employment

Gendered patterns also characterized the expansion of non-standard employment, as did patterns reflecting external boundaries of citizenship.

Previewing trends to be described and analysed in depth in Chapter 4, *part-time employment* rose as a percentage of total employment in many OECD countries in the late 20th century. Between 1973[9] and 2006,[10] it rose from 12% to 24% of total employment in Australia and from 10% to 18% in Canada, and between 1983 and 2006, it rose from 15% to 20% of total employment in the EU 15. In this period, laws and policies attempting to raise employment rates promoted part-time employment among women in particular and women's participation in part-time employment expanded even as their disproportionate responsibility for unpaid work remained in place (Duffy and Pupo 1992; Bosch et al. 1994; O'Reilly 1996; OECD 1998; Rubery 1998a; Bosch 1999; Anxo et al. 2004; see also contributions to O'Reilly and Fagan, eds., 1998).

Over the same period, especially in the 1980s and 1990s, foregrounding trends to be elaborated in Chapter 5, *temporary employment* also grew in many industrialized countries, with the key exception of the United States (ILO 1997c). It should be emphasized, however, that the effects of employment at will in the American context grew more acute, starting in the 1980s, such that rates of job separation increased (see e.g. Hyde 1998; Stone 2001). Defined as employment that does not allow for the prospect of an ongoing engagement, the expansion of temporary employment was greatest in contexts with extensive employment protection legislation, such as in Canada and among the EU 15, where it remained a significant feature of employment after 2000. By 2006 temporary employment constituted 10% of total employment in Canada and it represented 11% of total employment in the EU 15, where non-citizen workers were more likely to hold temporary jobs than citizens (Ambrosini and Barone 2007: 33).

Temporary employment varies by place of work, administrative control, and work timing or scheduling. It includes several forms, which may overlap. Beginning in the 1980s, two significant forms in the EU 15, the primary case to be investigated, were fixed-term and temporary agency work. *Fixed-term work* involves a contract or relationship between an employer and a worker, where the end is determined by reaching a specific date, completing a given task, or the occurrence of a pre-established event. In the EU 15, it represented 8% of total employment in 2006 (up from approximately 3% in 1983[11]). Women also had larger shares of fixed-term work than men in 2006 in members of the EU 15 with the highest rates of fixed-term work that year (i.e. France, the Netherlands, Portugal, and Sweden), with the exception of Spain.

Temporary agency work is characterized by a triangular employment relationship between a worker, an agency, and a user firm. Temporary agency workers lack a direct employment relationship with, and supervision by, a single employer on the employer's premises. In the early 2000s, temporary agency work represented a much smaller percentage of total employment than fixed-term work in the EU 15 (2% vs. 8% in 2006). However, it was quite significant numerically, as absolute numbers reached approximately 2.6 million in 2006.

Among the EU 15, men tended to predominate in temporary agency work in countries where it was concentrated in industrial sectors, such as Austria, Belgium, France, and the Netherlands, whereas women tended to predominate in countries where it was prevalent in public and private services and retail trade, such as in Denmark, Spain, Germany, and the United Kingdom. Yet in the early 2000s, shifts in the concentration of temporary agency work from male-dominated industrial to more female-dominated post-industrial sectors characterized labour markets in several countries of the EU 15. The prevalence of temporary agency work among migrant workers also marked the EU 15, where it reflected both the growth of internal EU migration, especially among workers migrating for employment from accession countries to countries such as the UK, Netherlands, and Finland, and the expansion of international migration for employment.

Self-employment, a focus of attention in Chapter 6, also expanded in the late 20th century, especially forms resembling paid employment (Curran and Burrows 1986; Dale 1991; Meager 1991; Eardley and Corden 1996; Fudge et al. 2002; Cranford et al. 2005). Between 1979 and 1997, it grew faster than paid employment in over half of all OECD countries, a change from previous decades when it fell in a majority of such countries (OECD 2000). Although the magnitude of its growth varied in these OECD contexts, this shift was particularly marked in Australia, Canada, and the EU 15, where self-employment grew or stabilized at relatively high levels as a percentage of total employment. By 2006, self-employment stood at 16% of total employment in Canada (up from 10% in 1979), 13% across the EU 15 (up from 7% in 1987[12]), and 15% in Australia (up from 10% in 1973).

Solo self-employment, where the self-employed person does not employ others, contributed significantly to its growth in these contexts. Until the late 1970s, OECD countries characterized by high shares of employers among the self-employed experienced greater job growth than those where solo self-employment was sizeable. However, employer self-employment grew in very few OECD countries beginning in the 1980s (OECD 2000: 159). Over the same period, solo self-employment became more common in many OECD countries, such as Canada, where it reached 11% of total employment in 2006. That year, it was also quite prevalent in Australia (9% of total employment), as well as among some countries belonging to the EU (e.g. Greece, Italy, and Portugal). Simultaneously, although employer self-employment remained male-dominated, solo self-employment became less so and, in settler societies, it remained quite common among immigrants.

SER-Centrism at the Margins of Late-Capitalist Labour Markets

With the deterioration of full-time permanent employment and the concomitant expansion of forms of employment labelled non-standard in industrialized contexts came concerns about rising labour market insecurity—concerns rooted in what had come, over the course of the 20th century, to be a close association between the form of the SER and its functions of providing access to training, regulatory protections and social benefits, sufficient income, and a social wage to support a male citizen and his family.

To be sure, concerns about the margins of labour markets were expressed earlier. In international labour regulation, early expressions of concern surfaced with the creation of the ILO's International Programme for the Improvement of Working Conditions and Environment (PIACT). Launched in 1975 via an ILO Resolution prompted by the report 'Making Work More Human', PIACT's role was to reinvigorate the ILO's constitutional mandate to 'improve "conditions of labour" that involve injustice, hardship and privation' (Clerc 1985: 311) (for a table of International Labour Regulations described in this chapter, see Appendix A).

Research conducted as part of the programme (ILO 1984: 91, emphasis added) illustrated that categories of workers falling outside the scope of traditional protection measures find themselves in 'particularly disadvantaged or *precarious* situations', especially, women and migrant workers, as well as children, young people, and people with disabilities (12, 103). On this basis, PIACT called for ILO regulations on 'certain types of economic activity in which normal measures for social protection are particularly difficult to apply...temporary or casual work, seasonal work, subcontracted work, home work, and clandestine or undeclared work' as part of a three-pronged programme of technical assistance and standard setting, which a myriad standards built upon subsequently, aimed at 'making work more human' by ensuring that it respects workers' life and health, leaves time for rest and leisure, and enables workers to serve society and achieve fulfilment (ILO 1984: 20 and 4).

Continuing Adjustments to the Crumbling Gender Contract, 1975–1990

Alongside PIACT's interventions, and parallel EU-level discussion of the phenomenon there described as 'atypical work', where calls for action by the Council of Ministers for the European Community drew particular attention to the situation of women (CEU 1982a and 1982b), there were moves to further address the crumbling gender contract in ILO regulation—several such initiatives addressed categories of workers falling outside the scope of 'normal' measures for protection. After making a Declaration on Equal Opportunity and Treatment of Women Workers (1975) echoing its precursors' concerns with non-discrimination, in 1981 the ILO adopted a Convention on Equal Opportunities and Equal Treatment for Men and Women Workers with Family Responsibilities. Significantly, this convention departed from the 1965 recommendation on this subject by addressing both men and women and embracing a broad conception of caregiving, but still emphasized eliminating gender inequalities in the labour force with limited attention to those in households and communities. On the assumption that many 'part-time workers, temporary workers and home-workers . . . have family responsibilities', its associated recommendation also called for adequately regulating and supervising 'the terms and conditions on which these types of employment are performed', a move towards enlarging the form of the now formally de-gendered SER (ILO 1981b: para. 21). However, given that this call supplemented a convention neglecting still gendered processes of social reproduction, it implicitly acknowledged, but failed to question, women's prevalence in such non-standard forms of employment. Similar limitations also characterized a 1985 ILO Resolution on Equal Opportunities for Men and Women in Employment calling on the ILO Governing Body to consider the need for additional standards on equality of opportunity and treatment, 'bear[ing] in mind the interests of women workers, for example, coverage of part-time and temporary work', and on 'the situation of home-based workers and contract workers' (ILO 1985: paras. 15a and 15b).

Indicative of the uneven crumbling of the gender contract, alongside these efforts towards a gender-neutral employment norm, the ILO adopted both a new and a revised convention on night work. The new instrument—the

Convention on Night Work (1990)—permitted it for *all* workers subject to health checks. However, instead of withdrawing its precursor, delegates passed a Protocol to the Night Work (Women) Convention (Revised) (1948), relaxing key provisions (e.g. providing for exemptions from the prohibition of night work and for variations in the duration of the night period by agreement between employers and workers) (Art. 1) while preserving this convention's framework for sex-specific prohibitions (Art. 2). The rationale for the two-pronged approach: on the one hand, international labour regulations espousing the equal opportunity and treatment, specifically, the CEDAW, the EU Equal Treatment Directive, and the European Social Charter, supported the principle that restrictions on women's employment at night are acceptable only in cases of maternity (Politakis 2001: 408–9). On the other hand, as the ILO Committee on the Application of Standards revealed, at least 50 countries effectively applied a general prohibition on the industrial employment of women at night at that time. Thus, many member states 'would not yet be prepared to dismantle all protective regimes for women in the name of gender equality' (ILO 2001: 134, para. 179, 53–6). Attesting to the resilience of norms of female caregiving in these 50 countries in particular, tasks fundamental to social reproduction (e.g. unpaid work at night in the home) still largely remained in women's hands, a justification for continuing the sex-specific ban on night work in many countries.

Consolidating a Multi-Tiered Framework for Migrant Workers' Protection

Corresponding tensions reflecting the neglect of processes integral to workers' social reproduction also shaped ILO standards protecting migrant workers, reworked in the late 20th century. In this instance, however, explicit exclusions remained and in some respects grew through the development of a multi-tiered framework for regulating migrant work. Recall member states' failure to ratify the 1939 Convention on Migration for Employment due to its (qualified) provisions for equal treatment for fear it would undermine the nation state order. Recall too the distinction, introduced in its 1949 successor, between migrant workers authorized to reside on a temporary basis and immigrants destined for permanent residency. Recall finally the exclusion of 'nationality' from the grounds of non-discrimination in the subsequent Convention on Discrimination.

ILO regulations focused on the treatment of migrants were adjusted, once again, with the Convention on Migrant Work (Supplementary Provisions) (1975), supplementing its 1949 precursor. Known formally as the

Convention Concerning Migrations in Abusive Conditions and the Promotion of Equality of Opportunity and Treatment of Migrant Workers (1975), this convention was motivated by growing concerns about abuse and by pressure to extend provisions for equality of opportunity and treatment for migrant workers. However, advancing the latter aim was complicated by the accelerating trend in the late 1960s among states in Western Europe and North America to resort to migrant workers entering as guest workers under time-limited arrangements. Drafters of the 1975 convention thus divided it into two parts, either of which ratifying states could exclude. The result permitted discrimination on the basis of workers' national citizenship.

Part I of the convention committed states to respect the basic human rights of all migrant workers and to limit their 'illegal movements'. Member states' concerns to address the abuse of migrant workers, such as the 'dubious recruitment practices' of concern since the adoption of the convention on unemployment in 1919, while preserving their autonomy in the arena of immigration policy, shaped this section (Böhning 1976: 147). Part II, in contrast, obliged states to promote 'equality of opportunity and treatment in respect of employment and occupation, of social security, of trade union and cultural rights and of individual and collective freedoms' for migrant workers and their families (ILO 1975a: Part I, Art. 6.1, and Part II, Art. 10). Despite this compromise, two-part, formulation, some Western states (e.g. Australia and the United States) opposed the passage of the convention, fearing that the free choice of employment provided for in Part II would undermine their guest worker programmes, programmes that, as numerous scholars show (see for example Arat-Koc 1990; Stasiulus and Bakan 2005), increasingly included those facilitating the temporary migration of domestic workers and caregivers around that time (Böhning 1991: 699). Consequently, of the few Western states that subsequently ratified the convention, many opted to exclude Part II.

Although there were many ILO-level discussions of migrant work in the 1980s and 1990s, the UN Convention on the Protection of the Rights of All Migrant Workers and Members of their Families adopted in 1990 carried this multi-tiered framework for protection forward. Taking 13 years to enter into force because of difficulties in securing ratification, this convention divided immigrant workers into 'irregular' workers or persons that are 'undocumented' (UN 1990: Art. 5b) and 'regular' workers or persons 'lawfully' employed within the territory of the receiving country. Under its terms, regular workers were further subdivided into those admitted on a permanent basis (or immigrants eligible ultimately for citizenship or residency in their country of employment) and those admitted on finite bases (i.e. migrant workers) (UN 1990: Art. 5a).

The first tier, designed to be universally applicable, unified a large body of human rights covering migrant workers and their families. It enumerated civil and political rights as well as economic, social, and cultural rights delineated elsewhere while naming those of particular importance to migrant workers, such as freedom of exit and the right to stay in one's country of origin. It also articulated a series of new rights and protections for all migrant workers, including protection from arbitrary expulsion (UN 1990: Arts. 22 and 56). Applicable to workers in a regular (i.e. legalized) situation, the second tier provided for access to education and social services. It also called for the extension of 'treatment no less favourable than' that which applies to nationals to so-called regular workers in a variety of areas (e.g. remuneration, hours of work, safety, etc.) (UN 1990: Part IV and Art. 25). The third tier, in turn, extended additional rights applicable to 'particular categories' of workers in a regular situation and their families regardless of the terms of their stay, such as a general right to freedom of movement within a state of employment and the right to be temporarily absent from that state (UN 1990: Arts. 40–2). To promote ratification among countries that might otherwise reject the terms of the convention due to concerns that they would undermine their guest worker programs, several provisions of this tier permitted receiving states to limit regular workers' free choice of employment and to set other conditions tied to their terms of employment (UN 1990: Art. 52.2a–b).[13] Carrying this logic further, the fourth tier provided for a range of exclusions from rights delineated in the third tier for certain subcategories of regular workers, such as migrant seasonal, itinerant, and project-tied workers.[14] Through this multi-tiered framework, this UN convention reinforced inclusions and exclusions associated with the territorially bounded conception of community membership attached to the SER. It provided for extensive protections to workers that are citizens of the countries in which they are employed, lesser protections to those that are not, especially those permitted only to reside temporarily, and still fewer for those that are undocumented.

Together, the PIACT's calls for ILO regulations on forms of employment where standard measures for social protection are difficult to apply, parallel moves to address the crumbling gender contract through equal employment opportunity and treatment, and the consolidation of a multi-tiered framework for regulating migrant work inaugurated contemporary approaches to managing the margins of the labour market aimed, on the one hand, at upholding the SER. On the other hand, as noted in the epigraph to this chapter, these initiatives sought to respond to 'a general increase in the precarious nature of employment and the decline in workers protection' (ILO 2000c: para. 104). Precarious employment became a central concern of international labour regulation, and it was understood in relation to the SER and the system of labour and social protection upholding this male citizen norm. The solution: compensating for deviation from the SER's central pillars of standardized working time, continuity, and employment status.

The Social Declaration (1998) and 'Decent Work' (1999, 2008)

Two contemporary developments in international labour regulation underscore tensions inherent in this strategy—the ILO's adoption of the Social Declaration and its pursuit of 'Decent Work' as the new strategic direction for international labour regulation. Adopted in 1998, the Social Declaration represented a pivotal 'constitutional moment' (Langille 1999: 232) in ILO history. It was introduced partly to respond to the failure to include social clauses in international trade agreements. Uniquely, it articulates a set of fundamental labour rights, casts the promotion of these rights as a constitutional obligation of ILO membership, and establishes a mechanism for monitoring adherence among member countries. The Social Declaration aims to promote freedom of association and the recognition of the right to collective bargaining, the elimination of all forms of forced or compulsory labour, and the abolition of child labour. It also reaffirms the ILO's commitment to the elimination of discrimination in respect of employment and occupation and to equal remuneration.

The organizational review producing 'Decent Work', in contrast, offered a new agenda for ILO action, one whose closest affinities lie with soft law mechanisms such as the EU's Open Method of Coordination (OMC), a means of synchronizing national strategies in complex policy fields, organized around principles of convergence, management by objectives, country surveillance, and an integrated approach to policy design (for further discussion of the OMC, see Chapter 5) (Lonnroth 2000). The goal of 'Decent Work' is to increase the influence of international labour regulations by rehabilitating old instruments, while adopting new ones. Its purpose is to improve the conditions of all workers, waged and unwaged, through the expansion of labour and social protections. To this end, 'Decent Work' identifies people at the margins of the labour market, for whom normal measures for labour and social protection are particularly difficult to apply, as requiring greater attention, naming migrant workers in particular. As an organizational agenda, 'Decent Work' therefore moves beyond the ILO's traditional sphere of activity—advancing rules to be applied by states—by fostering non-rule outcomes. It also recognizes that while ILO regulations have 'paid most attention to the needs of waged workers—the majority of them men...not everyone is employed' (ILO 1999: 3–4).[15] An unprecedented acknowledgement of unpaid work performed by women, as well as work in the so-called informal economy, this assertion offers an opening for greater regulatory attention to these areas. Accordingly, it was followed by the adoption of a Convention on Maternity (2000) retaining key protections introduced in 1919 and expanding others, while introducing new protections aimed at non-discrimination and extending coverage to all employed women, including those in 'atypical forms of dependent work' (ILO 2000a: Art. 2.1).[16] This last measure is particularly noteworthy in light of the ensuing discussion of the contemporary ILO efforts to preserve the employment relationship as the primary basis for labour protection (Chapter 6).

The almost simultaneous appearance of the Social Declaration and 'Decent Work' in the late 1990s was paradoxical. On the one hand, 'Decent Work' is a response to the significance of forms of employment differing from full-time permanent employment, of unpaid work, and of migrant work. On the other hand, the mandate of the Social Declaration is to reassert fundamental labour rights, a move responding to pressures to limit the creation and expansion of (especially social and economic) rights and the corpus of international labour regulations subject to ratification (Cooney 1999; Murray 2001b; Alston and Heenan 2004; see also Standing 2008a).[17] The Social Declaration gestures at equality of treatment of different forms of work (Sen 2000). However, it fails to employ the broader conceptions of work (paid and unpaid) embraced in 'Decent Work', affirming instead efforts to address longstanding exclusions from employment norms through formal equality as conceptualized in previous international labour regulations.

Almost a decade after the introduction of 'Decent Work', in attempt partly to enlarge this strategy, the ILO adopted the Declaration on Social Justice for a Fair Globalization. This 2008 declaration takes as its point of departure that globalization, defined as 'economic cooperation and integration', has led certain countries to 'benefit from economic growth and employment creation', while at the same time 'caus[ing] many countries and sectors to face major challenges', including 'both the growth of *unprotected work* and work in the *informal economy*' (ILO 2008: Preamble, para. 2, emphasis added). To address such challenges, the Declaration on Social Justice for a Fair Globalization formalizes four strategic objectives towards decent work: employment creation through fostering sustainable institutional and economic environments; enhanced measures of social protection (i.e. social security and labour protection); social dialogue and tripartism; and the promotion of the fundamental principles and rights at work named in the Social Declaration (ILO 2008: I. A). Under its terms, constituents are to develop labour and social policies advancing these objectives with the technical support of the International Labour Office. And they are to consider the four strategic objectives as 'interrelated and mutually supportive' and to view 'gender-equality and non-discrimination' as 'cross-cutting issues' (ILO 2008: I. B). More concretely, to enhance social protection, they are directed to extend social security to all, including measures to provide for basic income; in this way, this declaration carries forward the notion, integral to the 'Decent Work' agenda, that 'not every-one is employed' (ILO 2008: I. A(ii)). Consistent with this recognition, it also calls for adapting the scope and coverage of social security to reflect technological, societal, demographic, and economic changes and for policies regarding wages and earnings, hours and other conditions of work to ensure a minimum living wage to all employed (ILO 2008: I. A(ii)). The Declaration on Social Justice for a Fair Globalization thereby attempts to limit tensions taking contemporary expression in the juxtaposition of the Social Declaration and the 'Decent Work' agenda—that is, to the extent possible in a framework whose overriding emphasis is *employment* promotion.

Together with PIACT, ongoing efforts to respond to the crumbling gender contract through measures of formal equality and the consolidation of a multi-tiered framework for regulating migrant work, the Social Declaration and 'Decent Work', as well as the Declaration on Social Justice for a Fair Globalization, represent critical developments occurring alongside more specific efforts to manage the margins of contemporary labour markets— the creation of the 'hard' international labour regulations analysed in Chapters 4, 5, and 6 and previewed below.

Regulating Part-Time, Fixed-Term, Temporary Agency Work, and Self-Employment

When precarious employment became a focus of concern, international labour regulations were motivated by the idea that, within the context of a nation state, citizen-workers who are engaged in non-standard employment should not see their employment and occupational opportunities or working conditions limited by barriers erected on the basis of form of employment. There was recognition of the need to allow workers in part-time and temporary paid employment, as well as the nominally self-employed, the ability to access benefits and entitlements associated with the SER, even if such 'normal measures' for labour and social protection are difficult to implement.

The ILO Convention on Part-Time Work (1994) and the EU Directive on Fixed-Term Work (1999) reflect this understanding most closely. Their approach is to provide for equal treatment on the basis of form of employment among citizens.[18] These regulations pursue this aim in two ways: first, through the familiar notion of non-discrimination, interpreted in these instances as either equivalent treatment to or treatment no less favourable than a similarly situated worker, unless it is justified on 'objective grounds'. In both the ILO Convention on Part-Time Work and the EU Directive on Fixed-Term Work, non-discrimination means providing the same level of protection in some areas and proportional protection in others—that is, protection defined either in relation to hours in the case of the former and job tenure in the case of the latter. The second way is through the mechanism of the comparable worker whose employment relationship approximates the SER. The comparable worker is defined as the full-time permanent wage-earner in both cases.

Both the ILO Convention on Part-Time Work and the EU Directive on Fixed-Term Work seek to bring forms of paid employment lacking the benefits and entitlements conventionally associated with the SER into its range. However, the commitment to equal treatment on the basis of form of employment does not provide for minimum standards—that is, for attaching certain benefits and entitlements to all forms of employment. Furthermore, because of the requirement for a comparator, this approach is capable only of treating limited labour force insecurities and of addressing the situation of restricted categories of workers. The upshot is that the terms of the ILO Convention on Part-Time Work only apply fully to part-time permanent wage-earners and the EU Directive on Fixed-Term Work excludes temporary agency workers. For the limited categories of workers to whom they apply, entitlements are prorated by proximity to the full-time continuous employment relationship.

This approach also fails to acknowledge the significance of unpaid caregiving in households and of receiving states' externalization of costs associated with non-citizen workers' social reproduction. It does not account for the fact that so many women engage in part-time and temporary employment because of their caregiving responsibilities. Nor does it address the issue that so many migrant workers engage in temporary employment because receiving countries, and employers in them, derive extensive benefits from two features of their situation: first, sending countries' contribution to their daily and intergenerational reproduction; and, second, the particular form of powerlessness migrant workers experience as a result of the direct and structural controls to which they are subject, made possible by the combination of limits on their lengths of stay and their lack of national citizenship.

These are a few deficiencies of the framework for equal treatment on the basis of form of employment. However, in the EU Directive on Temporary Agency Work (2008), even this limited framework is qualified. The terms of this directive erode the baseline for comparison such that workers recruited directly by firms (broadly defined) qualify as 'standard workers' vis-à-vis temporary agency workers.

The ILO Recommendation on the Employment Relationship (2006) also shares with the ILO Convention on Part-Time Work (1994) and the EU Directive on Fixed-Term Work (1999) the aim of incorporating more employed workers falling outside the SER into the ambit of labour protection. However, as opposed to its precursors' emphasis on equal treatment, it uses the terminology of 'effective protection'. Marking the limit of SER-centrism, this shift means that only those workers in situations closely resembling the employment relationship at the core of the SER are to receive labour protection rather than all workers engaged in forms of work for remuneration falling outside the strictures of the employment relationship who are in need of protection.

The approaches to regulation adopted in international labour regulations on part-time work, fixed-term work, temporary agency work, and the employment relationship are capable of making some important adjustments. However, their SER-centric logic contributes to exacerbating the precariousness of employment situations diverging markedly from this model. The next three chapters probe this logic further through detailed analyses of these regulations vis-à-vis approaches to regulating such forms of employment where they are well-developed, beginning in Chapter 4 with an exploration of regulatory responses to precarious part-time employment in the ILO Convention and Recommendation on Part-Time Work and at the national level in Australia.

Notes

1. As it is used here, 'flexible accumulation' (Harvey 1989) refers to a mode of production defined by continuity through change—that is, the continuation of aspects of the system of mass production associated with Fordism alongside the

expansion of new productive technologies and greater specialization (Vosko 2000: 27). This notion is preferable to alternate terms, such as neo-Fordism and post-Fordism, which emphasize continuity and change respectively, since it is concerned with their dynamic interaction and attentive to geographic and temporal specificity.

2. Neoliberalism is taken here, on the one hand, to be a theory of political and economic practice, originating in the ideas of Frederick Von Hayek, proposing that 'human well-being is best advanced by the maximization of entrepreneurial freedoms within an institutional framework characterized by private property rights, individual liberty, free markets and free trade' (Harvey 2006: 145; see also Peters 1999). In this conception, the role of the state is to cultivate institutions and policies fostering such practices—hence, the association between neoliberalism, the demise of the Keynesian welfare state, and the rise of the global economy (i.e. the globalization of production, distribution, and exchange). On the other hand, neoliberalism is used to denote a series of projects emerging in the 1980s and often associated with Thatcherism, Reaganomics, and monetarism. The economic project of neoliberalism entails liberalizing and deregulating economic transactions within and across borders, privatizing state services, a process which often involves using market surrogates in the remaining public sector, and casting social spending as a cost of international production instead of an inducement for domestic demand, as was the case in the Keynesian era (see especially Jessop 2002: 454; see also Teeple 1995; on privatization, see especially Armstrong et al. 1997; and contributions to Fudge and Cossman, eds., 2002). As a political project, neoliberalism is associated with the elimination of forms of state intervention characteristic of a mixed economy (Jessop 2002: 454) and the introduction of 'new' forms of governance aimed at supporting marketization (on the latter, see especially Rose 1996; Larner 2000; Brown 2003; Ong 2006; on disciplinary neoliberalism, see Gill 1995). Finally, the social project of neoliberalism involves a simultaneous withdrawal and reconfiguration of collective responsibility and, more specifically, the dismantling of the Keynesian welfare state, and its partial socialization of production and social reproduction as well as its commitments to social equality and redistribution.

3. The sources listed in Appendix D for Figures 3.1–3.3 are also the sources for the narrative and footnotes corresponding with the discussion of trends in full-time permanent employment and total work in the subsection 'The Declining Significance of Full-Time Permanent Employment', unless otherwise indicated. In the subsection, 'The Expansion of Non-Standard Employment', unless otherwise indicated, data are based on custom tabulations derived for Australia, from the ABS Labor Force Survey (LFS) 2006, Catalogue Nos. 6202.0 and 2637, or Household, Income, and Labour Dynamics (HILDA) Survey, Wave F; for Canada, from StatsCan's LFS 2006; for the EU, from the EU LFS 1983–2006; and, for the United States, from the Contingent Work Supplement to the Current Population Survey, February 2005, or United States Bureau of Statistics (USBS) 2006, Current

Population Survey, 2006, News Release USDL 05-1433, Catalogue No. 2934. Data on temporary agency work in the United States are for 2005, the latest year for which they are available.

4. The significance of employment at will has varied over time. Its legal meaning and its effects on the security and durability of full-time permanent employment progressed through several phases in parallel with the rise and decline of the SER in the United States, fostered by the growth of internal labour markets (Doeringer and Piore 1971; Gordon et al. 1982) and large vertically integrated firms (Hyde 1998; Stone 2001).

   After World War II, implicit contracts for lifetime employment dominated in the United States. Employment at will prevailed, but employers 'routinely entered into contracts in which people were effectively guaranteed lifetime employment' (Hyde 1998: 104). Underpinning this practice was an implicit bargain between workers and employers that firms would invest in workers' acquisition of skills and knowledge, provide workers with a range of social benefits and entitlements, including back-loaded benefits such as pensions, and increase workers' wages incrementally—all in exchange for loyalty over the long term (Jacoby 1985).

   The lifetime employment model was, however, relatively short-lived. It began to wane in the 1970s and especially the 1980s, with the break-up of internal labour markets and vertically integrated firms, falling real wages, and declining rates of unionization.

   Into the early 2000s, with the exception of the state of Montana, legislatures remained at an impasse with regard to the adoption of statutes on this subject (Swinnerton and Wial 1995; see also Block and Roberts 2000: 293). Furthermore, while many unions still negotiated collective agreements prohibiting dismissal without just cause, enforcement continued to be a problem.

5. In Australia, between 1984 and 2006, full-time permanent employment dropped from 72% to 60% of total male and from 55% to 42% of total female employment. In Canada, between 1989 and 2006, it dropped from 71% to 67% of total male and from 63% to 62% of total female employment. Finally, across the EU 15, between 1983 and 2006, it dropped from 73% to 66% of total male and from 58% to 53% of total female employment.

   In the United States, between 1978 and 2006, full-time employment stabilized at roughly 89% of total male employment and rose from 72% to 75% of total female employment (USBS November 2007).

6. Both men and women spent on average a total of 8.8 hours per day engaged in paid and unpaid work in Canada in 2005, and 10.6 hours in the United States in 2006. Near gender parity in total hours of work also characterized many of the EU 15. Across the eight EU 15 countries represented in Figure 3.3, in the period 1998–2002, women averaged seven hours of total work per day while men averaged 6.5 (EUROSTAT 2004a) (note: National time use surveys for these countries took place in slightly different years. For further information, see notes to Figure 3.3 in Appendix D). The largest differences in men's and women's

total work was apparent in Australia, where, in 2006, men's and women's total hours of work per day were 7.9 and 8.9 hours respectively.

7. In Canada, for example, in 2001 women and men in two-parent households with children under age 6 performed an average of 5.7 and 3.2 hours of unpaid work daily respectively, while they performed an average of 5.5 and 6.8 hours of paid work daily respectively (StatsCan, Census 2001, Custom Tabulation). Similarly, in Australia, in 1997, the latest year for which data are available, women and men in households with children under age 15 performed an average of 4.6 and 3.4 hours of unpaid work daily and an average of 5.7 and 7.1 hours of paid work daily respectively (ABS Time Use Survey 1997). Parallel patterns also held across the eight EU 15 countries represented in Figure 3.3, where in the 1998–2002 period, women in families with children under age 7 spent, on average, twice as much time as men performing unpaid work daily (Aliaga and Winqvist 2003: 6).

8. In 2001, in Canada, the largest percentage of men employed 30 hours or more per week with children under 6 reported doing 5–14 hours of childcare per week. The largest percentage of women, in contrast, reported doing 30–59 hours of child-care per week. Men also reported doing less housework than women. That year, the largest percentage of men employed 30 hours or more per week with children under 6 reported doing 5–14 hours of housework per week. The largest percent-age of women, in contrast, reported doing 15–29 hours of housework per week. Shares of unpaid childcare and housework only equalized between employed men and women who were also lone parents, and women were the majority of lone parents (StatsCan, Census 2001, Custom Tabulation).

The gendered division of unpaid childcare was also apparent in Australia, where, in 1997, the latest year for which data are available (again, referring to individuals working more than 30 hours per week and with children under 6), the largest percentages of men reported doing 0–4 and 5–14 hours of unpaid childcare per week respectively, while the largest proportion of women reported doing 30–59 hours per week and 60+ hours respectively (ABS 1998: Catalogue. No. 2328140).

Similar patterns were discernible in the eight EU 15 countries represented in Figure 3.3. In the 1998–2002 period, women in employed couples (no informa-tion on the number of hours individuals are working is available) with children under 6 spent twice as much time as their male counterparts performing unpaid childcare daily (e.g. in France, on average, women in such households performed 1.41 hours of unpaid childcare care per day, whereas men performed 37 minutes) (EUROSTAT 2004b: 66).

9. For Australia and Canada, figures for 1973 are drawn from *ILO World Employment Report*, 1996/1997. Definitions of part-time employment varied considerably across OECD countries in the 1970s before harmonized data became available. Estimates for 1973 must therefore be approached with caution.

10. For 2006, part-time work is defined as 30 or fewer usual weekly hours at the main job.

11. This estimate of fixed-term work is based on the nine countries for which national data were available in the EU LFS for 1983.

12. This calculation excludes Austria, Finland, Portugal, and Sweden, because data for these countries is only available through the EU LFS in later years.

13. For example, states were permitted to make certain rights conditional on the fact that the regular worker has 'resided lawfully in its territory' for employment purposes for a prescribed period of no more than two years (UN 1990: Arts. 52.2a–b and 52.3).

14. For example, seasonal workers were to be entitled only to rights that are 'compatible with their status as seasonal workers, taking into account that they are present in that State for only part of the year' and the rights of itinerant workers were similarly constrained (UN 1990: Arts. 59 and 60).

    The convention also introduced the category 'specified-employment workers' and provided for excluding this 'hitherto internationally unknown' (Böhning 2003: 5) group from a variety of protections to be provided, in principle, to regular workers. Specified-employment workers were defined to include: migrant workers sent by their employers for restricted periods to a state of employment to undertake a specific assignment or duty; migrant workers engaging for finite periods in work that requires professional, commercial, technical, or other highly specialized skill; and, migrant workers who, at the request of their employers, engage for finite periods in work the nature of which is transitory or brief and who are required to depart at the expiration of their authorized periods of stay.

    The creation of the specified-employment worker category, and terms applicable it, arose from a debate between European delegations, on the one hand, and Australia and the United States, on the other hand. The former group took the position that 'a migrant worker whose labor input contributes to the economic performance of the State of employment would eventually earn a right to stay permanently in that State after a number of years' (Lonnroth 1991: 722). Australia and the United States took an opposing position in order to preserve admissions schemes permitting certain categories of migrant workers to enter for a specific type of work for a finite period, and to renew work permits for that purpose. They objected to extending the right to the free choice of employment to such workers. The compromise reached was the addition of the specified-employment worker category, which is to date a category in international law available to any State of employment (Böhning 2003: 5).

15. For an in-depth analysis of 'Decent Work' (1999), see Vosko (2002a).

16. The terms of this convention are paradoxical: on the one hand, it retains compulsory exclusions of women from employment after the birth of a child for the same six-week period provided for in the first convention on this subject and provides for an increased period of leave, albeit permitting a lower level of

pay to women while on compulsory leave (ILO 2000a: Arts. 4.4 and 6). On the other hand, in an unparalleled move advocated by feminist organizations well before the ILO's founding, as Chapter 1 showed, the convention also provides for guaranteeing women's return to the same or an equivalent position that is paid the same and also provides greater protections for pregnant workers (ILO 2000a: Art. 8.2).

17. Standing (2008a: 367, emphasis added) argues further that the weakness of the Social Declaration is not only its 'selection of a *small* number of standards as "core" and "fundamental"', but its 'inconsisten[cy] with the principle established by the 1948 Universal Declaration of Human Rights that rights are indivisible and interdependent'.

18. Neither of these regulations excludes migrant workers explicitly, but they reference other conventions that permit exclusions and partial exclusions on the basis of national citizenship: namely, the ILO Convention on Discrimination (1958), the ILO Convention on Migrant Work (Supplementary Provisions) (1975), and the UN Convention on the Protection of Migrant Workers and Members of their Families (1990).

4

Regulating Part-Time Employment: Equal Treatment and its Limits

When I was a casual employee I worked an average of 27 hours per week. During this time I was called to work with very short notice on a regular basis. This was very difficult for me due to family responsibilities, particularly with regards to my children... [but] my husband works full time so we needed my employment to be part time so that I could be available for my family.

> New South Wales (NSW) (2003) Testimony of Mary Vanderpool, *Exhibit. 63. Secure Employment Test Case.*

Standardized working time was central to the emergence of the SER. Through the sale of workers' labour power for a specified period of time, employers gained exclusivity and direct control and workers gained predictability and pay for job inactivity, providing time essential for recuperation. To be sure, even in national contexts where the SER was normative under Fordist-Keynesianism, the notion of 'normal' working hours was never fully institutionalized, particularly in small and medium-sized workplaces. Nor was it ever universal or indeed meant to be: recall the many early protective measures adopted at the national and international levels specifying exclusions for certain categories of workers—not only those unpaid workers whose time was perceived to be 'free' but workers in forms of employment deemed to be intermittent (e.g. casual employment) and in family businesses. Such exclusions were as significant as the stated aims of these regulations. Nonetheless, standard working time was normative, and its deterioration has figured prominently in the contraction of the SER.

This chapter examines the logic of contemporary regulations addressing forms of employment deviating from the temporal boundaries of the SER and the labour market insecurities associated with them. It begins by charting the deterioration of standardized working time since the 1970s, focusing principally on the expansion of part-time employment in a number of OECD countries. It then analyses the ILO Convention on Part-Time Work (1994), spurred by calls to improve the conditions of workers in 'precarious situations' who fall outside the scope of traditional measures of protection. This convention seeks to bring forms of part-time employment lacking the benefits and entitlements conventionally associated with the SER within its ambit. However, its terms only extend fully to *permanent* part-time wage-earners. Furthermore, for the workers to whom they apply, entitlements are prorated by proximity to the full-time continuous employment relationship.

The chapter uses the case of Australia to explore the logic and effects of such SER-centric responses to precariousness amongst part-time workers. In Australia, where rates of part-time employment are amongst the highest in the OECD, a sizeable group of part-time workers lack job certainty, indicated typically by an indefinite contract of employment. Many part-time workers are casual—like the worker quoted in the epigraph, who worked on a part-time casual basis for nine years before becoming permanent. Australia has not ratified the 1994 ILO Convention on Part-Time Work.[1] Still, the Australian government participated actively in negotiations towards its adoption and contemporary Australian approaches to regulating part-time employment, at both the federal and the state levels, reflect the tenor and the terms of the convention. Through a profile of part-time employment in Australia, an analysis of Australian policies and regulations, and interviews with workers, union representatives, and government officials involved in two key test-cases, the analysis highlights the limits of a regulatory framework employing the mechanism of equal treatment to bring forms of part-time employment falling just outside the SER into its range.[2]

The Deterioration of Standardized Working Time

By the late 1970s standardized working time arrangements were eroding in many industrialized countries where the SER had become normative. With fundamental structural changes occurring in the global economy, the resort to informal solutions to secure firm-centred flexibility intensified. Employers' growing emphasis on results-based employment relationships, on the one hand, and highly variable working time, on the other hand, cultivated these solutions. As Supiot observes, these twin measures mean that workers' 'surrender of their time ceases to be the primary purpose of the[ir] obligation [as] employees', and is replaced by greater self-regulation (Supiot

2001: 83; see also Boulin 2006: 197–8; Burchell 2006). Self-regulation supposedly gives workers greater control over their time, but, in practice, the erratic working hours, on-call hours, and annualization that ensue often translate into more time on the job (Perrons et al. 2006: 4; see also Brannen 2005). Together, these developments challenge the notion of paid on-the-job inactivity central to standardized working time: as Rubery et al. (2006: 126) comment, 'fragmented time is explicitly aimed at removing…the porosity of the working day, while a results-based system is aimed instead at removing the cost to employers of unproductive time'. Firms' demands for greater variability in hours contributed to the expansion of part-time employment in the 1970s and its growth in the 1980s, while their support for results-based employment relationships was central to fostering various forms of self-employment, discussed in Chapter 6.

Demand-side pressures were not alone in destabilizing standardized working time. The actions of many governments also contributed, especially labour and social policies promoting part-time employment as a response to women's collective struggles for access to the labour force and pressures to raise employment rates in an era of competitive austerity.

As Table 4.1 indicates, part-time employment grew in most OECD countries in the last quarter of the 20th century (Table 4.1). However, this aggregate trend masks a high degree of complexity; there was variation over whether countries promoted part-time employment per se and, if so, by what means, as well as the nature of part-time employment that they cultivated (Bosch et al. 1994; Tilly 1996; OECD 1998; Rubery 1998a; Bosch 1999). In the EU context, some governments emphasized reducing full-time hours (e.g. France), partly as a means of altering the terms of worker-citizenship within their borders to promote a more equitable distribution of work for remuneration among men and women (and, in some instances, a more equitable distribution of unpaid work as well). As a consequence, several states (e.g. Denmark) experienced convergence in the working hours of part-time and full-time workers, while retaining high but reduced levels of part-time employment (Bosch 1999; Jackson 2006). Others, especially states characterized by relatively high levels of income inequality (e.g. the United Kingdom), actively promoted part-time employment as a means of raising (especially women's) employment rates; as a result, part-time employment often was, and continues to be, characterized by short hours, viewed as a supplement to household income, and shaped by occupational and industrial sex segregation (see especially: Bosch 1999; Boulin et al. 2006). Still other countries, such as the Netherlands, experimented with a 'one-and-a-half earner model' (or two three-quarters jobs in dual-earner households),

Table 4.1. Part-Time Employment as a Percentage of Total Employment, Selected OECD Countries, 1973 and 2006

	1973	2006	Change
Australia	12	24	+12
Japan	14	18	+4
New Zealand	11	21	+10
EU 15	-	18	-
Netherlands	*17	36	+19
United Kingdom	16	23	+7
Germany	10	22	+12
Sweden	*24	13	−11
Denmark	*23	18	−5
Austria	6	17	+11
Belgium	4	19	+15
Ireland	*5	20	+15
Luxembourg	6	13	+7
France	6	13	+7
Spain	-	11	-
Italy	6	15	+9
Finland	*7	11	+4
Portugal	*8	9	+1
Greece	-	8	-
Canada	10	18	+8
United States	16	13	−3

*1979 figures used in lieu of 1973 where national data unavailable.

aimed at producing high quality part-time employment across industries and occupations (Burri 2006; Fouarge and Baaijens 2006).

The effects of these different approaches varied; for example, a maternal part-time model came to define the United Kingdom (Anxo et al. 2006a; see also Lewis 1992; O'Reilly and Fagan, eds., 1998), one in which short hours part-time employment characterized by high levels of labour market insecurity became the norm (Fagan 2001), especially among mothers, due partly to the limited availability of public childcare and the organization of the school day (Rubery 1998a). In contrast, in France, women's participation in part-time employment was less significant due to efforts to shorten the standard work week; in this context, many women, especially those with young children, sought full-time jobs involving shorter hours to avoid the labour market peripheralization associated with part-time employment (Fagnani and Letablier 2004, 2006; Boulin et al. 2006: 27; see also Jefferys

2003; Charpentier et al. 2006). Simultaneously, the Dutch model aimed to enable both women and men to reduce or increase their hours for caregiving reasons. However, despite extending greater value to caregiving, particularly among parents, the principal result was the dramatic increase in part-time employment among Dutch women (Fagan 2000; Burri 2005; Yerkes and Visser 2006). The Dutch 'combination model' has had some success if measured in terms of the high incidence of part-time employment with relatively small divergence in the occupational profiles and terms and conditions of employment of full- and part-time workers and the limited number of highly insecure part-time jobs (Fagan and Ward 2003). Its success has been more modest in terms of men's take-up rates (Plantenga 2002).

The United States did not promote part-time employment as actively as many European countries in the post-1970 period. Nor did it emphasize shorter-hours full-time employment. Rather, it stressed having 'every available adult engaged in paid employment', preferably full-time, while still expecting women to maintain 'the main responsibility for domestic homemaking and child and elder care' (Appelbaum 2002a: 94). Consequently, part-time employment actually declined in the United States, unlike in most other OECD countries, and flex-time or flexible scheduling, especially common among women in occupations with high levels of socially recognized skill, grew in prominence (Rosenfeld and Birkelund 1995), alongside a mounting 'time-bind' (Jacobs and Gerson 2004).

Part-time employment in Canada, where high quality public childcare was limited, expanded considerably over the last few decades of the 20th century and reached the same level as the EU 15 as a whole by 2006. In this context, there was a federal commission of inquiry into part-time employment in 1983 and several provincial governments investigated prospects for promoting high quality part-time employment thereafter (Wallace 1983; see also Saskatchewan 2006). Spurred partly by proposals arising from such inquiries and especially by women's growing militancy in public sector unions, the quality of part-time employment improved markedly in the public sector, making it a primary site of secure (i.e. permanent) part-time jobs for women (Duffy and Pupo 1992; Luxton and Reiter 1997).

Between 1973 and 2006, rates of part-time employment also rose steadily in Australia, placing the country second (after the Netherlands) among the OECD countries covered in Table 4.1. To the present, part-time employment is also more clearly gendered in Australia than other liberal welfare states; for example, almost half of all employed women in Australia are engaged part-time as opposed to about one-quarter of women in Canada and the United States.

The promotion and concomitant rise of part-time employment in many industrialized contexts signalled a movement away from measured conceptions of time towards greater fragmentation and a decline in social time (Probert 1997; see also Carnoy 2000). This shift challenges the dichotomy between 'free time' and 'working time' (i.e. time spent engaging in work for remuneration) and thus the temporal dimensions of the employment norm. As discussed in Chapter 3, there are nevertheless continuities in this change. While the de-standardization of working time is fostering alternatives to the full-time permanent worker as breadwinner, 'new' axes of gender inequality surrounding the *amount* of time spent in work for pay are emerging with the continuing failure to reduce women's disproportionate responsibility for unpaid work (Mutari and Figart 2000: 232; see also Picchio 2000; Anxo 2002; Vosko 2002b; Perrons et al. 2006). Compounded by workers' often limited scope of action in controlling their time,[3] these developments heighten the likelihood that SER-centric regulations will exacerbate precariousness in those part-time situations diverging sharply from this employment model.

SER-Centric Responses to Precariousness in Part-Time Employment: The ILO Convention on Part-Time Work (1994)

> When examining the rights, protections and terms and conditions of employment of part-time workers, the yardstick generally used, in the same way as for defining part-time work, is the treatment enjoyed by comparable full-time workers. In effect, this amounts to asking whether part-time workers are discriminated against in terms of their shorter hours of work.
>
> ILO (1993a) *ILC Report V(I): Part-Time Work*: 31.

A product of intense debate, the 1994 ILO Part-Time Work Convention, and its associated recommendation, responds to deviations from the 'normal' working hours integral to the SER. It does so by distinguishing between those who cannot find full-time employment and those who 'prefer' part-time employment, ostensibly due to family responsibilities (ILO 1994a: Art. 9). Its guiding premise, set out in a report preceding its adoption, is that 'although part-time work responds to the aspirations of many workers, there are those for whom it spells low wages, little protection and few prospects for improving their employment situation... This is partly because labour legislation and welfare systems... were designed largely for the full-time workforce' (ILO 1993a: 3). The convention thus aims to stretch the SER by extending improved protections to part-time workers in order to make their employment less precarious.

The Part-Time Work Convention builds on the acknowledgement that a growing segment of workers engage in part-time employment because of a shortage of full-time opportunities, even as it characterizes specific groups, such as workers with family responsibilities, as freely choosing part-time employment. This framing legitimizes sex/gender divisions of labour. The familiar language of 'choice' pervades the justificatory parts of the convention. Yet as Murray (1999a: 14) has observed, echoing key themes in feminist scholarship, 'for many workers, the fundamental issue of part-time employment is not their willingness to be flexible, but the price they have to pay for flexible work' (see for example Pollert 1988; Duffy and Pupo 1992).

The Part-Time Work Convention extends core elements of the SER to part-time workers, although it does so only for a subset of this group. According to its first clause, the convention includes within its purview 'employed person[s] whose normal hours of work are less than those of comparable full-time workers' (ILO 1994a: Art. 1a). The 'comparable full-time worker' is defined as one with the same type of employment relationship (e.g. permanent or temporary) who is engaged in the same or similar type of work or occupation and employed in the same establishment or, 'when there is no comparable full-time worker in that establishment, in the same enterprise' or, 'when there is no comparable full-time worker in that enterprise, in the same branch of activity' (ILO 1994a: Art. 1c). The convention also allows ratifying countries to 'exclude wholly or partly from its scope particular categories of workers or of establishments' (ILO 1994a: Art. 3.1).

Given the strategy of providing for equal treatment on the basis of form of employment, the convention places workers whose employment situations deviate slightly from the SER—on the basis of 'normal hours' alone—and who lack access to certain labour and social protections as a consequence on a par with 'standard' workers. At the same time, it permits the exclusion of many other, if not most, part-time workers engaged on temporary, seasonal, and casual bases. The framework offered is thus least likely to protect those most on the margins.

Early in the negotiations towards a convention, some member countries, including Australia, objected to creating a standard covering all part-time workers since, as one government delegate stated, 'what may be considered reasonable in the case of part-time workers employed for a large number of hours in relation to normal working time, may be unnecessary in cases where hours worked are minimal' (ILO 1993b: 24). Employers also called for excluding the self-employed, family workers, persons working a very small number of hours over a given period, and seasonal workers (ILO 1993b: 24). Such opposition led to the decision that 'part-time workers should not be grouped with other "non-standard" or "atypical" workers... the Governing Body did not intend the conference to include, under the item on part-time work, such questions as temporary, casual or seasonal work' (ILO 1993a: 9). Consequently, under the terms of the convention, procedural ILO standards (e.g. the 1958 Convention on Discrimination) offer the primary means through which part-time workers who are also employed on casual, seasonal, and/or temporary bases may have their rights enforced. To this end the Convention on Part-Time Work asserts that its provisions do not 'affect more favourable provisions applicable to part-time workers under other international labour Conventions' (ILO 1994a: Art. 2). This clause is designed partly to set limits on the exclusions that the convention permits for temporary, casual, and seasonal part-time workers. However, as Murray (1999a: 10) rightly points out in her analysis of the convention as a vehicle for social justice for women, 'those who rely on the savings clause to enforce their fundamental rights are at a disadvantage compared with those granted... positive right[s]... in light of their part-time status'. That the terms of this convention only extend fully to permanent part-time wage-earners reflects the maintenance of a singular employment norm despite the stated aim of promoting part-time employment characterized by a full range of social and labour protections.

For the part-time workers that the ILO convention does cover, terms equivalent to comparable full-time workers prevail. Under the convention, equal treatment is interpreted as equivalency. This means part-time workers are to have the same level of protection regarding the rights to organize and collective bargaining, basic wages, occupational health and safety, and discrimination in employment and occupation (ILO 1994a: Arts. 4 and 5). The convention prohibits the payment of differential wages, but provides for differential non-pecuniary benefits. In other areas, part-time workers are to 'enjoy conditions equivalent to those of comparable full-time workers' (ILO 1994a: Art. 6). Equivalency, here, is defined on a proportional basis: protections related to social security, certain types of paid leave, and maternity are to be determined in relation to hours, contributions, earnings, or by other means. Prorated entitlements are put forward as equivalent conditions with virtually no attempt to provide for minimum standards (ILO 1994a: Arts. 6 and 7). Reflecting the success of governments seeking to exclude short-hours part-time employment, the terms of the convention also provide for the disqualification of part-time workers falling below certain hours-thresholds from prorated social security schemes, with the exception of maternity and employment injury (ILO 1994a: Art. 8). Equal treatment on the basis of form of employment amounts to accepting a unitary baseline for all categories of workers. Only those part-time workers in employment relationships closely resembling the SER are assured of protections.

ILO regulations on part-time employment focus on the removal of barriers denying workers in particular forms of employment the opportunity to access benefits and entitlements attached to the employment norm. They also subscribe to the principle that workers who are similarly situated should not receive differential treatment on the basis of form of employment alone. But, by promoting equivalency through the notion of the comparable worker, the primary means through which equal treatment is to be achieved, they are capable only of addressing precariousness amongst part-time workers to a limited degree. This is so even among part-time permanent wage-earners, the group best served.

'Family responsibilities' assigned to women historically are a central justification for the ILO convention and its associated recommendation. Processes of accommodation within the ambit of the employment norm also have a gendered cast. Although they make room for wage-earning among women, they implicitly uphold male breadwinning and female caregiving norms surrounding the social wage by neglecting to address the equalization of unpaid work between men and women. ILO regulations on part-time employment overlook how gender structures cultivate paid work deviating from the SER and obscure the debt that the SER owes to the male breadwinner / female caregiver gender contract.

Regulating Part-Time Employment in Australia[4]

Representing a quarter of total employment, part-time employment is more prevalent in Australia than in many OECD countries, as the preceding discussion illustrated. Its gendered dynamics are also sharp: as Figure 4.1 shows, almost half of all employed women are part-time in Australia as opposed to only 15% of employed men. The magnitude of part-time employment for women reflects longstanding patterns in Australia, particularly the historic relationship between political and social citizenship, employment, and welfare, in which women's primary duty has been caregiving in households, accompanied by a modest degree of market activity

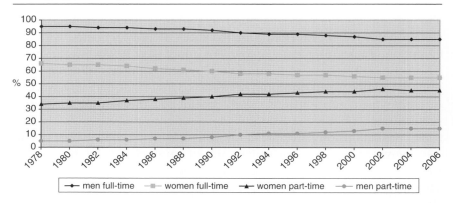

Figure 4.1 Part-Time Employment and Full-Time Employment as a Percentage of Total Employment by Sex, Australia, 1978–2006

(see for example Cass 1994: 106–7). Australian women's low level of participation in full-time employment, which declined between 1978 and 2006 at the virtually same rate as men's, further underscores the legacy of these patterns (Figure 4.1).

Where continuous employment denoted by an open-ended employment relationship is concerned, the composition of part-time employment also sets Australia apart from other industrialized countries. In Australia, only 29% of all part-time workers are permanent employees. The remaining 71% are employed on a casual and/or fixed-term basis or are self-employed.

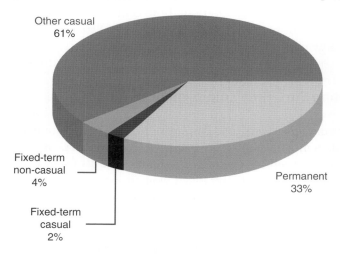

Figure 4.2 Composition of Part-Time Paid Employment, Australia, 2006

SER-centric approaches, exemplified by the Part-Time Work Convention, to regulating part-time employment exclude the self-employed. They also permit the full or partial exclusion of those engaged on temporary or casual bases (ILO 1994a: Arts. 1a, 3.1). These exclusions and permissible exclusions are significant in the Australian case, as Figure 4.2 illustrates: even among all part-time employees (i.e. excluding the self-employed), only 33% are permanent, while fully 63% are casual, and the remaining 4% are fixed-term non-casual. A large percentage of part-time employees thus fall into the casual category.

The Management of the Margins of the Australian Labour Market

The history of labour regulation in Australia has been marked by what Pocock et al. (2004: 20) call a peculiar and longstanding 'conjunction of permissive regulation of casual work with strict regulation of part-time work'. The roots of this conjunction lie in the means by which courts and tribunals crafted and sought to uphold Australia's version of the SER, on the one hand, and the partial citizenship of adult women, on the other hand. In late 19th-century Australia, few benefits flowed from the continuity of employment contracts (O'Donnell 2004). This changed with the actions of figures such Justice Higgins of the Conciliation and Arbitration Court, who remarked in 1921 that 'there is nothing that steady family men desire more than constant work, and some certainty as to their income for a week or more ahead' (Higgins, as cited by Pocock et al. 2004: 20) after having himself set a minimum wage for an unskilled man and his family, including a wife and three children, in the well-known *Harvester Judgement* (*H. v. McKay* 1907). Flowing from these pronouncements, as O'Donnell shows (2004: 11), by the 1920s courts began to express preferences for 'weekly hire' in order to 'systematize terms of engagement according to the nature of the work arrangements' and to extend security to male breadwinners. The shift to weekly hire gave rise to the payment of a weekly wage, even in instances of public holidays, illness, or temporary lack of work, and the provision of notice of one week. At the same time, courts affirmed their support for norms of male breadwinning and female caregiving; accordingly, in the 1912 *Fruit Pickers* case, Justice Higgins suggested that women 'should only be paid 54% of the basic wage' because they 'were not generally responsible to maintain a family' (McCallum 2005: 7–8).

As weekly hire expanded among breadwinning men, casual employment became a catchall category for all remaining hiring systems and the primary means through which many women participated in the labour force. Owens (2001: 125) shows that there were initially some efforts to limit casual employment to circumstances in which 'work . . . was urgent and could not be attended to adequately by "weekly hire" employees'. Such efforts, while of marginal success, were designed to treat it as a subset of temporary employment like seasonal, on-call, and fixed-term work as it was in many others countries. Yet in Australia, the defining feature of casual employment came to be the provision of 'casual loadings' or payments in lieu of entitlements designed to mitigate labour market insecurity, which had the effect of ascribing a distinct labour force status—akin to partial worker-citizenship—to workers unable to stake a claim to steady employment.

The catchall nature of the category, and the provision of casual loadings, contributed to the adoption of a vague definition of a 'casual employee' as 'an employee engaged as such' (AIRC 1997: Attachment F 15.2.1). This language aims to convey that casuals are paid at the end of each engagement, although this is not always the case. Awards[5] in male-dominated occupations and industries limited this ambiguity somewhat, by restricting the duration of casual employment so that it remained an exception to weekly hire. Yet awards in female-dominated industries and occupations contained few such limitations. It was also virtually impossible to be employed part-time except as a casual until the late 20th century because of the strength of breadwinning men's claims to continuity or permanent employment. Casual employment thereby 'grew necessarily as the means to part-time work' (Pocock et al. 2004: 20). For example, under the South Australian Clerks Award, which applied to a female-dominated occupation in this state, it was impossible to be employed part-time on a permanent basis before 1988. This limitation was accompanied by the restriction, introduced in 1948, that casual employment was to entail fewer hours than weekly hiring (Owens 2001: 125). For 40 years, the Clerks Award never required casual employment to be periodic or irregular; it simply required shorter (i.e. part-time) hours.

This vexed history continues to shape contemporary manifestations of casual employment in Australia, where casuals work under various types of employment contracts.[6] There are casuals engaged on a 'one-off' basis (Stewart 1992), for whom a host of social and labour protections simply do not apply. For other casuals, with fixed-term contracts, access to labour and social protections depends on the length of the term. Still others engage in casual employment on a more or less ongoing basis, cultivating a series of misperceptions, including among casuals themselves, 'an awful lot of [whom] don't think they're casuals cause they've been working at the same place for so long' (Allison Peters, 28 June 2006). Common across all forms of casual employment are both the absence of the full range of protections extended to full-time permanent employees—still the normative citizen-worker in Australia when it comes to labour market regulation—and the payment of loadings. Casuals have less protection against unfair dismissal than their permanent counterparts. Additionally, only a subset of casuals may access unpaid parental leave—those who have 12 months continuous service or are long-term casual employees.[7] Many casuals should technically have access to extensive statutory labour and social protections, as well as supplementary employer-sponsored schemes, since they are engaged in a continuous way. For example, 56% of all casuals (and 60% of part-time casuals) reported being in their present job for one year or more in 2004 (HILDA, Wave D, Custom Tabulation). However, enforcement is a major obstacle even after years of continuous service because courts often find it difficult to distinguish between one-off and ongoing engagements (Tham 2003: 8). Since small firms are notoriously lax in implementing rules and regulations, enforcement is also made more cumbersome by the high percentage of casuals (fully 50%) found in firms employing fewer than 20 workers.

Dynamics of Part-Time Casual Employment in Australia: Gendered Precariousness

In distinguishing between casual and permanent part-time workers, the objective is to develop an understanding of the socio-economic situation of part-time workers in Australia whose employment is precarious partly because they lack formal open-ended employment relationships, even though their employment may, in practice, be ongoing.

Part-time casuals are by far the largest group of part-time employees in Australia, and 64% of part-time casuals are women. Casual positions are the only options for many workers in part-time jobs because, as discussed above, permanent part-time employment remains relatively undeveloped in Australia. Trends by industry and occupation, moreover, show how regulatory practices, specifically mechanisms restricting access to part-time permanent employment, shape the gendered character of the part-time casual category and contribute to reproducing sex/gender divisions of paid and unpaid caregiving work. Historically, as Pocock et al. (2004: 24) illustrate, awards in key female-dominated occupations and industries rarely provided scope for expanding the number of part-time permanent employees, whereas awards in male-dominated industries and occupations routinely imposed rigid restrictions on the use of casuals. Reflecting such tendencies, two industries dominated by women have the highest levels of part-time casual employment—accommodation, cafes, and restaurants (46%) and retail trade (38%). Similar tendencies are evident at the level of occupation, although here part-time casual employment is most common among elementary sales workers (60%), a group dominated by women, and labourers (39%), a group composed mainly of men, followed closely by intermediate service workers (37%), a group dominated by women. Furthermore, amongst the occupations with the highest levels of female participation (intermediate clerical workers, intermediate service workers, education professionals, health professionals, and business and administration associate professionals), a majority of women part-time employees hold casual positions. Key awards originally cultivated this situation by restricting access to permanent part-time employment within these occupational groups. In professional occupations, such as those in education, part-time casual jobs are three times more common among women than men. The Deputy Assistant Secretary (Community Affairs) of the Labor Council of NSW (or Unions NSW) characterizes the situation as follows: 'in areas where there is a demand for it [part-time work] and where it is entirely suitable, you can't actually get it except as casual part-time work. The best example is probably . . . teachers, many of whom would like to work part-time but can only do so by becoming casual relief teachers . . .' (Allison Peters, 29 June 2006). The prevalence of part-time casual employment among women is characterized not only by continuity (e.g. longstanding practices in female-dominated occupations and industries), but also by change (e.g. the use of this category to *casualize* employment in various occupational groups).

Sex-based differences in income and access to extended benefits further reveal the gendering of part-time casual employment—they also underscore the resilience of norms of male breadwinning and female caregiving that give these differences legitimacy. Comparing women's gross annual income in their main job to men's, women part-time casuals earn 86% of their male counterparts.[8] This situation is due partly to Australia's strict regulation of forms of employment in certain sectors and its accommodating approach in others. Part-time casuals' independent access to extended health care coverage is similarly gendered; only a third of women in part-time casual jobs have such coverage, compared to over two-thirds of men.[9]

The gendered character of part-time casual employment is particularly marked among workers with young children (i.e. aged 0–6). In Australia, fully 41% of women in the labour force with young children are part-time employees, in contrast to just 16% of their male counterparts. These patterns mirror trends in other industrialized countries, in North America as well as in the EU, especially in the United Kingdom, where part-time employment is largely the domain of women with young children and students. What makes Australia unique is its large proportion of women employees with young children who are both part-time *and* casual. Out of all women employees with young children, 29% fall into this group, in contrast to just 15% of men.

Strategies for Limiting Precariousness amongst Part-Time Workers in Australia

Beginning in the 1980s, growing recognition of the gendered and precarious character of part-time casual employment in Australia led unions, union federations (known as 'peak' union bodies), and NGOs to step up efforts to dislodge the association between part-time and casual employment. These actors pursued several strategies that included challenging employer- and industry-level practices in specific awards, engaging in community-based campaigns, and pursuing across-the-board legal changes through test-cases then permissible under the industrial relations machinery of the arbitral system. With each of these strategies, their approach was two pronged. The first prong aimed to confine casual employment to intermittent and irregular employment and the second sought to limit labour market insecurity amongst part-time workers.

1. CONFINING CASUAL EMPLOYMENT TO INTERMITTENT AND IRREGULAR EMPLOYMENT: THE SECURE EMPLOYMENT TEST-CASE

The first prong rested on the premise that regulators have lost sight of the true meaning of casual. The proposed remedy, as Pocock et al. (2004: 47) note, seeks to: 'prevent "casual" employment status from being abused' by confining it 'to its proper place as just a minor component in the range of employment forms' (see also Campbell 2004). Attempts to secure conversion to permanent employment among long-term casuals echo this aim. One well-studied state-level example is found in modifications to the South Australia Clerks Award in 2000, finalized in 2002 after a successful appeal by employers to weaken provisions for conversion,[10] which granted casuals with 12-months service the right to request to become permanent, a right that employers could not refuse on unreasonable grounds (SAIRC 2002). A federal example is the 2000 Metal Industry Award. In this case, the Australian Industrial Relations Commission (AIRC) acknowledged that the growth of casual employment 'undermined the award's role and "integrity" as a safety net' (Pocock et al. 2004) and it granted casuals the right to convert to permanency after six months of 'regular and systematic' employment (on the proviso that employers could refuse to grant conversion on reasonable grounds), an order perceived as a 'major victory' by workers seeking to limit casual employment in this sector (Kentish, 29 June 2006).[11]

The 2006 Secure Employment test-case ruling in New South Wales mirrored both of these examples. However, its significance was more far-reaching, because it set a test-case standard in the state, which means its effects extended beyond a particular industry or occupation. In this case, Unions NSW, the peak state-level union body representing 64 unions operating in a wide array of industries and occupations, made an application with four unions to vary awards covering the private sector, local government, and the public sector. The decision to pursue a test-case reflected a conscious choice to build a long-term campaign for secure employment (Hughes, 29 June 2006). According to Mark Lennon, Assistant Secretary with Unions NSW, two linked developments motivated the test-case: first, 'the explosion in casual employment and also labour-hire'; and, second, the widespread use of casuals and employees of labour-hire businesses in the state government,[12] such that they were 'becoming . . . regular form[s] of employment in the public sector' (Lennon, 29 June 2006).

The test-case hinged on four issues: the conditions of work of labour-hire employees, contracting-out, occupational health and safety, and limits on long-term casual employment. The applicants in the test-case sought to ensure that labour-hire employees receive the same pay and working conditions as employees of the host employer, that employers consult with workers and unions prior to contracting-out, and that employees of labour-hire and contract companies (including casuals) are afforded proper protection in terms of occupational health and safety and rehabilitation in the workplace. To restrict casual employment, the goal was to grant long-term casuals the right to convert to permanent status. This multifaceted strategy for improving employment security recognized the many effects of casual employment, as well as its relationship to broader processes of casualization. According to Alisha Hughes, the industrial officer at Unions NSW who gathered testimony for the case:

The underlying feeling from all unions was that casual employment was increasing and it was undermining our ability to bargain. But it was appearing in different forms. In some places it was straight-out casual direct hire. In other places, it was increasing use of body hire [i.e. the use of labour hire employees on a casual basis] and, in the public and private sector, it was outsourcing work to other organizations that were using casual labour. (28 June 2006)

The ruling in the Secure Employment test-case delivered several gains to employees of labour hire and contract companies and long-term casuals. Foremost among them, the goal of limiting casual employment on a continuous basis, much of it part-time, met with some success: the Commission granted casuals (part-time and full-time) engaged for six months or more, the right to elect to convert to permanent employment. The exception, ironically, was the public servants employed under the Public Sector Employment and Management Act, due to the potentially high cost to the state (Peters, Unions NSW, 29 June 2006).[13]

In the wake of this ruling, Unions NSW made variations to 300 awards, a process completed one month after the decision. However, the variations to these awards had limited long-term effects[14] and several elements of the ruling were also limited by design, especially the hard-won provision providing for conversion among long-term casuals. As Alison Peters, Deputy Assistant Secretary (Community Affairs) of Unions NSW, later reflected, this provision still left employers with considerable discretion:

> The conversion issue, much to our annoyance, ended up being that the boss has to ask workers if they want to convert to permanent employment. What we wanted were provisions ... such as deeming provision, after three months ... The take-up rate of people electing to convert was therefore much lower than we'd anticipated ... There's [still] a lot of employer control over that [conversion]. (29 June 2006)

As these comments suggest, permitting casuals to *elect* to convert to permanent employment after a specified period of time and on the basis of employer invitation is a limited means of curtailing long-term casual employment. Like the South Australia Clerks Award (Owens 2002) and the Federal Metal Case, instead of extending the safety net to casuals automatically, the Secure Employment test-case ruling still required those casuals eligible for conversion to opt to convert, a 'choice' obscuring power imbalances between employer and employee.

2. STRETCHING THE EMPLOYMENT NORM: THE FAMILY PROVISIONS TEST-CASE

The second prong directing strategies aimed at minimizing labour market insecurity amongst part-time casuals involved increasing possibilities for part-time *permanent* employment. Such efforts focused on 'work–family' issues, and they reached their height in late 2005, with the decision of the AIRC in the federal Family Provisions test-case. In this test-case, the Australian Council of Trade Unions (ACTU) and four unions cutting across public and private sectors[15] sought four key changes: unpaid parental leave of up to two years following the birth of a child; an option for full-time employees returning from parental leave to be employed on a part-time permanent basis until the child is in school; an option for employees with school-aged children to 'buy out', through 'salary sacrificing', up to six weeks per year of extra leave to cover school holidays; and, finally, flexible start and finish times to enable parents and carers to pick up and deliver children to school and childcare. Initially, emergency leaves were also addressed, but before the test-case went forward unions and employers reached an agreement on a new right to take leave for family emergencies without threat of reprisal, a measure applicable to casuals (Bowtell, 26 June 2006; see also Catanzariti and Byrnes 2005: 361–2). The ACTU succeeded with each of these proposed variations in some measure. The main new entitlements affecting casuals in the ruling related to parental leave: for employees entitled to parental leave under federal awards (i.e. those with 12 months service), including casuals engaged continuously for this period of service, the decision provided for the right to request extensions of the periods of simultaneous unpaid parental leave to eight weeks and of unpaid parental leave to 24 months. In an effort to limit casual employment, for those it covered, the Family Provisions decision also granted parents re-turning from parental leave the right to request secure (i.e. non-casual) part-time employment until the child reaches school age on the condition that the request be 'genuinely based on the employee's parental responsi-bilities' (AIRC 2005 (Workplace Relations Act (WRA) 1996): para. 396, 2). Employers, however, were permitted to refuse such requests 'on reasonable grounds related to the effect on the workplace or the employer's business', defined broadly to encompass 'cost, lack of adequate replacement staff, loss of efficiency and the impact on customer service' (AIRC 2005 (Workplace Relations Act 1996): para. 396, 2). In making this order, the AIRC was careful neither to support the ACTU's preferred model for 'reconciling work and family responsibility' nor the case-by-case model advocated by employers' groups:

The ACTU claim that these conditions should constitute an employee entitlement is not one we are prepared to grant. We agree with the employers that an uncondi-tional right to additional parental leave is inappropriate. It would have the potential to increase costs, reduce efficiency and create disharmony in the workplace. The employers' proposal, one which is based purely on agreement, has some merit. To take an example, an award might provide that an employer and an employee may agree that an employee could return from parental leave on a part-time basis until the child commences school... On the other hand it is equally true that there is nothing to stop the employer and the employee reaching such an agreement now. Despite this fact, and consistent with our earlier conclusion that some positive step is required, we think it is necessary to go beyond simply providing for agreement between the parties. (AIRC 2005 (Workplace Relations Act 1996): para. 395)

Providing employers granted it, the resulting provision made it possible for new parents to engage in employment on a part-time and permanent basis, whereas in the past the trade-off for returning to employment part-time usually meant casual status. In this way, it represented an advance in dislodging the association between part-time and casual employment. Furthermore, following the lobbying efforts of unions and women's organizations, the NSW Industrial Relations Commission incorporated the orders of the Family Provisions test-case in state-level awards, a move justified by the community orientation of the test-case system (Gale, 27 June 2006). This right of parents of preschool-aged children to request part-time permanent employment is nevertheless gendered, because the Family Provisions test-case effectively presumed, in part by neglecting unequal sex/gender divisions surrounding unpaid caregiving work, that women principally confront the problems associated with juggling caregiving and paid employment. There has been little effort either to encourage men to engage in caregiving or to curtail the long hours associated with full-time (including non-casual) employment.

The two-pronged strategy for curtailing gendered precariousness among part-time workers (i.e. limiting the extent of casual employment and/or promoting part-time permanent employment) reflected the shortcomings of the strategy of equal treatment on the basis of form of employment. Neither prong addressed problems related to the requirement for a comparator. Consequently, even those part-time casuals who managed to convert to permanent status as a result of the Secure Employment test-case were only able to access labour and social protections available to full-time permanent employees on a pro-rata basis. Furthermore, neither prong challenged the notion that workers (principally women) perform unpaid work by 'choice' in their 'free' time. As a result, despite the AIRC's formal recognition of women's high levels of labour market insecurity, especially evident among mothers of young and school-aged children, the Family Provisions test-case ruling was limited in its capacity to alter the male baseline for regulation.

'Work Choices'

Even so, changes to Australia's industrial relations system under the Work-place Relations Amendment (Work Choices) Bill (2005) offset the gains flowing from the two-pronged approach.[16] Adopted by the Conservative government of John Howard in 2006, Work Choices introduced a host of changes heightening the insecure situation of part-time casuals and inten-sifying insecurity across the labour force. Endorsing a unitary system of industrial relations whose core elements resemble the North American or Wagnerist model, it scaled back Australia's longstanding arbitral laws and weakened collective bargaining.

De-collectivizing industrial relations and centralizing government au-thority at the federal level, Work Choices introduced a dramatically reduced national industrial relations scheme. It only permitted states to regulate the terms and conditions of their own employees and employees of unincorpo-rated entities by moving state awards covering employees of incorporated companies into the federal jurisdiction and by scaling back remaining awards.[17] It also created the Fair Pay Commission (FPC) to take over core functions of the independent AIRC and to administer an Australian Fair Pay and Conditions Standard (AFPCS) (Briggs 2005; Briggs and Buchanan 2005; Ellem et al. 2005; McCallum 2005; Waring et al. 2006).

The gradual replacement of the awards system with an AFPCS to operate in conjunction with individualized Australian Workplace Agreements (AWAs) or enterprise-level collective agreements was arguably the foremost change introduced by Work Choices and it was criticized widely (Briggs 2005; Murray 2005a; Waring et al. 2006). At the end of 2006, the AFPCS included entitlements to: a minimum pay rate (either a Federal rate or a rate set according to an Australian Pay and Classification Scale);[18] annual leave of four weeks (five weeks for continuous shift workers) with the possibility of cashing-out two weeks by agreement; ten days of personal carer's leave (with two days additional unpaid carer's leave where this is exhausted); two days unpaid carer's leave for casuals; two days paid compassionate leave per occasion; unpaid parental leave of 12 months for workers with at least 12 months continuous service with their employer; and, a 38-hour week to be averaged over 12 months[19] (while permitting 'reasonable additional hours') (Australia (WRA) 1996, amended 2006: Div. 3, Sched. 1, Subdiv. B). Exclud-ing parental leave, these minimum entitlements extended to 'part-time employees and those who [had] not yet worked for twelve months' through 'pro-rata arrangements' (DEWR 2005). Rights extended to employees with caring responsibilities in the Family Provisions test-case decision were omitted from the AFPCS and other Work Choices legislation. Consequently, although unions varied numerous federal awards to reflect its outcome before Work Choices came into force, only those awards varied retained such provisions and only for transitional periods.

Prior to Work Choices, awards set the floor for conditions in many occupations and industries—and part-time employees of all types as well as casuals of all types were among the highest award-reliant groups of workers. Indeed, in 2006, 34% of part-time workers and 45% of casuals were award-reliant (Women's Electoral Lobby Australia and the National Pay Equity Coalition 2006: 3). Yet Work Choices established the AFPCS to replace the superior, albeit criticized, 'no disadvantage test' introduced with AWAs, which measured these agreements against relevant awards and ensured that they did not leave employees worse off overall (Briggs 2005: 13).

Taken together, measures consolidating industrial relations at the Australian federal level and reconfiguring how minimum standards are regulated (i.e. by scaling back awards and introducing the AFPCS) prevented restrictions on the number of employees that an employer could engage in a particular type of employment—a feature that long kept a lid on the growth of casual employment in certain (principally male-dominated) industries and occupations. They also limited possibilities for conversion clauses for casuals[20] and maximum hours for part-time workers (Australia 2006 (Fact Sheet No. 3): 2, 4; Australia Human Rights and Equal Opportunity Commission 2005: A1.2). In these ways, Work Choices undermined the main achievements of the Secure Employment and Family Provisions test-cases, which could have contributed both to limiting casual employment and to extending new rights to part-time workers. Work Choices also fostered greater insecurity across the labour force by likening the conditions of a larger group of workers to those long identified with casual employment, by, for example, increasing firms' capacity to fragment employment through permitting averaging as well as additional hours.

The Australian Labor Party: Working with Work Choices

Many of the overarching changes initiated under Work Choices remained in place through to early 2009,[21] despite the November 2007 election of the Australian Labor Party (ALP). Upon its election, the ALP accepted the centralization of industrial relations, having promised in its pre-election platform to use 'all of the Constitutional powers available to it in government to legislate national industrial relations laws' and to achieve this end by encouraging state governments to refer their powers for private sector industrial relations to the federal level or through other types of harmonization and cooperation (ALP 2007a: 6). It also accepted the existing structure of the safety net for workers defined by legislated minimum standards and a 'modernized' awards system.

In contrast to its predecessor, however, the ALP sought to improve the content of minimum standards through the introduction of a series of legislated national minimum standards applicable to employees. Advanced under its Fair Work Act (FWA) in April 2009, these standards included maximum weekly hours, requests for flexible work arrangements, unpaid parental leave and related entitlements, annual leave, personal/carer's and compassionate leave, community service leave, long service leave, public holidays, notice of termination and redundancy pay, and a Fair Work Information Statement (Australia (FWA) 2009: chapter 2, Part 2.2, Div. 2, s. 61). Most revised pre-existing minima relatively modestly. For example, a new standard on hours set the standard week for a full-time employee at 38 hours, with the caveat that an employer must not request or require an employee to work more hours 'unless the additional hours are reasonable', and the FWA permitted averaging of weekly hours, albeit in a more constrained manner (Australia (FWA) 2009: chapter 2, Part 2.2, Div. 3, ss. 62–4). One standard on unpaid parental leave represented a notable improvement: it provided employed parents, so long as they have 12 months continuous service or are (familiarly) long-term casual employees, with an entitlement to 12 months unpaid leave associated with the birth of a child and one parent with the right to request an extra 12 months unpaid leave, a request that could only be refused on 'reasonable business grounds' (Australia (FWA) 2009: chapter 2, Part 2.2, Div. 5, Subdiv. B, s. 76). Furthermore, shortly after the passage of the FWA, in its 2009 budget proposals, the federal government committed to introducing a paid parental leave scheme in January 2011 (Australia 2009: 24).[22] Another standard on flexible working arrangements aimed, in turn, to provide employees with 12 months continuous service the right to request changes in work arrangements, including in hours, patterns, and location of work, a request that could also only be refused on 'reasonable business grounds' (Australia (FWA) 2009: chapter 2, Part 2.2, Div. 4, s. 65).

As of early 2009, the process of modernizing awards envisioned by the governing ALP entailed simplifying the 2,000 plus awards (excluding enterprise awards) in place upon its election and reducing this number to as low as 150 over a transition period up to 1 January 2010. The FWA stipulated that modern awards contain terms addressing coverage, flexibility, dispute settlement, ordinary hours of work, base and full rates of pay of pieceworkers (if applicable), and automatic variation of allowances (Australia (FWA) 2009: chapter 2, Part 2.3, Div. 3, Subdiv. C). It indicated that they may also include terms addressing minimum wages, including junior rates, training rates and skill-based classifications and incentive-based payments; the type of employment (e.g. full-time, part-time, and/or casual employment and shift work, and also the facilitation of flexible work arrangements); arrangements for when work is performed; overtime rates; penalty rates; annualized wage arrangements; allowances; leave, leave loadings, and arrangements for taking leave; superannuation; and procedures for representation, consultation, and dispute settling (Australia (FWA) 2009: chapter 2, Part 2.3, Div. 3, Subdiv. B, s. 139). Additionally, where appropriate, the FWA called for including industry-specific detail on the ten National Employment Standards in awards. Broadly speaking, the ALP's vision for modern awards was to provide the basis for a safety net for Australian workers, without being overly prescriptive or extending coverage to employees that have traditionally been 'award free' (e.g. managerial or high income employees) (Australia (FWB Memo) 2008: rr. 93–6, r. 103, r. 517; Australia (FWA) 2009: chapter 2, Part 2.3, Div. 2, s. 134).[23]

In addition to advancing the National Employment Standards and a modernized award system, as well as committing to the first scheme for paid maternity leave, the government established an improved unfair dismissal system in its April 2009 package, albeit a system that continued to provide for lesser protections for casuals.[24] Furthermore, it created Fair Work Australia, a scaled back institution designed partly to replace the AIRC and to take over several of its former roles.[25] It also phased out AWAs in favour of collective bargaining, largely at the enterprise level, while enabling Fair Work Australia to facilitate multiple-employer bargaining for employees who are low-paid and those who have not historically had access to the benefits of collective bargaining (Australia (FWA) 2009: chapter 2, Part 2.4, Div. 9, ss. 241–3; see also Australia (FWB Memo) 2008: rr. 177–81).

Lessons from Australia and Alternative Possibilities

> There's going to be a mix. The question is where the balance will lie... There's going to be casual employment. There's going to be part-time employment... Clearly there's more 'flexibility'... The question is whether it [part-time employment] actually accords with what people want and what protections they've got and to what extent it is run by what the employer wants... I hate to use the word 'choice'.
>
> Alison Peters, Labor Council NSW, Deputy Assistant Secretary, Sydney, 29 June 2006.

117

The Australian case reveals the limits of SER-centric approaches to curbing precariousness among part-time workers—before, during, and after Work Choices. In their aim to bring more otherwise 'regular' part-time employment situations within the range of the SER, such approaches to regulation leave intact those situations diverging most from this employment model. Their application is limited to permanent part-time employees. In the Australian context, this translates into neglecting not only the most sizeable segment of part-time employees but those who are worst off. Among part-time employees, it is part-time casuals whose employment situations are especially insecure along multiple dimensions—and women dominate this group.

Examined historically, the Australian case underscores the need for a more comprehensive approach. The movement to an industrial relations system centralized at the federal level strengthens this contention: consider the former AFPCS, whose substance the ALP's national employment standards sought to improve starting in 2008, under which a weak set of entitlements came to apply proportionally to part-time and temporary employees. The lack of access to leave entitlements and limited protection against unfair dismissal contributed to an expansion of part-time casual employment in the post-1980 period, with serious consequences for women. Given the legacy of a gender contract leaving women responsible for unpaid caregiving, it became common for women to engage in part-time casual employment, since shorter hours were typically available only on a casual basis. It is these workers who were (and are) most in need of minimum standards and least likely to receive them.

Nevertheless, even if Australia applied the regulatory framework advanced in the ILO Convention on Part-Time Work to all part-time workers, not just permanent ones, deficiencies would remain. In Australia, as elsewhere, patterns of occupational and industrial sex segregation make it difficult to identify comparable workers. Furthermore, where a comparable worker may be found, the pursuit of equal treatment defined as equivalency vis-à-vis a singular baseline fails to alleviate the problem of group disadvantage, since it amounts to the same levels of protection in only limited areas (i.e. the right to organize and collective bargaining, basic wages, occupational health and safety, and discrimination in employment and occupation). Elsewhere it entails only proportional protections (i.e. non-pecuniary or social wage benefits).

The most effective contemporary efforts to limit labour market insecurity amongst part-time workers at the state and federal levels in Australia have centred on regularizing part-time paid employment. They have extended select benefits and entitlements to those part-time workers whose employment relationships most closely approximate the SER. These efforts nevertheless largely leave in place the notion of standard weekly (or full-time) hours and the sex/gender divisions of labour (paid and unpaid) upholding this pillar of the employment norm.

At the level of employment regulation, responding to precariousness amongst part-time workers calls for advancing approaches embracing two principles, which Fudge and I (2001b) have developed elsewhere and applied to the Canadian case: parity and inclusivity. Achieving the first principle, *parity*, for part-time workers means crafting protections attentive to the diverse needs and situations of workers in different forms of employment rather than accepting pro-rata entitlements. It entails devising labour market policies that not only transcend an SER-centric approach but displace the baseline altogether. One promising avenue involves reducing working time for *all* people over the course of the entire lifecycle and reorganizing production for the market not only to reflect life's different phases but to reject the gendered segmentation of workers' lives into discreet sequences (Klammer et al. 2005). Inspired by Supiot's (2001) calls to move 'beyond employment', this approach embraces 'worker-time' to reconcile occupational and personal life, to encourage genuinely worker-centred flexibility through a new set of public rights, known as social drawing rights (84), linked to the notion of lifetime hours (Boulin 2006), and to promote the redistribution of employment. The call for 'differential consideration' (Vogel 1993) on the basis of workers' unpaid caregiving responsibilities at a given phase of the lifecycle, which shaped the arguments of Australian unions in the Family Provisions test-case, is consistent with this new direction. It should be emphasized, however, that in this test-case the notion of differential consideration was used to support what Molyneux (1985: 232–3) labels 'practical gender interests' (i.e. women's requirements for part-time employment in order to fulfil their socially prescribed responsibilities for pre-school-aged children) rather than to support what she calls 'strategic gender interests' addressing structural issues, as one union official interviewed confirmed (Bowtell, ACTU, 27 June 2006). Together, differential consideration and the redefinition of working time to reflect life's different phases are a potential antidote to the shortcomings of SER-centric approaches to limiting precarious employment among part-time workers: they provide guidance as to which social differences are significant and address questions, whose centrality in fostering gender equity is well-documented (see for example Fredman 1994; Picchio 1998), of who bears and who should bear the cost of caregiving.

In the early 1990s, at the outset of discussions towards the ILO Convention on Part-Time Work, several member states and worker representatives proposed fostering worker-centred working-time adjustments as a means of simultaneously increasing women's labour force participation rates and easing unemployment, but they were met with opposition (ILO 1993a). The Australian case highlights the need to revisit such proposals, particularly in reshaping Australia's emergent industrial relations system. Otherwise, there is a danger that the promotion of permanent part-time employment will reproduce *old* problems in the form of *new* patterns of gender inequality. For example, despite its greater security, part-time permanent employment still routinely fails to provide adequate incomes for individuals (Chalmers et al. 2005). Paradoxically, the risk of low income is magnified among part-time permanent workers who were formerly casual, since the shift to permanent status involves trading off casual loadings, and hence higher wage returns, for greater certainty. In all but a few professional occupations there is also no such thing as a part-time career; part-time permanent workers are confined to a relatively narrow band of job classifications (Burgess 2005: 34) and their hourly earnings on average slipped in relation to full-time permanent workers between 1990 and 2006 (from 0.98 to 0.86) (ABS 2007).

To address precariousness amongst part-time workers, a second principle—*inclusivity*—must also be integral to labour policies. This would mean adopting comprehensive minimum standards, from which no party may derogate, and covering all workers regardless of their hours, employment status, sector, occupation, or industry and regardless of the presence or absence of a comparator. The Australian case, where there is some movement in this direction, highlights the importance of an inclusive approach. Consider the requirement for 12 months' continuous service to access unpaid parental leave in the Family Provisions test-case ruling, compelling casuals to prove that their employment is continuing, an approach largely retained in the national employment standards introduced in 2009 and moderated only modestly in the paid parental leave scheme proposed in the subsequent budget. Why should workers' access to unpaid parental leave still be tied to continuity defined in accordance with tenure in a single employment relationship?

The union movement's response to changes introduced under Work Choices was broadly consistent with this inclusive approach. For example, in a 2006 policy brief, the ACTU (2006: 5–6, pt. 11) enumerated principles for future industrial relations policy aimed at inclusivity. Chief among them was the notion that any new system 'should apply throughout the labour market to all forms of [paid] employment covering all employers, employees and contactors'; in so doing, the ACTU called for discouraging 'artificial arrangements to exclude workers from the protection of the system'. It also called for a 'decent, relevant and secure safety net of fair and enforceable minimum standards' that included the terms previously won under the Family Provisions test-case, some of which informed the actions of the ALP government in late 2008 (ACTU 2006: 8, pt. 23).

As of 2006, the union movement recognized that the legal basis upon which awards historically stood had been altered for good. It opted to stress the quality of the industrial relations system itself, and the rights it confers on working people, rather than the jurisdiction (federal or state level). As the Assistant Secretary of Unions NSW noted:

We've developed a strategy which is partly reactive like everybody else's but it's also partly proactive. Presuming that we are going to be pushed further down that other path, we have a very firm policy principle of 'no less than'. So whatever you [workers] are called, however it [employment] is configured, you have certain conditions and rights no less than what essentially used to be [associated with] full-time secure employment. (Lennon, 28 June 2006)

Such responses symbolize the ACTU's reluctant acceptance of a North American-style bifurcated industrial relations system, characterized by minimum standards, on the one hand, and enterprise-level collective bargaining, on the other hand (ACTU 2006: 5, pt. 11, principle 3). This system is known for its gendered and polarizing tendencies (on the United States, see for example Cobble 1994 and Wial 1994; on Canada, see for example Fudge 1991; see also O'Grady 1991; Vosko 2000; Fudge and Vosko 2001a). The notion of 'no less than' represents a triumph of practical over strategic interests, which is not surprising, given the depth of structural changes in Australia and the tensions they have engendered. This tactic presses for the new system to apply to all workers in the labour force. The risk, however, is that, as Perrons et al. (2006: 260) demonstrate, based on their comparison of various EU countries, by steering away from 'transformative policies that reshape the distribution of opportunities' (e.g. policies recognizing the social value of caregiving work), shorter-term practical interests could contribute to gendered consequences in the long term.

Considered over the long term, the Australian case also underscores the importance of challenging norms of male breadwinning and female caregiving, and the partial internal citizenships they reflect and engender, by addressing unpaid work in tandem with employment regulation. Part-time casual employment heightens, rather than eases, the stresses and strains encountered by workers with caregiving responsibilities. Many workers in these employment situations are women like Mary Vanderpool, quoted at the beginning of this chapter. Their casual designation is made necessary by their parental role and the unpaid caregiving it involves, because, for them, casual employment has long been the only entrée into working part-time—their *only* choice. Rather than improving conditions for a limited number of part-time (permanent) workers compelled to trade off paid employment for unpaid work, why not opt for policies fostering the realignment of total work (Picchio 1998) among women and men? In Australia, characterized by especially sharp differences in men's and women's levels of unpaid and paid work (as Chapter 3 illustrated), such measures could go a considerable distance in forging gender equity and inclusive citizenship.

Notes

1. The reasons relate principally to Australian federalism, since certain issues covered by ILO standards have fallen historically within the jurisdiction of states (Creighton 1998; Ruskin and Smith 1998; Nyland and Castle 1999; Biffl and Isaac 2002).
2. For a full list of participants and representatives of organizations interviewed, see Appendix C.
3. As Boulin (2006: 200) observes, behind 'new' conceptions of control over time is a critical distinction between the quantity of free time workers have and their 'scope of action', that is, their ability to use it. To this end, he emphasizes, in particular, socio-spatial constraints such as waiting and commuting times, but also acknowledges 'economic reasons'.
4. The data referred to in this section were customized by the author from Wave F of the HILDA Survey and refer to the year 2006 unless otherwise noted. To reflect the Australian policy context, this section defines casual workers as employees lacking paid sick leave / holiday entitlements and the unit of analysis is the 'main job'.
5. In Australia, an award is a binding ruling of an industrial relations tribunal that prescribes the rights and obligations of parties, typically employees and employers in a given industry or occupation, through conciliation (see especially Brooks 2003: 74). Awards were the main form of industrial regulation in Australia until the 1990s, at which point there was a shift to enterprise agreements and individualized Australian Workplace Agreements became permissible (in 1993 and 1996 respectively) (Biffl and Isaac 2002). With the 2007 federal election of the Australian Labor Party, the tide shifted once again. At this juncture, the federal government began to gradually eliminate Australian Workplace Agreements (a process still under way at the time of writing) and made commitments to a

'modernized' award system (analysed below) and collective bargaining at the enterprise level (Australia (FWB Memo) 2008; Australia (FWA) 2009).

6. The ensuing discussion of casual workers' degree of access to statutory protections and social benefits refers to federal examples, except where otherwise noted.

7. Australian parents have historically lacked a government-supported scheme of paid parental leave. However, federal budget proposals (described below) were poised to change this situation at the time of this book's completion.

8. This percentage reflects the 'raw' (i.e. unadjusted) annual income gap.

9. This figure refers to 2005, the most recent year for which data are available (HILDA, Wave E, Custom Tabulation).

10. The original decision, which allowed automatic conversion, was rejected in *Clerks (SA) Award Casual Provisions Appeal* case (SAIRC 2002).

11. Notably, in making provision for conversion, the AIRC stated that 'the notion of permanent casual employment, if not a contradiction in terms, detracts from the integrity of an award safety net in which standards for annual leave, paid public holidays, sick leave and personal leave are fundamentals' (AIRC 2000: 47).

    Other orders of this decision also included an increased loading (from 20% to 25%), and a minimum shift of four hours (three hours for part-timers) (AIRC 2000: 86 and 59). Yet the AIRC rejected the union's application to permit the use of casuals only in short-term and emergency situations and 'when rostering permanent employees is impracticable' (AIRC 2000: 44–5).

12. According to Allister Kentish, National Research Officer for the Australian Manufacturing Workers' Union, this development was a product of caps on hiring permanent staff in the public sector in NSW initiated in the early 1990s, when 'managers were using part of their budget to employ day labour through labour hire . . . because they couldn't employ new staff' (29 June 2006).

13. Other successes included the requirements that firms engaging a labour-hire business to perform work on the client's premises consult with employees regarding occupational health and safety, provide employees of such businesses with training for job safety, as well as protective equipment and clothing that they supply to their own employees, and ensure that labour-hire employees are apprised of risks in the workplace and procedures to limit such risks. The NSW IRC did not, however, grant labour-hire employees and employees of the host employer equivalent wages and working conditions.

14. At a practical level, the National Agreement Preserving State Awards (NAPSAs), created in the transition from state-level awards to a consolidated federal industrial relations system, only protected the awards varied for a maximum of three years (i.e. until 2009).

15. Namely, the Shop, Distributive and Allied Employees Association, the Australian Municipal, Administrative, Clerical and Services Union, the Community

and Public Sector Union, and the Automotive, Food, Metals, Engineering, Printing and Kindred Industries Union.

16. The Work Choices Bill amended the Workplace Relations Act (WRA) (1996); therefore, subsequent references refer to the changes in this Act.

17. The process of scaling back remaining awards included fostering their expiry, permitting future limits on their numbers, and constraining their scope and content. The latter entailed, on the one hand, limiting allowable award matters, effectively disallowing matters formerly contained in awards, such as conversion clauses for casuals as well as restrictions on the engagement of independent contactors, and, on the other hand, freezing provisions outside the list of allowable matters during transitional periods (AIRC 2006a and 2006b).

18. Work Choices also deemed the AFPC responsible for regulating casual loading. According to Watson (2004: 13), casual loadings ranged between 15% and 33% in the early 2000s; under Work Choices, the default casual loading percentage was initially set at 20% (Australia (WRA) 1996 amended 2006: Part 7, Div. 2, Subdiv. C 186).

19. Work Choices allowed employers to require workers to submit to averaging; it also permitted them to require reasonable overtime with no requirement for supplementary compensation.

20. Unions, however, continued to struggle to secure conversion by inserting voluntaristic language, such as 'may request to be considered for conversion', in enterprise agreements; agreements between teaching staff at universities and employers are a case in point (Brown, NTEU, 29 June 2006; Game, National Tertiary Education Union (NTEU), 30 June 2006; Rosewarne, NTEU, 29 June 2006).

21. The ensuing discussion is up to date to May 2009.

22. According to its announcement in mid-May 2009, paid parental leave is to be available to primary carers at the rate of the minimum wage set by the FPC (then $543.78 per week) and recipients are to receive it over 18 weeks. Recipients, however, are neither to receive the $5,000 baby bonus nor to be paid superannuation, and their leave is to be taxed, unlike the baby bonus. Under terms proposed in May 2009, most people in the workforce are to be eligible for the entitlement after the birth or adoption of the child as long as they are the 'primary carer', a designation intended to be assumed by the mother due to her unique capacity to breastfeed, although the leave is to be transferable to the father or same-sex partner if s/he is the primary carer and meets other requirements. All employees, casuals, contractors, and the self-employed, earning $150,000 or less, are to qualify for the paid leave if they have been employed continuously (not necessarily for the same employer) for at least ten of the previous 13 months before the birth and have worked for pay for at least 330 hours in that period (Australia 2009: 24).

23. The FWA also stipulated that awards are to include a flexibility clause permitting individual arrangements enabling an employer and an individual employee to

agree on arrangements that meet their needs but that do not disadvantage the employee (Australia (FWA) 2009: chapter 2, Part 2.3, Div. 3, S. 144; O'Neill 2008; Australia (FWB Memo) 2008).

24. When the ALP came to power, protections against unfair dismissal applied only to employees employed by a business employing more than 101 employees. The system introduced under the FWA (2009) established new qualifying requirements for unfair dismissal—12 months for employees employed in firms with fewer than 15 employees and six months for employees employed in firms with 15 or more employees—and a simplified (six-paragraph) Small Business Fair Dismissal Code to guide employers (Australia (FWA) 2009: chapter 3, Part 3.2, Div. 2, 3). Casuals were also formally included in unfair dismissal protection. However, the effect of this change was primarily symbolic; to benefit from it, casuals were required to meet a series of qualifying requirements replicating old practices. Indeed, a period of casual employment did not count towards the period of employment required for unfair dismissal protection unless it was on a regular and systematic basis and the employee had a reasonable expectation of continuing employment by the employer on that basis (Australia (FWA) 2009: chapter 3, Part 3.2, Div. 2, s. 384; see also FWB Memo 2008: esp. rr. 1515–20).

25. The FWA assigned Fair Work Australia the following functions: minimum wage-setting and adjustment by a specialist Minimum Wage Panel; award variation; ensuring good faith bargaining; dealing with industrial action; approval of agreements; and resolution of disputes and unfair dismissal matters (Australia (FWB Memo) 2008: r. 329; see also Australia (FWA) 2009: chapter 5, Part 5.1, Div. 1, 2).

5

Regulating Temporary Employment: Equal Treatment, Qualified

On fixed-term work it was very, very hard to get an agreement. Then we came to agency work ... You couldn't treat agency work the same way as fixed-term contracts because there was this major question mark of who is the formal employer ... It's already difficult to achieve equal treatment ... in fixed-term work but a major question for agency work is also who are you allowed to compare these workers with.

> Catelene Passchier, Confederal Secretary, European Trade Union Congress, Brussels, 29 October 2006.

The open-ended relationship between a worker and an employer, in which the worker normally works on the employer's premises under direct supervision, was central to the development of the SER. Through it, workers granted employers their loyalty and willingness to retrain in exchange for stability and regularity (i.e. predictable wages and deferred benefits). The exchange was facilitated, on the one hand, by the firm-level identification of pre-specified ports of entry, job ladders, on-the-job training, and clear and enforceable terms and conditions of employment and, on the other hand, by protections against unfair or arbitrary dismissal. Even at the height of the SER, there were limits to the protective framework surrounding the open-ended employment relationship: for example, in many OECD countries, there were exceptions permitting employers to engage certain workers on finite bases (e.g. in fixed-term and temporary agency work), both occupational groups, such as clerical workers, and social groups, such as women and migrant workers (Parker 1994; Vosko 2000: chapter 3; Burgess and Connell, eds., 2004; Davidov 2004). As challenges to the open-ended employment relationship grew in the 1980s, these exceptions revealed themselves to be as important to the management of the margins of the labour market as the limits laid down by employment protections.

This chapter explores contemporary regulations addressing precariousness in forms of employment diverging from the SER's central pillar of continuous employment. It begins by sketching the erosion of the open-ended employment relationship in the post-1980 period, focusing on the expansion of temporary employment in a selection of OECD countries, placing an accent on its development in the EU 15, particularly the fixed-term and temporary agency work varieties.

After reviewing EU employment policy framing its emergence, the chapter analyses the EU Directive on Fixed-Term Work (1999). This directive extends certain protections and benefits identified with the SER to workers lacking open-ended employment relationships whose situations otherwise resemble this norm, providing for equal treatment on the basis of form of employment, broadly defined. However, it excludes temporary agency workers, a notable omission given that temporary agency work, since it is characterized typically by the lack of both an open-ended and a bilateral employment relationship, tends to be especially precarious.

It nevertheless took years of negotiations, and the adoption of a Directive on Services in the Internal Market (2006) excluding services provided by temporary work agencies, for the Council of the EU to agree on a Directive on Temporary Agency Work (2008). Furthermore, the directive adopted ultimately qualifies equal treatment, limiting it to basic working and employment conditions (i.e. working time and pay) and circumscribing it further by permitting national social partners and their equivalents to conclude collective agreements that differ from this principle, so long as they respect the protection of temporary agency workers overall.

EU-level regulation is not a complete regime governing temporary employment, since it represents only one aspect of labour market regulation shaping developments in member states. The EU 15 are also diverse, characterized by different levels of fixed-term and temporary agency work and distinct approaches to regulation due to their unique social, economic, political, and legal histories. While recognizing this diversity, an analysis of developments in the EU 15 vis-à-vis EU-level regulations shows how SER-centrism in the regulation of temporary employment has the capacity to moderate labour market insecurity associated with fixed-term work while extending an inferior protective framework to temporary agency work.[1]

The Erosion of the Open-Ended Employment Relationship

The open-ended employment relationship operated most effectively in periods of employment growth, when product markets were character-ized by high levels of demand. It reached its height in the decades following World War II. At this juncture, two principal mechanisms sustained the open-ended employment relationship: first, the terms of the contract of employment between employee and employer, which established work rules and benefits systems; and second, statutory em-ployment protections attached to the employment relationship, con-ceived as a status (and described in Chapter 2) arising from an unequal relationship between employer and employee. Bolstered by workers' col-lective struggles and the institutionalization of collective bargaining, the recognition of the power imbalance between workers and employers cultivated a 'floor of rights', operating typically at a national and/or sub-national level, independent of the terms of a given contract (Mück-enberger and Deakin 1989). Statutory protections establishing penalties for unfair or arbitrary dismissal, often pegged to the duration of the employment relationship, were integral to this floor in Western and Northern Europe, as well as in Canada and Australia, in contrast to the United States and, to a lesser extent, the United Kingdom.[2] So, too, were limits on fixed-term contracts and on temporary agency work regulated, for example, through requirements for specific reasons to engage workers on such bases.

The design of these protections varied by context but they all made 'ad hoc personnel decisions costly' for firms (Bosch 2004: 620). In this way, safeguards established for the open-ended employment relationship high-light the interplay between the economic, psychological, and legal settle-ments upholding the SER. Career pay systems, distributing profit-linked wages and benefits across the employment phase of workers' adult lives, and making retirement mandatory, complemented protections against unjust dismissal. Restrictions on the use of contracts of finite duration, together with a form of work organization premised on vertically integrated produc-tion, encouraged individuals 'to pursue continuous employment, and in the end to internalize this constraint as an intrinsic motivation' (Mücken-berger and Deakin 1989: 159).

The open-ended employment relationship nevertheless hinged on a set of historically contingent circumstances. It reflected not only the balance of gendered class relations in nation states, well-recognized in the scholarly literature on the dynamics of wage regulation under the SER (Clarke 1991; Deakin 1998; Picchio 1998), but the ways in which this balance shaped and was shaped by other elements of the post-World War II entente, especially mass production and domestic consumption. Originating with the structural changes in the global economy of the early 1970s, and intensified by the rise of new technologies, the shift to tertiary employment, the decline of the full-employment objective, and the attendant erosion of real wages, the late 20th century saw the introduction of neoliberal policies pursuing 'flexible' employment relationships through the removal of 'labour market rigidities'.[3] This so-called era of deregulation (Standing 1997: 8) signalled a partial turning back of postwar regulations: with 'de-regulation', as Mückenberger and Deakin (1989: 162) argue, 'there is a distinct "recontractualization" of the employment relationship and a return to the individual contract'. As a consequence, employment protections became more selective and more integrative (i.e. labour force participation became more central to workers' reproduction). It would be misleading, however, to suggest that the de-regulation characterizing the 1980s and 1990s amounted to a withdrawal of state regulatory powers. Nor were new measures aimed only at allowing employment relationships to respond quickly (or 'flexibly'). Many policies meant the continued influence of 'rigid' regulations (e.g. those promoting governments' active roles in training and education to assist in matching workers with employers' skills requirements) (Standing 1997).

The main developments characterizing this era were the introduction of firm-level practices encouraging 'employability security' (Kanter 1993), associated with the re-emergence of human resource practices resembling welfare capitalism but resting more heavily on worker consent than earlier control-oriented variants (Jacoby 1997), and the reconfiguration and weakening of employment protections. Employability security de-links employment security from the pooled social risk made possible by the open-ended employment relationship. On the employer side, it calls for providing workers with training opportunities as part of the employment relationship. However, training is not perceived as a long-term investment in the productivity of a given firm, but rather as meeting workers' needs to continually market themselves (Stone 2004: 110–11). For workers, employability security promotes the active pursuit of training and learning within and outside the confines of a given job, on the assumption that there is no long-term job but rather many episodic, short-term work opportunities (Sennett 1998: 22).

Complementing the 'new' emphasis on human capital investment was the reconfiguration of employment protections entailing not only investments in training but limitations on statutory protections against unfair dismissal.

This meant, in the case of the United States, for example, minimizing the significance of implied terms and, in the United Kingdom, constraining the strict statutory test of continuity (Evans et al. 1985; Mückenberger and Deakin 1989: 164; Stone 2004: 70). It also involved introducing regulations legitimizing employment relationships of finite duration and other measures that unhinge the open-ended employment relationship.

This twofold emphasis on employability security and the weakening employment protections originating in the 1980s coincided with stagnation in permanent (especially full-time) employment in some contexts in Europe and North America, such as in West Germany (Bosch 2004: 621) and Canada (Vosko 2006a: 11). In other contexts, most notably the United States, it amounted to the weakening salience of permanency. One explicit indication in the 1990s was the significant decline in job tenure among men over 25 with a high school diploma or less; this decline reflected the erosion of internal labour markets, especially in blue-collar sectors. Some scholarship exploring trends in job tenure in Europe and North America cautions against overstating the extent of the decline in long-term employment (see e.g. Auer and Cazes 2001; Doogan 2005). Equally critical, in examining the American case, Stone (2004; see also Piore 2002) highlights the limits of job tenure and job loss data itself. She (Stone 2004: 82–3) notes that neither

address whether there has been a decline in implicit promises of long-term employment. Job tenure data is an *ex post* measure of how long a worker holds a particular job. Job tenure data can tell us whether jobs today are in fact of shorter duration than they were in the past, but they do not show whether a worker has an *ex ante* expectation that his or her job will be long-term. What characterized internal labor markets, from an employer's point of view, was the *expectation* of long-term job security … If the prevalence of employment relationships that embody such an implicit understanding is declining, that fact might or might not show up in job tenure data.

Long job tenure may mean access to the full range of available statutory protections and social benefits, but it is not necessarily indicative of labour market security. Furthermore, if employment-linked health care, pension, and other benefits are not transferable to a worker's new job, then workers may also face powerful disincentives to change their employment situation even if they face dimensions of labour market insecurity, such as low income and a lack of control over the labour process (Stanford and Vosko 2004: 13).

The deterioration of permanency evident in many national contexts offers one lens through which to investigate challenges to the open-ended employment relationship. The extent and character of employment relationships of limited duration represents another. This second lens is particularly promising in discerning both quantitative and qualitative aspects of continuity and change in labour markets once characterized by extensive statutory employment protections.

In the post-1980 period, temporary employment grew in such contexts, especially in the EU, leading the European Commission (2002a: 8) to report that it had 'become an important cog in the machinery of the European labour market' because it fostered 'greater flexibility in job management'. In the EU 15, temporary employment rose from approximately 6% to 11% of total employment between 1983 and 2006, reaching particularly high levels in Spain, France, Sweden, Portugal, Finland, and the Netherlands (Table 5.1).[4] Among the countries in this group, women held particularly large shares of temporary employment and in 2006 they represented a majority of all temporary workers in all of the EU 15 except Portugal and Germany.

Furthermore, countries where temporary employment became most widespread exhibited greater differentials related to migrant status, leading authors of a study commissioned by the European Foundation for the Improvement of Living and Working Conditions to conclude that 'the increase in [such] flexible contracts is largely at the expense of migrants, since the higher the prevalence of flexible contracts the stronger the disadvantage for this group' (Ambrosini and Barone 2007: 33). In some cases, these differentials also intersected with migrant workers' country of origin. This study found that in the Netherlands, for example, 'migrants with a non-western background are less likely to have an open-ended contract... than Dutch natives...Conversely, the work careers of western non-nationals more closely resemble those of nationals' (33).

In the contemporary period, temporary employment is highly diverse in the EU, varying by place of work, the exercise of administrative control, and scheduling. It also has distinct social and legal meanings in different countries, including within the EU 15. For example, in Spain, temporary employment is associated with a particular legal form of contract designed to ensure that rights reserved for permanent workers, especially those related to dismissal, are not extended to temporary workers.[5] In contrast, in the Netherlands, a significant share of temporary employment involves work through temporary agencies; furthermore, in the late 1990s, in this context temporary agency work came to be uniquely associated with significant rights and entitlements channelled through agencies themselves.[6]

Table 5.1. Temporary Employment as a Percentage of Total Employment, Selected OECD Countries, 1983 and 2006

	1983	2006	Change
EU 15	6	11	+5
Spain	15*	21	+6
France	3	20	+17
Sweden	-	15	-
Portugal	13	14	+1
Finland	-	14	-
Netherlands	5	13	+8
Germany	10	7	−3
Denmark	-	6	-
Italy	4	8	+4
Belgium	4	7	+3
Greece	9	6	−3
Ireland	6	3	−3
Austria	-	4	-
Luxembourg	3	5	+2
United Kingdom	5	5	0
Canada	5*	10	+5
Australia	-	7	-
United States	-	3*	-

* Data drawn from a different year other than 1983 or 2006: Spain (1985); Canada (1989); United States (2005).
- = no data available.

Within the category of temporary employment in the EU, fixed-term work is particularly prominent. In the EU 15, it represented 8% of total employment in 2006 (up from 3% in 1983[7]). In countries where it was most prevalent, women also had larger shares of fixed-term work than men.[8] Additionally, although the basic hourly or monthly wages of fixed-term workers differ very little from those engaged in open-ended contracts, with the notable exceptions of Spain and Ireland, in countries where wage payments are tightly linked to length of service, fixed-term workers earn less than permanent workers (e.g. Belgium, Finland, France, and Greece) (Scheele 2002). They also have limited access to social benefits and statutory entitlements tied to the duration of employment.

Temporary agency work represented a much smaller percentage of total employment than fixed-term work in most EU countries—approximately 2% of total employment in the EU 15 in 2006. At the same time, with the gradual removal of longstanding restrictions on its use, its incidence has grown. It also continues to be characterized by low wages and workers continue to encounter difficulties in securing protections requiring the identification of an employer. Unlike fixed-term work, however, there was no uniform pattern of sex differentiation in temporary agency work in 2006.

SER-Centric Responses to Precariousness in Temporary Employment in the EU

EU-level measures on temporary employment were initiated in the late 1970s with calls for action by the EU Council of Ministers to monitor temporary employment and to ensure social protection for workers. They took shape in three phases, culminating in the adoption of the first directive on this subject on fixed-term work.

European Employment Policy Framing Directives on Fixed-Term and Temporary Agency Work

At the end of the 1970s, which marked the first phase, common employment policy was in its infancy. With only a Tripartite Standing Committee on Employment Issues in place, holding merely an advisory role, there was a dearth of institutional mechanisms that could facilitate its creation (Goetschy 1999: 118). Directives on employment protection (e.g. those on Collective Redundancies, 1975; Transfer of Enterprises, 1977; and Employee Protection in Cases of Insolvency, 1980), along with two on sex equality (on Equal Pay, 1975; and Equal Treatment, 1976), were nevertheless among the first 'hard' law initiatives. Early discussions of the need for substantive regulations on temporary employment thus occurred in a fragmented policy environment, but there was some recognition of the erosion of the open-ended employment relationship and the risks of rising insecurities for women workers in particular.

In 1982, the earliest concerted attempt at a directive on temporary employment took place at the instigation of the Commission. The directive was to cover both triangular relationships involving temporary work agencies and the bilateral relationship between an employer and an employee engaged in a fixed-duration contract (CEU 1982a: 1). A draft of the directive indicated that temporary employment could be used in instances of a short-term reduction in the workforce or a rare and temporary increase in production. Firms could only use fixed-term workers for these purposes or to carry out a clearly specified 'occasional task of a transient nature, where work is of a "special nature", or in connection with a "new activity of uncertain duration"' (CEU 1982b: Art. 15.1). It provided for a three-month maximum for all assignments through temporary agencies and permitted only one renewal, except under special circumstances (CEU 1982b: Art. 3.2). In instances of abuse, it prescribed deeming the contract 'to be of indefinite duration' (CEU 1982b: para. 15.3). However, this draft did not pass because member states were unable to reach the unanimous agreement required.

In the aftermath of this failure, institutional mechanisms fostering common employment policies slowly took shape. In this second phase, as concerns mounted over 'social dumping',[9] those opposing an exclusive emphasis on a common market envisioned for 1992 under the Single European Act (1986), led by the French under François Mitterand, pressed for a Social Charter as a counterbalance. The resulting Community Charter of the Fundamental Social Rights of Workers of 1989 covered freedom of movement for workers, fair remuneration, adequate income supports outside employment, equal treatment for women and men, and the right to strike. In tandem with the introduction of this Charter, in 1990 the Commission introduced a new proposal for three separate Council directives on 'atypical work'. Only one, on the safety and health of temporary workers, covering fixed-term and temporary agency workers, passed in 1991 and even then, only following reformulation. New institutional mechanisms for adopting directives introduced under the Single European Act facilitated its passage (Jeffery 1995),[10] but this directive's focus on only one form of 'atypical work' was, in retrospect, also critical. After its adoption, negotiations on temporary employment proceeded separately from those on part-time employment.

Efforts to regulate the working conditions of temporary workers paused for nearly a decade in the 1990s, during which time there was a sea-change in employment policy at the EU level. For example, an Agreement on Social Policy, annexed to the Maastricht Treaty (1992), provided for the negotiation of framework agreements, or pan-European collective agreements negotiated by the social partners, that could be transposed into EU directives (EU 1992: Arts. 3 and 4).

Subsequent to Maastricht, in the third phase, the impetus for change in common employment policy came from Jacques Delors's White Paper on 'Growth, Competitiveness, Employment: Challenges and Ways Forward into the 21st Century, 1993' and the Green Paper and subsequent White Paper on Social Policy. The White Paper on 'Growth, Competitiveness, Employment' set out a framework for putting EU social and employment policy, and especially the issue of job creation, on the supranational agenda. While Delors was concerned to meet the criteria for the monetary union, the White Paper on 'Growth, Competitiveness, Employment' also attempted to quell concerns that European integration was contributing to rising unemployment by promoting 'active' employment policy bringing features of Keynesianism, such as targeted spending on social protection, together with neoliberal fiscal policies (EC 1993a: 16, 130). Instead of recommending the tax measures necessary to secure the spending side of this policy equation (Gray 2004: 66), however, the White Paper on 'Growth, Competitiveness, Employment' advanced four independent targets: namely, identifying changes taking place in the labour market, especially concerning part-time and flexible work, to achieve a wider distribution of jobs and income; improving access to the labour market, especially among disadvantaged social groups through, for example, 'promoting...equal opportunities between men and women'; raising the stock of human capital to optimize community competitiveness; and accelerating the development of new jobs and new activities, 'particularly labour-intensive ones' (EC 1993a: 130). Representing a 'juggling act' (Deacon 2001: 70) akin to the White Paper on 'Growth, Competitiveness, Employment', the White Paper on Social Policy supported each of these targets, and it prioritized the first by casting flexible employment contracts as a measure of 'adaptation' and minimizing the implications for employment protections and job quality.

In the mid-1990s, these targets contributed to the emergence of more coordinated community employment policy or institutionally embedded efforts to devise synchronized 'soft' supranational employment policy (EC 2002a). Developments reflecting this shift included the Council's endorsement of measures bearing the imprint of the White Paper on 'Growth, Competitiveness, Employment' and a framework for monitoring progress at the national level at a 1994 summit at Essen. They also included the Extraordinary European Council Meeting on Employment in Luxembourg in 1997, where the Council launched a coordinated strategy for national employment policies in anticipation of the entry into force of the Amsterdam Treaty in 1998, which included an Employment Chapter setting out employment policy guidelines for the first time and laying the basis for the European Employment Strategy (EES)[11]and subsequently the Open Method of Coordination (OMC), whose adoption, as some scholars would come to argue, reduced pressure to secure harder EU-level measures (EU 1997: Title VIII, Arts. 125–30).[12]

That same year, after the adoption of the Directive on Part-Time Work (1997), talks on fixed-term and temporary agency work were separated when unions and employers could not agree to address them in one package (Passchier, 29 October 2006; van den Burg, 21 February 2007).[13] Still, the following sentiment, expressed at the Cardiff Council in 1998, shaped the tenor of both directives:

while strict EPL (employment protection legislation) should not be singled out as causing the high European unemployment, adequate job-security provisions, combining flexibility and security at work are important for increasing employment and adjusting to important shocks. Further EPL reforms in countries with strict regulations would reduce labour market segmentation . . . (CEU 1998: 15)

The Directive on Fixed-Term Work, negotiated first, initially took the form of a framework agreement between the social partners. The content of the final product, a hard directive informed by soft supranational employment policy, marked a shift away from limiting insecure jobs to minimizing abusive uses of this form of temporary work. Following the Cardiff Council as well, annual guidelines emanating from the EES increasingly cast equal opportunity as a productive factor or, as Barnard and Deakin (1999: 371) noted at the time, 'as a means of raising the employment rate', elevating the risk that 'the equality principle' would 'merely serve to buttress a policy aimed at the creation of employment'. When a Directive on Fixed-Term Work was adopted, there were signs that a form of temporary employment common among women was becoming more generalized.

The EU Directive on Fixed-Term Work (1999)

The 1999 EU Directive on Fixed-Term Work is a response to challenges to the notion of permanency associated with the SER, typified by the existence of an open-ended employment relationship. Placed on the EU agenda partly in recognition of the fact that women predominated in fixed-term work in the early stages of talks, it calls, on the one hand, for non-discrimination and, on the other hand, for limiting 'abuses arising from the use of successive fixed-term employment contracts or relationships' (CEU 1999: Annex, cl. 1, and General Considerations 9).

To advance these goals, it aims to extend various benefits and entitlements associated with the SER to temporary workers; however, it does so for only a subset of this group. The Directive on Fixed-Term Work applies to fixed-term workers who have an employment contract or employment relationship (CEU 1999: Annex, cl. 2.1). It includes within its purview employees and their equivalents—for example, persons defined as 'workers' in the United Kingdom—engaged in bilateral employment relationships whose duration is determined by 'objective conditions' such as 'reaching a specific date, completing a specific task, or the occurrence of a specific event' (CEU 1999: Annex, cl. 3.1). The directive explicitly excludes fixed-term workers placed at the disposition of a user firm by a temporary work agency (CEU 1999: Annex, Preamble, para. 4). It also permits the exclusion of other categories of workers in initial vocational training and apprentice-ship schemes and engaged in employment under a public, or publicly supported, training, integration, or vocational retraining programme (CEU 1999: Annex, cl. 2.2). Prior to the adoption of the directive, a particular issue of debate was whether, in contexts where civil servants are governed by special statute, such as in France, its terms would cover contractual workers 'hired to fill the holes' in the civil service, and viewed, by some, not to be employees (Alberg, 29 October 2006). In implementing the directive, some member states have included workers in the public service under laws, policies, and/or collective agreements on fixed-term work, whereas others have not (EC 2006d: 7). The terms of the directive thus only apply with certainty to fixed-term workers in the private sector in situations that deviate from the SER on the basis of the absence of an open-ended employment relationship.

For the fixed-term workers covered, the principle of non-discrimination is applied through the notion of a 'comparable permanent worker'. Resem-bling the approach adopted in the ILO Convention on Part-Time Work discussed in Chapter 4, this notion refers to 'a worker with an employment contract or relationship of indefinite duration', ideally in the same estab-lishment, engaged in the same or similar type of work/occupation (CEU 1999: Annex, cl. 3.2). Where there is no such worker in the same establish-ment, comparison is still to take place but by reference to the applicable collective agreement or, in the absence of such agreement, in accordance with national law, collective agreements, or practice.[14] In addition to nar-rowing the horizon of comparison, the stated preference for comparison to be worksite-based reinforces the centrality of control (i.e. direct supervision by the employer on the employer's premises) attached to the SER (ad-dressed in Chapter 6). The directive also requires that due regard be given to a variety of other conditions, suggesting that these may include 'seniori-ty and qualification/skills'; this qualifier makes such conditions bases for rejecting a comparison between certain fixed-term and permanent workers engaged in the same work (CEU 1999: Annex, cl. 3.2).[15]

Under the directive, the principle of non-discrimination is to apply to 'employment conditions', a notion whose meaning has been contentious. There is agreement that this notion covers health and safety and working time but not statutory social security and there is debate, particularly in the United Kingdom and Ireland, about whether it covers pay and, if so, to what extent (i.e. the aspects of pay that it encompasses). At the same time, according to a representative of the Commission, it is acknowledged that 'a lot of regulation, not the least on working time, has indirect effects on pay . . . and that it is a very artificial distinction to say that we can regulate working time but not regulate pay' (Berthiaume, 29 October 2006). In practice, therefore, legislation adopted by most member states interprets 'employment conditions' broadly, an understanding buoyed by the directive's emphasis on non-discrimination. As one expert observed:

[it] is a separate issue when you have a non-discrimination provision because this is not really regulating the level of pay. [Rather,] you have a standard of comparison which is set by the free market forces, which is the amount which is paid to the permanent workers. Then, it [the directive] says, if you have decided on this amount for the permanent workers, you should pay at least the same amount to the fixed-term workers. (Alberg, 29 October 2006)

Under the directive, non-discrimination means that fixed-term workers shall not be treated less favourably than comparable permanent workers unless differential treatment is justified on 'objective grounds' (CEU 1999: Annex, cl. 4.1). While the precise definition of non-discrimination is left to member states, this qualification makes possible the exclusion of some fixed-term workers from the employment conditions otherwise falling within the terms of the directive. Since the prohibited discrimination must be linked explicitly to the existence of a fixed-term contract, it also fails to encompass indirect discrimination. This distinguishes the directive, as well as its EU counterpart on part-time work, from other community-level legislation. In the other legislation, as another representative of the Commission observed, if there is a 'practical effect' of, for example, 'discriminat[ion] against women, even if it is not specifically on that particular ground that you introduce a certain measure . . . you will be caught by the requirement to justify it' (Alberg, 29 October 2006). Furthermore, *pro rata temporis* is used to apply this principle: proportional entitlements are the means of attaining 'equivalent conditions', although the modifier 'where appropriate' qualifies even this already limited principle (CEU 1999: Annex, cl. 4.2).[16]

The directive's provisions on the prevention of abuse focus on the use of successive fixed-term contracts. They require member states to establish 'objective reasons' that would justify the renewal of fixed-term contracts, the maximum total duration of successive fixed-term contracts, and/or the number of renewals. At the same time, member states are to establish the conditions under which such contracts are to be regarded as successive and which are to be deemed of indefinite duration (CEU 1999: Annex, cl. 5.2a and b). In response, member states have taken a variety of approaches, including distinguishing between the *renewal* and the *succession* of fixed-term contracts, and applying different rules for these situations.[17] The requirement that where there is 'abuse', member states 'determine under what conditions fixed-term employment contracts or relationships shall be deemed to be contracts or relationships of indefinite duration' (CEU 1999: cl. 5) is typically interpreted loosely as an aspiration for conversion, although it has been upheld by rulings of the European Court of Justice (ECJ) addressing the public sector (Cases C-53/04 and C-180/04, see also C-212/04, emphasis added), where the ECJ has said that the directive:

must be interpreted as *not in principle precluding national legislation* which, where there is abuse arising from the use of successive fixed-term employment contracts or relationships by a public-sector employer, *precludes their being converted into contracts of indeterminate* duration, even though such conversion is provided for in respect of employment contracts and relationships with a public-sector employer, *where that legislation includes another effective measure to prevent and, where relevant, punish the abuse of successive fixed-term contracts by a public-sectorc employer.*

The implementation process thus reflects the increasing influence of soft community employment policies in making harder EU regulations on temporary work less prescriptive than those adopted in the past (Jeffery 1998; Schömann et al. 2003: 81).

Of course, states may introduce or maintain more extensive protections through laws or collective agreements. The directive's terms are not to 'constitute valid grounds for reducing the general level of protection afforded to workers' and it is to be 'without prejudice' to 'in particular, Community provisos concerning equal treatment or opportunities for men and women' (CEU 1999: Annex, cls. 8.1–8.3). Still, as others have argued, they are permissive of this form of employment (Murray 1999b; see also Schömann et al. 2003). The directive's emphasis on promoting non-discrimination and preventing abuse only moderates the high level of uncertainty characterizing fixed-term work and the consequent insecurities. As one official with the ETUC involved in its negotiation stressed, 'the fact [is] that the job finishes. A fixed-term job is a fixed-term job is a fixed-term job' (Passchier, 29 October 2006).

Persistently high levels of fixed-term work across the EU amplify such uncertainties. In 2004, the year by which the 15 states comprising the EU at the time of its adoption had to implement its terms, the average EU share of fixed-term work (including temporary agency work)[18] was 9.1% of total employment, although the proportion of fixed-term work varied by country. In this period, according to the Commission's follow-up report, fixed-term work remained heavily concentrated among young people, standing at nearly 22% of total employment among workers aged 15–24 in 2004. It also remained common among workers with low levels of education and in the primary and especially construction sectors. However, in following up on its implementation, the Commission (2006d: 2) reported that while 'there is a slightly higher incidence of fixed-term contracts among women, the gender dimension of fixed-term work is weak'.

For the Commission (EC 2006d: 2), the growing prevalence of this type of temporary employment in the EU, as well as the approaching equal shares of men and women engaged in it, was a desirable trend contributing to 'making labour markets more flexible'. Yet it also acknowledged risks, particularly the risk of 'excessive career instability in the early life of young adults', which 'can be associated at a macro level with the lowering of consumption propensity and of the fertility rate' (2). This acknowledgment flowed from its finding that while a third of those in fixed-term work find stable jobs after one year, 16% are still in the same situation after six years and fully 20% had moved out of employment altogether (EC 2006d: 2). The Commission reported further that while the EU 15 had implemented most of the terms of the directive, several problems remained. Notably, many member states failed to implement the concept of the 'comparable permanent worker' (EC 2006d: 38). It found fault particularly with Spain, Italy, France, Luxembourg, the Netherlands, Austria, and Portugal for neglecting to provide guidelines for comparison where there is no comparable permanent worker in the same establishment. Familiarly, this weakness in member states' legislation affects those fixed-term workers covered by the directive but whose situations are most difficult to evaluate against a singular baseline—a challenge amplified in the case of temporary agency work as the ensuing discussion shall show.[19]

Regulating Temporary Agency Work in the EU 15

Like their counterparts in fixed-term work, temporary agency workers have limited access to social benefits and statutory entitlements linked to the duration of an employment relationship, since their paid working lives are often punctuated by multiple periods of unemployment. At the same time, the dimensions of labour market insecurity that temporary agency workers experience relate to both the short duration of employment compared to permanent workers and the triangular character of the employment relationship (i.e. between the agency, the client firm, and the worker), through which the agency takes on employment-related responsibilities such as hiring and dismissal, as well as administrative responsibilities related to pay and benefits (Vosko 2000: 134).

In accordance with the principle that 'labour is not a commodity', many national governments in Europe and elsewhere largely eliminated triangular employment relationships by prohibiting certain types of private employment agencies, starting in the second quarter of the 20th century. Consistent with the ILO Convention on Private Employment Agencies (1933) discussed in Chapter 2, temporary work agencies were prohibited in most sectors in a majority of European countries until the 1970s, partly in an attempt to institutionalize the open-ended employment relationship (Vosko 1997 and 2000; Clauwaert 2000). The principal exceptions were in occupations common among women, such as clerical work, for example in Sweden (ILO 1966: 391–6). However, exceptions became more widespread in the last quarter of the 20th century with the legitimization of temporary work agencies at the national and international levels, alongside the preservation of worker protection. Simultaneously, concern over the regulation of temporary agency work grew at the EU level.

National Regulations in the EU 15, Mid-1970s–Early 2000s [20]

The EU 15 opened possibilities for the expansion of temporary agency work in two phases.[21] In the first phase, beginning in the late 1960s, several countries introduced licensing and registry systems for temporary work agencies: first, the Netherlands (1965) (Jacobs 1999, 2005; Dunnewijk 2001; Zaal 2005) and then Denmark (1968) (Eklund 2002). Shortly thereafter, Ireland (1971), Germany (1972), France (1972), and the United Kingdom (1973) followed suit, developing distinct systems of regulation that also involved licensing (Ireland and the United Kingdom), rules governing the nature and duration of temporary agency work, and the contractual relationships required, as well as reasons for its use (Germany and France) (Vosko 1997; Weiss 1999; Michon 2005; Arrowsmith 2006: 14–15).

During the second phase, from the late 1980s, countries such as Austria (1988) and Portugal (1989) introduced regulations governing the nature of the employment contract in temporary agency work; Portugal also intervened directly in the wages and working conditions of temporary workers and Belgium (1987/2000), which had modelled its postwar regulatory architecture on the ILO Convention on Fee-Charging Employment Agencies, Revised (1949), relaxed restrictions by providing for the temporary posting of workers (Arrowsmith 2006: 16–17; see also Vosko 1997). Subsequently, Sweden (1993) and Luxembourg (1994) loosened restrictions on the provision of temporary agency workers, although in these contexts collective agreements governed regulation in practice (Berg 2005; see also Vosko 1997; Arrowsmith 2006: 17). So, too, did Spain (1993), Italy (1997/2003), Finland (2001), and Greece (2001) (Albarracín 2004; see also Arrowsmith 2006: 17).

In both phases, national regulations had the effect of legitimizing temporary agency work. However, the form of regulations varied, depending on the legal status of temporary agency work—specifically who is the employer (user or agency) and, if employment-related responsibilities are divided, which responsibilities rest with the respective parties (Vosko 1997; Davidov 2004 and 2005; Arrowsmith 2006). By the late 1990s, following the adoption of the ILO Convention on Private Employment Agencies (1997) directed at this end, most of the EU 15 were defining temporary agency workers as employees of the temporary agency who work under the supervision of the user firm; the chief exceptions were the United Kingdom, where temporary agency workers fell into a grey zone,[22] and Ireland, which deemed them to be the employees of the user (under the Unfair Dismissals (Amendment) Act 1993).[23] In a majority of countries, temporary agency workers were hired for the duration of a given assignment or posting. However, there were some exceptions: in Sweden, they were regarded as having open-ended employment relationships (Nystrom 1999; Berg 2005) and, in Germany, it was common to hire workers on this basis (Weinkopf 2006). Finally, in Denmark, Greece, and Finland, temporary agency workers were engaged on fixed-term contracts (Arrowsmith 2006: 19).[24]

Most of the EU 15 continued to operate licensing schemes for temporary work agencies in the early 2000s. Some also continued to maintain restrictions on temporary agency work, which usually supplemented protections such as the prohibition of direct fee-charging and the requirement that the worker agree to be placed on assignment, as well as prohibitions on no-hiring clauses (i.e. preventing the user from hiring the worker directly and/or on a permanent basis) (Vosko 1997; Clauwaert 2000; Davidov 2005; Arrowsmith 2006). The restrictions took three general forms. First, many established rules governing sectors and occupations in which temporary agency work is permissible. Second, some retained measures limiting the maximum duration of a given assignment and/or successive assignments, although such limitations waned in the late 1990s and early 2000s in some countries, such as in Germany (Weinkopf 2006). Third, consistent with the failed proposals for the earliest directive addressing temporary agency work in 1982, some countries identified reasons and circumstances under which user firms could resort to temporary agency workers, limiting their use to unexpected and finite increases in workloads, and in most cases prohibiting their use as replacement workers.

By 2000, many of the EU 15 (the United Kingdom and Ireland being the chief exceptions) were also providing for equal treatment to temporary agency workers, especially in the areas of pay and occupational benefits, although accessing the latter was difficult because many state-provided and employer-sponsored benefits remained tied to the duration of a given employment relationship. In some contexts, such as in Germany and the Netherlands, provisions for equal treatment only came to apply after a given time period (e.g. six weeks), whereas in others, such as in France, 'parity of pay' applied from the outset (Michon 2005: pt. 5). French regulation also provided for precarity pay, a premium for uncertainty (akin to casual loadings in Australia, described in Chapter 4), paid at the end of the assignment and amounting to 10% of the total gross pay.

In most cases where equal treatment came to apply, the baseline for comparison was the equivalent permanent worker in the user firm, although there were occasionally provisions for comparison by sectoral collective agreement (e.g. in Spain) (Albarracín 2005). In still other cases, such as Finland, fixed-term workers served as comparators (Kuusisto 2005; on Denmark and Greece, see also Arrowsmith 2006). This variation in the form and effectiveness of measures fostering equal treatment reflected the different approaches to temporary agency work throughout the EU, ultimately affecting coordinated community action. Yet regardless of the approach adopted, by the early 2000s, temporary agency work had secured legitimacy across the EU 15.

Contemporary Dynamics of Temporary Agency Work in the EU 15

In 2006, the first year for which standardized data are available, temporary agency work accounted for between 0.2% and 3.4% of total employment in the EU 15. As Table 5.2 shows, Spain had the highest percentage (at 3.4%) followed by the Netherlands (at 3.0%). According to data from the EU Labour Force Survey (LFS) (which is likely to underestimate the number of

Table 5.2. Temporary Agency Work in the EU 15, 2006^

	Number of Workers	% of Total Employment	% of Total Temporary Employment
EU 15	2,628,570	1.5	12.5
Spain	676,800	3.4	13.2
Netherlands	240,800	3.0	21.6
France	599,620	2.2	10.8
Germany	595,300	1.6	22.5
Belgium	64,938	1.5	21.9
Ireland*	30,000	1.5	46.1
Austria	55,737	1.4	28.0
Denmark	36,650	1.3	19.4
Finland**	30,000	1.2	8.3
Portugal***	45,000	0.9	6.0
Sweden	34,854	0.8	5.0
UK	144,600	0.5	11.0
Luxembourg	626	0.3	7.6
Italy	65,870	0.3	3.8
Greece	7,775	0.2	2.7

Notes:
^Numbers of temporary agency workers reported in this table are estimates drawn from the EU LFS 2006, except for countries noted below. EU LFS estimates of the number of temporary agency workers should be interpreted with caution. In many cases (e.g., the UK), they likely underestimate the size of this workforce. Appendix D provides further details about the challenges of estimating the number of temporary agency workers, sources used, and alternative estimates, where available.
*In column 1, the number for Ireland refers to full-time equivalents, the only estimates available. Calculations in columns two and three use these counts.
**In column 1, the number of workers reported for Finland refers to 2004. Calculations in columns two and three use these counts.
***In column 1, the number of workers reported for Portugal refers to 2004 and to full-time equivalents, the only estimates available. Calculations in columns two and three use these counts.

temporary agency workers—see notes in Appendix D), such percentages translated into over 2.6 million temporary agency workers in the EU 15.

There is considerable variation in the duration of the average placement through a temporary work agency within and across member states. In one group of countries, assignments tend to be of short duration; for example, in France, the average assignment was 9.5 days in 2005 and, in Luxembourg, it lasted approximately a month. In another group, there is greater dispersion in assignment length. For example, in Ireland, one-fifth last less than a month, but the same proportion last more than five months and similar patterns characterize temporary agency work in Belgium. For a third set of countries, a significant number of assignments are of longer duration, such as in the Netherlands, where the typical assignment is five months; in the United Kingdom, where one-fifth are between six months and a year; and, in Austria, where nearly half of all placements in white-collar work last more than a year (Arrowsmith 2006: 9–10; see also Clauwaert 2000; Jacobs 2005; Michon 2005; Winchester 2005; Zaal 2005; Weinkopf 2006).

In terms of the industrial distribution of temporary agency work, in some countries (e.g. Austria, France, the Netherlands, and Portugal) it is most common in manufacturing and in others (e.g. Spain and in Sweden) it is most common in services, whereas in the remainder it is more varied. Except in a few Nordic countries and the United Kingdom, temporary agency work is uncommon in the public sector (unlike fixed-term work), reflecting the high proportion of temporary agency workers assigned to occupations with low levels of socially recognized skills (Arrowsmith 2006: 7–8).

Temporary agency work tends to be precarious in many of the EU 15, even more so than fixed-term work, a chief exception being the Netherlands. Temporary agency workers have lower average wages than workers in other forms of employment,[25] a product partly of the mark-up (the difference between the rates clients pay agencies for their services and workers' wages), and they are particularly disadvantaged in countries where seniority is not included in the wage structure of agencies. They are more commonly engaged in 'unsocial' work arrangements than their permanent counterparts, such as shift, evening, and night work.[26] They encounter difficulties in securing protections—such as wages in the case of insolvency or default on the part of the agency, as well as occupational health and safety measures—due to the need to identify a single employer in most labour laws, regulations, and policies. The nature of their employment relationship also hampers temporary agency workers' ability to organize and bargain collectively and to secure effective protection (see for example Vosko 1997; Smith-Vidal 1999; Davidov 2005; Forde and Slater 2005). It is therefore not surprising that in 2006, 72% of temporary agency workers in the EU 15 reported engaging in this form of employment because they were unable to find permanent positions (10% more than temporary workers as a whole).

Temporary agency work came to be increasingly characterized by a gender balance at the turn of the 21st century across the EU 15, although there was considerable variation by country, mostly reflecting industrial distributions.[27] Still, even though men's and women's shares of temporary agency work approached parity, it remained gendered. For example, in 2006, 28% of all women temporary agency workers in the EU 15 engaged in this type of temporary employment for periods exceeding seven months (as opposed to 20% of their male counterparts). A slightly higher percentage of women

145

than men (73% compared to 70%) also performed temporary agency work because they had no other alternative.

Considering their shares of permanent as well as temporary employment as a whole, participation by 'non-national citizens'[28] in temporary agency work is significant. In 2006, 11% of all temporary agency workers in the EU 15 were non-national citizens of the countries in which they were employed, as opposed to 5% of permanent workers and 7% of all temporary workers. Non-national citizens' overrepresentation in temporary agency work is quite marked in Austria, Belgium, Spain, and France. However, the figures are most dramatic in the United Kingdom, where they make up 25% of temporary agency workers, compared to 14% of temporary workers as a whole and 5% of permanent workers. This figure represents fully five times non-national citizens' percentage of the employed population in the United Kingdom. Studies illustrate further that (im)migrants from non-Western backgrounds are comparatively overrepresented in temporary agency work. According to Ambrosini and Barone (2007: 33), in Sweden, for example, it is common for immigrants from Africa and South America to work for temporary work agencies and, in the Netherlands, temporary agency work is more prevalent among 'migrants with non-Western backgrounds' than Dutch natives and non-citizens from other EU or Western countries.

Although the data available preclude detailed analyses of the situation of non-citizen workers engaged in temporary agency work, agencies have been challenged over their treatment of migrant workers, particularly in Finland, the Netherlands, the United Kingdom, and Portugal (Zaal 2005; Arrowsmith 2006: 20; TUC 2007a). Such criticism has prompted calls to tighten licensing and enforcement mechanisms. In the Netherlands, for example, the labour inspectorate investigated so-called illegal practices in the early 2000s and reported that 'a quarter of agencies provided illegal [i.e., undocumented] workers', a term used by the government to encompass both EU citizens without work permits and workers from outside the EU who lack work permits (Zaal 2005: pt. 8). In 2004, these findings led the Dutch cabinet to propose reintroducing a licensing system, including a requirement for a £75,000 bond, although it failed to pass.[29] The United Kingdom introduced the Gangmasters (Licensing) Act in 2004 in response to similar concerns, and more immediately a work-related accident in Lancashire's Morecambe Bay that killed 18 migrant cocklers from China.[30] This Act makes mandatory 'licensing of activities involving the supply or use of workers in connection with agricultural work, the gathering of wild creatures or wild plants, the harvesting of fish from fish farms, and certain processing and packaging; and for connected purposes' (UK 2004: chapter 11, para. 1).

EU-Level Attempts at Regulating Temporary Agency Work, 2000–2008

After the adoption of the Directive on Fixed-Term Work in 1999, formally excluding temporary agency workers from its scope, negotiations on temporary agency work took shape. The earliest negotiations took place between UNICE and ETUC from May 2000 to May 2001, but these talks broke off due to insurmountable differences over questions of equal treatment. In retrospect, the Commission (2002a: 9) stated that 'the real bone of contention is the concept of the "comparable worker"'. According to a negotiator for ETUC, 'because the agency worker is made available to a user enterprise to provide for labour, trade unions everywhere have always taken the same position . . . equal treatment with the worker in the user enterprise' (Passchier, 29 October 2006). Yet the UNICE (2002: 1) objected to introducing a comparison with a worker of the user company on the ground that:

Temporary agency work has the unique feature of implying a triangular relationship involving a temporary worker, an agency (who is the employer of that worker), and a user company (where that worker is sent on assignment). Non-discrimination can therefore be established, in comparison either with a worker of the user company, or with a temporary worker employed by the same agency.

The ETUC insisted on the former option and the UNICE on the latter. However, their disagreement did not translate to the positions of the EU-level representatives of temporary agency workers and businesses. Rather, the UNIEUROPA, the EU-level union representing temporary agency workers, and the EUROCIETT, the EU-level industry association representing temporary help agency businesses, in 2001 issued a joint declaration of common objectives, affirming their commitment to 'establish the principle of equal treatment, both in terms of the relationship between the agency and the worker and the relationship between the worker and the user company' (EUROCIETT and UNIEUROPA 2001: 1). For the EUROCIETT, according to one of its representatives, the idea was 'that there should be a kind of equal treatment principle between agency workers and permanent workers in a company and, at the same time, that our industry should . . . have the possibility to develop itself within the EU' (Pennel, 29 October 2006). In exchange for legitimizing temporary agency work, the UNIEUROPA sought minimum conditions.[31]

At the sector level, the ETUC backed the UNIEUROPA's position. Yet the UNICE withheld its support for the EUROCIETT's position on equal treatment because of disagreement, inherent in temporary agency work, over splitting the 'invisible fee' (i.e. the mark-up between what agency workers are paid and costs charged to the user company) (Parker 1994; Vosko 2000; Gonos and Freeman 2005). As an official with the EUROCIETT reflected:

sometimes...we say we have some kind of conflict of interest [with client firms] because, of course, for us, we do consider that it should be the user company who will take over the charges for the equal treatment and, of course, the UNICE and the business community was not in favour of [including] this equal treatment provision [in the directive]. (Pennel, 29 October 2006)

The initial negotiations thus failed because of intra-industry disagreement between the UNICE and the EUROCIETT.

Starting in summer 2001, the Commission undertook to craft a directive building on the momentum of the UNIEUROPA-EUROCIETT joint declaration. For the Commission, a directive on temporary agency work was required to address the movement (or internal migration) of workers within the EU and the related need to advance the aims initiated by the Posted Workers Directive (1996), which obliges temporary work agencies that wish to post their workers in user companies in another member state to apply the minimum statutory rights in force in the host country. Accordingly, it noted that the proposal for a directive 'can be seen as an extension of arrangements already in force for transnational posting of temporary workers. In a proper internal market, it is only logical for the rules for posting temporary workers to be aligned with each other, irrespective of whether a posting is national or transnational' (EC 2002a: 10).

A directive was also essential to fulfilling the terms of the ILO Convention on Private Employment Agencies (1997) (EC 2002a: 10) as well as of the Treaty Establishing the European Community itself, which called for action on the basis of its commitment to improving working conditions (Art. 136); according to the Commission (2002a: 10, 11), this commitment required the extension of 'the principle of non-discrimination between temporary [agency] workers and comparable workers in user undertakings' at the community level to supplement existing community law that 'already lay[s] down the principle of non-discrimination as regards non-standard employment relationships'.

The resulting draft directive of 2002 called for non-discrimination in basic working and employment conditions between a temporary agency worker and a comparable worker, defining the latter as 'a worker in the user undertaking in an identical or similar job' (EC 2002a: 12). To address the emerging concerns of member states, such as Germany, which objected to extending the principle of non-discrimination to temporary agency workers with open-ended contracts, as well as to resolve the impasse between the UNICE and the ETUC, it provided for the waiving of this principle under several circumstances: where workers are paid between postings, for 'objective reasons', by collective agreement as long as an 'adequate' level of protection is ensured,[32] and for assignments of fewer than six weeks (EC 2002a: 12). These were the core elements of the Commission's self-described 'flexible response' to the disagreement over equal treatment upon which prior negotiations had foundered (EC 2002a: 13).

The ETUC criticized the Commission's draft harshly for introducing a qualifying period and excluding permanent agency workers; at the same time, unions recognized the challenges of discussing this issue among 15 member states, including seven or eight without extensive restrictions on temporary agency work (Passchier, 29 October 2006). For the EURO-CIETT, the draft was acceptable, but for the UNICE the qualifying period was too short. It called for six months and the government of the United Kingdom called for 12 (Pennel, 29 October 2006; van den Burg, 19 February 2007). All of these concerns were secondary to equal treatment, however, which remained the fault line in the negotiations.

In response to the Commission's draft, as well as an opinion by the EU Economic and Social Committee (EESC 2002), the EU Parliament proposed amendments aimed at forging a consensus, focusing on narrowing the parameters of the directive and the application of the principle of non-discrimination. On the one hand, it sought to define temporary agency work on the basis of postings of limited duration rather than the absence of an open-ended employment relationship (EC 2002b: Amendment 23). On the other hand, Parliament recommended deleting reference to 'comparable worker' and introducing, in its place, the notion of a worker 'recruited directly by that enterprise to occupy the same job' (EC 2002b: Amendments 15, 87, Art. 5.1). To appease certain member states as well as the UNICE, it also proposed limiting non-discrimination to pay and working time and providing for restrictions on temporary agency work only for reasons of health and safety at work, the smooth functioning of the labour market, and protections against abuse (EC 2002b: Amendments 34 and 35).

The redrafted text was approved in second reading. However, in June 2003 a blocking minority of Denmark, Germany, the United Kingdom, and Ireland prevented its adoption by the Council, placing community action in the form of a directive officially on hold. The main objections were the length of the derogation period and the inclusion of an explicit reference to pay—and they emanated principally from the United Kingdom and Ireland,[33] shaped, in the case of the former, by strong opposition from the national temporary agency industry (Green 2008).

It would be five years before this logjam would be broken. In the meantime, precipitating an eventual agreement, and significant on its own terms, a Directive on Services in the Internal Market (2006) ('Services Directive') was adopted, formally establishing an internal market for the provision of services in the EU, completing the creation of a market in which persons, goods, capital, and services circulate freely. Covering business-to-business services, services provided both to businesses and consumers, and consumer services, the Services Directive requires member states to respect the rights of the services provider to provide services in a member state other than that in which they are established, that is, to 'ensure free access to and free exercise of service activity within its territory' (CEU 2006a: Art. 16. 1). No restrictions are to be imposed by member states unless access to or exercise of a service activity fails to respect principles of non-discrimination, necessity, or proportionality (CEU 2006a: Art. 16.1a–c).

Under the directive, member states are to continue to apply their own rules regarding work and employment conditions and social security in conformity with community practices (CEU 2006a: Preamble, para. 14). In the lead-up to its passage, in 2004–2005, however, a tension surfaced between the regulation of labour and employment conditions, on the one hand, and service provision, on the other hand. At a community level, the 'country of destination principle' guides employment policy—the notion that non-national workers working in a given country should receive the same protections as nationals working in that jurisdiction. In contrast, the 'freedom to provide services' under the Services Directive requires states to allow non-national businesses to establish themselves in their territories and to provide the same conditions for service provision as those received by national providers.

In negotiations towards this directive, initial proposals were for a 'country of origin principle' for the provision of services—that is, that '[service] providers [be] subject only to the national provisions of their Member State of origin' (EC 2004b: Art. 16.1). Yet member states, especially those belonging to the EU 15, as well as trade unions and public interest groups, raised concerns about the proposed country of origin principle. They feared that it would lead to social dumping (Broughton 2004; Social Platform 2005; Fichtner 2006) and devoted particular attention to its potential effects on posted workers and temporary agency workers. Recall that the Posted

Workers Directive requires that employees (and their equivalents) who are posted by their employer to work in an EU member state other than that in which they are normally employed receive, at a minimum, the labour protections applicable in the host state (CEU 1996: Art. 3). Trade unions were concerned that the proposed country of origin principle would transform this provision into 'maximum protection as opposed to a minimum floor of rights' with potentially severe consequences for EU migrants (Representative of UK TUC, 23 November 2006; TUC 2006: 4). They also feared that the Services Directive would weaken the enforcement of the Posted Workers Directive since, as originally drafted, it prohibited the member state to which the worker is posted from 'imposing any conditions on the company posting the worker to hold and keep employment records or documents in its territory or to register with its authorities' (TUC 2006: 4). Additionally, the ETUC (2004: 6) argued that, if the Services Directive only 'provide[d] for simplistic derogation of the Posting Directive . . . , while allowing for a free choice of law in all other cases, the effects would—again—be unacceptable'. Such concerns contributed to the exclusion of matters covered under the Posted Workers Directive from the Services Directive (CEU 2006a: para. 86).[34] They also shifted the emphasis of the Services Directive away from the country of origin principle to 'removing unjustified barriers faced by service providers' or 'freedom' to provide services, to be achieved through the reduction of barriers to cross-border trade, provision, and direct investment in services (TUC 2006: 9; CEU 2006a and 2006b).[35]

Prior to the adoption of the Services Directive, unions also called for excluding temporary agency work from its scope to prevent deregulation. The UNIEUROPA argued that 'if Member States apply systems of licensing etc. to their national service providers but not to foreign ones, this would create unfair competition between national and non-national operators' (Ségol 2004: 1). Once the shift from the country of origin principle seemed imminent, unions began to argue that even a watered-down free provision of services, if applied to temporary work agencies, would 'make control of the employment conditions of posted-temporary workers near impossible' (Ségol 2004: 2). To contextualize this objection, they characterized temporary agencies as 'service providers [that] sell workers to their clients' (Ségol 2004: 1). The EUROCIETT interpreted such concerns as reflecting unions' 'political agenda . . . to have us excluded in order to revive discussion on the agency work directive' (Pennel, 29 October 2006), an interpretation whose accuracy was confirmed by officials in the trade union movement (Passchier, 29 October 2006; Warneck, 29 November 2006).

Unions' strategy of using the exclusion of services provided by temporary work agencies from the Services Directive to revive negotiations towards a directive on temporary agency work proved successful when, in spring 2008, British unions and employers arrived at a joint declaration, supported by the government, resolving several issues behind the United Kingdom's previous objections. They agreed to extend equal treatment to temporary agency workers after 12 weeks in a given job (i.e. on an assignment), and they concurred that equal treatment would mean 'at least the *basic working and employment conditions* that would apply to the workers concerned if they had been recruited directly by that undertaking to occupy the same job' (UK Government et al. 2008: (b), emphasis added). Basic working and employment conditions included pay and working time but excluded occupational social security schemes. Furthermore, their declaration provided for the possibility of comparing temporary agency workers to workers in a variety of forms of employment. In supporting this joint declaration, the United Kingdom government indicated that it would move quickly to seek an agreement on these terms with its European partners on a directive on temporary agency work. Shortly thereafter, and after the EUROCIETT and UNIEUROPA issued a more extensive 'Joint Declaration on the Directive on working conditions for temporary agency workers', the Council reached an agreement on the Directive on Temporary Agency Work (2008), as part of an overall package which also included a revised Working Time Directive (CEU 2008a: 12).

The Directive on Temporary Agency Work (2008)

Accepted by Council and the European Parliament in Fall 2008, the Directive on Temporary Agency Work pertains to a form of temporary employment defined typically by a lack of permanency, where an agency posts the worker at the worksite of a client firm.

The directive aims explicitly to protect temporary agency workers against abuse by affirming the employment relationship as a basis for labour protection. It sets out conditions for the free operation of temporary work agencies and, in so doing, constructs an employment relationship between a worker and an agency (CEU 2008b: Arts. 1 and 2). Yet it advances a protective framework inferior to the Directive on Fixed-Term Work, even as it is hinged to it.

The terms of the directive extend strictly to employees and their equivalents 'who are assigned to a user undertaking to work temporarily under their supervision and direction' (CEU 2008b: Art. 1.1). They address what

I label elsewhere a 'temporary employment relationship' (Vosko 2000), in which the worker establishes connections with several entities rather than one, is rarely party to an indefinite contract of employment, and often may be dismissed with little notice.

Under the terms of the directive, the mechanism of the 'comparable permanent worker' is set aside in favour of providing to temporary agency workers conditions, 'at least those that would apply if the worker had been recruited directly by the user firm to occupy the same job' (CEU 2008b: Art. 5.1). By introducing the phrase 'recruited directly by that enterprise', the directive opens the possibility to compare temporary agency workers with not only permanent workers but other workers employed by the user company. As an official from the EUROCIETT observed during the negotiations that ultimately led to the directive, 'in this new version there is no comparable worker any longer. It is just if you hire an agency worker then he should have the same minimum working conditions as if [he had] . . . been recruited directly . . . That would mean either on a fixed- term contract or on a permanent contract' (Pennel, 29 October 2006). Union officials at the national and European levels concurred with this assessment, even as they objected vehemently to the omission of the words 'comparable *permanent* worker' in the directive (Representative of UK TUC, 23 November 2006; Warneck, 29 November 2006). This language also raises a further danger, which had been articulated by one of the union negotiators during the talks: 'the question arises [whether] you would get into a kind of pass card thinking because the fixed-term worker has to be treated equally to the permanent worker, but the agency worker has to be treated equally to the fixed-term worker' (Passchier, 29 October 2006). Accordingly, before it passed formally, UNIEUROPA expressed concern 'in particular about the legal uncertainty created by the loose definition of the comparable worker' (UNIEUROPA 2008).

With regard to the mechanism of comparison, although the directive departs from the baseline of the 'comparable permanent worker' which underpins the Directive on Fixed-Term Work, it expresses an analogous preference that comparison be undertaken at the establishment level because the user firm is responsible for supervising the temporary agency worker while s/he is on his or her premises. At the same time, it does not cover all temporary agency workers, but rather retains the possibilities for excluding, from provisions governing basic working and employment conditions, workers with permanent employment contracts with a temporary work agency who are paid between postings (CEU 2008b: Art. 5.2).

For the workers covered, the principle of equal treatment is to extend to 'basic working and employment conditions', encompassing exclusively working time and pay, the latter of which is to be 'without prejudice to national law as to the definition of pay' (CEU 2008b: Arts. 3.1f, 3.2). This provision also differentiates the directive from the broader 'employment conditions' covered in the Directive on Fixed-Term Work.

The equal treatment mechanism is circumscribed further by an exception allowing member states to permit the social partners to conclude collective agreements establishing working and employment conditions which may differ from the principle of equal treatment so long as they respect 'the overall protection of temporary agency workers' (CEU 2008b: Art. 5.3). Where 'there is no system in law for declaring collective agreements universally applicable or no such system in law or practice for extending their provisions to all similar undertakings in a certain sector or geographical area', member states are permitted to 'establish arrangements concerning basic working and employment conditions' diverging from equal treatment on the basis of an agreement with social partners at the national level 'provided that an adequate level of protection is provided for temporary agency workers' (CEU 2008b: Art. 5.4). Notably, the latter arrangements may 'include a qualifying period for equal treatment' (CEU 2008b: Art. 5.4). The main caveat: member states are also to take measures to prevent misuse of such arrangements, in particular, 'successive assignments designed to circumvent the provisions of the directive', a provision referring to the misuse of the qualifying period (CEU 2008b: Art. 5.5).

There are several other broad provisions for the prevention of abuse in the directive. For example, it prohibits charging workers direct fees (CEU 2008b: Art. 6.3). Temporary agency workers are also to be given information about vacancies in the user undertaking and to have opportunities identical to other workers in the undertaking to find permanent employment and to have access to amenities or collective facilities of the user firm, such as childcare, cafeteria, and transport services, under the same conditions as workers employed directly by the user, unless the 'difference in treatment is justified by objective reasons' (CEU 2008b: Art. 6). The directive also aims to prevent no-hiring clauses; however, such measures are not to interfere with 'a reasonable level of recompense for [agencies'] services rendered to user undertakings for the assignment, recruitment, and training of temporary agency workers' (CEU 2008b: Art. 6.2). Furthermore, building on another proposal contained in the 2008 EUROCIETT and UNIEUROPA Joint Declaration (2008: 2, 14), there is to be regular review of any restrictions or prohibitions imposed at the national level on the use of temporary agency workers to ensure that they are justified only on the grounds of 'the protection of temporary agency workers, the requirements of health and safety at work or the need to ensure that the labour market functions properly and abuses are prevented' (CEU 2008b: Art. 4).

Unlike the Directive on Fixed-Term Work's instruction to member states to establish conditions under which fixed-term contracts or relationships might be transformed into permanent or open-ended employment relationships, there is no mention of circumstances requiring, or even warranting, conversion in this case, either into open-ended nor bilateral employment relationships.

In addition to its substantively inferior protective framework compared to its forerunner on fixed-term work, the Directive on Temporary Agency Work increases the likelihood that services provided by temporary agencies, that is, the provision of workers to third parties, will ultimately fall within the scope of the Services Directive. Indeed, in their 2008 Joint Declaration, EUROCIETT and UNIEUROPA (pt. 5) linked their collective call for 'secur[ing] the equal treatment principle for temporary agency workers with regard to their basic working and employment conditions' to support for 'the development of a well functioning European market for temporary agency work services'. This linkage risks making the already porous distinction between commercial and employment regulation in the case of temporary agency work even more so. A Green Paper on the Future of Labour Law in the EU, launched after the passage of the Services Directive in late 2006, acknowledged this danger by linking the 'free provision of services in the Internal Market' to the phenomenon of temporary agency work and to so-called dependent self-employment (EC 2006b: 13; Cullen, 30 October 2006). For Ieke van den Berg (19 February 2006, emphasis added), rapporteur for the EU Parliament on the issue of temporary agency work in 2002–2003 (when the blocking minority had prevented the adoption of the directive otherwise acceptable to the Council), it is precisely such developments that necessitate principled EU-level action in the employment field:

One of the biggest problems is the reluctance to deal with this type of issue at the European level [i.e. to develop 'hard' employment policies]. Many member states say 'this is our business, we don't want any European involvement' but *in the meantime the European internal market rules and the Service Directive are creating a European labour market and it's attacking the national labour market ... from the outside.* Employment policy is not an isolated issue anymore.

In the context of making these remarks, van den Berg emphasized that the Posted Workers Directive only covers employees. Thus, even though it provides irrevocably for a floor of minimum labour protections for temporary agency workers in most of the EU 15 (i.e. where they are defined as employees), it leaves a loophole where self-employment is concerned. This acknowledgement points as well to growing pressure to manage the division between the sphere of competition, a universe presumed to be populated by businesses, and that of the labour market, where workers are to be protected, the subject of Chapter 6.

Lessons from the EU 15 and Alternative Possibilities

> You have the core in the labour market and then you have an outer layer of maybe fixed-term workers, you have agency workers, you have grey zone workers, you have self-employed, and you have illegal workers and migrants. The more you tighten up this core, the more there will be a natural tendency in the labour market to resort to these so-called flexible forms of work. In a sense, if you tighten up the regulation of fixed-term work, obviously . . . there will be an increase in agency work. If you try to tighten up agency work, there will be a resort to other kinds of work, like self-employment . . .
>
> Jonas Alberg, Legal Officer—EU Labour Law; Commission of the European Union, Brussels, 29 October 2006.

The terms of the Directives on Fixed-Term Work and Temporary Agency Work support the conclusion that SER-centrism in the regulation of temporary employment fosters the extension of fewer and more limited protections to those forms deviating most from the employment norm.

They also threaten to perpetuate longstanding social inequalities because the baseline they assume is gendered and premised on national citizenship. The acutely precarious character of temporary agency work in most of the EU 15, combined with the fact that non-citizens are overrepresented in this form of employment, underscore this threat. So, too, do concerns expressed by Parliament in a resolution on the Green Paper (EP 2007: J), that 'many workers are falling outside the scope of fundamental labour and social rights, thereby undermining the principle of equal treatment'. Parliament's notable decision to exclude matters covered under the Posted Workers Directive from the Services Directive along with services provided by temporary work agencies sought to limit this threat. However, with the passage of the Directive on Temporary Agency Work and the Services Directive scheduled for implementation by the end of 2009, it is unclear how long the exclusion of the latter will remain, reinforcing the need for alternative strategies.

At the level of employment policy, limiting precariousness in fixed-term and temporary agency work calls for strategies that replace the narrowly conceived principle of equal treatment on the basis of form of employment, itself found only in some EU-level regulations on temporary work, with a broader conception of equity. Building on the principles and policy strategies identified in Chapter 4, developing this conception involves supplementing the requirement for finding 'similarly situated' workers in order to extend labour protection.

One avenue in this direction involves extending benefits and entitlements beyond job tenure. Why should workers' access to benefits, such as maternity or parental benefits, dental or medical benefits, vacation or other pay premiums be limited to an open-ended employment relationship between an employee and an employer? Why not extend benefits to workers regardless of the duration of a given job? This solution would be preferable to pro entitlements for principled and pragmatic reasons.

To avoid reproducing a hierarchy of forms of temporary employment, or, in the words of the ETUC official cited above, to refuse 'pass card thinking', it is also necessary to reject comparators. The SER-centric approach informing EU Directives on Fixed-Term Work and Temporary Agency Work shows how modes of comparison reinforce a labour force structured in tiers based on form of employment, shaped by social relations of inequality. In the interest of inclusivity (Fudge and Vosko 2001b: 335), there is a need for comprehensive minimum labour standards from which no party may derogate, covering all workers regardless of the existence of an open-ended employment relationship, job tenure, or multiple parties and regardless of the presence of a suitable comparator.

A broader conception of labour market membership and its attendant public rights, complementing the notion of 'worker time' introduced in Chapter 4, would augment this approach. It would also offer an antidote to the gendered character of precarious temporary employment. Furthermore, alongside the development of EU citizenship, in the case of internal EU migration, it could address the bouts of unemployment prompted increasingly by the expectation that workers be mobile or migrate to locales where jobs are available. Popularized by Supiot (2001: p. x), labour force membership (or *statut professionnel* in the original French) is the idea that 'an individual is a member of the labour force even if he or she does not currently have a job'. Placing labour market membership (broadly defined) at the centre of labour policy entails assuming that the *typical* worker has gaps in employment, fluctuating levels of employment intensity, and jobs of varying duration over the life-course—and its potential is explored in greater detail in Chapter 7.

Notes

1. For a full list of participants interviewed for this investigation, see Appendix C. See Appendix D for a list of statistical sources for each statistical table in the chapter, and more detail on how particular variables have been constructed. The EU LFS 1983–2006 is the source of data referred to in the sections 'The Open-Ended Employment Relationship Integral to the SER' and 'Temporary Agency Work in the EU 15' unless otherwise noted.

2. In the United States, as discussed in Chapter 3, there was never either a broad protection against unfair dismissal or discharge without just cause (except in Montana) or any period of notice through the common law or by statute (Swinnerton and Wial 1995; see also Block and Roberts 2000). Yet at the height of the SER, employers and workers often entered into contacts and collective agreements providing such protections (Hyde 1998: 104).

   British labour regulation in this area also historically relied heavily on voluntary collective bargaining and especially on union power for securing job protection (Deakin and Wilkinson 1989; Mückenberger and Deakin 1989: 158).

3. I place 'flexible' in quotation marks here because studies show that labour markets in many national contexts, especially in small countries in Europe as well as in Canada, were already characterized by a high degree of flexibility in the 1980s and 1990s, illustrating that the use of the term is often indicative of the introduction of neoliberal employment policies rather than the rigidity of employment structures (Pollert 1988; Stanford 2001).

4. See notes to Tables 5.1 and 5.2 in Appendix D for a discussion of the measures of temporary employment, fixed-term work, and temporary agency work for the EU 15 used throughout this book.

5. Spurred by an economic crisis commencing in 1975, Spain introduced new types of training and practice contracts as well as 'employment promotion fixed-term contracts' in the 1980s; these contracts allowed for short-term engagements absent of dismissal restrictions applicable to permanent contracts (Toharia and Malo 2000). Directed, in particular, to individuals outside the labour market, such as women and young people, these contracts contributed to segmentation along two axes (i.e. between permanent and fixed-term employment and between the employed and the unemployed). In the ensuing decades, the broad contours of this employment system remained but, beginning in the late 1990s, with nearly 30% of all employees holding fixed-term contracts (Schömann et al. 1998), the government launched reforms attempting to revive permanent employment by weakening regulations governing dismissal and improving the conditions of fixed-term work by, for example, increasing the minimum length of positions (for an extensive review, see Golsch 2003).

6. In 1998 and 1999, under the new 'Polder Model' of cooperation between employers' organizations and national trade unions, two statutes were passed in the Netherlands, an Act on Allocation of Workers by Intermediaries (1998) and an

Act on Flexibility and Security (1999). These Acts altered legislation governing temporary agency work fundamentally. Most notable among the changes introduced under the Act on Flexibility and Security (1999) were the exclusion of restrictions on dismissals of temporary contracts in the first 26 weeks of employment, and the provision for employers and unions to agree on a clause that terminates the contract immediately in instances where the client-firm terminates its assignment during this period. At the same time, under the Act on Allocation of Workers by Intermediaries (1998), temporary agency workers were not to be used as strike breakers, were to receive the same wages as workers performing the same work as an employee of the client firm (although this rule could be set aside by collective agreement), and were to accrue seniority (and associated dismissal protections) with temporary work agencies through successive assignments with one or more clients. As a result, a dual system emerged for controlling dismissals of permanent workers, on the one hand, and temporary workers on the other hand (van Voss 1999).

7. This estimate of fixed-term work is based on the nine countries for which national data were available for 1983.

8. Furthermore, between 2000 and 2006, the percentage of women employed in fixed-term work in the EU 15 also increased from 10% to 12% (as compared to the percentage of men, which increased from 8% to 9%).

9. Social dumping is a shorthand for policies and practices encouraging firms to operate in countries with the weakest labour and social protections due to the absence of a floor of protections.

10. Foremost was, as Jeffery (1995) illustrates, a new procedure permitting a qualified majority vote in Council for measures addressing public health under the Single European Act. Ultimately, the Working Time Directive of 1993 was also adopted on the basis of this procedure.

11. This Employment Chapter formally introduced three features of EU employment policy: the establishment of annual community employment policy guidelines, based on a joint report by the Council and the Commission and accepted by a qualified majority (European Union 1997: Title VIII, Arts. 128.1 and 128.2); the requirement that member states prepare annual national reports (known as 'National Action Plans') reporting on measures taken to implement common employment guidelines (European Union 1997: Title VIII, Art. 128.3); and, provision for the Council, upon examining national reports, to make recommendations to member states on the basis of a qualified majority vote (European Union 1997: Title VIII, Art. 128.4). It also established an Employment Committee, and its broader provisions permitted Council to adopt incentives to 'encourage cooperation between Member States and to support their action in the field of employment' (EU 1997: Title VIII, Art. 129).

The chapter is also the institutional basis for the EES, whose introduction marked a shift away from harmonization through mainly 'hard' measures such as the Directive on Fixed-Term Work then under negotiation, to a consensus model characterized by a mix of 'hard' and 'soft' laws to 'establish minimum standards at the community level while leaving a wide range of discretion to Member States' (Kenner 1999: 34). Under the EES, the new logic became 'management by objectives' (Biagi 2000: 161; see also Regent 2003). This logic, and the EES specifically, is criticized widely for its failure to incorporate sanctions for states not adhering to common guidelines, its limited resources for implementation, its 'high politics' process of devising supranational employment policy guidelines, its emphasis on quantitative measures of job creation, and its subordination of employment to monetary policy (see especially Goetschy 1999; see also Daguerre and Larsen 2003; Gray 2004; Ashiagbor 2006).

The criticism about job creation at the cost of job quality was addressed in the wake of the Lisbon Summit of 2000, an impact evaluation of the EES in 2002, revisions to the EES in 2003, and in the significant revisions to the EES in 2005 (CEU 2000; EC 2002c, 2003b, 2005b). The Kok Report (2003) also took up the issue, shifting the emphasis to 'more and better jobs', and thus on 'flexicurity'.

12. Introduced at the Lisbon Summit in 2000, the OMC is a policy tool taking inspiration from the EES, aimed at advancing an integrated supranational approach to renewing economic and social policy. It is a prototypical example of soft law measures aimed at advancing supranational action where legislative solutions have either failed or are unlikely to succeed through traditional means. In theory, OMC attempts to develop European strategies in complex policy fields, organized around the principles of convergence, management by objectives, country surveillance, and an integrated approach to policy design (Lonnroth 2000). In practice, its goal is coordination through a flexible and participatory approach (Trubek and Mosher 2001), rather than uniform regulations, through such activities as mutual learning, benchmarking, best practices, and peer pressure advanced in the EU White Paper on Governance (EC 2001), although the concrete effects of this coordination are questionable (Ashiagbor 2006). The OMC involves three distinct steps: the identification of common aims to guide national policy; the conversion of EU guidelines into national action plans; and the mobilization of key actors (state and non-state) from local to supranational levels, including, in particular, actors in the third sector or social economy (Regent 2003). (On the OMC and social policy, see especially O'Connor 2005; on the OMC's application and potential application in specific areas, such as childcare, pensions, and immigration, see also Mahon 2002; Rubery et al. 2004).

13. Reflecting on the significance of this disagreement, one trade union official observed that in hindsight, the order of negotiations, from part-time work to fixed-term work to temporary agency work, was not necessarily in workers' favour:

With regard to part-time work, that was something that you could at least say okay, there is something positive about it to give more options for part-time work as long as it's voluntary options because a lot of people want to work part-time. Maybe they do not want to work under bad conditions but they do really want to work part-time and they want equal treatment. With fixed-term work that's much more difficult. Maybe you could say, young people would like to have the opportunity but even young people after three fixed-term jobs have had enough. By also making it a separate debate, separate from agency work, it was even more difficult. (Passchier, 29 October 2006)

14. The direction given to member states in such instances is vague, however. Consequently, the Commission has not lodged infringement proceedings against any state for failure to implement the directive in this respect (Alberg, 29 October 2006).

15. Murray (2001b: 165) makes a similar analytical point in her assessment of the EU Directive on Part-Time Work.

16. The directive also provides for the same period-of-service qualifications for fixed-term and permanent workers, which aims to prevent employers from using fixed-term workers to avoid employment protections. However, it fails to specify the conditions of employment covered and permits 'different length-of service qualifications on objective grounds' (CEU 1999: Annex, cl. 4.4).

17. According to the Commission (EC 2006d: 19–20), in most national legislation 'the extension of the same contract... normally entails the application of the rules applicable to open-ended contracts, but in some... the continuation of work under the same contract beyond its terms is possible during a certain period'.

18. The percentages cited in this sentence and the next encompass temporary agency workers because the EU LFS only made it possible to disaggregate data on temporary agency work in 2006.

19. The Commission also found other problems of implementation, including issues related to the period of service qualifications required in the directive and extensive challenges in preventing abuse, the focus of the majority of ECJ rulings on the directive.

20. The framework for this discussion builds on Vosko (1997, 2000) and Arrow-smith (2006: 13–17), especially his synthesis of contributing country studies.

21. While this discussion focuses on statutory law because it was the central back-drop to debates over the draft directive on temporary agency work, in some EU countries, collective bargaining is the preferred mode of regulation and in many it serves to regulate temporary agency work extensively. This is the case in Sweden, where there is a long tradition of regulation via collective agreement, and in Denmark, where statutory law was effectively dismantled in 1990, as well as increasingly in Germany (Nystrom 1999; Berg 2005; Arrowsmith 2006: 21; Weinkopf 2006).

22. See McCann (2008: 147–52) for an in-depth discussion of how UK courts and tribunals have left temporary agency workers in limbo.

23. Notably, despite the practice of deeming temporary agency workers employees of the user, in this period temporary agency work represented a large share of temporary employment in Ireland, as Table 5.2 illustrates. Some commentators

suggest that this is because of Ireland's weak employment protection legislation, which makes fixed-term work less desirable to employers than in other member states of the EU 15 (CESifo 2002: 47).

24. Other national laws and practices affect the character of the employment relationships associated with temporary agency work. In Spain, for example, there is a distinction between 'assigned' and 'structural' workers. The latter, including management, administration, and support staff in the temporary agency, must be permanent (Arrowsmith 2006: 19; see also Albarracín 2004).

25. Unfortunately, data on the wages of temporary agency workers are not available in microdata from the EU LFS 2006. However, other studies show that their relative wages are particularly low in Germany, where a national report cites cases in which average hourly earnings are 30% below the comparable user-firm rates; in Portugal, where the state inspection body documents salaries below those defined by law, collective agreements, or practice in the user company; and in the United Kingdom, where the average weekly income of full-time agency workers in 1999 was just 68% of all employees (the comparable figure for fixed-term workers in the United Kingdom was 89% that year) (Storrie 2002: 54–5).

26. In 2006, 24% of temporary agency workers in the EU 15 engaged in shift work (compared to 17% of their permanent counterparts and 18% of temporary workers as a whole), 22% normally worked evenings (compared to 16% of their permanent counterparts and 18% of temporary workers as a whole), and 10% usually engaged in night work (compared to 7% of their permanent counterparts and 7% of temporary workers as a whole).

27. Data from the EU LFS indicate that in member states where temporary agency work is common in industries such as manufacturing and construction (e.g. Austria, Belgium, France, and the Netherlands), men dominate, whereas in others, where it is common in public and private services and retail (e.g. Denmark, Spain, and the United Kingdom), women dominate. For country case studies, see also Albarracín 2005; Berg 2005; Forde and Slater 2005; Kuusisto 2005; Michon 2005; Weinkopf 2006.

28. This discussion refers to 'non-national citizens' because of the way the EU LFS collects and codes data.

29. Employer organizations questioned the proposal's effectiveness, suggesting that 'maladfide temporary agencies can buy off a bonafide status by paying the deposit', opposed the administrative expenses they would incur, and called instead for better enforcement of existing laws (Zaal 2005: pt. 8).

30. Further reports followed of so-called gangmasters engaging mainly migrant workers from Eastern Europe in industries ranging from fish processing and hospitality to farming and meat packing. Such gangmasters were charged with violating minimum wage laws, overtime rules, and unfair dismissal provisions, as well as charging fines for workers calling in sick, and requiring unpaid

training days (see e.g. TUC 2007a: 22–3; Hyland 2007; Lawrence 2007a and 2007b).

31. The same industry representative noted further that:

> our industry ha[d] been very much attacked for many years . . . At the beginning, because we were creating a kind of a new form of employment relationship, there had been a lot of concern. In many countries the people who were in charge of our industry realized that if we want to be recognized . . . we need to get this balance between the need for . . . flexible work [and], at the same time, because they don't have an open-ended contract, the agency workers should get some kind of compensation. This was the equal treatment [objective].
> (Pennel, 29 October 2006)

32. The precedent for this provision lay in the Directive on fixed-term Work; it was meant to ease member states' and national employers' associations' discomfort with the principle, while appealing to unions by mandating adequate levels of protection (van den Burg, 19 February 2006). However, it had the effect of qualifying the equal treatment objective, which would become a pattern in subsequent negotiations.

33. At the time, Germany supported the United Kingdom and Ireland in blocking the passage of the directive in exchange for these governments' support in blocking a different piece of EU legislation on codetermination. The timing of this bargain was ironic considering Germany was then in the process of redrafting its own legislation to conform with the proposed text (van den Burg, 19 February 2006).

34. Using the case of construction, trade unions also raised the potential pitfalls of adopting measures for the free provision of services in sectors where service provision often involves workers engaged in fixed-term contracts. According to the British Trades Union Congress (TUC) (2006: 9):

> Although the construction sector is by definition creating products designed to be permanent, and many construction projects last for years, construction is regarded as temporary service provision because the contracts are fixed-term. Construction is one of the most dangerous sectors to work in and one in which standards of work have major implications for consumers and the public at large. For standards to be regulated effectively, it is essential that construction companies are working to one set of rules at any one site. If the CoOP (Country of Origin Principle) rules were to be applied in this sector, the construction of Wembley Stadium would be subject to the regulations of over 10 different Member States. This would create considerable confusion about which standards should be adhered to, creating vast difficulties in terms of enforcement and an unacceptable risk of lowering of quality and safety.

Such concerns had particular salience in the EU 15, where disputes over the application of domestic law on construction sites had become commonplace (Woolfson and Sommers 2006).

35. As Chapter 6 will show, this shift also shaped terms governing transnational movement of workers in the ILO Recommendation on the Employment Relationship (2006). Indeed, at the request of the EU, paragraph 12 of this recommendation's preamble notes that 'the globalized economy has increased the mobility of workers who are in need of protection, at least against the circumvention of national protection by choice of law'.

6

Self-Employment and the Regulation of the Employment Relationship: From Equal Treatment to Effective Protection

It can be expected that in the future employment relations and cases of self-employment will become more varied. People will e.g. hold a job as a dependent employee and at the same time have a small company or work as self-employed. Employees will become self-employed while their former employer becomes their client (and in the beginning of the new business often the most important client). Temporary work arrangement[s] for which the borderline between employment and self-employment is unclear will also become more common . . . more work arrangements for which the traditional dichotomy of employed and self-employed no longer fits can be expected.

> European Commission (2004c) *Second Career: Overcoming the Obstacles Faced by Dependent Employees Who Want to Become Self-Employed and/or Start their Own Business.* Brussels, Enterprise-Directorate: 30.

Marking the dividing line between the labour market and the commercial sphere, the employment relationship served historically as a central mechanism for shielding workers selling their labour power from unfettered product markets. Over the course of the 20th century, some groups of workers fell outside its range—such as freelance workers, farmers, and certain craftspeople, many of whom perform work for multiple parties due to the nature of their trade. The dominant trajectory was nevertheless one in which paid or subordinate employment rose steadily, alongside the decline of other mechanisms for organizing the exchange of labour power for remuneration (see e.g. Hyde 1998; Supiot 2001: 3; Fudge et al. 2002; Cranford et al. 2005: chapter 1). This pillar of the SER remains today the foremost basis for organizing labour and social protection in industrialized market economies. At the same time, together with the deterioration of both standardized working time and the open-ended employment relationship documented in Chapters 4 and 5, the employment relationship has grown increasingly unstable, leaving the very existence of the SER threatened.

This chapter examines contemporary regulations addressing the destabilization of the employment relationship and the labour market insecurities coming in its trail. After briefly reviewing prevalent mechanisms used for establishing the existence of an employment relationship, it outlines sources of contemporary instability in the employment relationship in OECD countries. Next it analyses the ILO Recommendation on the Employment Relationship, adopted in June 2006 after years of difficult negotiations. The overarching aim of this recommendation is to sustain the employment relationship as the basis of labour protection. It seeks to combat disguised employment relationships and to ensure that standards applicable to all forms of contractual arrangements protect employed workers. To this end, the recommendation recognizes the 'gender dimension' of disguised employment relationships as well as the need to protect migrant workers from abusive and fraudulent practices and to take 'particular account' of workers 'especially affected' by uncertainty as to the existence of an employment relationship (ILO 2006a: paras. 5, 6, and 7). Its defining challenge, however, is to protect employed workers without interfering with 'true civil and commercial relationships' (ILO 2006a: para. 8). The result is a precarious balancing act on the margins of the employment relationship.

Whereas ILO and EU regulations addressing part-time work and fixed-term work adopted in the 1990s operated through equal treatment (Chapters 4 and 5), the ILO Recommendation on the Employment Relationship eschews this mechanism and, indeed, the use of a comparator altogether. Instead, it pursues 'effective protection'. This shift from equal to 'effective protection' marks the limit of SER-centrism: only those workers in situations closely resembling the employment relationship at the core of the SER are to receive labour protection. The corollary is the neglect of workers engaged in forms of work for remuneration that fall outside the strictures of the employment relationship, many of whom are especially in need of protection.

The second half of the chapter explores national developments concerning the employment relationship, focusing on the Industrialized Market Economy Countries (IMEC) group of the ILO, an influential set of OECD countries including EU member states, Norway, Switzerland, Japan, New Zealand, Australia, Canada, and the United States.[1] IMEC members participated actively in negotiations towards the recommendation. Their common interest in these talks flowed from developments in their national labour markets and the OECD as a whole, specifically the stagnation or decline of paid employment, associated typically with a bilateral employment relationship, and the development of other forms of work for remuneration, such as self-employment. IMEC members did not respond uniformly to such developments. Although most were committed to supporting self-employment, one approach embraced by some IMEC members involved extending legitimacy to independent contracting in the name of the freedom to contract and the need for certainty in commercial relationships. Regulations adopted at the federal level in Australia exemplify this approach; they entailed the withdrawal of protections for workers in precarious work situations falling outside the employment relationship, including protections directed at women and workers from non-English-speaking backgrounds, and the introduction of policies fostering enterprise work. A contrasting approach involved adopting policies promoting entrepreneurship while simultaneously exploring possibilities for extending rights to a subset of the self-employed known as 'economically dependent workers'. This approach developed most extensively in the EU, given its orientation to 'flexicurity'. These distinct approaches to self-employment were crystallizing as the final ILO recommendation was crafted. They therefore offer insight into the logic of approaches to addressing instabilities in the employment relationship, focused on maintaining the binary division between paid or subordinate employment and self-employment rather than on extending labour protection to all workers.[2]

The Destabilization of the Employment Relationship at the Crux of the SER[3]

What has long differentiated employees from self-employed business entrepreneurs, where both groups perform work for remuneration themselves, is whether the purchaser of the labour power exercises control, defined typically as personal subordination of one person to another at a given worksite (Ocran 1997; Fudge 1999). When the SER was at its apex, control was the foremost criterion for establishing the existence of an employment relationship in common-law legal tests in Britain, Canada, the United States, and Australia and in the case law approach prevalent in much of continental Europe (Dunlop 1994: 63–4; Davies 1999: 166; Fudge et al. 2002: 10; Perulli 2003: 13). In response to the different legal and policy contexts in which the question of employee status was raised and the evolving meaning of control itself, other criteria, such as ownership of tools, chance of profit, risk of loss, integration into the firm, and terms of payment, arose gradually to supplement control (Davidov 2002).[4]

Around mid-century, in response to the expansion of contractual arrangements surrounding the performance of work designed to evade employment-related rights and obligations, two types of strategies also emerged to distinguish between employees and independent contractors (Fudge et al. 2002: 50–1, see also 87–91):[5] the first centred on reducing the significance of the employee/independent contractor distinction or, in the case of continental jurisdictions, the subordinate employment/self-employment distinction, by extending rights and protections to persons not classified as employees (or by deeming them employees). This approach normally involved legislative or administrative action. The second approach entailed altering legal tests or case law approaches used to ascertain who is an employee so as to enable the category to shift to encompass groups of people viewed as requiring protection; and it was frequently pursued by way of adjudicative processes. The first approach had the effect of making employee status less relevant in accessing certain types of protection, such as under human rights legislation and occupational health and safety standards in Canada, Australia, and the United Kingdom, as well as at the EU level.[6] The second approach largely meant giving weight to economic dependence in establishing employee status in order to extend labour protection to workers.[7]

Both approaches contributed to the creation of new categories of workers not traditionally viewed to be employees, but distinct from the stereotypical business entrepreneur. One early example is found in Canada, where, since the 1970s, many jurisdictions extended collective bargaining rights to 'dependent contractors', persons who are 'legally contractors but economically dependent' (Arthurs 1965: 89; see also Bendel 1982: 374–6). Another example is the category 'employee-like persons' in Germany, encompassing workers under obligation personally to provide the work and to do the majority of it or who receive more than half of their income from a single client.[8]

Despite the creation of such new categories, the employment relationship remained at the crux of the SER through to the early 21st century, and the presence of control, associated with direct supervision, continued to be vital to its determination. Still, this pillar began to exhibit growing signs of instability in the late 1970s and early 1980s as a result of several developments related to the tendency to shift risk from employers to workers (Cappelli et al. 1997; Gallie et al. 1998; Davies 1999). This '"recontractualization" of the employment relationship' (Mückenberger and Deakin 1989: 162) is evident in four linked trends: first, the growth of market-mediated employment relationships (Abraham 1990: 85) often tied to networks of firms, of which temporary agency work is one example.

A second trend is the rebirth of subcontracting, where firms outsource activities formerly performed in-house to business entities with which they have no formal relationship. Subcontracting is deeply implicated in the changing nature of the employment relationship. As Supiot (2001: 20) observes, even though under 'legal sub-contracting there is in principle no legal relationship between one company and the employees of another ... employees' lot may be dependent more on the decisions made by the principal than on their actual employer'.[9]

A third trend relates to work organization inside firms. Taylorized production techniques common under Fordism contributed to the vertical integration and hierarchical organization of production. In contrast, processes of work organization associated with flexible accumulation require employees in open-ended bilateral employment relationships both to multitask and to cooperate more extensively with their co-workers. The result for workers in this employment situation is paradoxical: on the one hand, hierarchical structures of authority are weakening, such that 'subordinate employment' is said to increasingly 'resemble self-employment in that it is more independent in terms of execution' than under Fordism (Perulli 2003: 29). On the other hand, employer control is transforming into internalized constraint.[10]

A fourth trend, and an empirical focus in this chapter, is the development of self-employment, especially the expansion of varieties resembling paid employment and exhibiting dimensions of labour market insecurity. According to the OECD (2000), between 1973 and 1997 self-employment grew faster than paid employment in a majority of OECD countries, including Australia, Canada, and many of the EU 15. Bringing these trends up to date, Table 6.1 depicts rates of self-employment in select OECD countries in 1973 and 2006.

On account of these four trends, there is widespread recognition that the distinction between self-employment and paid employment is blurring—and especially that, for many people, self-employment is not equivalent to entrepreneurship (Burchell et al. 1999; Clayton and Mitchell 1999; Fudge et al. 2002; Perulli 2003; Tham 2004; Weiler 2004; Davidov and Langille 2006; EC 2006b). The OECD (2000: 187) has pointed to the increased use of self-employment as a 'device to reduce total taxes paid by the firms and the workers involved'. Some self-employed people have paid employees

Table 6.1. Self-Employment as a Percentage of Total Employment, Selected OECD Countries, 1973 and 2006

	1973	2006	Change
EU 15	-	13	n/a
Greece*	32	30	−2
Italy	23	24	+1
Portugal	13	19	+6
Spain	16	16	0
Ireland	10	15	+5
Belgium	11	13	+2
United Kingdom	7	12	+5
Austria	12	12	0
Netherlands*	9	12	+3
Germany	9	11	+2
France	11	10	−1
Sweden	5	10	+5
Luxembourg	11	9	−2
Denmark	9	8	−1
Finland	6	7	+1
Canada*	10	16	+6
Australia	10	15	+5
United States	7	10	+3

* = 1979 figures used in lieu of 1973.
- = no data available.

(i.e. they are employers), but in many countries a considerable majority work alone (i.e. the solo self-employed). Until the 1970s, OECD countries characterized by high shares of employers among the self-employed experienced greater job growth than those where solo self-employment was sizeable. Yet between 1983 and 1997, employer self-employment grew in very few OECD countries and, in the 1990s, it fell or levelled off in many, such as in Canada and Germany (OECD 2000: 162). In many contexts where self-employment grew or plateaued, the solo variety contributed to its vitality. For example, as Table 6.2 illustrates, in Australia, solo self-employment represented 9% of total employment in 2006 and 10% or higher in the United Kingdom, Ireland, Spain, Portugal, Italy, Greece, and Canada.

The self-employed are a diverse group, cutting across a range of occupations and sectors, although in many OECD countries, self-employment is quite common in services occupations.[11] Self-employment has always been

Table 6.2. OECD Countries and Country Groupings with the Highest Rates of Solo Self-Employment as a Percentage of Total Employment, 2006

	% of Total Employment
EU 15 (selected)	
Greece	22
Italy	21
Portugal	17
Spain	11
Ireland	10
United Kingdom*	10
Belgium	9
Austria	7
Sweden*	6
Germany	6
France	6
Luxembourg*	4
Canada	11
Australia	9
US*	5

* Data drawn from a different year other than 2006: UK (2003), Sweden (2004), Luxembourg (2004), US (2002).

gendered. Before the late 20th century, across most OECD countries, self-employment was a male domain, especially the employer variety. While this continued to be the case after 1979, growth rates for women outstripped those for men in a majority of countries.[12] In OECD countries, such as Canada and Australia, women's increased shares of self-employment were most pronounced in the solo variety. Over the same period, self-employment also remained common among immigrants, especially men, in such OECD countries (on Canada, see for example Frenette 2002).

Further attesting to the diversity of self-employment, in the 1990s and early 2000s, the income distributions of the self-employed were more varied than paid employees in most OECD countries (Robson 1997: 502; Firebaugh 2003).[13] Where working conditions are concerned, the self-employed also tend to work longer and more unsocial hours than paid employees (see e.g. OECD 1998; OECD 2000: 170; EIRO 2002). For example, in the EU, compared to employees, the self-employed are more likely to work weekends and at night and to work long hours (Weiler 2004). Similarly, in Australia, the self-employed (particularly those working in services and administrative and professional occupations) have a higher probability of working at night (HILDA 2004: Wave D).

Other aspects of the working conditions of the self-employed in industrialized market economies also reflect precariousness, such as gaps in health and safety and perceived job security. For example, in the EU, the self-employed are less likely than employees to wear protective equipment, to receive supplemental training, and to consider their jobs secure (the solo self-employed, in particular, reported low levels of job security) and more likely to work in painful positions (Weiler 2004). Additionally, roughly two-thirds of the solo self-employed in the EU 25 cater to small and medium-sized enterprises, with over 50% servicing exclusively small or micro businesses with fewer than ten persons employed (EUROSTAT 2006).[14]

The development of self-employment in many OECD countries in the post-1980 period reflects the growing convergence of certain forms, especially the solo variety, with paid employment (see especially Fudge et al. 2002: 16–19; see also Burchell et al. 1999; Clayton and Mitchell 1999; Hyde 2000: Perulli 2003). Still, in the early 2000s, the self-employed as a whole remained less likely than employees to have access to labour and social protections, given the persistent assumption that their activities fall properly in the commercial sphere.

SER-Centric Responses to Precariousness in Work for Remuneration at Cusp of the Employment Relationship: ILO Actions, 1990–2006

ILO efforts to address instability in the employment relationship took shape between 1990 and 2006, beginning with the adoption of the Resolution Concerning Self-Employment Promotion (1990). A report prepared for the international labour conference that year had drawn attention to the diverse nature of self-employment and to the rise of what it labelled 'nominal self-employment', leading the conference to conclude:

Employment relationships are complex and do not fit all into neat conceptual categories. While the polar cases of pure wage and self-employment are simple to categorise, there are hybrid and intermediate cases which need to be recognised. Among these an important category is the nominal self-employed—those who are sometimes classified as self-employed in national statistics and who may consider themselves to be such, but who are in reality engaged in dependent employment relationships more akin to wage employment than to genuine autonomous self-employment. (ILO 1990b: para. 4)

In this way, notions of 'dependent employment' and 'nominal self-employment' found their way onto the ILO agenda. The resolution embraced 'freely chosen and productive forms of self-employment' while calling for action against 'the growth of precarious and dependent forms of nominal self-employment stemming from attempts to bypass protective social legislation and erode the employment security and earnings of affected workers' (ILO 1990b: paras. 6a, 12). Notably, the resolution also stated that the nominal self-employed should enjoy levels of social and labour protection '*comparable* to those enjoyed by wage employees' (ILO 1990b: para. 17c, emphasis added, see also para. 6d).

Following the passage of the Resolution on Self-Employment Promotion, in 1996 the ILO adopted a Convention on Home Work, along with a recommendation, modifying the definition of 'employment relationship' and 'worksite'. Adopted in spite of the objections of employers, this convention identified the relationship between a home worker and an employer and/or an intermediary as an employment relationship (ILO 1996a, Art. 1). It also advanced a broad notion of the worksite, permitting its extension into the home, and ascribed a wage relationship to what had historically been characterized as piecework.[15] In this process, the convention characterized an employer as a person who 'either directly or through an intermediary' assigns home work supporting his or her business and it encouraged the re-allocation of employment-related responsibilities by categorizing those who purchase products or services as employers and by drawing a link between employers and intermediaries. Recognizing the possibility of multiple parties to an employment relationship, the convention also promoted accountability up the subcontracting chain (ILO 1996a: Arts. 1c, 8).[16] Where the employment relationship is concerned, on the one hand, the convention retained the traditional test for employee status by excluding from its terms those home workers who have 'the degree of autonomy and economic independence necessary to be considered an independent worker under national laws' (ILO 1996a: Art. 1a(iii)). On the other hand, it introduced a presumption in favour of employee status or subordinate employment for homeworkers on account of their vulnerability; in this way, regulations on home work maintained yet weakened the distinction between employees and independent contractors. Furthermore, under the convention, signatories were to promote 'equality of treatment between homeworkers and other wage-earners', considering conditions applied to the 'same or similar types of work carried out in an enterprise' (ILO 1996a: Art. 4.1).

Adopted a year after the Convention on Home Work, the Convention on Private Employment Agencies (1997) was amongst the most controversial regulations introduced in the 1990s because it defined workers in triangular employment relationships as employees of private employment agencies whose services consist of making workers available to a third party responsible for assigning specific tasks and for direct supervision (ILO 1997a: Art. 1.1b). It thereby constructed an employment relationship between a worker and an intermediary and called on national governments to allocate responsibility between the agency and the user firm (ILO 1997a: Art. 12). The result was a modified basis for the employment relationship. Still, while it required private employment agencies to 'treat workers without discrimination' and to promote 'equality of opportunity' in employment and occupations (ILO 1997a: Art. 5.1), the convention made no provision for equal treatment with a 'comparable permanent worker', as in the subsequent EU Directive on Fixed-Term Work, nor with a worker hired directly by the user-enterprise as in the subsequent EU Directive on Temporary Agency Work (Chapter 5). Instead, it called only for 'adequate protections' for workers employed by private employment agencies (ILO 1997a: Arts. 11, 12).

By 1998, following the passage of the Conventions on Home Work and Private Employment Agencies, the ILO attempted to adopt a convention on contract labour covering bilateral and triangular contract labour or, in the words of an early draft, 'all situations in which work is performed for a person who is not the worker's employer under labour law but in conditions of subordination and dependency that are close to an employment relationship under that law' (ILO 1998b: 2). It sought to address the situation of workers engaged directly by a user enterprise as well as by subcontractors or a third party, excluding workers employed by private employment agencies (ILO 1998b: 2; see also 1998c: Art. 1).[17] A primary aim was to eliminate 'disguised employment relationships', a less controversial notion than 'nominal self-employment', as it implies wilful attempts to cast employment relationships as commercial (ILO 1998c: Art. 7).

The draft convention on contract labour promoted what it called 'adequate' protection in a host of areas identified with the features of an employment relationship, including the right to organize, the right to bargain collectively, freedom from discrimination, minimum wage, payment of wages, occupational safety and health, compensation in case of injury or disease, and payment of social insurance contributions, defining 'adequate' in a relational fashion, as affording protection to contract workers 'to correspond to the degree of the worker's subordination to and/or dependency on the user enterprise' (ILO 1998b: 65). The employment relationship continued to serve as a reference point in advancing a model of graduated protection. At the same time, the draft recommendation set out a process for allocating 'the respective responsibilities of the user enterprise and the other enterprises in relation to employees' in triangular employment relationships (ILO 1998c: Art. 9). It also attempted to improve protections accorded to workers in such relationships *regardless* of the nature of the contract labour arrangement. Still, it stopped short of making them employees of the user enterprise, proposing, instead, a hybrid test for establishing subordination and dependency, covering the various forms of contract labour. Its tenor thereby reflected a desire among some to extend labour protection to 'dependent workers', a term then coming into greater usage.

Employers blocked the adoption of a convention on contract labour, rejecting its version of 'adequate protection', its provisions inscribing shared responsibilities between the user and other enterprises, and its definition of contract labour, which would loosen the relationship between labour protection and the employment relationship. In turn, workers refused to accept a recommendation in the place of a convention, due to the severity of the problem of contract labour (Parrot, 17 June 1997; ILO 2000c: para. 72). As a result, deliberations failed.

In the wake of the failure to adopt a convention on contract labour, an ILO Committee of Experts was struck to inquire into 'workers in situations needing protection'. On the basis of its extensive research,[18] this committee advanced a typology of 'dependent work' organized around disguised, ambiguous, and triangular relationships. This typology defined dependent workers as workers lacking labour protection because of one or a combination of the following factors: the scope of the law is too narrow or too narrowly interpreted; the law is poorly or ambiguously formulated; the employment relationship is disguised; the relationship is objectively ambiguous; and the law is not enforced (ILO 2003a: 2). The Committee of Experts also surveyed criteria for defining the employment relationship, examined the consequences of the absence of labour and social protections for workers in the situations concerned, and proposed several alternative models for regulation. In the end, it concluded that the employment relationship remains a universal concept and an appropriate basis for extending labour protection; at the same time, the committee recognized the need to adapt outmoded policies to improve protection for dependent workers (ILO 2003a: 53).

In 2003, in response to the conclusions of the ILO Committee of Experts, ILO constituents agreed to engage in negotiations towards a recommendation on the employment relationship. This recommendation, they concurred, would outline mechanisms for ensuring that persons in employment relationships have access to its associated protections and address disguised employment relationships, although constituents could not at first agree on whether it would cover triangular employment relationships (ILO 2003b: paras. 9–25; ILO 2003a: 32).

In the same negotiations, employers claimed that 'there was no evidence . . . demonstrating that lack of labour protection exacerbated gender inequalities' despite formal acknowledgements of this tendency in previous ILO regulations pertinent to the employment relationship, such as the Convention on Home Work (ILO 2003b: para. 123). In response, government and worker representatives marshalled evidence of women's high concentration in various forms of what were then labelled dependent work, affirming findings of the ILO's (2000c: para. 90) own synthesis report (ILO 2003b: para. 53). These efforts led to the conclusion that 'the lack of labour protection of dependent workers exacerbates gender inequalities in the labour market' (ILO 2003b: para. 123). Another was a directive for clearer policies on gender equality and better enforcement of laws and agreements based on the notion that the Convention on Discrimination (1958) applies to all workers. ILO constituents agreed that the recommendation to be drafted for discussion in 2006 would 'address the gender dimension' (ILO 2003b: Conclusion, paras. 16, 25; see also ILO 2004: 14).

The period preceding the adoption of the Recommendation on the Employment Relationship brought home workers and private employment agency workers into the range of labour protection, providing for the extension of select protections associated with the SER to them. While the Convention on Homework aimed at 'equality of treatment', the Convention on Private Employment Agencies provided for 'adequate protection' only. The subsequent failure to adopt a convention on contract labour prompted the creation of a recommendation clarifying the scope of the employment relationship and calling for 'effective protection'.

The ILO Recommendation on the Employment Relationship (2006)

> The situation of workers who are unprotected because of a lack of clarity about their employment status undermines the impact of national and international labour standards whose application depends mainly on the existence of an employment relationship.
>
> ILO (2004) *ILC: Date, Place and Agenda of the 95th Session 2006 of the International Labour Conference*: para. 57.

On 12 June 2006, the ILO adopted the Recommendation on the Employ-ment Relationship, affirming the employment relationship as the basis of labour protection. This recommendation emerged from intensive nego-tiations during which Workers' and Employers' Groups disagreed strongly over the placement of the dividing line between the sphere of commerce and that of the labour market. On the one hand, the Employers' Group rejected any 'wording that interfered with legitimate subcontracting and outsour-cing, and burdened enterprises as well as the workers servicing them', suggesting that it infringed upon the freedom of contract (ILO 2006c: para. 10).[19] On the other hand, the Workers' Group sought to draw atten-tion to workers compelled to become independent contractors and then 'forced to work long hours for low wages in exploitative conditions' (ILO 2006c: para. 14). To mediate this tension, the first segment of the recom-mendation sets out a framework for national policies on the employment relationship and states that those addressing its scope, coverage, and responsibility for application and enforcement should be clear as well as 'adequate to ensure effective protection for workers in an employment relationship' (ILO 2006a: para. 2). It also calls for national policies on establishing the existence of an employment relationship, distinguishing between employees and the self-employed, combating disguised employ-ment relationships, and ensuring that labour standards are applicable to all forms of contractual relationships, including those involving multiple parties.

The broad objective of the recommendation is to ensure that employed workers have access to protections that they are due. At the same time, drafters recognized that meeting this aim may entail establishing 'who is responsible' for labour protection, which may involve more than one entity (ILO 2006a: paras. 4a–d).

During the final negotiations, the notion of shared employment-related responsibilities was a major subject of debate, particularly since the Inter-national Confederation of Private Employment Agencies (CIETT) sought to preserve, at the level of international labour regulation, temporary work agencies' status as employers required to abide by labour regulations, and the parallel universe of user firms as businesses subject to the rules of competition, to whom agencies provide services on the basis of commercial agreements.[20] The force with which it made its case stemmed partly from the exclusion of services provided by temporary work agencies in the EU Services Directive that occurred that year, discussed in Chapter 5. In at-tempting to exclude temporary agency workers from the scope of the recommendation, CIETT also sought to preserve the framework of limited rights extended to agency workers under the Convention on Private Employment Agencies.[21]

CIETT's lobbying efforts amplified the focus on the triangular employment relationship in the ILO negotiations of June 2006. It led the Workers' Group to call for addressing without distinction 'the difficulties associated with triangular relationships',[22] a proposal opposed by the Employer's Group (ILO 2006c: para. 42). The workers and employers ultimately resolved their dispute by replacing references to triangular employment relationships with 'contractual arrangements, including those involving multiple parties', and inserting a paragraph noting that nothing in the recommendation alters the meaning or application of the Convention and Recommendation on the Private Employment Agencies (ILO 2006a: paras. 4c and 23; ILO 2006c: paras. 537, 539).

Under the framework offered by the Recommendation on the Employment Relationship, national policies protecting workers in an employment relationship are not to 'interfere with true civil and commercial relationships' (ILO 2006a: para. 8). During negotiations, workers and employers debated the wording of this provision extensively. Workers and EU member states wanted reference to 'genuine' civil and commercial relationships and employers preferred 'legitimate' since it meant legal, while 'genuine' implied that some relationships might be legal but are, in principle, 'false, lacking sincerity, etc.' (ILO 2006c: paras. 364 and 365). The compromise terminology was 'true'. Despite attempts by the Workers' Group, as well as most EU member states and Norway, to incorporate a broader conception of who is a worker and thus who should have access to labour protection, under the recommendation the traditional employment relationship continues to mark the dividing line between commerce and the labour market.

Further demarcating this line, the recommendation's second part addresses the determination of the existence of an employment relationship. Above all, this process is to be governed by the facts surrounding the performance of work and how the worker is remunerated, references that refer implicitly to indicators used traditionally to distinguish employment from commercial relationships (ILO 2000c: para. 9). At the same time, the recommendation supports providing for a legal presumption that an employment relationship exists in instances where pertinent indicators are present and for determining that 'workers with certain characteristics, in general or in a particular sector, must be deemed to be either employed or self-employed' (ILO 2006a: paras. 10 and 11). National policies are also to define conditions to be used in the determination process and 'subordination or dependence' are named as suggested conditions (ILO 2006a: paras. 12–13). Furthermore, the list of possible indicators of such criteria emphasizes control as well as remuneration (ILO 2006a: para. 13a–b).

This package of provisions was also a source of contestation: employers, backed by the United States and Australia, sought language referring to the 'intentions of the parties' in the list of suggested criteria for determining the existence of an employment relationship, but workers objected, refusing to place this criterion on a par with 'the facts of the relationship' (ILO 2006c: para. 375). Workers and employers also disagreed on suggested 'indicators' of the employment relationship. Initially, employers called for deleting the examples of 'subordination and dependence' and subsequently for deleting a suggested list of criteria altogether, on the basis that they 'could be abused to characterize many independent contractor relationships as employment relationships' (ILO 2006a: 8; ILO 2006c: paras. 399 and 576). Here, however, IMEC members backed workers.

The third and least debated segment of the recommendation on 'monitoring and implementation' directs national governments to monitor policies relevant to the employment relationship, as well as their application and enforcement.[23]

The Recommendation on the Employment Relationship also includes various measures addressing gender. Foremost amongst these, national policies are to take 'special account' of the fact that women specifically 'predominate in certain occupations and sectors where there is a high proportion of disguised employment relationships' (ILO 2006a: para. 6a). It also suggests that labour administrations pay 'special attention' to occupations and sectors in which there are high proportions of women in determining the existence of an employment relationship (ILO 2006a: para. 15). In a separate provision, it calls for 'clear policies on gender equality and better enforcement of the relevant laws and agreements' to address the gender dimension of uncertainty (ILO 2006a: para. 6b). In these ways, the recommendation goes some distance towards linking the lack of labour protection to gender inequalities in the labour market. However, its terms fall short of calls by workers, during the negotiations, for extending equal protection on the basis of form of employment to dependent workers. Initially, the Workers' Group proposed a paragraph for insertion in the preamble, stating that 'the lack of labour protection of dependent workers exacerbates gender inequalities', and recalling that the Convention on

Discrimination (Employment and Occupation) (1958) 'appl[ies] to all workers' and that the Maternity Convention (2000) applies to all employed women, 'including those in atypical forms of dependent work' (ILO 2006c: para. 179). In response, employers opposed this provision for fear it could make the dependent worker into a 'new type of *worker* recognized by international labour standards' (ILO 2006c: para. 180, emphasis added). They also objected to naming the Convention on Discrimination (Employment and Occupation) because the recommendation was to deal '*exclusively with employees*, which represented only one category of workers' and in making this objection they were supported by the IMEC group (ILO 2006c: paras. 180 and 182, emphasis added). Other governments nevertheless sought to retain some specific references to the protection of women. The agreement ultimately reached involved inserting a broad reference in the preamble drawing attention to 'all relevant international labour standards, particularly those addressing the protection of women' (ILO 2006c: para. 188).

Despite this resolution, there persisted a deep-seated tension over the sharpness and placement of the dividing line, which rose to the surface in debates over gender issues. As it had been constructed by the international labour office, the draft recommendation included provision for extending '*equal protection* to workers *especially affected* by uncertainty as to the existence of an employment relationship, including women workers, young workers, older workers, workers in the informal economy, migrant workers and, in general, the most vulnerable workers...' (ILO 2006b: para. 4m, emphasis added). Employers, however, opposed the reference to 'equal' and insisted on the word 'adequate' on the basis that any call for equal protection could be used to justify extending the reach of labour protection to workers engaged in forms of work falling outside the employment relationship. The employers' proposal received support from every country in the world, except Norway and member states of the EU (excluding the United Kingdom). In response, focusing on the situation of women in particular, the Workers' Group argued that the term 'adequate' might be misunderstood 'to mean that lower standards were acceptable in relation to vulnerable groups of workers', emphasizing gender inequalities. They reluctantly proposed the word 'effective' instead—and this became the compromise position (ILO 2006c: paras. 310–11).

The addition of provisions for taking 'special account' of women's predominance in industries and occupations characterized by high rates of disguised employment relationships, and for 'clear policies on gender equality', followed this outcome. 'Effective protection' for women was interpreted to mean providing clarity where there is uncertainty as to the existence of an employment relationship and, in instances of disguised employment relationships, ensuring that employed workers have access to protections associated with employee status.

The recommendation includes provisions directed explicitly to migrant workers as well. Its preamble highlights that 'the globalized economy has increased the mobility of workers who are in need of protection, at least against circumvention of national protection by choice of law' and exposes the link between the needs of this group of workers and the 'transnational provision of services' (ILO 2006a: preamble, paras. 12–13). The body of the recommendation also contains provisions directing national governments to consider adopting measures within their own jurisdictions and, as appropriate, in conjunction with other national governments, 'to provide *effective protection* and prevent abuses of migrant workers *in its territory* who may be affected by uncertainty as to the existence of an employment relationship' (ILO 2006a: para. 7a, emphasis added). In addition, continuing a theme characterizing international labour regulations since 1919 (as outlined in Chapter 2), 'where workers are recruited in one country for work in another', the recommendation encourages countries to enter into agreements aimed at preventing 'abuses and fraudulent practices which have as their purpose the evasion of the existing arrangements for the protection of workers in the context of an employment relationship' (ILO 2006a: para. 7b).

These provisions were also the product of considerable debate. During the negotiations, the EU (excluding the United Kingdom) and Norway sought to have the recommendation meaningfully address the link between migrant work and the deterioration of the employment relationship. Shaped by the related debate over the EU Services Directive (discussed in Chapter 5), part of their aim was to protect workers working in a country other than their own from the imposition of laws other than those applied in that country. These countries also attempted to promote clarity and accountability in work relationships in the interest of migrant workers affected by the transnational provision of services. Workers, in turn, lobbied for a provision calling for, at a minimum, 'effective protection' of migrant workers confronting uncertainty.

Employers objected to these proposals based on familiar concerns about the possibility of enlarging the group to whom the recommendation was addressed and entering into the territory of triangular employment relationships (ILO 2006c: paras. 134, 136, 140, and 145). Speaking to the EU drafters of the relevant amendment, the Employers' Vice-Chair argued that 'firms or agencies which recruited and placed workers in other countries were often, as in Europe, well-established and regulated businesses' (ILO 2006c: para. 336). At the same time, he applauded legislation addressing gangmasters that had just been introduced by the United Kingdom (see Chapter 5), emphasizing that the problem was 'illegally operating gangmasters' (ILO 2006c: paras. 335–6). His claims led the Vice-Chair of the Workers' Group to note that even 'legitimate placement companies did not stop abuses of migrant workers' (ILO 2006c: para. 337). It was therefore necessary for the recommendation to cover the entire process of recruitment, placement, and employment: the Workers' Group feared that the deletion of the words 'recruited or placed' would 'result in a gap in the protection being offered' (ILO 2006c: para. 340). Workers' response suggested that behind the employers' call for their deletion was an attempt to maintain the 'adequate' level of protection provided for, in processes of recruitment and placement, in the Convention on Private Employment Agencies, but this was insufficient. Still, EU drafters, unaffected by workers' arguments, clarified that their 'amendment did not intend to deal with temporary agency work' and omitted mention of triangular employment relationships and references to 'recruited or placed' in provisions devoted to protecting migrant workers (ILO 2006c: paras. 338 and 335).

Provisions for 'effective protection to workers especially affected by uncertainty as to the existence of an employment relationship' (i.e. women workers, migrant workers, older workers, younger workers, and workers in the informal economy) nevertheless survived (ILO 2006a: para. 5). The recommendation recognizes that it is common for workers belonging to equity-seeking groups to lack clarity in their employment status. Its call to address the situation of groups facing uncertainty in their employment status could meaningfully shape determination processes, but provisions addressing these 'most vulnerable workers' gain their greatest force after the determination process if an employment relationship is found to exist, given the clear directives not to interfere with true civil and commercial relationships (ILO 2006a: para. 5).

The recommendation's emphasis on women workers and migrant workers is notable, given employers' and some governments' objections to addressing both the gender dimension and migrant work. But more significant is the way in which disagreements over equal protection crystallized on this terrain, and the degree to which IMEC members backed employers' rejection of provisions for extending equal labour protection to workers affected by uncertainty over the existence of an employment relationship in order to retain the employment relationship as the basis for labour protection and to confine the responsibility for labour protection to countries of employment (i.e. to exclude processes of recruitment and placement).

The main outcome of such disagreements, and specifically the endorsement of 'effective' protection, is the maintenance of the employment relationship at the basis of the SER as the dividing line between the sphere of commerce and that of the labour market. The result is a regulatory approach lending continued support to the idea that it is acceptable to extend different protections to workers on the basis of whether or not they are employees. In this way, its framework simultaneously reinforces SER-centrism and denotes its limit.

Approaches to Regulating Self-Employment in Industrialized Market Economy Countries

The Recommendation on the Employment Relationship leaves intact a key phenomenon undermining the basis of labour protection worldwide: forms of work for remuneration that do not fit neatly into the employment relationship, especially self-employment resembling dependent employment. The changing composition of employment in IMEC member countries attests to the significance of this omission. And yet the IMEC group supported retaining a sharp dividing line, reflecting the distinct approaches to self-employment among core members. Two divergent approaches to the development of self-employment, exemplified by federal policies in Australia, on the one hand, and the EU, on the other hand, prevailed among IMEC countries when the Recommendation on the Employment Relationship was adopted in 2006. In Australia, federal laws and policies encouraged the growth of self-employment through measures legitimizing independent contracting as part of a larger 'enterprise agenda'. The EU, in contrast, took self-employment as a challenge and opportunity for its 'flexicurity' agenda, viewing its growth as a vehicle for both promoting entrepreneurship and extending rights and protections to a subset known as 'economically dependent workers'. Despite their divergence, both approaches are premised on retaining the employment relationship as the basis of labour protection.

Maximizing Enterprise Work: The Australian Case

> A party's freedom to contract must be upheld and there must be certainty
> in commercial relationships.
>
> > Howard, J. (2004) *A Stronger Economy: A Stronger Australia. The
> > Howard Government Election 2004 Policy: Protecting and Supporting
> > Independent Contractors*. Barton: The Liberal Party of Australia.

As in other common-law contexts, in early 20th century Australia the employment relationship 'became the platform around which a range of statutory and common law rights and obligations are granted and imposed' (Australia, DEWR 2005: 13). Common-law legal tests in which control was the foremost criteria for establishing the existence of an employment relationship were applied in various jurisdictions at the federal and state levels. Late-century, as work contracts aimed at evading employment-related rights became more widespread, Australian states and territories adopted two further means of protecting the welfare of workers: deeming and unfair contracts provisions.

Developed most fully in Queensland and New South Wales, deeming involved the power to declare persons or groups of persons who work under independent contracting arrangements to be employees. For example, Queensland's Industrial Relations Act (1999) defined an employee to include workers who might not normally be characterized as such, namely outworkers, lessees of equipment or vehicles, and owner-drivers. It also gave its Industrial Relations Commission the power to deem other persons who work under a commercial contract to be employees on the bases of their relative bargaining power, economic dependency, the particular circumstances and needs of low-paid workers, whether the contract is designed to, or does, avoid the provisions of an industrial agreement, and the particular circumstances and needs of women, persons from a non-English-speaking backgrounds, young persons, and outworkers. As such, this Act aimed to limit insecurity among equity-seeking groups and recognized the relationship between social location and forms of employment characterized by dimensions of labour market insecurity.[24]

In addition to deeming provisions, unfair contracts laws at the state and federal levels[25] allowed industrial relations commissions to review or investigate contracts involving independent contractor arrangements and contracts of service not covered by industrial relations laws. Such laws defined an unfair contract as 'harsh, unconscionable or against the public interest' and they empowered the industrial relations commission to vary the contract or to declare all or part of it null and void, as well as to make orders for the payment of money (Neilsen 2006). At the state level, unfair contract laws were also most extensive in New South Wales and Queensland (Riley 2007a; Sarina and Riley 2007). At the federal level, the Workplace Relations Act (WRA) (1996) empowered the Federal Court to examine contracts involving an independent contractor relating to performance of work and to intervene by providing remedies in the case of those determined to be unfair.

In the early 2000s, with the election of the Howard government at the federal level, Australia's emphasis on protecting the workers at the margins of the employment relationship through deeming and unfair contracts laws was replaced by concerted efforts to promote self-employment. Indeed, a discussion paper on the regulation of independent contracting and 'labour hire' arrangements (or temporary agency work), released shortly after Howard's re-election, asked the question: 'how can genuine independent contracting arrangements be better protected under the federal system?' (Australia, DEWR 2005: 12). The answer was an overhaul of laws and policies at the interface of workplace and commercial regulation, aimed at extending greater legitimacy to independent contractors, while preventing so-called 'sham' arrangements, akin to the illegal practices of concern to the Employers' Group during the ILO negotiations of 2006.

1. MEASURES LEGITIMIZING INDEPENDENT CONTRACTING

In 2006, the federal government created a new commercial law on independent contracting that aimed to 'move contracting relationships as far as possible away from the realm of employment and to place these relationships as far as possible under commercial regulation' (Neilsen 2006; see also Australia (ICB) 2006: 1). Adopted two weeks after the ILO Recommendation on the Employment Relationship, the federal Independent Contractors Act (ICA) (2006) is compatible with it and it was retained by the Labor government after its election in late 2007.[26] It seeks to protect the freedom of independent contactors to enter into services contracts, recognize independent contracting as a legitimate form of work arrangement that is primarily commercial, and prevent interference with the terms of independent contracting arrangements (Australia (ICA) 2006: Part 1.3).

To advance these ends, while the ICA does little to regulate the engagement of independent contractors,[27] it excludes provisions in state and territorial laws deeming certain categories of independent contractors to be employees for the purpose of a 'workplace relation matter' (defined very broadly)[28] and granting employee-related entitlements to independent contractors (Australia (ICA) 2006: Part 2.7(1)a–b). However, due to the successful efforts of outworkers and their advocates, the Act exempts current, and permits future, state and federal laws on outwork, including deeming provisions (Rawling 2007); it also exempts, subject to review, legislation protecting owner-drivers in Victoria and New South Wales from the override of deeming provisions for fear of the significant costs they would incur (Australia (ICA) 2006: Part 2.7(2)b).

In addition to excluding state-level deeming provisions, federal legislation excludes state laws, applicable to employees of and independent contractors with corporations (also exempting outworkers and owner-drivers), permitting the review of work contracts on the basis of unfairness, leaving only a small jurisdiction covering public sector employees, employees of unincorporated businesses, and independent contractors with state governments or corporations under state laws, in states where such laws existed (e.g. Queensland and NSW) (Australia (ICA) 2006: Parts 2.7(1)c, 2.7(2), and 2.9(2); Riley 2007a: 33). In their place, it creates a new unfair contracts review jurisdiction applicable to independent contractors to replace the scheme for unfair contracts provided under the federal WRA (1996) (Australia (ICA): Parts 3.11–12).

The unfair contracts jurisdiction created by the ICA is weaker than the state/territorial and federal laws it replaced because it only covers independent contractors (not employees) (Riley 2007a: 33). Federal unfair contract laws are also more limited in their scope because they apply exclusively to legally valid contracts and exclude services contracts for the performance of work for private or domestic work purposes (Australia (ICA) 2006: Part 3.11); they thereby do nothing to discourage the resort to independent contracting in a gendered set of occupations known also to be precarious. Furthermore, they do not give the court the explicit power to make orders for the payment of money (Riley 2007b; Sarina and Riley 2007: 357). The assignment of the power of review to a federal court rather than a specialized body, such as an industrial relations commission, amplifies these shortcomings since, according to the Australian Democrat's Minority Report to the Senate Employment, Workplace Relations and Education Legislation Committee (2006: 21) 'access to courts rather than industrial tribunals invariably swings the advantage to those with deep pockets and resources'.

2. NEW PENALTIES FOR SHAM ARRANGEMENTS

Australia's commitment to fostering 'genuine' independent contracting also involved introducing new legislative penalties for so-called 'sham arrangements' in workplace relations regulations (Australia (WRA) 1996 amended 2006: Part 22). When the ICA was enacted, the WRA was amended to prohibit three types of conduct among employers: misrepresenting an employment relationship as an independent contracting arrangement; making false statements to a worker with the intention of persuading that worker to become an independent contractor; and dismissing or threatening to dismiss a person, where the sole or main purpose is to re-engage the person as an independent contractor to perform substantially similar work (Australia (ICB) 2006: 1; Australia (WRA) 1996 amended 2006: Part 22). However, the first two types of conduct are defensible under the amendment if subjective and objective tests of ignorance are met. The WRA amendment also includes a series of civil penalties for such action.[29]

These new measures on sham arrangements aim ostensibly to ensure that workers in disguised employment relationships have their rights enforced (Australia, DEWR 2005: 23). In this way, too, they place independent contracting as far as possible under commercial regulation, fostering a particular form of self-employment—'legitimate independent contacting'—by restricting the range of contracts for the performance of work where labour protections apply. This outcome echoes the position of the Australian Chamber of Commerce and Industry, which noted in 2005 that 'regulating independent or dependent contractors as employees is a regulation of entrepreneurship, and not something that even the International Labour Organisation has recommended' (ACCI 2005: 6).

Just as the ILO Recommendation on the Employment Relationship was adopted, and congruent with its terms, new Australian policies promoting self-employment upheld the employment relationship as the basis of labour protection; they effectively reduced the sphere of labour protection for precariously employed independent contractors, many of whom would have once been deemed to merit such protection under state-level industrial legislation.

Promoting Entrepreneurship and Protecting Economically Dependent Workers: EU Approaches

> '[E]conomic dependence' appears to be a socially important criterion which raises the question of the protection of these workers but cannot justify per se their assimilation as dependent employees.
>
> EIRO (2002) *Economically Dependent Workers: Employment Law and Industrial Relations*. Paris, Eurofound: 2.

EU-level policy action on self-employment at the time of the adoption of the ILO Recommendation on the Employment Relationship differed considerably from Australia's enterprise agenda. It was shaped by a dual commitment to cultivating entrepreneurship by removing barriers to running a small business and extending rights and protections to so-called economically dependent workers. In this way, it was consistent with the goal of the flexicurity agenda, that is, to 'enhance, at the same time and deliberately, the flexibility of labour markets, work organization and labour relations...and...employment security and social security' (Expert Group on Flexicurity 2007: 2).

1. PROMOTING ENTREPRENEURSHIP

The promotion of entrepreneurship became a focus for the EU when the EC launched a Green Paper on 'Entrepreneurship in Europe' (2003), which argued that Europe faced an 'entrepreneurial challenge' (EC 2003a: 4). It identified obstacles to entrepreneurship, including administrative hurdles and the financial and legal risks associated with business start-up, the 'regulatory environment', and overly burdensome tax regimes. While it received less emphasis, the Green Paper also recognized the risk factors associated with self-employment as particularly acute among women and ethnic minorities given these groups' concentration in so-called low-entry threshold activities (EC 2003a: 14). In the process, it noted the lack of social protection for the self-employed as a challenge to the viability of entrepreneurship (12). Given this, the paper raised the question of what EU member states could do to 'make the balance between risk and reward more favourable to promoting entrepreneurship' (24).

The Green Paper generated significant debate, but one intervention receiving particular attention was the study, quoted in the epigraph to this chapter, 'Second Career: Overcoming the Obstacles Faced by Dependent Employees Who Want to Become Self-Employed and/or Start their Own Business' (2004), commissioned by the Enterprise-Directorate of the EC, which argued that there was a direct link between the weak entrepreneurial culture characterizing the EU and member states' well-developed labour and social protection systems (EC 2004c: 7). The latter contributed to a high 'degree of risk aversion' among Europeans and the perception that dependent employment offers 'a more or less foreseeable future more favourable than the uncertainty of self-employment' (7, 44). The loss of unemployment insurance, pensions, health insurance, disability insurance, and, among women, lower maternity benefits, were all found to cultivate risk aversion. Based on its research findings, the study therefore recommended measures enabling employees who want to become self-employed to avoid 'all or nothing' decisions (9). For example, it called for ensuring that former employees retain access to unemployment insurance during transition periods and for basic insurance against some of the consequences of business failure, especially for new entrepreneurs (44). It also proposed reducing uncertainties over to whom various protections and rights apply by adopting clearer definitions of employment and self-employment (30). Rather than pursuing greater clarity in the distinction between employment and self-employment, the study advocated reducing the importance of definitions of employment and self-employment in social security, taxation, and labour protection regimes.

Such recommendations had an effect on the follow-up to the Green Paper. Indeed, the resulting action plan, 'The European Agenda for Entrepreneurship', called for improving social security for the self-employed and small business owners under its core theme of 'encouraging more people to become entrepreneurs'. The Commission, in conjunction with national and regional policy-makers, was to explore means of extending coverage to these groups (EC 2005c, Key Action Sheet 4).

2. EXTENDING PROTECTIONS TO ECONOMICALLY DEPENDENT WORKERS

At the same time as EU-level policy-makers promoted entrepreneurship, they explored alternative approaches to extending protections and rights to economically dependent workers who do not have a contract of employment but depend mainly on a single client for their source of income. The formal rationale: economically dependent work was a distinct and significant phenomenon, not to be confused with disguised employment, which laws and policies are ill-equipped to address (EIRO 2002; Perulli 2003).

The roots of the notion of 'economically dependent work' rest in approaches to identifying dependent employment in difficult cases in EU member states. Among EU member states, subordination is the defining element of employee status. This notion, equivalent to an employer's control over the worker, is used to distinguish between different types of employment relationships. In cases where it is difficult to identify 'dependent employment', the approaches of EU member states may be placed into four categories (see especially EIRO 2002; Perulli 2003). First, the standard response is case law applying agreed-upon criteria for defining the employment relationship. Case law is important everywhere, but especially where there is no statutory definition of dependent employment or where the legal definition is general (Ireland, Norway, Sweden, and the

United Kingdom). Amongst the range of legal tests, economic risk is the foremost criterion for assessing whether a relationship entails dependent employment or self-employment (EIRO 2002: 2–3). A second, less common, approach involves 'soft regulation' and it is most developed in Ireland, which in 2001 introduced a Code of Practice outlining indicators of employee status and of self-employment, using criteria established by common law.[30]

A third approach involves legislative interventions to extend rights and supports to workers in situations where it is difficult to establish subordination, but where protection is required. Such interventions may either reverse the burden of proof, which would normally lie with the self-employed person, or provide for a mandatory presumption of subordination where certain factors are present. A number of EU member states pursue such strategies, including Austria, France, and Germany.[31]

A fourth approach involves establishing new legal categories of employment, and it takes two forms. One form—extending rights and protections to a subset of the self-employed—is particularly well-developed in Italy and Germany. In the 1970s, Italy introduced the notion of 'quasi-subordinate employment' to define forms of self-employment 'involving continuous and coordinated work, performed mainly in a personal capacity' that make them similar to subordinate employment; it then gradually extended protections to this group (Perulli 2003: 79; see also Tiraboschi and Del Conte 2004). For example, in 1995, it reformed its pension system to create a special social security fund for workers employed through 'continuous and coordinated contractual relations' (or 'employer-coordinated freelance work'). Such interventions remained in place in the early 2000s, as did others, such as the extension to this group of rules governing occupational accidents and diseases.[32] In Italy, quasi-subordinate workers are not 'synonymous with that of the "weaker contracting party"' (Perulli 2003: 79). Hence, the extension of rights and protections to them does not attempt to make them equivalent to subordinate employees, but rather casts them as a subgroup of the self-employed characterized by continuity, coordination, and the mainly personal nature of the work.[33] The same may be said of 'worker-like persons' in Germany, a parallel notion originating in the 1970s referring to self-employed workers who are economically dependent and in need of similar types and levels of social protection to there-named subordinate employees (Daübler 1999: 88; Böheim and Muehlberger 2006: 6–7).[34]

A second form of establishing new legal categories of employment is most well-developed in the United Kingdom and involves introducing a third category midway between self-employment and dependent employment. In 1996, building upon pre-existing conceptions in anti-discrimination laws and policies, the United Kingdom introduced the category 'worker' under its Employment Rights Act to include both employees and individuals who work under any other contract, 'whereby the individual undertakes to do or perform personally any work or services for another party to the contract whose status is not by virtue of the contract that of a client or customer of any profession or business undertaking carried on by the individual' (United Kingdom 1996: s. 230(3)).[35] This category includes a group often labelled by analysts as the 'dependent self-employed', encompassing 'freelance workers, sole traders, home workers and casual workers' (Barnard 2004: 134).[36] In the UK, 'workers' are entitled to some rights and protections traditionally reserved for employees, including, but not limited, to those with respect to discrimination, minimum wages, and working time.[37]

Among these four approaches, those establishing new legal categories of employment were most influential in EU-level efforts to identify the subset of self-employed workers in need of protection. In devising the concept 'economically dependent work', EU analysts drew inspiration from the notions of quasi-subordinate workers and worker-like persons. Their influence is evident in the features commonly identified with it: in the main, economically dependent work is done personally and the worker does not hire others. There is continuity in the relationship between the worker and the client over time. The work is typically coordinated with the client's activity. Finally, the work is done for one principal only, on whom the worker relies for most of his or her income (see especially, EIRO 2002: 1; see also Perulli 2003: chapter 2; Sciarra 2005: chapter 5). Like quasi-subordinate workers and worker-like persons, economically dependent workers are nevertheless self-employed because of the absence of subordination.

EU-level analysts were also drawn to the system of protection evolving in the United Kingdom, organized in 'concentric circles moving away, to some extent, from the traditional binary division of subordinate employment and self-employment' (Perulli 2003: 86). This model recognized that economically dependent work can be precarious but provided a template for addressing the situation of those self-employed viewed to be economically dependent without extending to this group the full range of protections flowing from the employment relationship.

EU-level investigation of economically dependent work in the early 2000s grew with a study, titled 'Economically Dependent/Quasi-Subordinate (Parasubordinate) Employment: Legal, Social and Economic Aspects', exploring whether EU-level policies should embrace this notion and, if so, how and to what extent they should extend protection to workers in such situations. Authored by Perulli, its main conclusion was that 'if the regulation of economically dependent work is left to the mercy of market forces there is a risk of social dumping' (EP 2003: 12). After finding a growing 'osmosis' between national approaches to regulating self-employment and subordinate employment, the study called for 'soft' and programmatic EU-level interventions giving member states scope for adaptation in the fields of social protection (especially pensions), training, and health and safety, and 'harder' rules at the national level requiring written contracts that identify 'the self-employed characteristics of the service' and supranational rules to support national action (EP 2003: 13; Perulli 2003: 118).[38]

Adding to such interventions, a subsequent large-scale study, entitled 'The Evolution of Labour Law (1992–2003)' (2005), made further proposals for action. Building on 13 country studies, its synthesis report, prepared by Sciarra, argued that the distinction between labour and commercial regulation was becoming more porous due to attempts to encourage self-employment, on the one hand, and the expansion of non-standard contracts, on the other hand. Like its precursor, it emphasized the inadequacy of prevailing approaches to identifying dependent employment in difficult cases.[39] As a result, there was a need to assess 'under which circumstances a grey area emerges, in which certain criteria of subordination are not immediately visible and yet dependence is an indisputable feature' requiring attention (Sciarra 2005: 21).

The report defined employment as a 'key word' around which various entitlements should be extended, but it supported forging a path bringing together 'all essential means to expand human rights' (Sciarra 2005: 34). In developing this path, the report cautioned that 'the notion of protection may perhaps not be appropriate in this regard', indicating that economically dependent workers require various supports, but labour protections are not the appropriate vehicle since they are self-employed (Sciarra 2005: 34). Freedland's (2003: 26) notion of the 'personal employment contract', a new definitional category attempting to bring together contracts of employment and semi-dependent work contracts, and influencing developments in the United Kingdom, shaped its approach (see also Davies and Freedland 2000a).

'The Evolution of Labour Law (1992–2003)' called for three sorts of action at the EU-level: namely, the extension of economic support mechanisms to economically dependent workers, such as pensions, bank credits, and social security provisions, as well as access to training, maternity and parental leave, and childcare; the establishment of a set of 'permanent and generalized obligations for whoever engages in a personal employment contract where one party is economically dependent' (i.e., in essence, an obligation to ensure a 'floor of rights' relating to 'dignity, health and safety, access to training and reconciliation of work and family life'); and a framework directive clarifying criteria for economic dependence and identifying benefits and entitlements unique to the employment relationship (Sciarra 2005: 34).[40]

Both Sciarra's 'The Evolution of Labour Law (1992–2003)' and Perulli's 'Economically Dependent/Quasi-Subordinate (Parasubordinate) Employment: Legal, Social and Economic Aspects' informed a Green Paper on 'Modernizing Labour Law to Meet the Challenges of the 21st Century'. A draft of this Green Paper, initially entitled 'Adapting Labour Law to Ensure Flexibility and Security for All', was leaked during the final negotiations of the ILO Recommendation on the Employment Relationship in early June 2006, prompting serious criticism, a six-month delay of its official release and ultimately, as a comparison of texts and interviews with EU officials reveal, significant modifications. The original draft echoed the concerns of the 2003 report of the European Employment Task Force, chaired by Wim Kok, about the emergence of 'a two-tier labour market where "insiders" benefit from high levels of employment protection, while an increasing number of "outsiders" are recruited under alternative forms of contracts with lower protection' (Kok 2003: 9). It also suggested that the 'outsiders', to which the Kok report referred, 'occupy a grey area where basic employment or social protection rights may be significantly reduced, giving rise to a situation of uncertainty about future employment prospects and also affecting crucial choices in their private lives (e.g., securing accommodation, planning a family, etc)' (EC 2006b: 3). According to the draft, the growing numbers of these 'outsiders' called for a '"flexicurity" agenda in support of a labour market which is fairer, more responsive and more inclusive, as well as making Europe more competitive' (EC 2006a: 3). By the time the final version went public, however, the goal had changed to 'adapt[ing] the standard employment contract to facilitate greater flexibility to both workers and enterprises' due to political pressures (EC 2006b: 3; Cullen, 30 October 2006). Moreover, measures it identified for fostering this adaptation echoed the Kok report's call to increase the flexibility of standard employment contracts with regard to notice requirements, procedures for individual and collective dismissal, and definitions of unfair dismissal (EC 2006b: 3).

In this way, the final Green Paper still supported a 'flexicurity approach', driven to accommodate the opposing concerns that 'the traditional model of the employment relationship may not prove well-suited to all workers...' and that overly protective measures can deter hiring in periods of economic growth (EC 2006b: 5; Fieldnotes, 8–11 June 2006; Cullen, 30 October 2006; Pennel, 29 October 2006). It recognized that EU-level reforms of the early 1990s (e.g. the Directive on Fixed-Term Work) had increased flexibility 'on the margins', with the undesirable outcome of labour market segmentation with a 'strong gender dimension', since women workers 'engaged on non-standard contracts have fewer chances to improve their position in the labour market' (EC 2006b: 5 and 8). At the same time, it suggested that 'stringent employment protection legislation tends to reduce the dynamism of the labour market, worsening the prospects of women' (8). It thus sought to test out alternative models of contractual relations.

Accordingly, the final Green Paper identified economically dependent work as a potential area for intervention because 'self-employed workers in the EU-25 numbered 31.4 million in 2005 or 15.6% of total employment', and 'those who were self-employed on their own account [i.e., solo self-employed] and without employees constitute 10% of all workers' (EC 2006b: 8). It also devoted attention to this issue because some member states had already introduced legislative measures related to the legal status of economically dependent and 'vulnerable self-employed workers' (EC 2006b: 11). The Green Paper nevertheless carefully noted that 'this does not mean that these workers are necessarily in a vulnerable position' (EC 2006b: 11). Questions raised for discussion thus included: 'is there a need for a "floor of rights" dealing with working conditions of all workers regardless of the form of their work contract?' and for more convergent definitions of 'worker' in the EU directives (EC 2006b: 12, 14)?

Although, in its final form, the Green Paper contained only an abbreviated discussion of economically dependent work compared to the earlier draft,[41] it prompted extensive responses from unions, employers' groups, and member states over whether it is a suitable concept to embrace at the EU level and, if so, to what ends. In addressing its question about the floor of rights, unions, led by ETUC (2007: 5), argued that working people should have access to a core of essential rights, including the right to freedom of association and collective bargaining, regardless of their employment status (ETUC 2007: 5). ETUC also supported more convergent definitions of 'worker' and the creation of common criteria and guidelines on the definition of employment and self-employment, making explicit reference to the ILO's 2006 recommendation (ETUC 2007: 5). In contrast, employers' groups, such as UNICE, renamed BusinessEurope in 2007, and the European Association of Craft, Small and Medium-Sized Enterprises (UEAPME), opposed an EU-wide definition of 'worker'. BusinessEurope (2007: 1, pt. 2) characterized this type of legislative approach as 'top–down', suggesting that 'the green paper presents an unjustified negative picture of flexible forms of work' (pt. 3). UEAPME (2007: 7), however, welcomed the Green Paper's references to self-employment because they acknowledged its development. In opposing an EU-wide definition of worker and the notion of economically dependent workers, it was nevertheless careful to suggest that the self-employed, because they are defined by autonomy and independence, were not seeking labour protections (7).

Member states were generally favourable to the Green Paper's broad objective of 'flexicurity', although most rejected anything resembling a 'hard' legislative agenda aimed at convergence. For example, while stressing that it did not support equal rights for all, the United Kingdom (DTI 2007: 1) applauded the focus on minimum standards of security. At the same time, it asserted that its own definitions of employment and self-employment did not require amendment and emphasized that the variety of definitions across the EU did not lend themselves to harmonization (UK DTI 2007: 8–9).[42] Other governments and governmental bodies were more open to the Green Paper. For example, Italy supported the flexicurity emphasis. It praised the initiative to develop the concept of economically dependent work, while recognizing the difficulty of arriving at a 'univocal definition' and creating a 'core of rights extended to all workers, regardless of their contracts' (Italy 2007: 5–6).

At the conclusion of this round of discussion, creating a 'floor of rights' for all workers regardless of the form of their work contract was included amongst the options for EU-level action. While there was no consensus on the rights to be included, those favourable to such action called for rights to protections against discrimination, health and safety, access to training, and minimum wages. At the same time, even among advocates, there was also a concern that a floor could become a ceiling (GMB 2007: 12). Proposals for creating a common definition of 'worker' also received some support, principally among unions, although this support was tempered by concerns about the definition of 'worker' and the types of rights and supports to be associated with this status. Rights and social protections for economically dependent workers remained on the agenda,[43] but EU-level actions were poised to be 'soft' measures complementing self-employment promotion. Possibilities for extending economic support mechanisms and rights to economically dependent workers at the EU level had not been foreclosed, but the employment relationship was to remain the basis of labour protection.[44]

Lessons from Industrialized Market Economy Countries and Alternative Possibilities

> For a comprehensive approach to the issue of the protection of workers . . . the situation of workers who are not dependent and basic protection for all workers remains to be examined.
>
> > Marin, E., (2006) 'The Employment Relationship: The Issue at the International Level', in G. Davidov and B. Langille, eds., *Boundaries and Frontiers of Labour Law*. Portland Ore., Hart Publishing: 354.

Reflecting divergent approaches to self-employment among IMEC members, the Australian and the EU cases provide insight into the limits of SER-centric responses to the destabilization of the employment relationship and the rise of forms of self-employment resembling paid employment, many of which are characterized by precariousness. The main commonality in contemporary Australian and EU policies has been the commitment to retain the employment relationship as the basis of labour protection. The Australian federal government's enterprise agenda sought to legitimize and make greater space for independent contracting, and in the process it eroded pre-existing employment-related protections for workers whose employment status is uncertain. To quote Ieke van den Berg, trade union negotiator for the Convention on Home Work and then Member of the European Parliament acting as the liaison to 2002 talks on temporary agency work, this agenda reflected attempts to 'make labour smaller', to shrink the sphere of labour protection. However, it still supported enterprise workers' 'choice' to be employees. Consequently, the most extensive labour protections available still flow from this status. EU policy interventions, in contrast, made some efforts to transcend the dichotomy between subordinate employment and self-employment, but they focused mainly on economically dependent workers. And even there, the most innovative proposals involved extending only limited economic support mechanisms and rights to this group.

These two approaches to developing self-employment point to the potentially distinct interpretations of the notion of 'effective protection' so central to the Recommendation on the Employment Relationship. Applied in Australia, 'effective protection' could be interpreted to mean protecting independent contractors' freedom to enter into service contracts and legitimizing independent contracting as a work arrangement that is commercial. It could be taken as support for the removal of unfair contract provisions in workplace regulations, and their placement in commercial regulations, on the grounds of clarity. Since an SER-centric approach to regulation, such as that advanced in the ILO Recommendation on the Employment Relationship, provides for several possibilities for remedying uncertainty, of which deeming is only one, it could also lend support to Australia's decision to withdraw deeming provisions in favour of provisions prohibiting sham arrangements and to reconfigure unfair contracts laws. Applied in the EU, 'effective protection' could, in contrast, provide openings for future laws and policies to introduce a broader concept of 'worker' at the supranational level and to extend select rights and protections to persons so labelled. Still, even here, mechanisms of effective protection are likely to deliver only 'adequate' or basic protection to this group, alongside the continued exclusion of many self-employed workers confronting high levels of labour market insecurity from labour protections.

Even the most forward-looking policy proposals, such as those under discussion in the EU, are insufficient in responding to the growth of precarious forms of self-employment, because they treat only a subset of self-employed workers—economically dependent workers who, in the main, perform work personally and continuously for a single principal and whose work activities are coordinated with that client. While economically dependent workers certainly require attention, they represent only a portion of all self-employed workers in need of protection—a larger group that includes those who work for more than one client.

Combating precariousness amongst this larger group requires rethinking the dividing line between the sphere of the labour market and that of commerce.[45] Building on the principles advanced in the concluding sections of Chapters 4 and 5, it requires an inclusive approach extending labour protections to all workers—defined as persons economically dependent on the sale of their capacity to work—unless there is a principled reason for doing otherwise, as Fudge, Tucker, and I (2002: 105) argue elsewhere. This approach calls for devising tests for defining labour force membership (Supiot 2001: p. x), rather than employee status, and for moving away from the notion of subordination or, for that matter, economic dependence, towards one using criteria for establishing whether or not a person is a business entrepreneur. Rather than emphasizing control, such tests would define a business entrepreneur as someone, typically employing others, with capital assets and an income sufficient to place him or her in the commercial sphere (Fudge et al. 2002). If the goal is—

truly—to enable workers, especially those from equity-seeking groups, to change status without a loss of protection or to encourage dependent employees to consider a 'second career' in self-employment, it is essential to abandon the dependent employment/self-employment dichotomy. While it goes some distance towards transcending this dichotomy, introducing the notion of 'economically dependent work', and attaching rights and entitlements to it, fails to provide for protecting the full range of workers engaged in forms of work for remuneration falling outside the strictures of the employment relationship. It is necessary to broaden such notions beyond workers dependent on a single client for the majority of their income. For example, in responding to the Green Paper on Modernizing Labour Law, the Broadcasting Entertainment Cinematograph and Theatre Union (BECTU), the British trade union for workers in the audiovisual and live entertainment sectors (2007: 3), supported broader notions to encompass freelancers, such as the many self-employed workers in the arts who 'are not entrepreneurs who create their own work . . . [and] are entirely dependent on the employers operating in this labour market'. Other unions also criticized this Green Paper's reference to the 'targeted approach', operating in the United Kingdom, because it excludes workers who are neither employees nor workers (e.g. temporary agency workers) and because even for those it covers, this approach provides a limited set of protections and rights. It thereby risks 'setting an inferior and lower floor of rights for economically dependent workers' (BECTU 2007; see also GMB 2007: 12). As responses to the EU Green Paper on Entrepreneurship also demonstrate, few dependent employees with genuine options will risk 'choosing' self-employment unless they can retain access to protections of various sorts.

Only once adjustments are made to the dividing line to ensure that commercial regulations apply exclusively to business entrepreneurs and that labour protections are accessible to all workers dependent on the capacity to sell their labour power, does extending labour protections and social protections become possible. Recall that in the early 2000s, 'Second Career' identified the loss of unemployment insurance, pensions, health insurance, disability insurance, and, among women, lower maternity benefits as the foremost barriers preventing dependent employees from becoming self-employed. In response, the European Agenda on Entrepreneurship directed EU member states as well as the Commission to explore means for providing social insurance coverage to the self-employed. Similarly, 'The Evolution of Labour Law (1992–2003)' called for extending various economic support mechanisms to economically dependent workers. The power of these proposals stemmed from the fact that social protections, especially in the area of pensions, already existed in many member states. Yet each of these reports identified cost as an obstacle to the introduction of social protection for the self-employed and they pointed especially to the problem of revenue losses among firms.

Such preoccupations with the firm-level costs of extending social protections to self-employed workers underpin proposals requiring self-employed workers to contribute more to social insurance and/or to receive lower levels of coverage than their employee counterparts. Yet concern with the financial situation of firms obscures the larger issue of public costs—both the increasingly acknowledged costs of the failure to extend protections to self-employed workers, including the effects on state revenues, and the social costs of introducing a graduated system of social protection further entrenching differentiation on the basis of employment status. The Green Paper on Modernizing Labour Law recognized the undesirable outcomes of EU-level labour market reforms of the 1990s, which, by increasing flexibility 'on the margins' through fostering fixed-term work, reproduced labour market segmentation along gendered lines (EC 2006b: 5). There is a risk that EU-level endorsement of a graduated system of protection, whereby self-employed workers access lower levels of protection than their employee counterparts, will contribute to labour market segmentation along parallel lines, albeit with a different form of employment.

This danger highlights the need to challenge the longstanding basis for distributing employment-related benefits. One alternative, taken up in the recommendations of the review of Part III of Canada's Federal Labour Code (2006: Recommendation 4.3), entails designating various sectors and assigning firms using self-employed workers to their appropriate sector and requiring them to pay levies to cover their share of social benefits owed to self-employed workers (see also Fudge and Vosko 2001b). Another involves creating structures to support the establishment of self-employed workers' organizations to organize and administer various social benefits. This scenario could involve setting rates of minimum pay (or scale rates), building in the worker and client contributions necessary to maintain the benefits packages. Common in the arts in Canada and various parts of Europe, it is particularly well-suited to self-employed workers who may, on average, work full-time but are engaged by multiple clients (Staines 2004; Vosko 2005; Bernier 2006; see also Cranford et al. 2005: conclusion). These are but a few options for curtailing precarious self-employed work that reject employee status as the principal (or the most extensive) basis for labour protection.

Notes

1. Collectively, this group of countries provides 97% of the ILO's base budget. Thus, while there are other ILO subgroups, such as the Asia Group and the Africa group, IMEC's financial contribution puts it in a powerful position.

   The year of the Recommendation on the Employment Relationship, 2006, was the last year that member states of the EU participated in IMEC. Thereafter, these states withdrew from this subgroup to foster greater policy coordination within the EU, a decision motivated by the introduction of the EES described in Chapter 5.

2. For a full list of sessions observed and participants interviewed in conducting research for this chapter, see Appendices B and C. See Appendix D for a list of sources for each statistical table in the chapter documenting these trends. The remaining references to statistical data are cited in the text.

3. This section draws and builds on research conducted jointly with Fudge and Tucker (especially Fudge et al. 2002 and 2003a).

4. In Canada, for example, a fourfold test—considering control, ownership of tools, chance of profit, and risk of loss—grew up and, shortly thereafter, the 'organization test', introduced by Lord Denning, emerged to take better account of the integration of the work performed into the employer's business (Fudge et al. 2002: 51–3).

   Such a test was also influential in Britain, where common criteria for distinguishing between a contract of service and contract for services came to include control, integration in a business, economic reality (a notion encompassing chance of profit and risk of loss), and mutuality of obligation (Perulli 2003: 24–5).

   In the United States, in turn, by the early 20th century, a 'common law agency test' emphasizing the right of control prevailed in many jurisdictions. Yet some used an 'economic realities test' (e.g. the federal Fair Labour Standards Act and the Occupational Health and Safety Act), which allows for fuller examination of other factors suggestive of 'economic dependence', and still others applied hybrid tests (for a concise summary of the list of factors normally considered under the common-law agency test or 13-factor test, see Commission for Labor Cooperation 2003: 32).

5. Fudge, Tucker, and I (2002) describe these two approaches largely in relation to the Canadian case, but they are broadly consistent with those identified in Australia, the United States, and many EU member states (see also Dunlop 1994; Clayton and Mitchell 1999; Stewart 2002; Commission for Labor Cooperation 2003; Perulli 2003).

6. For discussion of the first approach in the Australian context, see Clayton and Mitchell (1999: 29); for the United Kingdom and EU level contexts, see Perulli (2003: especially 118); and for an assessment in the Canadian context, see Fudge et al. (2002: 66–73).

7. For discussion of the second approach in the United Kingdom context, see Davies (1999: 183); for the Australian context, see Creighton (1994: 68–70); and for an assessment in the Canadian context, see Fudge et al. (2002: 88–90).

8. Employee-like persons in Germany, whose situation is described in greater detail below, have access to procedural rights and a few substantive rights (e.g. holiday entitlements) (Daübler 1999; Davies 1999: 186; ILO 2000c). However, as is true of dependent contractors in Canada, workers in this category can only access some of the labour and social protections available to employees.

9. See also Tucker (2005) for an instructive case study of newspaper carriers illustrating this point.

10. This is particularly the case with the introduction of managerial techniques, such as Total Quality Management, designed to flatten hierarchies and shift authority to cross-functional work teams, so that jobs widen and oversight is more horizontal (Stone 2004: 105). Such techniques mean that some workers have greater independence from management but, given collective or peer oversight, independence does not necessarily amount to greater control over the labour process. It is therefore important, as Davies (1999: 169) argues, to distinguish specialized labour from labour flexibility. The flipside of greater demands for 'functional flexibility' (Atkinson 1984; Piore and Sable 1984) and teamwork among specialized workers is, of course, the increasing weight of subordination among workers without open-ended or permanent employment relationships. As Chapter 5 illustrated, a source of increased power among employers in this area is rooted, in the case of fixed-term work, in their discretion to renew such contracts on their expiry or, in the case of temporary agency work, in their option of extending or cancelling assignments without notice.

11. There was an overall tendency towards growth in self-employment in services in OECD countries in the 1990s, much of which was concentrated in financial intermediation, real estate, renting and business services, and business and community services (OECD 2000: 160).

12. In most OECD countries, between the 1980s and the 2000, the share of total male employment made up by those who are self-employed decreased or remained stable, while the share of total female employment made up by those who are self-employed increased (OECD 2000: 156).

13. According to OECD (2005) national accounts data, the trend towards increased within-nation income inequality is especially pronounced among the self-employed. Furthermore, Förster (2000: 16) shows that not only is the market income of the self-employed within OECD countries more diverse than that of employees, their income dispersion rates are higher, suggesting that their incomes are likely to become even more variable than those of employees in the future.

14. In the EU, employers are more likely than their solo counterparts to service large enterprises, although many also service small and medium-sized enterprises. In

2006, only 18% of self-employed employers catered exclusively to client businesses employing more than 100 employees (EUROSTAT 2006).

15. By labelling it a potential worksite, the convention encouraged registration and labour inspection in the home. Its associated recommendation went further, asserting that homeworkers should receive compensation for a variety of production-related costs (ILO 1996b: paras. 8, 16).

16. The non-binding recommendation called as well for joint and several liability for remuneration due to homeworkers, where an intermediary is involved (ILO 1996b: para. 18).

17. This exclusion followed from a deal struck between employers and workers in advance of negotiations on private employment agencies and contract labour (Fieldnotes, 17 June 1997).

18. This committee commissioned 39 country studies, as well as prepared a synthesis document, to explore four types of situations: 'subordinate work' defined with reference to notions of control and subordination associated with the employment relationship, 'triangular employment relationships', self-employment, and self-employment under conditions of dependence (ILO 2003a: 44).

19. To make their case, they used the Industrial Relations Act of Queensland, Australia as an example of legislation extending labour protection too far (ILO 2006c: para. 43). They argued that this legislation (analysed below) brought within its purview workers who 'had a variety of reasons for remaining independent contractors—including using their own equipment and flexible working hours—not the least of which was that it was the individual's own free choice'.

20. In a position paper prepared for the negotiations, CIETT (2006: 1) argued for formal recognition of the distinction between temporary agency work and other triangular employment relationships. For CIETT (2006: 3), making such a distinction was necessary in the recommendation because 'the legal uncertainty that may arise in relation to the employer's identity, the workers' rights and who is responsible for them in the case of "triangular" relationships does not arise in the case of Agency Work'. These elements, it argued, are already addressed through the Convention on Private Employment Agencies, which also defines the employer of the agency worker as the private employment agency and outlines agency workers' rights 'unambiguously'.

21. The draft EU directive addressed to temporary agency workers under discussion at that time motivated the latter concern since, as Chapter 5 also illustrated, in 2006 trade unionists and some EU parliamentarians were still seeking stronger protections than those accorded under the ILO Convention on Private Employment Agencies (van den Burg, 19 February 2007; Passchier, 29 October 2006).

22. The Worker Vice-Chair rationalized this proposal on the basis that many of the 'some 23 government members sharing insights and examples in their opening

statements' had 'referred to the problems associated with triangular relation-ships' (ILO 2006c: paras. 44–5).

23. A resolution adopted with the recommendation strengthens this call by inviting the International Labour Office to support constituents by maintaining up-to-date information as well as conduct comparative studies to support great-er understanding and to 'promote good practices' (ILO 2006c: paras. 1–2).

   EU members and Norway originally proposed that the text of this resolution be incorporated in the body of the recommendation on the basis of a prior claim of the Committee of Experts that it cannot be expected that nation states will make the first move at a policy level (ILO 2000c: para. 68). However, employers rejected giving the International Labour Office such a central role, leading to the creation of a resolution.

24. The Industrial Relations Act (1996) of New South Wales also deemed workers in certain occupations to be employees, recognizing that certain categories of workers are in weak negotiating positions—for example, cleaners, carpenters, bread and milk vendors, joiners or bricklayers, plumbers, drainers or plasterers, painters and clothing outworkers—and included a power to deem other workers to be employees by regulation.

   In the case of the South Australian Fair Work Act (1994), section 4 contained a definition of 'contract of employment' deeming certain kinds of independent contracting arrangements to involve employment relationships even if they would not have otherwise be defined as such.

25. My understanding of the nature and significance of unfair contracts laws at the state and federal levels in Australia, particularly their import for protecting independent contactors, is informed especially by the work of Sarina and Riley (2006 and 2007) and Riley (2007a and 2007b).

26. In its pre-election platform, the ALP (2007d: 64, no. 148) went so far as to endorse the ICA on the grounds that 'labour recognizes, as recognized by the ILO, that genuine independent contractors are governed by commercial law, while employees are governed by employment law'.

27. For example, rather than introduce a statutory definition of 'independent con-tractor', it continues the reliance on common-law tests. As Sarina and Riley (2007: 355) illustrate, this approach reflects the Act's aim of undoing state initiatives to limit 'employer strategies to outsource work previously done by employees to armies of tied dependent contractors'.

28. Under the ICA (Part 2.8(1)), 'workplace matters' include remuneration and allowances, leave entitlements, hours of work, enforcing or terminating con-tracts of employment or agreements determining terms and conditions of employment, disputes between employees and employers, industrial action, and any other matter relating to employees or employers dealt with under the WRA (1996) or state or territorial industrial legislation.

   Social and anti-discrimination protections are defined not to be workplace matters and, therefore, the federal government and states/territories retain authority over deeming provisions under superannuation, workers' compensation, and occupational health and safety, as well as matters relating to the 'prevention of discrimination or promotion of EEO (Equal Employment Opportunity)' (Australia (ICA) 2006: Part 2.8(2)(a)).

29. It empowers the court to levy fines, grant injunctions, and make orders, including reinstating dismissed employees in the position they occupied before their dismissal or a position no less favourable, and paying dismissed persons or persons threatened with dismissal compensation for loss suffered as a result of the dismissal or threatened dismissal (Australia (WRA) 1996 amended 2006: Part 22, s. 904).

30. Crafted by a special Employment Status Group, this code aims to address concerns about the increasing numbers of individuals categorized as self-employed 'when the "indicators" may be that "employee" status would be more appropriate' (Ireland 2001: 2). The group opted for this method because of a fear that a statutory approach would interfere with the flexibility offered by a case law approach.

31. In Austria, for example, a presumption of subordination applies to a number of designated groups, including sales representatives, pharmacists, and sports people (EIRO 2002: 4). Similarly, France has a provision that covers journalists, artists, and writers, among others (Staines 2004: 24; see also Lokiec 2004).

   In the late 1990s Germany introduced an Act on the Advancement of Self-Employment, after finding social security funds directed to employees were shrinking due to the misclassification of subordinate employees as self-employed. This Act established new criteria to assess employment status for this purpose (Daübler 1999: 87; EIRO 2002: 4). The Act was short-lived, however; in December 2002, the Red/Green coalition struck it down and initiated various activities promoting self-employment as a means of curbing unemployment. One such measure was the introduction of legislation promoting 'me-inc companies', or small businesses of one, in January 2003. This legislation is designed to encourage unemployed people to become self-employed by creating a state-financed scheme to cover pensions and social security contributions for the first three years that a formerly unemployed person engages in self-employment. Another measure, introduced shortly before this me-inc legislation, was new legislation promoting 'mini jobs' by raising the monthly pay threshold to which workers pay no social security contributions, contributing to an increase in such jobs from an estimated two million in 1991 to 4.7 million in 2005 (Ebbinghaus and Eichhorst 2006: 15).

32. In 2003, however, to prevent improper resort to 'employer-coordinated freelance work', a new legislative decree replaced the concept of 'employer-coordinated freelance work' in the private sector with the notion of 'project work' (or 'programme work'). Under the new legislation, contracts for project or programme work are to make reference to at least one specific work programme or programmes or phases of work established by the contractor. Furthermore, a

'project' must foresee a specific final result, which may be connected to the undertaking's principal activity or an ancillary one and a 'programme' is an activity which does not necessarily see a final result (Muratore 2004).

33. As Perulli explains (2003: 80), continuity reflects the notion that 'the requirement of the other party...will take time to complete'. Distinct from the notion of control, coordination is, in turn, a 'functional relationship, a necessary connection between the execution of the work and the organization of the work by the beneficiary (entrepreneur or not)' (80). Finally, the notion of work of a mainly personal nature is quantitative, in the sense of the provision of equipment, capital, or the involvement of other workers, and qualitative, in terms of the importance of the service for the business involved. Its quantitative connotation provides for including relationships involving third-party work, while its qualitative meaning makes it possible to exclude purely entrepreneurial activities.

34. The earliest German interventions also extended procedural rules, in this case concerning labour law, to worker-like persons, and they subsequently gained entitlements to holidays, collective bargaining rights, protections against sexual harassment in the workplace, and social security (Perulli 2003: 83–5).

German laws and policies do not define worker-like persons as clearly as their Italian counterparts, but they typically refer to indicators such as the absence of economic independence, the presence of economic dependence (as distinct from personal dependence), the need for social protection (often indicated by the presence of low income), the personal performance of work, and the fact that the worker either performs work solely for one person or relies on one person for more than half of his or her total income (Daübler 1999: 89–90; Perulli 2003: 85).

35. Shortly thereafter, it modified s. 23 of its Employment Relations Act (1999), giving the government the power to extend the protection of employment rights, by secondary legislation, to these vulnerable workers (Barnard 2004: 134).

36. As Chapter 5 noted, the classification of temporary agency workers is uncertain. For helpful discussions of this uncertainty, see especially Barnard (2004: 134–5); and TUC (2007a: 8–9); see also Davidov (2004).

37. For a perceptive discussion of the strengths and limitations of the 'worker' concept, see McCann (2008: 41–8).

38. Such contracts, it argued, should: include rules on remuneration, such that rates of pay are assessed 'using a criterion of proportionality with the quality and quantity of the work performed'; extend the right to suspend the relationship in the event of maternity, sickness, accident, or serious family reasons (i.e. keep the post open with or without payment of compensation); address termination (i.e. mandate compulsory notice and justifiable reasons for termination, such as serious breaches of the contract or a lack of economically viability); and extend rights to training, and guarantees of the right to organize and participate in trade union activities (Perulli 2003: 118–19).

39. For example, it noted that the mechanism of a legal presumption of employee status does not 'capture the subtleties of situations in which, rather than expanding labour law principles, it is necessary to find new ways to adapt them to economically dependent workers' (Sciarra 2005: 22).

40. This proposal was for a directive similar to the Council Directive on an employer's obligation to inform employees of the conditions applicable to the contract or employment relationship (1991), which sets out employers' obligations to paid employees with a contract of employment or employment relationship.

    The criteria of economic dependence it proposed and the entitlements it sought mirrored those identified in the report's immediate precursor (Perulli 2003), as well as those used in Italy, Germany, and the United Kingdom in defining new categories of employment.

41. The original draft stated that establishing rights for economically dependent workers does not require extending the full range of entitlements associated with standard work contracts and, specifically, that anti-discrimination rights, health and safety protection, minimum wage guarantees, and safeguards for collective bargaining rights could be sufficient (EC 2006a: 9). As well, rights to notice of dismissal might be restricted, as they are in most member states, to 'regular employees' after a qualifying period of continuous employment. The original draft also asked if there is to be a '"floor of rights" to be put in place to safeguard the working conditions of all workers regardless of the form of their work contract . . . , what should those rights be?' (EC 2006a: 10). This question took its lead from Perulli's proposal for minimum requirements for personal work contracts for services undertaken by the economically dependent workers.

42. While the United Kingdom's brief took great pains to indicate that all British workers are entitled to certain rights, it objected to establishing something akin to its worker concept and a floor of rights at the EU level on the basis that 'it is a matter for individual member states as to what the "floor of rights" should be' (UK DTI 2007: 9). Other countries, such as Denmark (2007), took similar positions.

43. This was evidenced by a resolution adopted by the European Parliament in July 2007 (pts. 1 and 4), which welcomed a new approach to labour policy 'cover[ing] all workers regardless of their contractual status' and identified 'secure contractual arrangements in the context of modern organization of work' as a priority.

44. Notably, as EU-level policy-makers were assessing possible new legal categories of employment, parallel developments were occurring elsewhere, such as in Canada. Indeed, like the EU case, in the early 2000s the Canadian situation was marked by modest efforts to promote self-employment, especially among women, and the related concern to preserve social protection. For example, in 2004, a Canadian federal taskforce proposed that the government extend maternity leave benefits to self-employed women, noting that 'women

entrepreneurs would gladly pay into Employment Insurance [the program through which maternity benefits are provided in Canada] if it meant that they would have access to these benefits' (Canada 2003: Recommendation 4.01). It also called for improved pension provisions, observing that 'many [self-employed women] are in lower income categories than their male counterparts' and that their socio-economic situation unfairly compromises their ability to save for retirement (Canada 2003: Recommendation 12.06). Simultaneously, Canadian policy-makers explored avenues for extending protections and rights to a new category of 'autonomous worker', or 'persons who perform services comparable to those provided by employees and under similar conditions, but whose contractual arrangements with the employer distinguish them from "employees"' (Canada 2006: 64). Indeed, the 2006 report 'Fairness at Work: Federal Labour Standards for the 21st Century', a review of minimum terms of employment under the federal labour code, chaired by Harry Arthurs, proposed extending measures to protect their 'basic right to decent working conditions'; it also called for giving the government power to enact regulations delineating sector-specific criteria for defining 'autonomous worker status' and determining which protections are to be extended to this group in a given industry (Canada 2006: Recommendations 4.2 and 4.3).

45. The discussion of alternatives for moving beyond the dichotomy of employed and self-employed as a basis for establishing who should and should not be entitled to labour protection in the remainder of this section builds conceptually on research conducted jointly with Cranford, Fudge, and Tucker (especially Fudge and Vosko 2001b; Fudge et al. 2002; and Cranford et al. 2005: conclusion).

7

Alternatives to the SER

This book has attempted to illustrate the manner in which contemporary efforts to regulate the precarious margins of late-capitalist labour markets contribute to their reproduction. Despite the range of approaches taken across different contexts, they largely operate according to a common SER-centric logic: the greater the deviation from the SER, the lesser the protection they provide. There is, therefore, an urgent need for a radical rethinking of labour market regulation. The challenge, as stated at the outset, is not simply to manage the precarious margins of the labour market but to eliminate them. One place to begin, and where this book ends, is by considering alternatives to the SER—and to SER-centrism.

This chapter evaluates three broad approaches to regulation, designating them under the headings 'tiered SER', 'flexible SER', and 'beyond employment'. Taken together, these approaches are by no means exhaustive of the myriad potential alternatives. Rather, they reflect the menu of available options, and thereby provide a basis for exploring possibilities. The 'tiered SER' encapsulates the SER-centric approaches examined in Chapters 4 to 6. The 'flexible SER', developed by Bosch (2004), is also SER-centric. However, it supports a greater diversity in the forms of employment encompassed by the SER and thus has the potential to limit the sharp tiering associated with SER-centrism. Finally, the third approach, associated with Supiot (2001), seeks to move 'beyond employment' as a basis for labour and social protection. The beyond employment approach is most promising, especially in its attempts to de-link employment status and form of employment from dimensions of labour market insecurity, while simultaneously addressing the relationship between employment norms and gender relations and extending citizenship's boundaries. It nevertheless has limitations. What is required is an alternative imaginary that builds towards transformative visions of caregiving and community membership.

Why there is No Returning to the SER

Before turning to discuss the three approaches, it is important to explain why returning to the SER of old is not itself an option.

Chapters 3 to 6 charted the partial eclipse of the SER over the last several decades, while illustrating considerable variation in the nature and extent of change across contexts. Between the early 1980s and the early 2000s, full-time paid employment declined in Australia, Canada, and the EU 15 and, after having decreased modestly in the 1970s, its levels remained relatively constant in the United States (Chapter 3). Furthermore, full-time permanent employment, identified with an open-ended employment relationship, decreased markedly in Australia, Canada, and the EU 15 (Chapters 3 and 5). At the same time, in some contexts, in its place, part-time paid employment has been a particularly significant phenomenon, whereas in others the growth of temporary paid employment has been more dramatic. In still others, work for remuneration falling outside the employment relationship, such as self-employment, is quite prevalent. It is therefore important neither to overstate the pace and the extent of the decline of the SER nor to assume uniformity in its character across different contexts (Chapters 4–6).

If the eclipse of the full-time continuous job is only partial, why not bolster the old SER? After all, sceptics might argue, moving too far away from this employment norm is akin to 'throwing the baby out with the bathwater', such that the security and protection long provided via employment would decline. Rather than move away from the SER, why not return to it, renormalizing its pillars and prohibiting forms of employment deviating from them, much as temporary agency work was once banned in many jurisdictions?

There is, however, no returning to the SER. This is so for several reasons. To begin with, the male breadwinner/female caregiver gender contract upon which it was built is crumbling. Women have entered the labour force in large numbers—women's participation rates were 69%, 74%, 65%, and 69% in Australia, Canada, the EU 15, and the United States in 2007—and there is every indication that they will remain high (OECD 2008). Even though gender relations remain a site of contestation, the notion of a normative citizen male worker unencumbered by caregiving responsibilities is, thankfully, 'history'.

External citizenship boundaries are also transforming. Countries such as Canada and the United States are enlarging entry categories for temporary migrant workers. Simultaneously, the EU is closing off its external boundaries to many third country nationals[1] in favour of internal migration.[2] In these ways, (supra)national borders are being reinforced and yet international migration for employment to industrialized countries continues to expand. Attesting to its growth, according to the International Organization for Migration (2005: 379), excluding the Soviet Union, nine million people migrated to industrialized countries in the 1970s, 15 million in the 1980s, and over 21 million in the 1990s.

Even if it were possible to revive the SER, there is no reason to expect that this employment model would not be characterized by its old exclusions. The point to emphasize is that fundamental changes in gender relations and citizenship boundaries make a return to the SER a recipe for crisis in social reproduction. Additionally, not everyone aspires to holding a full-time continuous employment relationship in which they work for a single employer on the employer's premises under direct supervision. Nor are all types of work for remuneration suited to such arrangements. To question the rhetoric surrounding 'choice' is not to dismiss many workers' desire for flexibility.

There is also good reason to anticipate that a revived SER would only be a degraded facsimile of the original. In this regard, the United States is an instructive case. Full-time employment, much of it ongoing, remains significant in the United States. However, 'contingent work', a moniker connoting temporary or transitory employment, has received considerable attention in the contemporary period—and for good reason (Barker and Christensen, eds., 1998; see also Polivka 1996). In the face of high levels of full-time employment, the focus on contingency reflects, as Chapters 3 and 5 illustrated, the mounting significance of employment at will in the United States, with the decline of internal labour markets, the break-up of vertically integrated firms, decreasing rates of unionization, falling real wages, and contracting social wage protections after the early 1970s (Hyde 1998; Summers 2000: 69; Stone 2001).

A high level of uncertainty surrounds full-time ongoing employment in the United States. One reason is that union membership, long serving as a means of securing protection against unfair dismissal or discharge without just cause, dropped precipitously starting in the 1980s (Mishel et al. 2008: chapter 3), such that just 7.5% of all employees in the private sector were union members in 2007, a decline of 9.3 percentage points from 1983 (Walker 2008: 30). Among all wage and salary workers, union membership dropped from 20.1% in 1983 to just 12.1% in 2007 (Walker 2008: 29). Even among full-time wage and salary workers, union membership rates are low—only 13.2% were members of unions in 2007 (14.5% were represented by unions) (USBS January 2008; table 1).

Alongside the decline in union membership in the United States, wages stagnated. While real hourly earnings rose by more than half for production and non-supervisory workers in private non-agricultural industries after World War II, most of this growth occurred in the 1950s and 1960s (United States Department of Labor (USDL) 1999). After peaking in 1973, real hourly earnings fell or stagnated for two decades—and they only began to stabilize in the late 1990s (USDL 1999; see also Boushey et al. 2007: 8). Wage inequality also grew in the 1980s and the 1990s; according to the United States Department of Labor (1999: 19), 'after forty years of narrowing inequality, the high-to-low wage ratio[3] increased by 19 percent between 1979 and 1999 (from 3.7 to 4.4), largely because low-wage workers' earnings fell dramatically [in the 1980s]'. This polarization over the past two decades divided employment into 'high-wage and low-wage jobs at the expense of middle-wage work' (Autor et al. 2006: 1). Furthermore, in 2005, inflation-adjusted wages of low-wage workers (i.e. earning lower than 66% of the median wage for male workers) had fallen back almost to 1979 levels (Boushey et al. 2007: 8; see also Appelbaum et al., eds., 2003).

Many full-time wage and salary workers not only lack the protection afforded by a collective agreement, along with formal protections against unjust dismissal, they earn low wages. There is no standard definition of a low-wage job in the United States. However, the widely used modified social-inclusion approach (Boushey et al. 2007) calculates low wages on an hourly basis, and defines them as less than two-thirds of the median hourly wage for men; it characterizes a low-wage job as one paying lower hourly wages than jobs in the middle and upper shares of the labour force and it references men's median wage to offset 'the extent to which gender inequality in wages affects the definition of low wage jobs' (20). In 2006, this low-wage threshold was $11.11 per hour. Using this approach, more than one-quarter of full-time wage and salary workers held low-waged jobs (King et al. 2006).

Many workers with sustained labour force attachment also lacked employer-provided social wage benefits, such as health insurance; indeed, between 1979 and 2006, private sector wage and salary workers (aged 18–64) who worked at least 20 hours per week and at least 26 weeks per year endured a 13.9 percentage point decline in employer-provided health insurance, a decline more dramatic for men (17.3 percentage points) than for women (8.2 percentage points), but still leaving more women without independent sources of health insurance (48.2% of women compared to 41.9% of men in this group) (Mishel et al. 2008: 3.12). This downward trend is especially significant since health insurance is arguably the foremost social wage benefit linked to employment in the United States, in contrast to other industrialized countries, where it is not attached to the contract of employment, the employer, or the workplace.[4] That is, most Americans with such coverage access it through plans provided by their employers and requiring employee contributions.

In the United States, employment that is full-time and ongoing still dominates. However, many workers in this situation, and situations closely approximating it, lack certainty of continuing work and protections afforded by union membership, earn low wages, and are without social wage benefits such as employer-sponsored health insurance. The American case highlights the threats of a degraded SER and the necessity of exploring alternative options, which following from the integrated approach pursued in this book, necessarily entails examining their assumptions about gender relations and citizenship boundaries.

A Tiered SER

The tiered SER approach seeks to redress the misfit between the changing realities of employment and labour and social protection systems by reviving norms of wage-earning and tying access to protection to a single job. In this way, it is SER-centric. This approach encompasses the range of efforts to address precariousness in post-1990 international and national labour regulations examined in Chapters 4 to 6 insofar as they address deviation from the SER's central pillars of the employment relationship, standardized working time, and continuous employment. It envisions a stretched employment norm, embracing the idea that all adults should engage in employment, preferably, but not necessarily, full-time and on an ongoing basis. The tiered SER approach calls, in some instances, for partial or prorated protections and benefits for part-time and temporary workers. It also provides for exclusions and/or upholds thresholds (i.e. minimum daily or weekly hours-requirements or qualifying periods) for their acquisition.

As Chapter 4's exploration showed, a tiered SER approach draws part-time permanent wage-earners into the orbit of the employment norm through the mechanism of equal treatment. The limitations of this approach, epitomized by the ILO Convention on Part-Time Work, are acute in Australia, given the magnitude of part-time casual employment there. Similarly, as Chapter 5's investigation of EU-level regulations indicated, adjusting the SER in response to the deterioration of continuous employment entails extending some protections and benefits to fixed-term workers, also on the basis of equal treatment vis-à-vis a comparable permanent worker, but fewer to temporary agency workers—and yet, as developments in the EU 15 attest, these workers are particularly precarious because they lack both an open-ended and a bilateral employment relationship. The tiered SER approach also authorizes the continued exclusion of certain workers from labour protection on the basis of occupational location and category of employment; for example, Chapter 6's examination of ILO regulations addressing instabilities in the employment relationship illustrates that this approach is capable of extending protection to employed workers and addressing uncertainties as to the existence of an employment relationship. However, marking the limit of SER-centrism, it focuses on drawing the distinction between commercial and employment relationships 'effectively'. The overarching logic of the tiered approach is to bring those forms of work for remuneration falling just outside the employment relationship at the crux of the SER within its ambit, while leaving the precarious margins of the labour market intact.

The tiered SER approach continues to treat gender relations as ancillary to employment norms. It assumes a gender contract characterized by dual breadwinning, with caregiving remaining marginal in policy terms. The result, variously associated with the 'ideal worker' (Appelbaum 2001 and 2002a) or the 'adult worker' models (Lewis and Guillari 2005), is that women assumed to reside in nuclear family households (hence 'dual' breadwinning), must be 'flexible'; they must bear a disproportionate share of the costs (e.g. the double day) and 'dependencies' associated with accepting forms of employment that enable them to accommodate caregiving. Hence, the persistently gendered character of part-time casual employment in Australia documented in Chapter 4. While a tiered SER approach might oppose the use of particular forms of employment, such as disguised employment, as a means for firms to abdicate from employment-related responsibilities, it takes a positive view of the 'flexibility' that others, such as part-time and temporary employment, provide for workers who must 'balance' work for remuneration with caregiving responsibilities.

With the application of a tiered SER approach, the gender contract could take several different forms. It could result in a situation in which dual breadwinning is defined by long-hours full-time paid employment among men and high rates of part-time employment characterized by labour market insecurity among women. Under this scenario, caregiving functions integral to social reproduction would remain private household responsibilities, resembling the state of affairs in Australia. Alternatively, it does nothing to prevent a situation, defined, on the one hand, by long hours of full-time continuous employment among both men and women and, on the other hand, by a combination of the 'third shift' (Hochschild 2000) and the intensified commodification of caregiving activities performed in both private households and institutional settings (public and private), in part, by migrant women care workers holding partial citizenship. This scenario approximates the American case (as well as the Canadian case outside Quebec) (Arat-Koc 2006; Bergmann 2008)—and it contributes to the tendency, among states, of using exploitative global care chains (Hochschild 2000), premised on the extension of partial citizenship to migrant women care workers, as a means of coping with tensions in social reproduction, producing a situation in which certain women's (i.e. highly educated national citizens) participation in the SER is founded on the labour of temporary migrant workers.

Although some combination of both outcomes is also imaginable, the second is made possible by the fact that the tiered SER approach retains national citizenship boundaries. It does little to alter existing practices of limiting full employment rights and protections, as well as other civil, political, and social rights and entitlements, to national citizens (i.e. native born or naturalized) and providing lesser employment rights, as well as other civil, social, and political rights, to migrant workers; as Chapter 5 showed, in the EU 15, temporary agency workers that are also migrant workers, especially those from accession countries, encounter acute difficulties in securing protections under this approach. Furthermore, as Chapter 6 indicated, although the recognition of the need to protect migrant workers helped put the instability of the employment relationship on the international agenda, as well as on the agendas of policy-makers in the EU and Canada, the resulting ILO recommendation focuses narrowly on addressing abusive and fraudulent practices in employment exclusively (i.e. it stops short of addressing processes of recruitment and placement)—and the workers of focal concern are those affected by uncertainty in the existence of an employment relationship.

In these ways, although it is more aware of, and concerned with, the precarious margins of the labour market than SER-centrism of old, the tiered SER approach can do little more than manage them.

A 'Flexible SER'

The second approach aims to forge a new flexible SER. The product of a widely cited scholarly intervention by Bosch (2004), 'Towards a New Standard Employment Relationship in Western Europe', and similar interventions by other scholars (see e.g. Esping-Andersen 2002), the flexible SER approach is a response to debates about successors to the SER. This approach locates the need for an alternative to the old SER in growing flexibilization of product markets leading firms to return to early industrial forms of hiring and firing, the linked trends of rising educational levels and the combining of education and employment,[5] and high unemployment rates in OECD countries. At the same time, proponents of this approach identify 'overregulation' as a concern. As Bosch (2004: 631) asserts, 'deregulation of the SER is not the only problem, since excessive regulation, as well as the regulations governing other employment forms, can have similar effects'. Here, Spain's historically strong employment protection legislation is criticized for creating an SER that is too rigid and the magnitude of fixed-term work therein is attributed to this legislative approach rather than to the dissolution of long-term employment (Auer and Cazes 2001; Doogan 2005). Rising employment rates of women are seen as another precipitating factor. In contrast to the tiered SER, however, the flexible SER approach supports greater diversity in the forms of employment encompassed by the employment norm partly as a means of maintaining women's high employment rates.

The flexible SER approach is an attempt to replace the SER of old with a more decommodified alternative for workers in employment situations formerly falling outside its range. It seeks 'a flexible framework for self-organized diversity, in which the differing interests of individuals, firms and society are balanced out and the social security system is linked to economic efficiency' (Bosch 2004: 635). The flexible SER encompasses an expanded range of forms of work for remuneration. Although employment is to remain the basis for most labour and many social protections, under this approach its form is to matter less in their content and design. This logic resembles that of the ILO Declaration on Social Justice for a Fair Globalization (2008) described in Chapter 3. In its aim to institutionalize the 'Decent Work' programme, this declaration seeks to respond to challenges posed by the growth of unprotected work and work in the informal economy. More specifically, it calls for adapting the scope and coverage of social security and creating policies ensuring a minimum living wage to all employed, as well as a basic income to all in need of such protection—two objectives congruent with this alternative.

Distinct from the tiered SER, the flexible SER makes way for a 'new bargain' between employers and workers. It pursues two additional avenues to improve the functioning of the SER: first, flexible work organization, specifically, increased opportunities for adjusting paid working hours in an attempt partly to 'share out the volume of paid work not only among women, but also between the sexes', counterbalanced by a shift to individual from derived rights, with the goal of encouraging women, in particular, to build 'independent' social protection through paid work, although minimum pensions are also to extend protections against poverty in old age (Bosch 2004: 634). The emphasis on flexible work organization aims, in addition, to support lifelong learning, where the accent is on 'active transfers' for persons experiencing difficulty in achieving labour force integration.

The second area of intervention emphasized is the development of public childcare infrastructure for children under 6 years of age and all-day schooling for those of school age. This requirement is driven by the recognition that 'an increase in women's employment that is not accompanied by changes in the wider social environment is a phenomenon with the capacity to blow apart the traditional SER, albeit one that is concealed by the decline of the birth rate' (Bosch 2004: 628). This justification, in its emphasis on women and declining birth rates, corresponds with the stance adopted by Esping-Andersen (2002: 95), who, in contemplating scenarios for a post-industrial gender contract, notes that 'we can abstractly imagine a world in which women begin to embrace the typical male life cycle model, lock, stock and barrel. In this world there would be almost no children'. Thus, Esping-Andersen's (2002: 94) vision of an egalitarian project, defined effectively as a Scandinavian model minus sex segregation, entails 'women-friendly policy' that includes affordable day care, justified on the basis that its provision is 'fundamental for mothers' capacity to remain employed', as well as eldercare (see also Esping-Anderson 2000; see also Myles 2002).

In this way, the flexible SER approach supports a different gender contract than its tiered SER counterpart—one defined by dual breadwinning (still assuming a particular family form) in which certain forms of caregiving (e.g. childcare and eldercare) are valued. At the same time, as is evident in the proposed shift from derived to individual rights, where social protection for men and women is built through labour force activity, proponents of a new flexible SER put their faith in equal employment opportunity. The path to addressing the gender of precarious employment lies in providing mechanisms for both men and women to engage in a range of forms of employment and work arrangements. For example, for Esping-Andersen (2002: 88, emphasis added), who observes that the 'masculinization of female biographies that we see in educational attainment and in participation curves hides persistent *feminine life choices*', there is a need for a 'new gender contract' for a new welfare state, one characterized by a more equitable domestic division of tasks. However, with the exception of Esping-Anderson's (2002) support for explicit incentives for fathers to take leaves after the birth of a child (akin to 'daddy leaves' available in Nordic countries, where men's share of total child leave days is modest but rising), the flexible SER approach does not treat the ongoing division of domestic responsibilities as an integral matter for public policy. Rather, it is implicitly assumed that once childcare (and other care infrastructure) is in place and once women no longer derive their rights as dependants, it is sufficient to treat men and women as if they are similarly situated. The flexible SER approach does not address structural issues tied to persistent gender divisions inside and especially outside the labour force. It does not acknowledge sufficiently the limits of care policies directed at sustaining women's employment, specifically, as Lewis argues (2003: 181, emphasis added), that they do little 'either to promote a more equal gendered division of the care work that *remains* to be done or to promote the valuing and recognition of that work at the household or workplace level'. It also overlooks imbalances in men's and women's ability to care for themselves or to rest (i.e. leisure time inequalities) (Fraser 1997).

Without strong incentives for the equalization of caregiving responsibilities that cannot be fully shifted outside of households, there is some risk that a flexible SER approach would cultivate strategies mediating tensions in social reproduction through the resort to migrant women care workers. In practice, however, a flexible SER could accommodate residence-based denizenship or the extension of considerable employment, social, and civil rights and select political rights, based on legal domicile. Brought into contemporary usage by Hammar (1985) to describe the situation of migrant workers who came to Western and Northern Europe from the 1960s onwards and stayed on as long-term residents, denizenship is an intermediary status in which immigrants from a variety of entry classes are neither total foreigners nor full citizens. This status stretches the bounds of national citizenship, and the rights and obligations attached to it by increasing the 'socio-economic life-chances' of permanent residents (Lister 1997: 48; see also Soysal 1994). At the same time, in a world dominated by nation states, denizenship is a less secure

217

status than national citizenship. Indeed, denizens typically lack full political rights, formal citizenship rights critical to democracy (Brubaker 1989). In Sweden, for example, where denizenship is longstanding, virtually the same rules govern immigrants' and native-born people's abilities to participate in economic life (e.g. equal pay and working conditions, unemployment insurance, and occupational injury benefits, etc.). With regard to political rights, immigrants residing in Sweden for more than three years are also permitted to vote and to run for office in regional and local elections. And the social rights of immigrants are extensive, given the country's strong mix of universal benefits and contributory schemes, which, while tied to employment, do not involve arduous work tests. Immigrants have access to national health insurance, child and housing allowances, and social assistance after a short period of residence. They also have relatively generous access to basic pensions. Consistent with the emphasis on individual rather than derived rights, Sweden additionally grants immigrant workers' family members individual entitlements so long as they are residents (e.g. maternity benefits for immigrant (and other) mothers who are not in the paid labour force are an individual right) (Sainsbury 2006: 238). Furthermore, the working and employment conditions of immigrant and non-immigrant care workers are equivalent in Sweden, effectively limiting the development of exploitative global care chains (Hassim 2008).

The commitment to a diversity of forms of employment without a loss of protection characterizing the flexible SER approach, coupled with its support for dual breadwinning and its capacity to accommodate denizenship, make it a more promising approach to regulation than the tiered SER approach. At the same time, because it remains SER-centric, it is incapable of dispensing with tiers altogether.

'Beyond Employment'

A third approach to regulation, introduced briefly in the conclusions to Chapters 4 to 6, emanates from a 'prospective and constructive survey' on the future of work and labour policy across the European Community, known in the original French as *Au-delà de l'emploi: Transformations du travail et devenir du droit du travail en Europe* (Supiot et al. 1999a; see also Supiot 2001). Calling attention to the crisis of the Fordist model, the originators of the beyond employment approach, a group of experts led by Supiot and convened by the European Commission, identify the following developments as cause for action: the internal reorganization of business towards customized production of products and services, women's entry into the labour force *en masse*, the need of trade unions to redefine their functions in the face of high unemployment, and states' abandonment of Keynesian policies in favour of anti-inflationary measures (Supiot et al. 1999b: 622–3).

The beyond employment approach pursues a vision of labour and social protection inclusive of all people, regardless of their labour force status, from birth to death, in periods of training, employment, self-employment, and work outside the labour force, including voluntary work and unpaid caregiving. It seeks to spread social risks, to be attentive to transitions in the lifecycle, such as movements from paid employment to retirement and from school to work, and to value civic engagement. The approach assumes that every worker should be able, as required, to reduce (or increase) paid working hours at certain points in his or her lifecycle, while retaining access to protections and income supports. It seeks to normalize working-time adjustments to accommodate shorter working hours in periods of weak demand, ongoing voluntary community activities, periodic skills upgrading, and phased-in retirement, as well as extended leaves, such as maternity and parental leaves, and to ensure that workers can maintain longer hours in peak periods of labour force participation. The idea, taking expression in the notion of labour force membership—that is, that 'an individual is a member of the labour force even if he or she does not currently have a job'—is to reject a linear and homogeneous conception of working life tied to the employment contract and thus the notion of a baseline altogether (Supiot 2001: p. x).

At the level of employment regulation, adopting the beyond employment approach would entail moving away from the uniform pillars of the SER as bases for protection. For example, as Chapter 6 suggested, pursuing this approach in its purest form would mean taking up the suggestion, which Fudge, Tucker, and I advance elsewhere (2002: 105), of extending labour protections to all persons engaged in work for pay and economically dependent on the sale of their capacity to work unless there is a principled reason for doing otherwise. By abandoning the dependent employment/self-employment distinction, this approach aims to enable paid workers to change employment status without a loss of protection. Likewise, as Chapter 4 indicated, instead of treating 'regular' part-time employment as a variation on the employment norm and prorating labour and social protections accordingly, the beyond employment approach proposes 'worker time', that is, organizing paid working time to better reflect both life's different phases and changing employment norms. Similarly, as Chapter 5 suggested, rather than tying benefits to job tenure, this approach calls for extending benefits to workers regardless of the duration of a given job; its starting premise is that gaps in employment, fluctuating levels of employment intensity, and jobs of varying duration are typical. As Anxo et al. (2006: 94) illustrate in elaborating this vision, individuals would 'consider their life course as a project in which they perform paid work with varying intensity depending on their circumstances and preferences' and, in turn, 'a new social system would have to offer citizens the possibility to design their own projects', by which they mean that discontinuities would no longer involve precariousness. This aspect of the new social system would serve as a corrective to one of the problems with SER-centric approaches, only addressed partially by the flexible SER's commitment to active transfers, under which individuals making transitions incur significant risks and costs, in the form of income loss, constrained access to training, and ultimately, in some instances, exclusion from the labour force (Schmid 2006).

The beyond employment approach proposes social drawing rights as the main mechanism for realizing its vision of 'worker time', and working-time adjustments in particular. As they are interpreted here, these rights are to supplement, not replace, benefits related to other risks (e.g. illness, occupational injury, layoffs, etc.), which remain essential to sustaining strong systems of labour and social protection. They are also assumed to be both public and collective, that is, social drawing rights are to be distinguished sharply from individual investment accounts.

As described by Supiot (2001: 56), social drawing rights aim to allow people to draw on their prior labour force contribution, on the basis of a 'free decision' rather than on account of risk, at times when they are required to engage in other forms of labour (e.g. unpaid caregiving work) or civic participation. These rights are imagined as 'a new type of social right related to work in general' (56). They are social in a double sense, in the way they are established (i.e. the process of building up the reserve) and in their aims (i.e. their social usefulness to the community).

To the limited extent that practical mechanisms for developing social drawing rights are considered, they are to operate by releasing an individual's time, normally during an employment contract or following its completion, and they are to be funded principally outside the market (narrowly defined); the reserve for these rights is to emanate either from the state directly (i.e. for tasks of public interest), from social security (e.g. by virtue of having a dependent child), from joint insurance (e.g. training leave funded by unions and employers' associations), from firms on the basis of the continuity of an employment contract (e.g. parental leave or sabbaticals), or from workers themselves, who may contribute, in whole or in part, to 'time-accounts' through various means (e.g. overtime or income reductions) (Supiot 2001: 57; see also Schmid 2006: 16). In this way, although their utilization embraces a broad conception of work, employment (and indeed continuity in employment) remains quite central to their operation; for example, the conditionality attached to social drawing rights distinguishes them from the notion of a citizen's income, which, in its purest (i.e. universal) form, is unconditional (McKay 2007; Standing 2008b). Furthermore, the last two means identified for securing the reserves necessary to exercise social drawing rights (i.e. on the basis of job tenure or self-funding through overtime or salary-sacrificing) make these rights, which aim to be public and collective, vulnerable to privatization and individualization.

The beyond employment approach effectively prescribes a gender contract defined by a more equitable distribution of work (paid and unpaid) among men and women. To this end, it supports a move from derived to individual rights for women, but sees it as insufficient. Indeed, to ensure that individual rights do not translate into individualization, it seeks to recast social rights based on a new concept of solidarity neither 'thought of as solidarity in the face of individual need nor on the basis of a closed list of risks' (Supiot 2001: 227), but, rather, as a vehicle connecting social rights (e.g. equal access to high quality services in the general interest, occupational freedom, and lifelong learning) and group-based guarantees to social equality. In its call for social drawing rights, the beyond employment approach also elevates the value of socially useful activities or work in the public interest, so that workers are not compelled to trade off precariousness for the capacity to perform tasks essential to social reproduction, such as unpaid caregiving and training. In these ways, it offers the promise of recognizing care obligations that women have long 'self-managed' (Murray 2005b) (e.g. childcare, eldercare, etc.) through the employment contract in the absence of formal provisions for them. In contrast to the flexible SER approach, however, publicly provided care services are not a focus under the beyond employment option. This omission raises the question of whether, in practice, mechanisms supported by this approach could effectively prioritize income replacement over the development of public infrastructure for socially necessary care work. This oversight is also critical to confront given the importance of labour force participation to women's equality, in addition to the fundamental reorganization and reallocation of paid and unpaid work among women and men more generally. Addressing it is also integral to confirming social drawing rights as supplementary to, rather than a replacement for, strong social protection systems covering involuntary risks.

Despite these qualifiers, the beyond employment approach goes a fair distance towards answering feminist calls for new 'reproductive bargains' (Gottfried 2009) and 'gender settlements' (Lewis 2003). It is also compatible with Fraser's (1997) widely discussed and elaborated universal caregiver model and Appelbaum's (2001: 313) parallel conception of 'shared work and valued care'. Fraser's (1997: 45) universal caregiver model is defined by gender equity—a 'complex notion comprising a plurality of different normative principles' to be 'respected simultaneously'. It entails the development of policies founded on the principles of anti-poverty, anti-exploitation, income equality, leisure-time equality, equality of respect, anti-marginalization, and anti-androcentrism. Under this model, all jobs are designed on the assumption that workers are caregivers, shortening hours of work for pay across-the-board, and extensive employment-enabling services are provided. Some informal care work is supported publicly, and merged with work for pay under social insurance, whereas other state-supported care work is located in civil society (e.g. in locally organized institutions) (Fraser 1997: 60, 61). By dismantling oppositions between breadwinning and caregiving and public and private responsibilities, the universal caregiver model offers possibilities for transforming gender relations. Taken to its logical conclusion, it dispenses with the need for a gender contract altogether.

The beyond employment approach also recognizes the need to recast citizenship boundaries. It assumes a version of citizenship extending further than the nation state, while still upholding the fusion of community membership and territory. Under this approach, rights previously attached solely to citizenship in a given state are supplemented by those tied to citizenship in a larger geopolitical entity comprised of a number of states (i.e. continentally). And this enlarged citizenship takes effect mainly through cross-border movement. The reference point is EU citizenship, which extends considerable extensive economic, especially work/employment rights, civil and social rights, as well as select political rights, to citizens of the Union, defined as 'every person holding the nationality of a Member State' (EU 1992: Art. 8.1),[6] and lesser rights, tied principally to employment, to third country nationals entitled to become permanent residents of EU member states. Beyond employment thereby supports a notion of citizenship resembling a supranational form of membership akin to a 'supra-nationality' (Delanty 1997). In the EU context, one potential result is a reduction in certain exclusions contributing historically to the prevalence of precarious employment among migrant workers holding EU citizenship (or EU long-term residence permits), moving between member states. Another potential outcome is the extension of elements of residence-based denizenship to third country national long-term residents of EU member states, a process (albeit limited) initiated in the 2003 Directive Concerning the Status of Third-Country Nationals who are Long-Term Residents, which seeks to enlarge work/employment rights (and economic rights more broadly) as well as social, political, and civil rights among this group.[7]

Still, the overriding logic of the European 'supranationality' reproduces pre-existing problems at a different scale. EU citizenship prioritizes the interests of paid over unpaid workers (and persons engaged in 'non-economic' activities). Additionally, while 'supranational denizenship' is emerging, obstacles to gaining entry through EU citizenship's gates are numerous, given strict external border controls. The EU context is characterized by pressures from within—that is, local nationalism—and from without—that is, entry into the EU (Lister 1997: 52–4). For these reasons, even this best-case scenario for post-national membership (Soysal 1994: 148) continues to hinge on a territorially delimited (supra) state-centred conception of community membership.

Much like the beyond employment approach itself, the version of gender justice informing the universal caregiver model is also insufficiently attentive to the relationship between gender relations and citizenship boundaries. The universal caregiver model is justly criticized for neglecting global sex/gender divisions, specifically for focusing on revaluing caregiving work among women who care for their own children without sufficient attention to the many migrant women care workers who care for other people's children in high-income countries (Weir 2005: 311). The geopolitics of its 'universal' vision is suspect, given its lack of attention to gendered processes of global exploitation and economic polarization (Beneria 2008; Hassim 2008). There is therefore a danger that, even with the realization of something like a beyond employment approach, migrant women would continue to perform a considerable share of paid care work in the contexts (national and supranational) from which this approach emanates (i.e. high-income countries and regions), in part because there is simply not enough labour to supply the number of workers, especially childcare workers, required (Hassim 2008). Furthermore, even if the working and employment conditions of care workers are fully valued through public care infrastructure, along with the extension of full citizenship rights to migrant care workers, this does nothing to redress the drain on sending economies. Nor does it respond to women's limited access to paid employment in the formal economy in low-income countries, which compels many workers to migrate in the first place (Beneria 2008; Hassim 2008).

Towards an Alternative Imaginary

The limits of the beyond employment approach necessitate an alternative imaginary combining its best elements with new normative principles for organizing the work/care/community membership nexus.

Pursuing this imaginary requires developing visions for gender relations and community membership towards *global* 'universal caregiving' (Fraser 1997; see also Weir 2005; Beneria 2008; Hassim 2008) and 'inclusive citizenship' (Lister 1997 and 2007; see also Bosniak 2002; Ong 2006) in tandem with expanded mechanisms for de-linking employment status and form of employment and access to labour and social protections.

It is necessary to rework the normative principles for gender equity underpinning the universal caregiver model such that they foster *global* universal caregiving. The difficult task is to deepen the anti-poverty, anti-androcentrism, and income equality principles critical to improving women's access to paid employment in the formal economy in low-income countries (Beneria 2008), to expand the anti-exploitation principle to respond to the harsh (and discriminatory) treatment of women workers employed by foreign-owned firms in such contexts (Hassim 2008), to develop the anti-marginalization principle to improve low-income states' capabilities to deliver social supports necessary for limiting gendered poverty, and, returning to the lessons of Chapters 1 and 2, to enlarge the equality of respect principle to strengthen (especially women) workers' power to shape the content of international regulatory frameworks around the world (Pearson 2004).

Denationalizing citizenship is a necessary complement to realizing this vision for global universal caregiving. To this end, a number of scholars in citizenship and migration studies are attempting to rethink place of birth, lineage, and residence as primary bases for accessing rights and protections (Lister 1997; Bosniak 2002; Sassen 2005; Ong 2006). One example is found in the work of Lister (1997: 63), who aims to 'free the concept of citizenship from the confines of the nation-state without losing sight of the continued power of the nation-state to delineate and control boundaries of exclusion'. Building on critiques of existing models of national and supranational citizenship (see especially Yeatman 1994; see also Meehan 1993; Isin 2005), Lister (2007) advocates what she calls 'inclusive citizenship', attempting to 'use international human rights measures and the development of an infrastructure of global citizenship to substitute a more just "order of exclusions and inclusions" [citing Yeatman 1994: p. ix] than national citizenship' (Lister 1997: 63). Her approach amounts to a radical framework for reconfiguring entry categories, residence rights, and citizenship. To such ends, Lister (1997: 63–4) identifies five guiding principles: non-discrimination so that rules governing entry do not disadvantage particular social groups; observance of basic human rights along the lines of international conventions, such as the UN Convention on the Rights of Migrant Workers and Members of their Families (1990) (on the right to stay and to move, see also Baines and Sharma 2002); autonomous legal status of migrants as individuals regardless of gender or marital status; internationalism, especially high-income countries' obligations to migrants in 'an economically polarized world'; and transculturalism or the affirmation of cultural differences and their fluidity. These principles aim to address external as well as internal inclusions and exclusions of citizenship, resulting in a framework complementary to visions for global universal caregiving.

The notion of labour force membership, aimed at weakening the link between employment status and form of employment and dimensions of labour market insecurity, together with the related mechanism of social drawing rights, is well-suited to integration with principles for pursuing global universal caregiving and inclusive citizenship. The beyond employment approach conceives of labour force membership as a means of responding to the situation of workers located in a particular national or supranational economy encountering bouts of unemployment or between jobs. However, this notion could extend more fully to workers who are unpaid carers in between and during phases of extensive labour force participation (i.e. part-time or full-time). Expanded in this way, labour *market* membership would lessen the compulsion, common among workers with caregiving responsibilities, to participate in precarious employment. To go one step further, stretching this notion to encompass persons moving from one country to another for work and/or employment could contribute to reducing the salience of entry category in shaping workers' access to social and economic rights in particular places. *Global* labour market membership would address gaps in the extension of rights and protections accorded to migrating workers falling in between different regulatory regimes; for example, it would promote the extension of protections to migrant workers in the recruitment and placement processes via agreements between sending and receiving countries of the sort rejected in debates preceding the adoption of the ILO Recommendation on the Employment Relationship (2006). Realized in practice, it would mean that migrant workers would no longer be captive groups of workers. It would reduce the *distinct* role of migrant labour as a component of the labour supply long defined by the institutional differentiation of its processes of reproduction and maintenance, and especially its specific form of powerlessness (Buroway 1976; Sassen-Koob 1978, 1981). Thus enlarged, labour market membership would limit precarious employment by fostering both gender equity and post-national citizenship.

The beyond employment approach proposes social drawing rights, interpreted here as public rights, as a means for realizing labour force membership and, in particular, for supporting work in the public interest. However, social drawing rights, specifically collective supports for the release of individuals' time, are designed to be attainable among all paid workers in a territory on the basis of a prior contribution to the labour force. They are imagined as social citizenship rights to be accessed by national and supranational citizens or denizens with (presumably extensive) employment histories in a given territory. This design element is out of sync with a much-needed recognition of the value of work, broadly conceived, since persons lacking reserves from which to draw, such as unpaid caregivers and migrant workers, could not access supports for work in the public interest. Furthermore, as emphasized above, although work in the public interest is to be funded outside the market, modes of potential funding identified for the utilization of social drawing rights are not fully public; most depend, at least in part, on market mechanisms (e.g. supports from joint insurance or from firms made available to workers on the basis of the continuity of an employment contract). Yet social drawing rights could be developed to support the unpaid caregiving work of women and men lacking sufficient reserves from which to draw due to their work/employment and/or citizenship status.

For those with care responsibilities in the territory in which they are employed, the obvious means of delivering social drawing rights are state social security systems. For those with care responsibilities outside the territory in which they work, creative modes of delivery are imaginable. One possibility, proposed for migrant women workers from low-income countries, particularly those engaged in paid caregiving work in high-income countries, involves taxing receiving countries to fund public physical and social (including care) infrastructure in sending economies (Beneria 2008: 17; see also Pearson 2004). Some such monies could then be devoted to enabling migrant workers to exercise social drawing rights.

Developing an alternative imaginary requires challenging the organization of caregiving and dominant notions of community membership. Approaches to regulation dislodging SER-centrism have the potential to contribute to this imaginary and political movements for social change are critical to seizing its potential. By illustrating the integrated historical roots of employment norms, gender, and citizenship boundaries and their lasting effects, my aim herein has been to begin to point the way to using a feminist political economy of the labour market to advance this process.

Notes

1. Third country nationals are persons resident in the EU who are neither citizens of the member state where they live nor citizens of another EU member state, but citizens of a third country. As they are defined in EU policy, third country nationals include immigrants who entered a member state with a valid work permit and subsequently gained residency status under the laws of their member state of residence and their family members who migrated to the EU via family reunification laws. They may also include children of third country nationals where member states do not grant citizenship automatically to those born in their territories.

2. On the expansion of temporary migrant work in Canada, see e.g. Boyd and Pikkov 2005; Sharma 2006; and Trumper and Wong 2007; and in the US, Smith 1999; and Lowell 2001. On limiting external migration to the EU, see e.g. Lister 1997; and Morris 2002.

3. The wage ratio is measured by the Bureau of Labor Statistics as the ratio of a high wage worker's earnings (in the 90th percentile of the wage distribution) to that of the low wage worker's earnings (in the 10th percentile). The figures cited here reflect weekly earnings ratios.

4. In Canada, for example, while there are various means of extending labour and social protections, medical care and health insurance flow from what Langille (2002: 140) describes as a citizenship platform, which provides social infrastructure regardless of an individual's labour force status.

5. The expansion of the education system, and the consequent extension of the youth phase of life, together with high unemployment, leads Bosch (2004: 628) to suggest that 'temporary and part-time jobs have become standard, albeit temporary, employment forms that are not the last stop on an individual's career trajectory'.

6. While there is no necessary analytical connection between citizenship and nationality, given the historical relationship between them, in the Treaty on the European Union (1992), 'nationality' refers to the affiliation of an individual with a state and the reciprocal rights and duties attached to it (Guild 1996: 32–3;

Meehan 2000: 4). As Close (1994: 6) helpfully explains, nationality is 'the external face of a complex concept which also possesses an internal face which is [national] citizenship'.

7. In 2003, in a move to create a supranational status akin to residence-based denizenship, the EU adopted a Directive Concerning the Status of Third-Country Nationals who are Long-Term Residents (2003). Introducing an EC long-term residence permit, this directive proceeds in two steps: first, it provides for the harmonization of rules for conferring (or withdrawing) permanent resident status to third country nationals in the 'first member state' (i.e. the EU member state which for the first time grants long-term resident status to a third country national). Under its terms, third country nationals residing legally within the first member state's territory for five years are eligible for permanent resident status, subject to certain mandatory conditions (i.e. evidence that long-term residents have, for themselves and for dependent family members, stable and regular resources sufficient to maintain themselves and their families, as well as sickness insurance) and certain optional requirements (i.e. the requirement that third country nationals comply with integration conditions) (CEU 2003b: Art. 5). Third country nationals holding this status are to be treated equally to nationals with regard to various rights and entitlements (e.g. access to employment and self-employment, education, credential recognition, social security, social assistance, and social protection, tax benefits, access to goods and services, freedom of association, and free access to the entire territory of the member state), subject to certain qualifiers (e.g. member states may limit equal treatment in respect of social assistance and social protection to core benefits) (CEU 2003b: Art. 11.4). Upon receipt of such national residence permits, member states are required to issue long-term residents with EC residence permits valid for five years and renewable automatically upon application.

Second, the directive advances a framework for the extension of residence rights in a 'second member state' (i.e. any member state other than the one which for the first time granted long-term resident status to a third country national) to third country nationals holding EC long-term residence permits. Here, the goal is to enable third country nationals holding permanent residence status in a first member state, and thus EC long-term residence permits, to acquire the right to reside in the territory of the second member state for economic (i.e. employment), training, and other purposes. This right is, however, subject to conditions established by the second member state. For example, the directive permits the second member state to limit the total number of persons entitled to be granted right of residence, provided that such rules existed when the directive was adopted (CEU 2003b: Art. 14.4). In cases of an economic activity in an employed or self-employed capacity, the second member state may also examine the situation in their labour market and apply national procedures regarding requirements for filling vacancies and it is permitted to give preference to Union citizens (CEU 2003b: Art 14.3; on broader conditions permissible, which resemble those qualifying access to long-term residence status in the first member state, see Art. 15).

This tiered formulation means both that the supranational citizenship rights of third country national permanent residents are more limited than those of nationals of EU member states, and that their rights vary on the basis of national rules.

Appendix A: Table of Selected^ International Labour Regulations, 1906–2008*

	1900s	1910s	1920s	1930s	1940s	1950s	1960s	1970s	1980s	1990s	2000s
	Forging a Male Breadwinner / Female Caregiver Contract		Constructing the Pillars of the SER			Stripping the SER of its Exclusions: The Era of Equality		Regulating Non-Standard Forms of Employment			
GENDER RELATIONS	IALL "Berne Convention" 1906 (C) IALL Limiting Women's Workday to 10-Hours 1906 (Resolution) IALL Prohibition of the Use of White (Yellow) Phosphorus in the Manufacture of Matches 1906 (C)	Night Work (Women) 1919 (C4) Maternity Protection 1919 (C3) Lead Poisoning (Women and Children) 1919 (R4) Prohibition of White Phosphorous 1919 (R6)		Night Work (Women) (Revised) 1934 (C41)	Night Work (Women) (Revised) 1948 (C89)	Equal Remuneration 1951 (C100/R90) Maternity Protection (Revised) 1952 (C103/R95) Social Security (Minimum Standards) 1952 (C102) Discrimination (Employment & Occupation) 1958 (C111/R111)	Employment (Women with Family Responsibilities) 1965 (R123)	EU Equal Treatment Directive 1976 UN Elimination of All Forms of Discrimination Against Women 1979 (C)	Equal Opportunities and Equal Treatment for Men and Women Workers with Family Responsibilities 1981 (C156/R165) Equal Opportunities for Men and Women in Employment 1985 (Resolution)	Night Work 1990 (C171/R178) Protocol to the Night Work (Women) Convention (Revised) 1948 (No. 89) 1990	Maternity Protection 2000 (C183/R191)
CITIZENSHIP BOUNDARIES		Reciprocity of Treatment of Foreign Workers 1919 (R2)	Equality of Treatment (Accident Compensation) 1925 (C19/R25)	Migration for Employment 1939 (C66 Insufficient Ratification/R61)	Migration for Employment 1949 (C97/R86)			Migrant Workers (Supplementary Provisions) 1975 (C143) Migrant Workers 1975 (R151)		UN Protection of the Rights of All Migrant Workers and Members of Their Families 1990 (C)	

SER dimension								
SER—(BILATERAL) EMPLOYMENT RELATIONSHIP	Unemployment 1919 (C2/R1)		Fee-Charging Employment Agencies 1933 (C34/R42)	Organization of the Employment Service 1948 (C88/R83); Fee-Charging Employment Agencies (Revised) 1949 (C96)		Employment Promotion and Protection against Unemployment 1988 (C168)	Self-Employment Promotion 1990 (Resolution); Home Work 1996 (C177/R184); Private Employment Agencies 1997 (C181/R188)	Employment Relationship 2006 (R181)
SER—STANDARDIZED WORKING TIME	Hours of Work (Industry) 1919 (C1)	Weekly Rest (Industry) 1921 (C14) & (Comm.) 1921 (R18); Utilization of Spare Time 1924 (R21)	Hours of Work (Commerce & Offices) 1930 (C30); Forty-Hour Week 1935 (C47)				Part-Time Work 1994 (C175/R182); EU Part-Time Work Directive 1997	
SER—CONTINUOUS EMPLOYMENT			Unemployment Provision 1934 (C144); Holidays with Pay 1936 (C52/R47)	Holidays with Pay 1954 (R98)	Holidays with Pay (Revised) 1970 (C132)		EU Fixed-Term Work Directive 1999	EU Temporary Agency Work Directive 2008

(Continued)

Appendix A (Continued)

	1900s	1910s	1920s	1930s	1940s	1950s	1960s	1970	1980s	1990s	2000s
CONSTITUTIONAL, PROGRAMMATIC & OTHER CORE INSTRUMENTS		ILO Constitution 1919			Philadelphia Declaration 1944 Charter of the United Nations 1945 UN Universal Declaration of Human Rights 1948 Freedom of Association & Protection of the Right to Organize 1948 (C87) Right to Organize & Collective Bargaining 1949 (C98)	European Convention for the Protection of Human Rights and Fundamental Freedoms (1950)	European Social Charter 1961	International Programme for the Improvement of Working Conditions and Environment (PIACT) 1975		Social Declaration 1998 Decent Work 1999	Social Justice for a Fair Globalization Declaration 2008

Notes:
^ Discussed in book.
* ILO unless otherwise indicated.
IALL = International Association of Labour Legislation.
(C) = Convention (ILO conventions numbered according to ILO system).
(R) = Recommendation (ILO recommendations numbered according to ILO system).

Appendix B: List of International Labour Conferences Observed

Negotiation of the ILO Convention on Private Employment Agencies; International Labour Conference; Geneva, Switzerland; 1–30 June 1997

Stage 1 Negotiation of the ILO Convention on Contract Labour; International Labour Conference; Geneva, Switzerland; 1–30 June 1997

Collection of Data on Stage 2 of Negotiation of the ILO Convention on Contract Labour and Activities of Committee of Experts; ILO; Geneva, Switzerland; 10–31 July 2000

General Discussion on the Informal Economy; International Labour Conference; Geneva, Switzerland; 1–20 June 2002

General Discussion on the Scope of the Employment Relationship; International Labour Conference; Geneva, Switzerland; 1–20 June 2003

Negotiation of the ILO Recommendation on the Employment Relationship; International Labour Conference; Geneva, Switzerland; 1–20 June 2006

Appendix C: List of Interviews

Alberg, Jonas	Commission of the European Union; Legal Officer—EU Labour Law; Brussels, Belgium; 31 October 2006.
Berthiaume, Francoise	Commission of the European Union; Senior Administrator or Legal Officer—EU Labour Law; Brussels, Belgium; 31 October 2006.
Brown, Tony	National Tertiary Education Industry Union; Vice-President Academic; Sydney, Australia; 30 June 2006.
Bowtell, Cath	Australian Confederation of Trade Unions; Industrial Officer; Melbourne, Australia; 27 June 2006.
Cullen, Paul	Commission of the European Union; Legal Officer—EU Labour Law; Brussels, Belgium; 2 November 2006.
Gale, Linda	Australian Education Union; Federal Industrial Officer; Melbourne, Australia; 27 June 2006.
Game, Chris	National Tertiary Education Industry Union; State Secretary; Sydney, Australia; 30 June 2006.
Harvey, Keith	Australian Services Union; Industrial Officer; Melbourne, Australia; 27 June 2006.
Hughes, Alisha	Labor Council New South Wales; Industrial Officer; Sydney, Australia; 29 June 2006.
Kentish, Alister	Australian Manufacturing Workers' Union; National Research Officer; Sydney, Australia; 29 June 2006.
Lawrence, Jeff	Liquor, Hospitality and Miscellaneous Union; National Secretary; Sydney, Australia; 29 June 2006.
Lennon, Mark	Labor Council New South Wales; Assistant Secretary; Sydney, Australia; 29 June 2006.
Morris, Jo	Trade Union Congress, UK; Senior Policy Officer; Reading, UK; 21 November 2006.
Parrot, Jean Claude	Vice-President, External, Canadian Labour Congress; Chief Trade; Union Negotiator in Failed Negotiations on Contract Labour; Geneva, Switzerland; 17 June 1997.
Passchier, Catelene	European Trade Union Congress; Confederal Secretary; Brussels, Belgium; 31 October 2006.

Pennel, Denis	EUROCIETT/CIETT; Managing Director; Brussels, Belgium; 31 October 2006.
Peters, Alison	Labor Council New South Wales; Deputy Assistant Secretary (Community Affairs); Sydney, Australia; 29 June 2006.
Representative	Textile Clothing and Footwear Union of Australia; Sydney, Australia; 29 June 2006.
Representative	Trade Union Congress, UK; London, UK; 23 November 2006.
Roberts, Tom	Construction Forestry Mining Energy Union; Senior Legal Officer; Sydney, Australia; 29 June 2006.
Rosewarne, Stuart	National Tertiary Education Industry Union; State President; Sydney, Australia; 30 June 2006.
Van den Burg, Ieke	Parliamentary Reporter for the draft EU Directive on Temporary Agency Work; European Parliamentarian; The Hague, Netherlands; 19 February 2007.
Van Leur, Alette	Ministry of Social Affairs and Employment; Deputy Director for International Affairs; The Netherlands; 19 February 2007.
Warneck, Fabrice	UniEuropa; Property Services Secretary; Berlin, Germany; 29 November 2006.
Yasokawa, Keiko	National Tertiary Education Industry Union; Secretary; Sydney, Australia; 30 June 2006.

Appendix D: Data Sources and Notes for Statistical Figures and Tables

This appendix lists the sources for each statistical figure and table in the book by chapter. It also explains how certain variables were constructed, where appropriate.

Chapter 3

Figure 3.1: Full-Time Paid Employment as a Percentage of Total Employment, Australia, Canada, the EU 15, and the United States, 1983–2006

SOURCES
Australia: Australian Bureau of Statistics (ABS) 1983–2006, LFS.
Canada: Statistics Canada (StatsCan) 1983–2006, LFS.
The EU 15: EUROSTAT 1983–2006, EU LFS.
The United States: United States Bureau of Statistics (USBS) 2006a, CPS.

NOTES
Data for several countries belonging to the EU 15 are missing from several early years of the EUROSTAT EU LFS. For this reason, data reported for the EU 15 in Figure 3.1 omit the following countries for the following years: Austria (1983–1994), Finland (1983–1985), Germany (1983–2001), the Netherlands (1984), Portugal (1983–1985), Spain (1983–1985), and Sweden (1983–1984). The most significant omission, from this data set, given its large labour force, is for Germany between 1983 and 2001. Fortunately, the most recent data referred to from the EUROSTAT EU LFS (i.e., for the early 2000s) include Germany.

Figure 3.2: Full-Time Permanent Employment as a Percentage of Total Employment, Australia, Canada, and the EU 15, 1980s*–2006

SOURCES
Australia: Figures for total employment for 1984–1995 are from ABS 1978–1995; for 1996–2002 are from ABS 1996–2002; and for 2003–2006 are from ABS 2003–2006. Figures for full-time permanent employment for 1982 are from ABS 2006; for 1984–1987 are from ABS 1984–1987; for 1988 and 1990 are from unpublished data derived from ABS, Weekly Earnings of Employees (Distribution), Cat. No. 6310.0 (Romeyn 1992);

236

for 1989, 1991–1995, and 1997 are from ABS (1989, 1991–1995, 1997); for 1996 are from ABS 1996; and for 1998–2006 are from ABS 1998–2006.

Canada: StatsCan 1989, 1990, 1992, 1993 and 1994, GSS; StatsCan 1991 and 1995 Survey of Work Arrangements; StatsCan 1996–2006, LFS.

The EU 15: EUROSTAT 1983–2006, EU LFS.

Notes

The measure for full-time permanent employment in Australia attempts to represent all employment characterized by standard full-time hours that is in no way perceived to be temporary; this requires creating a measure excluding both casual employment and employment of finite duration.

Depicting trends in full-time permanent employment in Australia is complicated by both the unique character of casual employment in this context, which Chapter 4 explores, and the changing approaches to measuring part-time and full-time employment and casual and non-casual employment adopted by the ABS over the period covered in Figure 3.2. For this reason, the percentages represented in the figure until 2002 draw on estimates using the above sources produced by Campbell (2008), which depict employees whose hours equal or exceed 35 per week and whose employment is perceived as permanent. I am grateful to Iain Campbell for sharing both his expertise and these estimates with me for this purpose.

Until 2002, ABS surveys relied on self-identification for determining both workers' status as full-time or part-time and their tenure as permanent or temporary. From 2002 onwards, actual hours worked became the basis for standard classifications of employment status such that full-time came to be defined as 35 hours or more per week. Simultaneously, in most measures the presence of leave entitlements for sickness or holidays, two central indicators that employment is *not* casual, became a key proxy for permanency. Campbell's estimates for the years prior to 2002 seek to develop a measure of full-time permanent employment that approximates this contemporary understanding (i.e. all full-time employment that is accompanied by leave entitlements for sickness or holidays and/or is not in any way of a limited duration), which this figure carries through to 2006 based on the sources identified above. This approach mirrors the approach to measurement used in examining part-time casual work in Chapter 4.

Figure 3.3: Men's and Women's Shares of Total Paid and Unpaid Work, Australia (2006), Canada (2005), Selected EU 15 Countries (1998–2002),* and the United States (2006)

Sources

Australia: ABS 2006 (Cat. No. 4153.0), TUS.

Canada: StatsCan 2006.

The EU 15 (selected countries): EUROSTAT 2004a (National Tables for Belgium, Finland, France, Germany, Italy, Spain, Sweden, and the UK).

The United States: USBS 2006, ATUS.

NOTES

Australia, Canada, and the United States rely on similar approaches to measuring total work (i.e. all paid work added together with unpaid work). There are three key components of unpaid work: childcare, housework, and senior care. For instance, StatsCan's GSS defines unpaid work as the sum of time spent looking after one or more children in or outside the household without pay; unpaid housework, yard-work or home maintenance for your household or for persons who live outside your household; unpaid care or assistance to one or more seniors who live in or outside your household. In contrast, paid work encompasses all activities that are performed for pay, in primary and secondary jobs, including self-employment and waged employment.

As for the EU 15, the calculation is based on estimates drawn from EUROSTAT (2004a). Countries included in this estimate are Belgium, Finland, France, Germany, Italy, Spain, Sweden, and the UK. Estimates published in EUROSTAT (2004a) are extracted from national time use surveys conducted during the period 1998–2002. This source does not indicate which specific years are included for the countries covered but rather refers to the range 1998–2002 (EUROSTAT 2005: 5).

Chapter 4

Table 4.1: Part-Time Employment as a Percentage of Total Employment, Selected OECD Countries, 1973 and 2006

SOURCES

Australia: For 1973, ILO 1997c; and for 2006, OECD 2008.
Canada: For 1973, ILO 1997c; for 2006, OECD 2008.
The EU 15: For 1973 (1979 for Denmark, Netherlands, Ireland, Portugal, and Sweden), ILO 1997c (except Luxembourg); for 2006, OECD 2008.
Luxembourg: For 1973, OECD 1996.
Japan: For 1973, ILO 1997c; for 2006, OECD 2008.
New Zealand: For 1973, ILO 1997c; for 2006, OECD 2008.
The United States: For 1973, ILO 1997c; for 2006, OECD 2008.

NOTES

Definitions of part-time employment varied considerably across all OECD countries in the 1970s before harmonized data became available. For 2006, part-time employment is defined as 30 or fewer usual weekly hours at the main job.

Although HILDA Wave F is the primary source for the in-depth profile of part-time employment in Australia in 2006 in this chapter, the OECD data are used in Table 4.1 because they permit direct comparison between countries (i.e. the source refers to 30 or fewer usual hours per week). Consistent with the national definition of part-time employment in Australia, however, the HILDA Wave F defines it as 35 or fewer usual weekly hours at one's main job. Hence, estimates in Table 4.1 differ slightly from those drawn from HILDA Wave F.

Figure 4.1: Part-Time Employment and Full-Time Employment as a Percentage of Total Employment by Sex, Australia, 1978–2006

SOURCE

For 1978–1980, ILO 1997c; for 1981–2006, OECD 2007.

Figure 4.2: Composition of Part-Time Paid Employment, Australia, 2006

SOURCE

HILDA 2006, Wave F, Custom Tabulation.

Chapter 5

Table 5.1: Temporary Employment as a Percentage of Total Employment, Selected OECD Countries, 1983 and 2006

SOURCES

Australia: For 2006, HILDA Wave F, Custom Tabulation.
Canada: For 1989, StatsCan 1989; and for 2006, StatsCan 1983–2006, LFS.
The EU 15: For 1983, OECD 2006; for 2006, EUROSTAT 1983–2006.
The United States: For 2005, USBS 2005, CWS.

NOTES

The measure used for temporary employment in Australia in 2006 in Table 5.1 encompasses fixed-term and temporary agency workers (both casual and non-casual), the types of temporary employment of focus in the chapter. It excludes other casuals because, as Chapter 4 demonstrates, a sizeable percentage of casuals in Australia are engaged on an ongoing (though not technically permanent) basis, although this proportion is difficult to quantify. Were the measure to include all casuals, temporary employment would represent fully 33% of total employment in 2006 in Australia as opposed to the 7% noted in Table 5.1. The percentages for Australia should thus be read with these issues in mind.

The measure of temporary employment in Canada includes all seasonal, fixed-term/contract, and casual jobs, and work done through a temporary agency.

Where the EU 15 are concerned, the EU LFS, the best source available for measuring temporary employment, suffers from a well-recognized lack of conceptual and empirical clarity. Because of the way data are collected, analyses tend to treat temporary employment and fixed-term work synonymously, unlike in Canada, as well as the United States and Australia, where fixed-term work is treated, more accurately, as a subset of temporary employment (see for example Clauwaert et al. 2003; Hardason and Romans 2005; Jouhette and Romans 2006).

The reason for this slippage is that the EU LFS harmonizes responses from EU country-level labour force surveys on the 'permanency of the job' (EUROSTAT, 2008: 14, question 52) by dividing them into 'a permanent job/work contract of unlimited duration' or 'a temporary job/*work contract of limited duration*' (EUROSTAT 2008: 52, emphasis added). Although the latter category is likely broader than fixed-term work, there is no means of separating out fixed-term work using this data source.

Fortunately, the EU LFS permits disaggregating some subgroups of temporary workers from the catchall category, such as persons on probationary contracts, contracts covering a period of training (i.e. apprentices, trainees, research assistants, etc.) and temporary agency workers.

To advance as nuanced an understanding of temporary employment and its component parts as possible, the measure of *temporary employment* for the EU 15 used in Table 5.1 (and throughout this book) encompasses all temporary jobs/work contracts of limited duration excluding probationary contracts, a definition closely resembling the definition of fixed-term work elsewhere. In the analysis developed in Chapter 5, *fixed-term work* is defined as all temporary jobs/work contracts of limited duration (i.e. temporary employment), excluding persons on contracts covering a period of training and persons engaged in temporary agency work, and *temporary agency work* encompasses the employment situations of all persons responding 'yes' to the question 'do you work for a temporary agency work hire firm?'

The rationale for excluding contracts covering a period of training from the definition of fixed-term work is that, as Chapter 5 shows, countries are permitted to exclude them from the provisions of the Directive on Fixed-Term Work and, hence, at a policy level they fall outside the regulations advanced therein (CEU 1999: Annex, cl. 2.2). Despite these attempts at clarification, the operationalization of fixed-term work through the EUROSTAT EU LFS remains imprecise. Still, fixed-term work, as it is measured in Chapter 5, represents a smaller subset of temporary employment in the EU than is often reported in studies using the EU LFS which treat temporary employment and fixed-term work synonymously.

On the limitations of estimates of the number of temporary agency workers derived from the EU LFS, see notes to Table 5.2 below.

Finally, in the United States, the measure for 'temporary' employment in Table 5.1 encompasses all paid employment with a specific end date or specified to last until the completion of a project. According to the CWS, this measure of 'temporary employment' includes work that is paid through a temporary work agency, of fixed duration (fixed term or contract), seasonal, on-call, or completed and paid on a daily basis (i.e. day labour).

*Table 5.2: Temporary Agency Work in the EU 15, 2006^*

SOURCES
The EU 15: Unless otherwise specified, estimates of numbers of temporary agency workers, temporary agency workers as a percentage of total employment, and temporary agency workers as a percentage of temporary employment in each member state in this table are based on the EUROSTAT EU LFS, 1983–2006.
Finland: The absolute number of workers reported for Finland refers to the year 2004 and is drawn from Arrowsmith (2006).

Ireland: The number of workers reported for Ireland is an estimate of full-time equivalents for 2006 and is drawn from CIETT (2006).

Portugal: The number of workers reported for Portugal is an estimate of full-time equivalents for 2004 and is drawn from CIETT (2006).

NOTES

Except where noted, estimates of the number of temporary agency workers refer to absolute numbers. Estimates include all temporary agency workers, including those that are permanent.

As indicated in the notes to Table 5.1 above, the reliability of data estimating the number of temporary agency workers in the EU LFS is questionable for several reasons which are not unique to this source but relate to national sources as well. One reason is the prevalence of temporary agency work among migrant workers as well as frontier workers (e.g. in Luxembourg), whose numbers are difficult to capture. Another reason is that estimates are drawn from self-reports, and temporary workers often have difficulty identifying their employer or confuse their employment situation with self-employment or fixed-term work. Together with a review of estimates provided by both trade unions and employers' associations where they are available, these reasons suggest that the EU LFS underestimates the number of temporary agency workers in many contexts. With regard to the United Kingdom, for example, as Arrowsmith (2006: 41) shows, estimates of the number of temporary agency workers provided through the EU LFS are considerably lower than those provided by both employer and trade union bodies. For example, the Trades Union Congress estimated the number to be 600,000 for 2005 (an estimate resembling that reported by the Confederation of British Industry) and the Recruitment and Employment Council (an industry-specific employer organization) estimated the number to be to be 1,434,098, including workers recruited on a permanent basis. If either of these numbers more accurately reflect the number of temporary agency workers in the UK, their proportion of total employment is considerably higher, rising to 2.6% or 5.1% respectively. The numbers reported in column 1 of Table 5.2 should therefore be approached with caution.

Chapter 6

Table 6.1: Self-Employment as a Percentage of Total Employment, Selected OECD Countries, 1973 and 2006

SOURCES

Australia: For 1973, OECD 2000; for 2006, HILDA Wave F.

Canada: For 1979, OECD 2000; for 2006, StatsCan LFS.

The EU 15: For 1973 (1979 for Greece and the Netherlands), OECD 2000; for 2006, EUROSTAT 1983–2006, LFS.

The United States: For 1973, OECD 2000; for 2006, USBS 2006b.

Table 6.2: OECD Countries and Country Groupings with Highest Rates of Solo Self-Employment as a Percentage of Total Employment, 2006

SOURCES

Australia: ILO, LABORSTA statistical database, 'Employment, Yearly Statistics,' Table 2D 'Total Employment by Employment Status'.

Canada: StatsCan 1983–2006, LFS.

The EU 15, selected (except Germany, Sweden, Luxembourg, and the UK): ILO, LABORSTA statistical database.

Germany: For 2006, Federal Statistical Office of Germany 2006.

Luxembourg: For 2004, Statec Luxembourg 2008: 17.

Sweden: For 2004, Statistics Sweden 2004.

The UK: For 2004, Office of National Statistics, UK 2005: 360.

The United States: For 2002, US Census Bureau 2006: 29.

NOTES

Germany, Luxembourg, the United Kingdom, and the United States do not publish statistics for self-employment that permit disaggregating employer or solo self-employment. For this reason, surveys of business activity recording the number of employees at establishments were used to develop the estimates included in Table 6.2. The estimate for Germany refers to the number of businesses that are 'sole proprietorships'. The estimate for Luxembourg refers to the number of enterprises where there are no employees. The estimate for the UK refers to enterprises without employees, sole proprietorships and partnerships comprising only the self-employed owner-manager(s), and companies comprising only an employee director. Finally, for the United States, the estimate refers to the number of sole owners of businesses/firms without employees.

Bibliography of Primary Sources

National Government Documents

Australia

Australia (1896) *Factories and Shops Act.* Vic. No. 29. Rep. 1900, 64 Vic No. 28, s. 3.
—— Australian House of Representatives (HOR) (1996) *Workplace Relations Act (WRA).* As amended by *Workplace Relations Amendment (WorkChoices) Bill 2005, Workplace Relations Amendment (WorkChoices) Act 2006* (no. 153), *Workplace Relations Amendment (Transition to Forward with Fairness) Bill 2008.* At: <http://www.austlii.edu.au/au/legis/cth/consol_act/wra1996220>.
—— DEWR (Department of Employment and Workplace Relations) (2005) 'Discussion Paper: Proposals for Legislative Reforms in Independent Contracting and Labour Hire Arrangements'. Canberra.
—— (ICB) (2006) *Independent Contractors Bill.* Parliament of the Commonwealth of Australia, HOR.
—— (ICA) (2006) *Independent Contractors Act.* Parliament of the Commonwealth of Australia, HOR. No. 162. At: <http:parlinfo.aph.gov.au/parlInfo/download/legislation/bills/ r2584_act/tocpdf/06101b01.pdf>.
—— (2006) 'Work Choices and State Awards and Agreements: Fact Sheet 3'. Australian Government.
—— (FWB) (2008) *Fair Work Bill.* Parliament of the Commonwealth of Australia, HOR.
—— (FWA) (2009) *Fair Work Act (No. 28, 2009). An Act relating to workplace relations, and for related purposes.* Parliament of the Commonwealth of Australia, HOR.
—— (2009) *Budget Overview, 12 May 2009.* Commonwealth of Australia.
Australia Human Rights and Equal Opportunity Commission (2005) Submission to Senate Employment, Workplace Relations and Education Legislation Committee, Inquiry into the Workplace Relations Amendment (WorkChoices) Bill 2005. Submitted by Jon von Doussa, Sydney.
Australian Democrats (2006) 'Australian Democrats' Minority Report' in *Provisions of the Independent Contractors Bill 2006 and the Workplace Relations Legislation— Amendment (Independent Contractors) Bill 2006.* Senate Education, Employment and Workplace Relations Commission. Canberra. At: <http://www.aph.gov.au/

Senate/Committee/eet_ctte/completed_inquiries/2004–07/contractors06/report/c04.pdf>.

Australian Industrial Relations Commission (AIRC) (1997) *Award Simplification Decision*. H0008 1533/97.

—— (2000) *Metal, Engineering and Associated Industries Award, 1998—Part I*. M1913 1572/00.

—— (2005) *Workplace Relations Act 1996*, s.113. Applications for Variations. C2001/5845.

—— (2005) *Family Provisions* case 2005. Fact Sheet. At: <http://www.airc.gov.au/familyprovisions/fp_fact.pdf>.

—— (2006a) *Federal and State Awards*. Australian Industrial Registry (AIR).

—— (2006b) 'Federal and State Awards—Fact Sheet'. AIR.

Australian Senate Employment, Workplace Relations and Education Legislation Committee (2006) *Provisions of the Independent Contractors Bill 2006 and the Workplace Relations Legislation Amendment (Independent Contractors) Bill 2006*, Aug.

H. v. McKay (Harvester Case) (1907) 2 CAR 1. AIR, Australian Parliamentary Library.

New South Wales (NSW) (1996) *Industrial Relations Act*. No. 17. Office of Industrial Relations.

—— (2003) *Secure Employment* test-case. Industrial Relations Commission.

—— (2003) Testimony of M. Vanderpool, Exhibit 63. *Secure Employment* test-case.

—— (2006) Submission to the Senate Employment, Workplace Relations and Education References and Legislation Committee: Inquiry into the *Independent Contractors Bill 2006* and the *WRA (Independent Contractors) Bill 2006*. 21 July.

Queensland (1999) *Industrial Relations Act*. Office of the Queensland Parliamentary Counsel.

—— (2006) Response to Federal Department of Employment and Workplace Relations Discussion Paper on 'Proposals for Legislative Reforms in Independent Contracting and Labour Hire Arrangements'.

South Australia (1994) *Fair Work Act 1994*. Ver. 1.9.2008. Industrial Relations: Gazette 5.3.

South Australian Industrial Relations Commission (SAIRC) (2002) *Clerks (SA) Award Casual Provisions Appeal* case. SAIRC 39.

Canada

Canada (2003) *The Prime Minister's Task Force on Women Entrepreneurs: Report and Recommendations*. Ottawa.

—— (2006) *Fairness at Work: Federal Labour Standards for the 21st Century*, by H. W. Arthurs. Ottawa: Human Resources and Skills Development Canada.

Ontario (1884) *Ontario Factories Act*. R.S.O. 1884.

Saskatchewan (2006) *Final Report and Recommendations of the Commission on Improving Work Opportunities for Saskatchewan Residents*. Regina: Saskatchewan Ministry of Labour.

Denmark

Denmark (2007) *The Danish Government's Comments and Answers to the Questions Posed in the Commission's Green Paper: Modernising Labour Law to Meet the Challenges of the 21st Century.* COM(2006) 708 final, 22 Nov. Kobenhavn.

France

France (1892) *Millerand-Colliard Law.* Ministry of Labour and Social Security.

Ireland

Ireland (2001) *Employment Status Group Report.* Department of Social and Family Affairs.

Italy

Italy (2007) *Italian Position on the Green Paper of the European Commission on Modernising Labour Law.* Ministero del Lavoro e della Previdenza Sociale.

United Kingdom

United Kingdom (UK) (1891) *Factory and Workshop Act.* HC Deb., 8 Feb. 1895, vol. 30, c. 320.
—— (1901) *Factory and Workshop Act.* HL Deb., 13 Mar. 1902, vol. 104 cc. 1207–14.
—— (1970) *The Equal Pay Act,* c. 41. HMSO.
—— (1975) *The Sex Discrimination Act,* no. 2420. HMSO.
—— (1976) *The Race Relations Act,* no. 3111. HMSO.
—— (1995) *The Disability Discrimination Act.* HMSO.
—— (1996) *Employment Rights Act.* HMSO.
—— (1998) *The National Minimum Wage Act,* c. 39. HMSO.
—— (1998) *The Working Time Regulations,* no. 1833. HMSO.
—— (1999) *Employment Relations Act,* no. 3374. HMSO.
—— (2000) *The Part-time Workers (Prevention of Less Favourable Treatment) Regulations,* no. 1551. HMSO.
—— (2004) *Gangmasters (Licensing) Act,* no. 2857. HMSO.
—— DTI (Department of Trade and Industry) (2007) UK Response: European Commission Green Paper, 'Modernising labour law to meet the challenges of the 21st century'.
UK Government, CBI and TUC (2008) 'Agency Workers: Joint Declaration by the Government, the CBI and the TUC'.

United States

Supreme Court (1905) *Lochner v. New York.* US 45.
Dunlop, J. (Commissioner) (1994) Dunlop Commission on the Future of Worker-Management Relations: Final Report. Washington Secretary of Labor and Secretary of Commerce.

European Union Documents

European Union (EU) Treaties, Parliamentary Resolutions, Committee Reports, etc.

Council of Europe (1961) *European Social Charter.* Turin, 18 Oct.

European Union (1987) *The Single European Act.* Signed in Luxembourg (1986). OJ L 169 of 29.06.1987.

—— (1992) *Treaty of Maastricht (Treaty on European Union).* OJ C 191 of 29.07.1992.

—— (1997) *Treaty of Amsterdam.* Luxembourg. OJ C 340 of 10.11.1997.

European Economic and Social Committee (EESC) (2002) *Opinion of the Economic and Social Committee on the 'Proposal for a Directive of the European Parliament and the Council on Working Conditions for Temporary Workers'.* COM (2002) 149 final— 2002/0072 (COD). Brussels.

EP (European Parliament) (2003) Economically Dependent/Quasi-Subordinate (Parasubordinate) Employment: Legal, Social and Economic Aspects. At: <http://www.europarl.europa.eu/meetdocs/committees/empl/20030619/study_en.pdf>.

—— (2006) *European Parliament Legislative Resolution on the Proposal for a Directive of the European Parliament and of the Council on Services in the Internal Market.* C6–0270/2006—2004/0001(COD)).

—— (2007) *European Parliament Resolution of 11 July 2007 on Modernising Labour Law to Meet the Challenges of the 21st Century* (2023(INI)).

Council of the EU (CEU), Office for Official Publications of the European Communities, Brussels

CEU (1976) *Council Directive 76/207/EEC of 9 February 1976 on the Implementation of the Principle of Equal Treatment for Men and Women as Regards Access to Employment, Vocational Training and Promotion, and Working Conditions.*

—— (1982a) Proposal for a council directive concerning temporary work: Explanatory memorandum. COM(82).

—— (1982b) Proposal for a council directive concerning temporary work. COM(82).

—— (1991) *Council Directive 91/383/EEC of 25 June 1991 Supplementing the Measures to Encourage Improvements in the Safety and Health at Work of Workers with a Fixed-Duration Employment Relationship or a Temporary Employment Relationship.*

—— (1993) *Council Directive 93/104/EC of 23 November 1993 Concerning Certain Aspects of the Organization of Working Time.*

—— (1996) *Directive 96/71/EC of the European Parliament and of the Council of 16 December 1996 Concerning the Posting of Workers in the Framework of the Provision of Services* (Posted Workers Directive).

—— (1998) Presidency Conclusions. Cardiff European Council, 15–16 June.

—— (1999) *Council Directive 1999/70/EC of 28 June 1999 Concerning the Framework Agreement on Fixed-Term Work Concluded by ETUC, UNICE and CEEP.*

—— (2000) Presidency Conclusions. Lisbon European Council, 23–4 March.

—— (2003a) *Council Recommendation of 18 February 2003 Concerning the Improvement of the Protection of the Health and Safety at Work of Self-Employed Workers.*

—— (2003b) *Council Directive 2003/109/EC of 25 November 2003 Concerning the Status of Third-Country Nationals Who are Long-Term Residents.*

—— (2006a) *Directive 2006/123/EC of the European Parliament and of the Council of 12 December on Services in the Internal Market* (Services Directive).

—— (2006b) *Amended Proposal for a Directive of the European Parliament and the Council on Services in the Internal Market.* COM(2006).

—— (2008a) *Draft Directive on Temporary Agency Work (Items debated). Employment, Social Policy, Health and Consumer Affairs: 2876th Council meeting.* Luxembourg: 10414/08 (Presse 166).

—— (2008b) *Directive 2008/104/EC of the European Parliament and of the Council of 22 October 2008 on Temporary Agency Work.*

European Commission (EC), Brussels

EC (1993a) *White Paper: Growth, Competitiveness, Employment: The Challenges and Ways Forward into the 21st Century.* COM(93) 700.

—— (1993b) *Green Paper: European Social Policy—Options for the Union.* COM(93) 551.

—— (1994) *White Paper: European Social Policy—A Way Forward for the Union.* COM (94) 333.

—— (2001) *White Paper: European Governance.* COM(2001) 428.

—— (2002a) *Proposal for a Directive of the European Parliament and the Council on Working Conditions for Temporary Workers.* COM(2002) 149 final.

—— (2002b) *Amended Proposal for a Directive of the European Parliament and the Council on Working Conditions for Temporary Workers.*

—— (2002c) *Taking Stock of Five Years of the EES. Communication from the Commission to the Council, the European Parliament, the Economic and Social Committee and the Committee of the Regions.* COM(2002) 416.

—— (2003a) *Green Paper: Entrepreneurship in Europe.* COM(2003) 27.

—— (2003b) *Communication from the Commission to the Council, the European Parliament, the Economic and Social Committee and the Committee of the Regions: 'The Future of the EES. A Strategy for Full Employment and Better Jobs for All'.* COM(2003).

—— (2004a) *Report From the Commission to the Spring European Council. Delivering Lisbon: Reforms for the Enlarged Union.* COM(2004).

—— (2004b) *Proposal for a Directive of the European Parliament and of the Council on Services in the Internal Market.* COM(2004).

—— (2004c) *Second Career: Overcoming the Obstacles Faced by Dependent Employees Who Want to Become Self-Employed and/or Start their Own Business.* Enterprise-Directorate.

—— (2005a) *Amended Proposal for a Directive of the European Parliament and of the Council Amending Directive 2003/88/EC Concerning Certain Aspects of the Organization of Working Time.*

—— (2005b) *Working Together for Growth and Jobs. A New Start for the Lisbon Strategy. Communication to the Spring European Council of 02 February 2005.* Communication from President Barroso in Agreement with Vice-President Vergeugen. COM(2005) 24 final.

—— (2005c) 'Entrepreneurship Action Plan: Key Action Sheets'. At: <http://ec.europa.eu/enterprise/entrepreneurship/action_plan/doc/keyactionsheets.pdf>.

—— (2006a) Communication from the Commission. *Green Paper Adapting Labour Law to Ensure Flexibility and Security for All.*

—— (2006b) *Green Paper: Modernising Labour Law to Meet the Challenges of the 21st Century.* COM(2006) 708.

—— (2006c) Joint Employment Report 2005/2006. *More and Better Jobs: Delivering the Priorities of the European Employment Strategy.*

—— (2006d) Commission Staff Working Document. *Report by the Commission Services on the Implementation of Council Directive 1999/70/EC of 28 June 1999 Concerning the Framework Agreement on Fixed-term Work Concluded by ETUC, UNICE and CEEP (EU-15).*

—— (2006e) Commission Staff Working Paper. *Report on the Implementation of the Entrepreneurship Action Plan.* SEC(2006) 1132, July 2009.

International Labour Organization (ILO) and its Precursor Documents

Reports, International Labour Conference (ILC) Proceedings, Conventions, Recommendations, and Resolutions (at Geneva unless otherwise noted)

IALL (International Association for Labour Legislation) (1906a) *Convention Respecting the Prohibition of Night Work for Women in Industrial Employment.* Berne.

—— (1906b) *Convention for the Prohibition of the Use of White (Yellow) Phosphorus in the Manufacture of Matches.* Berne.

—— (1906c) *Resolution on Limiting Women's Workday to 10 Hours.* Berne.

ILO (International Labour Organization) (1919a) *C4 Night Work (Women).* Washington.

—— (1919b) *C3 Maternity Protection.* Washington.

—— (1919c) *R4 Lead Poisoning (Women and Children).* Washington.

—— (1919d) *C1 Hours of Work (Industry).* Washington.

—— (1919e) *R2 Reciprocity of Treatment of Foreign Workers.* Washington.

—— (1919f) ILC: Minutes of the Commission on Hours of Labour. 1st Session. Washington.

—— (1919g) *C2 Unemployment.* Washington.

—— (1919h) *R1 Unemployment.* Washington.

—— (1919i) *R6 Prohibition of White Phosphorus.* Washington.

—— (1919j) *International Labour Conference: First Annual Meeting (Proceedings).* Washington.

—— (1919k) *ILC: Organising Committee Report on Unemployment (Item II of the Agenda).* Washington.

——(1921a) The International Protection of Women Workers. *Studies and Reports, Series I*, No. 1.

——(1921b) The International Emigration Commission. *International Labour Review* 4(3): 537–62.

——(1921c) *C14 Weekly Rest (Industry).*

——(1921d) *R18 (Withdrawn) Weekly Rest (Commerce).*

——(1921e) *ILC: Report on the Weekly Rest-Day in Industrial and Commercial Employment* (Report VII).

——(1922) *R19 Migration Statistics.*

——(1923) International Labour Office: *Official Bulletin* 1. Apr. 1919 – Aug. 1920.

——(1924) *R21 Utilisation of Spare Time.*

——(1925a) *C19 Equality of Treatment (Accident Compensation).*

——(1925b) *R25 Equality of Treatment (Accident Compensation).*

——(1927) *ILC: Migration in its Various Forms.* Report.

——(1928a) *C26 Minimum Wage-Fixing Machinery.*

——(1928b) *R30 Minimum Wage-Fixing Machinery.*

——(1928c) *ILC: Report on Minimum Wage Fixing Machinery* (Second Discussion).

——(1929) *Migration Laws and Treaties, Volume III: International Treaties and Conventions.*

——(1930) *C30 Hours of Work (Commerce and Offices).*

——(1932) 'Women's Work under Labour Law: A Survey of Protective Legislation'. *Studies and Reports*, Series I (Employment of Women and Children), No. 2.

——(1933a) *C34 (Shelved) Fee-Charging Employment Agencies.*

——(1933b) *R42 (Withdrawn) Fee-Charging Employment Agencies.*

——(1934a) *C41 (Shelved) Night Work (Women) (Revised).*

——(1934b) *C44 (Shelved) Unemployment Provision.*

——(1934c) *ILC: Record of Proceedings.* 18th Session.

——(1935a) *C47 Forty-Hour Week.*

——(1935b) *ILC: Holidays with Pay.* Fifth Item on the Agenda. Report V.

——(1936a) *C52 Holidays with Pay.*

——(1936b) *R47 Holidays with Pay.*

——(1939) *C66 Migration for Employment.*

——(1944a) *Declaration Concerning the Aims and Purposes of the International Labour Organization* (Philadelphia Declaration). Philadelphia.

——(1944b) *Future Policy, Programme and Status of the International Labour Organisation: First Item on the Agenda (Report I).* Montreal.

——(1944c) *'A New Era': The Philadelphia Conference and the Future of the ILO.* Montreal.

——(1947) *ILC: Freedom of Association and Industrial Relations (Collective Bargaining).* Report (VII).

——(1948a) *C87 Freedom of Association and Protection of the Right to Organise.*

——(1948b) Replies of the Governments. *ILC: Industrial Relations. Freedom of Association and Protection of the Right to Organise.* Report VIII(2).

ILO (1948c) *ILC: Industrial Relations. Application of the Principles of the Right to Organize and to Bargain Collectively, Collective Agreements, Conciliation and Arbitration, and Co-operation between Public Authorities, Employers' and Workers' Organizations: Eighth Item on the Agenda.* Report VIII(2). San Francisco.

—— (1948d) *Partial Revision of the Convention (No. 4) Concerning Employment of Women During the Night (1919) and of the Convention (No. 14) Concerning Employment of Women During the Night (Revised 1934).* San Francisco.

—— (1948e) *C89 Night Work (Women) (Revised).*

—— (1948f) *C88 Organisation of the Employment Service.*

—— (1948g) *R83 Organisation of the Employment Service.*

—— (1949a) *C98 Right to Organise and Collective Bargaining.*

—— (1949b) *C97 Migration for Employment (Revised).*

—— (1949c) *R86 Migration for Employment (Revised).*

—— (1949d) *C96 Fee-Charging Employment Agencies (Revised).*

—— (1951) *C100 Equal Remuneration.*

—— (1952a) *C102 Social Security (Minimum Standards).*

—— (1952b) *ILC: Minimum Standards of Social Security: Fifth Item on the Agenda.* Report V(a)(2).

—— (1952c) *C103 Maternity Protection (Revised).*

—— (1952d) *ILC: Record of Proceedings. Revision of the Maternity Protection Convention 1919 (Item 3).*

—— (1954a) *R98 Holidays with Pay.*

—— (1954b) *ILC: Appendix IV. Fourth Item on the Agenda: Discrimination in the Field of Employment & Occupation.*

—— (1956) *Discrimination in the Field of Employment and Occupation.* Report VII(1).

—— (1957) *Discrimination in the Field of Employment and Occupation.* Report VII(2).

—— (1958a) *C111 Discrimination (Employment and Occupation).*

—— (1958b) *R111 Discrimination (Employment and Occupation).*

—— (1958c) *ILC: Fourth Item on the Agenda: Discrimination in the Field of Employment and Occupation.* Report IV.

—— (1963) *ILC: Women Workers in a Changing World: Sixth Item on the Agenda.* Report VI(1+2).

—— (1965) *R123 Employment (Women with Family Responsibilities).*

—— (1966) Memorandum Sent by the ILO to the Ministry of Health & Social Affairs of Sweden. International Labour Office. *Official Bulletin* 49(3).

—— (1970) *C132 Holidays with Pay (Revised).*

—— (1975a) *C143 Concerning Migrations in Abusive Conditions & the Promotion of Equality of Opportunity and Treatment of Migrant Workers.*

—— (1975b) *Declaration on Equality of Opportunity and Treatment of Women Workers.*

—— (1975c) *International Programme for the Improvement of Working Conditions and Environment (PIACT).*

—— (1981a) *C156 Workers with Family Responsibilities.*

—— (1981b) *R165 Workers with Family Responsibilities.*

—— (1984) *ILC: Evaluation of the International Programme for the Improvement of Working Conditions and Environment (PIACT)*. Seventh Item on the Agenda. Report VII.

—— (1985) *Resolution on Equal Opportunities for Men and Women in Employment.*

—— (1988) *C168 Employment Promotion and Protection Against Unemployment.*

—— (1990a) *C171 Night Work.*

—— (1990b) *Resolution Concerning Self-Employment Promotion.* Committee on Self-Employment.

—— (1990c) *Protocol of 1990 to the Night Work (Women) Convention (Revised), 1948.*

—— (1993a) *ILC: Part-Time Work.* Report V(1).

—— (1993b) *ILC: Part-Time Work.* Report V(2).

—— (1994a) *C175 Part-Time Work.*

—— (1994b) *R182 Part-Time Work.*

—— (1996a) *C177 Home Work.*

—— (1996b) *R184 Home Work.*

—— (1996c) *General Survey: Equality in Employment and Occupation.* Report III (Committee of Experts).

—— (1997a) *C181 Private Employment Agencies.*

—— (1997b) *R188 Private Employment Agencies.*

—— (1997c) *World Employment Report 1996/97: National Policies in a Global Context.* Geneva.

—— (1998a) *Declaration on Fundamental Principles and Rights at Work* (Social Declaration).

—— (1998b) *ILC: Committee on Contract Labour. Addendum.* Report V(2B).

—— (1998c) *ILC: Committee on Contract Labour.* Report V(2B).

—— (1998d) *Constitution of the International Labour Organization and Standing Orders of the International Labour Conference* (February).

—— (1999) *Decent Work.* Report of the Director General.

—— (2000a) *C183 Maternity Protection.*

—— (2000b) *R191 Maternity Protection.*

—— (2000c) *Meeting of Experts on Workers in Situations Needing Protection (The Scope of the Employment Relationship):* Basic Technical Document.

—— (2001) *ILC: Information and Reports on the Application of Conventions and Recommendations, Third Item on the Agenda.* Report III(IB).

—— (2003a) *ILC: The Scope of the Employment Relationship.* Report V.

—— (2003b) *Report of the Committee on the Employment Relationship.*

—— (2004) *ILC: Date, Place and Agenda of the 95th Session (2006) of the International Labour Conference: Second Item on the Agenda.*

—— (2005) *Application of International Labour Standards: Report of the Committee of Experts on the Application of Conventions and Recommendations.*

—— (2006a) *R198 Employment Relationship.*

—— (2006b) *The Employment Relationship.* Report V(2A+B).

ILO (2006c) *ILC: Provisional Record. The Employment Relationship: Report of the Committee of the Employment Relationship.*

—— (2008) *ILO Declaration on Social Justice for a Fair Globalization.* Adopted by the ILC 97th Session, 10 June.

League of Nations (1919a) *League of Nations Report on The Eight-Hours Day or Forty-Eight Hours Week (Item I of the Agenda).* Prepared by the Organising Committee for the ILC.

—— (1919b) *Treaty of Versailles.*

—— (1919c) *Report on the Employment of Women and Children and the Berne Conventions of League of Nations, 1906.* Prepared by the Organising Committee for the ILC, Washington.

United Nations (UN) Documents

UN (1945) *Charter of the United Nations* (Founding Charter).

—— (1948) *Universal Declaration of Human Rights.* General Assembly Resolution 217 A (III).

—— (1979) *Convention on the Elimination of All Forms of Discrimination against Women.* Division for the Advancement of Women, Department of Economic and Social Affairs. New York.

—— (1990) *Convention on the Protection of the Rights of All Migrant Workers and Members of their Families.* General Assembly Resolution 45/158.

Primary Statistical Sources

Australian Bureau of Statistics (ABS) (1978–95) *The Labour Force Australia, 1978–1995,* Cat. No. 6204.0.

—— (1983–2006) *Labour Force Survey (LFS),* Cat. No. 6291.0.55.001.

—— (1984–1987) *Employment Benefits Australia, 1984–1987,* Cat. No. 6334.0.

—— (1989, 1991–1995, 1997) *Weekly Earnings of Employees (Distribution), Australia,* Cat. No. 6310.0.

—— (1990–2006) *Weekly Earnings of Employees (Distribution), Australia,* Cat. No. 6310.0.

—— (1996) *Trade Union Members, Australia (August),* Cat. No. 6325.0.

—— (1996–2002) *The Labour Force Australia, 1996–2002,* Cat. No. 6203.0.

—— (1997, 2006) *Time Use Survey (TUS), 'How Australians Use their Time'.* Cat. No. 4153.0.

—— (1998–2006) *Employee Earnings, Benefits and Trade Union Membership, Australia,* Cat. No. 6310.0.

—— (2003–2006) *The Labour Force Australia, 2003–2006,* Cat. No. 6202.0.

—— (2006) *Alternative Working Arrangements (March to May 1982),* Cat. No. 6341.0.

—— (2007) *Yearbook Australia,* No. 1310.0.

Australian Household, Income and Labour Dynamics Survey (HILDA) (2006) *Wave F.*
——(2004) *Wave D.*

CIETT (2006) *Agency Work Statistics for 2006.* Accessed 15 Dec. 2008. At: <http://www.ciett.org/fileadmin/templates/ciett/docs/CIETT_2006_Statistics.pdf>.

EUROSTAT (1983–2006) *European Union Labour Force Survey (EU LFS), 1983–2006.* EU.

——(2004a) *National Tables.* Working Paper on Comparative Time Use Statistics Database. EU. At: <http://circa.europa.eu/Public/irc/dsis/tus/library?l=/comparable_statistics&vm=detailed&sb=Title>.

——(2004b) *How Europeans Spend their Time—Everyday Life of Women and Men.* EU.

——(2005) *Comparable Time Use Statistics—National Tables from 10 European Countries.* EU.

——(2006) *The Non-Financial Business Economy in the EU25: One in Six Workers Self-Employed, Two-Thirds of Persons Employed in Small and Medium Businesses.* EU.

——(2007) *EU Labour Force Survey Database User Guide.* EU.

Australian Bureau of Statistics (ABS) (2008) *EU LFS User Guide.* EU.

Federal Statistical Office of Germany (2006) *Taxpayers, Their Deliveries and Other Performances 2006 by Economic Sections and Legal Forms: Business Liable to Pay Turnover Tax.* Accessed 8 Dec. 2008. At: <http://www.destatis.de/jetspeed/portal/_ns:YWl3bXMtY29udGVudDo6Q29udGVudFBvcnRsZXQ6OjF8ZDF8ZW-NoYW5nZVdpbmRvd1N0YXRlPT9dHJ1ZQ__/cms/Sites/destatis/Internet/EN/Content/Statistics/FinanzenSteuern/Steuern/Umsatzsteuer/Tabellen/Content100/SteuerpflichtigeRechtsformenGK,templateId=renderPrint.psml>.

ILO Bureau of Labour Statistics, LABORSTA statistical database. *Main Statistics (Annual).* Multidimensional Table 2D: Total Employment by Status in Employment, 1969–2007. Accessed 8 Dec. 2008. At: <http://laborsta.ilo.org/data_topic_E.html>.

King, M., S. Ruggles, T. Alexander, D. Leicach, and M. Sobek (2006) *Integrated Public Use Microdata Series, Current Population Survey: Version 2.0.* (Machine-readable database). Minneapolis, MN: Minnesota Population Center [producer and distributor]. At: <http://cps.ipums.org/cps/citation.shtml>.

OECD (Organisation for Economic Co-operation and Development) (2006) Multidimensional table, Employment by Permanency of the Job.

——(2007) Multidimensional table, Employment and Labour Market Statistics, Full-Time/Part-Time Employment Based on a Common Definition.

Office of National Statistics, UK.(2004) *UK 2005: Official Yearbook of the UK of Great Britain and Northern Ireland.* London.

Romeyn, J. (1992) *Flexible Working Time: Part-time and Casual Employment.* Industrial Relations Research Monograph No. 1. Department of Industrial Relations, Canberra.

Statec Luxembourg (2008) *Luxembourg in Figures: September 2008.* Accessed 12 Dec. 2008. At: <www.statistiques.public.lu/fr/publications/horizontales/luxChiffresEN/luxChiffresEN.pdf>.

Statistics Canada (StatsCan) (1983–2006) *LFS 1983–2006*. CANSIM, Table Nos. V1540489, V1540508, V13682073.

—— (1989) *General Social Survey (GSS) on Education and Work, Cycle 4, 1989*. GSS Division. Ottawa: Statistics Canada. Data Liberation Initiative, 14 Aug. 1990. At: <http://r1.chass.utoronto.ca/sdaweb/html/gss.htm>.

—— (1990) *GSS on Family and Friends, Cycle 5, 1990*. GSS Division. Ottawa: Statistics Canada. Data Liberation Initiative, 4 June 1991. At: <http://r1.chass.utoronto.ca/sdaweb/html/gss.htm>.

—— (1991) *Survey of Work Arrangements*. Ottawa: Statistics Canada. Data Liberation Initiative, Mar. 1998. At: <http://r1.chass.utoronto.ca/sdaweb/html/was.htm>.

—— (1992) *GSS on Time Use, Cycle 7, 1992*. GSS Division. Ottawa: Statistics Canada. Data Liberation Initiative, 30 Sep. 1993. At: <http://r1.chass.utoronto.ca/sdaweb/html/gss.htm>.

—— (1993) *GSS on Personal Risk, Cycle 8, 1993*. GSS Division. Ottawa: Statistics Canada. Data Liberation Initiative, 8 Sep. 1994. At: <http://r1.chass.utoronto.ca/sdaweb/html/gss.htm>.

—— (1994) *GSS on Education, Work, and Retirement, Cycle 9, 1994*. GSS Division. Ottawa: Statistics Canada. Data Liberation Initiative, 4 Oct. 1995. At: <http://r1.chass.utoronto.ca/sdaweb/html/gss.htm>.

—— (1995) *Survey of Work Arrangements*. Ottawa: Statistics Canada. Data Liberation Initiative. Mar. 1998. At: <http://r1.chass.utoronto.ca/sdaweb/html/was.htm>.

—— (2001) *Census of Canada*. Public Use Microdata. Files for Individuals. Revision 2. Ottawa. Data Liberation Initiative (STC 95M0016XCB).

—— (2006) 'General Social Survey: Paid and Unpaid Work, 2005'. *The Daily*, 19 July 2006.

Statistics Denmark (2006) *Business Demography by Type of Ownership and Unit*. Multi-dimensional table, Demo 5, 2001–2006. Statbank Denmark. Accessed: 8 Dec. 2008. At: <http://www.statistikbanken.dk/statbank5a/SelectVarVal/Define.asp?Maintable=DEMO5&PLanguage=1>.

Statistics Sweden (2004) *Labour Force Survey (LFS)*, Table 4, 2004. Stockholm.

United States Census Bureau, Department of Commerce, Economics and Statistics Administration (2006) Nonemployer Firms, Primary Source of Income. Table 8: Statistics for Owners of Respondent Firms by Whether the Business Provided the Owner's Primary Source of Personal Income and Business Interest, 2002. Characteristics of Business Owners: 2002. Economic Census, Company Statistics Series, issued Sept. 2006.

United States Department of Labor, Bureau of Labor Statistics (USBS) (1998–2008) *Current Population Survey, (Unadjusted) Employed, Usually Work Full Time*. Series ID: LNU02500000. Accessed 8 Dec. 2008. At: <http://data.bls.gov/PDQ/servlet/SurveyOutputServlet?series_id=LNU02500000>.

—— (2001) *Current Population Survey*. Labor Force Statistics.

—— (2005) *US Contingent Work Supplement (CWS) of CPS*. Custom Tabulation

—— (2006a) *Current Population Survey (CPS)*. Series Id:LNS12000000, LNS12000002, LNS12500000.

—— (2006b) *Current Population Survey (CPS)*. Custom Tabulation.

—— (2006) *American Time-Use Survey (ATUS)*.

—— (2008) *1998–2008 Current Population Survey (CPS), (Unadjusted) Employment Level*. Series ID: LNU02000000. Accessed 8 Dec. 2008. At: <http://data.bls.gov/PDQ/servlet/SurveyOutputServlet?series_id=LNU02000000>.

—— (2008) Labour Force Statistics 2006–7: Weekly Earnings Data. *Current Population Survey (CPS)*. Accessed 26 Jan. 2008. At: <http://www.bls.gov/cps/cpsaat37.pdf>.

—— (2008) Union Membership (Annual): Economic News Release (Jan.). Accessed 26 Jan. 2009. <http://www.bls.gov/news.release/union2.toc.htm>.

—— (2008) Employee Benefits in the United States (Mar.). Accessed 28 Jan. 2009. <http://www.bls.gov/news.release/pdf/ebs2.pdf>.

United States Department of Labor, Bureau of Labor Statistics (USBS) (2008) *Profile of the Working Poor, 2006*. Report 1006 (Aug.). Accessed 28 Jan. 2009. At: <http://www.bls.gov/cps/cpswp2006.pdf>.

—— (2008) *Highlights of Women's Earnings in 2007*. Report 1008 (Oct.). Accessed 26 Jan. 2009. At: <http://www.bls.gov/cps/cpswom2007.pdf>.

Bibliography of Secondary Sources

Abraham, K. (1990) 'Restructuring the Employment Relationship: The Growth of Market-Mediated Employment Relationships', in K. Abraham and R.B. McKersie, eds., *New Developments in the Labor Market: Toward a New Institutional Paradigm.* Boston, MA: MIT, 85–119.

ABS (Australian Bureau of Statistics) (1988) *Alternative Working Arrangements.* Canberra: Cat. no. 6341.0.

Abu-Laban, Y. and C. Gabriel (2002) *Selling Diversity: Immigration, Multiculturalism, Employment Equity and Globalization.* Peterborough: Broadview Press.

ACCI (Australian Chamber of Commerce and Industry) (2005) Submission to House of Representatives Standing Committee on Employment, Workplace Relations and Workforce Participation. *Inquiry Into Independent Contractors and Labour Hire Arrangements.* ACCI.

Acker, J. (1988) 'Class, Gender, and the Relations of Distribution'. *Signs* 13: 473–97.

ACTU (Australian Council of Trade Unions) (2006) *Industrial Relations Legislation Policy.* Melbourne: ACTU.

Aglietta, M. (1979) *A Theory of Capitalist Regulation: The US Experience.* London: NLB.

Albarracín, D. (2004) *New Agreement Signed for Temporary Employment Agencies.* Brussels: EIRO (European Industrial Relations Observatory).

—— (2005) *Spain's Contribution to 'Temporary Agency Work in an Enlarged European Union'.* Brussels: EIRO.

Albo, G. (1994) 'Competitive Austerity and the Impasse of Capitalist Employment Policy', in R. Miliband and L. Panitch, eds., *The Socialist Register 1994.* London: Merlin Press, 144–70.

Alcock, A. (1971) *History of the International Labour Organisation.* New York: Octagon Books.

Aliaga, C. and K. Winqvist (2003) 'How Women and Men Spend their Time: Results from 13 European Countries'. *Statistics in Focus: Population and Social Conditions (Theme 3).* Eurostat. Cat. no: KS-NK-03–012-EN-N.

ALP (Australian Labor Party) (2007a) *Forward with Fairness: Labor's Plan for Fairer and More Productive Australian Workplaces.* Canberra City: ALP. At: <http://www.alp.org.au/download/now/fwf_finala.pdf>.

ALP (2007b) *Forward With Fairness: Policy Implementation Plan.* Canberra City: ALP. At: <http://www.alp.org.au/download/now/070828_dp_forward_with_fairness___policy_implementation_plan.pdf>.

—— (2007c) *Fresh Ideas for Work and Family.* With J. Gillard. Canberra City: ALP. At: <http://www.alp.org.au/download/now/20071016_work_and_family_xx.pdf>.

—— (2007d) *Pre-election Platform of October 2007.* Canberra City: ALP. At: <http://www.alp.org.au/download/now/2007_national_platform.pdf>.

Alston, P. (2005) 'Facing up to the Complexities of the ILO's Core Labour Standards Agenda'. *European Journal of International Law* 16(3): 467–80.

—— and J. Heenan (2004) 'Shrinking the International Labour Code'. *New York University International Law and Policy Journal* 36(2/3): 221–64.

Ambrosini, M. and C. Barone (2007) *Employment and Working Conditions of Migrant Workers.* Dublin: Eurofound, MZES, University of Milan.

Anderson, M. and M.M. Winslow (1951) 'International Congresses of Working Women'. *Woman at Work: The Autobiography of Mary Anderson as told to Mary M. Winslow.* Minneapolis: University of Minnesota Press, 125–33.

André, I. and P. Areosa Feio (2006) 'Temporary Agency Work—National Reports: Portugal'. Eurofound. At: <http://www.eurofound.europa.eu/pubdocs/2002/33/en/1/ef0233en.pdf>.

Anxo, D. (2002) 'Time Allocation and the Division of Work in France and Sweden', in P. Auer and B. Gazier, eds., *The Future of Work, Employment and Social Protection: The Dynamics of Change and the Protection of Workers.* Geneva: Proceedings of the France/ILO Symposium 2002, International Institute for Labour Studies, 99–108.

—— J.-Y. Boulin, and C. Fagan (2006) 'Decent Working Time in a Life-Course Perspective', in J.-Y. Boulin, M. Lallement, J. C. Messenger, and F. Michon, eds., *Decent Working Time—New Trends, New Issues.* Geneva: ILO, 93–122.

—— C. Erhel, and S. Carcillo (2001) 'Aggregate Impact of Active Labour Market Policy in France and Sweden: A Regional Approach', in J. de Koning and H. Mosley, eds., *Labour Market Policy and Unemployment: Impact and Process Evaluations in Selected European Countries.* Cheltenham: Edward Elgar, 49–76.

—— C. Erhel, and J. J. Schippers, eds. (2006) *Labour Market Transitions and Time Adjustment over the Life Course.* Amsterdam: Dutch University Press.

—— C. Fagan, D. McCann, S. Lee, and J. C. Messenger (2004) 'Introduction: Working Time in Industrialized Countries', in J. C. Messenger, ed., *Working Time and Workers' Preferences in Industrialized Countries.* Abingdon: Routledge, 1–9.

Appelbaum, E. (2001) 'Transformation of Work and Employment and New Insecurities', in P. Auer and C. Daniel, eds., *The Future of Work, Employment and Social Protection: The Search for New Securities in a World of Growing Uncertainties.* Geneva: Proceedings of the France/ILO Symposium 2001, International Institute for Labour Studies, 17–36.

—— (2002a) 'Introductory Remarks: Shared Work/Valued Care: New Norms for Organizing Market Work and Unpaid Care Work', in P. Auer and B. Gazier, eds., *The Future of Work, Employment and Social Protection: The Dynamics of Change and the Protection of Workers.* Geneva: Proceedings of the France/ILO Symposium 2002, International Institute for Labour Studies, 93–8.

——(2002b) 'Synthesis', in P. Auer and B. Gazier, eds., *The Future of Work, Employment and Social Protection: The Dynamics of Change and the Protection of Workers.* Geneva: Proceedings of the France/ILO Symposium 2002, International Institute for Labour Studies, 141–5.

——T. Bailey, P. Berg, and A.L. Kalleberg (2002) 'Shared Work/Valued Care: New Norms for Organizing Market Work and Unpaid Care Work', in H. Mosley, J. O'Reilly, and K. Schömann, eds., *Labour Markets, Gender and Institutional Change: Essays in Honour of Günther Schmid.* Cheltenham: Edward Elgar, 136–65.

——A. Bernhardt and R. Mumane (2003) *Low Wage America: How Employers Are Reshaping Economic Opportunity in the Workplace.* New York: Russell Sage Foundation.

Arat-Koc, S. (1990) 'Importing Housewives: Non-citizen Domestic Workers and the Crisis of the Domestic Sphere in Canada', in M. Luxton, H. Rosenberg, and S. Arat-Koc, eds., *Through the Kitchen Window.* Toronto: Garamond Press, 81–103.

——(2006) 'Whose Social Reproduction? Transnational Motherhood and Challenges to Feminist Political Economy', in M. Luxton and K. Bezanson, eds., *Social Reproduction: Feminist Political Economy Challenges Neo-liberalism.* Montreal and Kingston: McGill-Queen's University Press, 75–92.

Archibald, K. (1970) *Sex and the Public Service.* Ottawa: Queen's Printer.

Arendt, H. (1958) *The Human Condition.* Chicago: University of Chicago Press.

Armstrong, H. and P. Armstrong (1983) 'Beyond Sexless Class and Classless Sex: Towards Feminist Marxism'. *Studies in Political Economy* 10: 7–43.

————(1994) *The Double Ghetto: Canadian Women and their Segregated Work,* 3rd edn. Toronto: McClelland and Stewart.

————and M. P. Connelly (1997) 'The Many Forms of Privatization'. *Studies in Political Economy* 53: 3–9.

Arrowsmith, J. (2006) *Temporary Agency Work in an Enlarged European Union.* Luxembourg: Eurofound.

Arthurs, H. W. (1965) 'The Dependent Contractor: A Study of the Legal Problems of Countervailing Power'. *University of Toronto Law Journal* 16: 89–117.

Ashiagbor, D. (2006) 'Promoting Precariousness? The Response of EU Employment Policies to Precarious Work', in J. Fudge and R. Owens, eds., *Precarious Work, Women, and the New Economy: The Challenge to Legal Norms.* Portland, OR: Hart Publishing, 77–98.

Atkinson, J. (1984) 'Manpower Strategies for Flexible Organisations'. *Personnel Management* August: 28–31.

Auer, P. and S. Cazes (2001) 'The Resilience of the Long-Term Employment Relationship: Evidence from Industrialised Countries'. *International Labour Review* 193(4): 379–410.

Autor, D. H., L. F. Katz, and M. S. Kearney (2006) 'The Polarization of the U.S. Labor Market'. NBER Working Papers no. JEL No. J3, D3, O3. At: <http://www.economics.harvard.edu/faculty/katz/files/akk-polarization-nber-txt.pdf>.

Baines, D. and N. Sharma (2002) 'Migrant Workers as Non-citizens: The Case against Citizenship as a Social Policy Concept'. *Studies in Political Economy* 69(Autumn): 75–107.

Barker, K. and K. Christensen, eds. (1998) *Contingent Work: American Employment Relations in Transition*. Ithaca, NY: ILR Press.

Barnard, C. (2004) 'The Personal Scope of the Employment Relationship'. The Japan Institute for Labour Policy and Training. At: <http://www.jil.go.jp/english/documents/JILPTRNo1.pdf>.

—— and S. Deakin (1999) 'A Year of Living Dangerously? EC Social Rights, Employment Policy, and EMU'. *Industrial Relations Journal* 30(4): 355–72.

Bartlett, K. T., A. Harris, and D. Rhode (2002) *Gender and Law: Theory, Doctrine, Commentary*, 3rd edn. New York: Aspen Law & Business.

Baxter, J. (2002) 'Patterns of Change and Stability in the Gender Division of Labour in Australia, 1986–1997'. *Journal of Sociology* 38(4): 399–424.

—— B. Hewitt and M. Western (2005) 'Post-familial Families and the Domestic Division of Labour'. *Journal of Comparative Family Studies* 36: 583–600.

Beck, U. (1992) *Risk Society: Towards a New Modernity*. London: Sage Publishing.

BECTU (Broadcasting Entertainment Cinematograph and Theatre Union) (2007) *European Commission Green Paper—Modernising Labour Law to Meet the Challenges of the 21st Century*. BECTU Response.

Bell, S. G. and K. M. Offen, eds. (1983) *Women, the Family and Freedom: The Debate in Documents*. Stanford, CA: Stanford University Press.

Belous, R. (1989) *The Contingent Economy: The Growth of the Temporary, Part-Time and Subcontracted Workforce*. Washington: National Planning Association.

Bendel, M. (1982) 'The Dependent Contractor: An Unnecessary and Flawed Development in Canadian Labour Law'. *University of Toronto Law Journal* 32: 374–411.

Beneria, L. (2008) 'The Crisis of Care, International Migration, and Public Policy'. *Feminist Economics* 14(3): 1–21.

Benyon, H., D. Grimshaw, J. Rubery, and K. Ward (2002) *Managing Employment Change: The New Realities of Work*. Oxford: Oxford University Press.

Berg, A. (2005) *Sweden's Contribution to 'Temporary Agency Work in an Enlarged European Union'*. Brussels: EIRO.

Bergmann, B. R. (2008) 'Long Leaves, Child Well-Being, and Gender Equality'. *Politics and Society* 36(3): 350–9.

Berkovitch, N. (1999) *From Motherhood to Citizenship: Women's Rights and International Organizations*. Baltimore: Johns Hopkins University Press.

Bernier, J. (2006) *Social Protection for Non-traditional Workers outside the Employment Relationship*. Quebec City: Federal Labour Standards Review Commission.

259

Bernstein, S., K. Lippel, E. Tucker, and L. F. Vosko (2006) 'Precarious Employment and the Law's Flaws: Identifying Regulatory Failure and Securing Effective Protection for Workers', in Vosko, ed. (2006b), 203–20.

Bettio, F. and P. Villa (1989) 'Non-wage Work and Disguised Wage Employment in Italy', in G. R. J. Rodgers, ed., *Precarious Jobs in Labour Market Regulation: The Growth of Atypical Employment in Western Europe*. Geneva: International Institute for Labour Studies, 149–78.

Biagi, M. (2000) 'The Impact of European Employment Strategy on the Role of Labour Law and Industrial Relations'. *International Journal of Comparative Labour Law and Industrial Relations* 16(2): 155–73.

Biffl, G., and J. Isaac (2002) 'How Effective are the ILO's Labour Standards under Globalisation?' *International Industrial Relations Association/CIRA 4th Regional Congress of the Americas Centre for Industrial Relations*. Toronto: University of Toronto.

Bittman, M. (1999) 'Parenthood without Penalty: Time Use and Public Policy in Australia and Finland'. *Feminist Economics* 5(3): 27–42.

—— P. England, L. Sayer, and N. Folbre (2003) 'When Does Gender Trump Money? Bargaining and Time in Household Work'. *American Journal of Sociology* 109: 186–214.

Block, R. N. and K. Roberts (2000) 'A Comparison of Labour Standards in the United States and Canada'. *Relations Industrielles/Industrial Relations* 55(2): 273–307.

Böheim, R. and U. Muehlberger (2006) 'Dependent Forms of Self-Employment in the UK: Identifying Workers on the Border between Employment and Self-Employment'. Bonn: IZA Discussion Paper No. 1963.

Böhning, W. R. (1976) 'The ILO and Contemporary International Economic Migration'. *International Migration Review* 10(2): 147–56.

—— (1991) 'The ILO and the New UN Convention on Migrant Workers: The Past and Future'. *International Migration Review* 25(4): 698–709.

—— (2003) 'The Protection of Temporary Migrants by Conventions of the ILO and the UN'. Workshop on Temporary Migration: Assessment and Practical Proposals for Overcoming Protection Gaps. Geneva, 18–19 Sept.

Bonefeld, W. (2001) 'European Monetary Union: Ideology and Class', in W. Bonefeld, ed., *The Politics of Europe: Monetary Union and Class*. Basingstoke: Palgrave Macmillan, 64–106.

Bosch, G. (1999) 'Working Time: Tendencies and Emerging Issues'. *International Labour Review* 138(2): 131–50.

—— (2004) 'Towards a New Standard Employment Relationship in Western Europe'. *British Journal of Industrial Relations* 42(2): 617–36.

—— (2006) 'Working Time and the Standard Employment Relationship', in J.-Y. Boulin, M. Lallement, J. C. Messenger, and F. Michon, eds., *Decent Working Time: New Trends, New Issues*. Geneva: ILO, 41–64.

—— P. Dawkins, and F. Michon (1994) 'Overview', in G. Bosch, P. Dawkins and F. Michon, eds., *Times are Changing: Working Time in 14 Industrialized Countries*. Geneva: International Institute for Labour Studies.

Bosniak, L. S. (2002) *The Citizen and the Alien: Dilemmas of Contemporary Membership*. Princeton: Princeton University Press.

Boulin, J.-Y. (2006) 'Local Time Policies in Europe', in D. Perrons, C. Fagan, L. McDowell, K. Ray, and K. Ward, eds., *Gender Divisions and Working Time in the New Economy: Changing Patterns of Work, Care and Public Policy in Europe and North America*. Cheltenham: Edward Elgar, 193–206.

——M. Lallement, and F. Michon (2006) 'Decent Working Time in Industrialized Countries: Issues, Scopes and Paradoxes', in J.-Y. Boulin, M. Lallement, J. C. Messenger, and F. Michon, eds., *Decent Working Time: New Trends, New Issues*. Geneva: ILO, 13–40.

Boushey, H., S. Fremstad, R. Gragg, and M. Waller (2007) 'Understanding Low-Wage Work in the United States'. Washington: Center for Economic Policy and Research and the Mobility Agenda.

Boxer, M. (1986) 'Protective Legislation and Home Industry: The Marginalization of Women Workers in Late Nineteenth- and Early Twentieth-Century France'. *Journal of Social History* 20: 45–65.

Boyd, M. and D. Pikkov (2005) 'Gendering Migration, Livelihood and Entitlements: Migrant Women in Canada and the United States'. United Nations Research Institute for Social Development. At: <http://www.unrisd.org/publications/opgp6>.

Brannen, J. (2005) 'Time and the Negotiation of Work–Family Boundaries: Autonomy or Illusion?' *Time and Society* 14: 113–31.

Briggs, C. (2005) *Federal IR Reform: The Shape of Things to Come*. Sydney: University of New South Wales.

——and J. Buchanan (2005) 'Work, Commerce and the Law: A New Australian Model?' *The Australian Economic Review* 38(2): 182–91.

Brodie, J. (2002) 'Three Stories of Canadian Citizenship', in R. Adamoski, D. E. Chunn, and R. Menzies, eds., *Contesting Canadian Citizenship: Historical Readings*. Toronto: Broadview Press, 43–66.

Brooks, B. T. (2003) *Labour Law in Australia*. The Hague: Kluwer Law International.

Broughton, A. (2004) 'Controversy over Draft Directive on Services'. EIRO: EU0407206F, 21 July. At: <http://www.eurofound.europa.eu/eiro/2004/07/feature/eu0407206f.htm>.

Brown, W. (2003) 'Neoliberalism and the End of Liberal Democracy'. *Theory and Event* 1(7): 1–43.

Brubaker, R. (1989) 'Membership without Citizenship: The Economic and Social Rights of Non-citizens', in W. R. Brubaker, ed., *Immigration and the Politics of Citizenship in Europe and North America*. Lanham, MD: University Press of America, 145–62.

——(1994) 'Are Immigration Control Efforts Really Failing?' in W. Cornelius, P. Martin, and J. Hollifield, eds., *Controlling Immigration: A Global Perspective*. Stanford, CA: Stanford University Press, 227–31.

Bryson, V. (2003) 'Socialist Feminism in Britain and the United States; Marxist Feminism in Germany', in *Feminist Political Theory: An Introduction*. Basingstoke: Palgrave Macmillan, 94–113.

Büchtemann, C. F. and S. Quack (1990) 'How Precarious Is "Non-Standard" Employment? Evidence for West Germany'. *Cambridge Journal of Economics* 14: 315–29.

Buckley, K. and T. Wheelwright (1988) *No Paradise for Workers: Capitalism and the Common People in Australia 1788–1914*. Melbourne: Oxford University Press.

Burchell, B. J. (2006) 'Work Intensification in the UK', in C. Fagan, D. Perrons, L. McDowell, K. Ray, and K. Ward, eds., *Gender Divisions and Working Time in the New Economy*. Cheltenham: Edward Elgar, 21–34.

—— S. Deakin, and S. Honey (1999) *The Employment Status of Workers in Non-standard Employment*. London: Department of Trade and Industry.

Burda, M. C., D. S. Hamermesh, and P. Weil (2006) 'The Distribution of Total Work in the EU and US'. *Discussion Paper Series*. Bonn: Institute for the Study of Labor.

—— —— —— (2007) 'Total Work, Gender and Social Norms'. *Discussion Paper Series*. Bonn: Institute for the Study of Labor.

Burgess, J. (2005) 'Exploring Job Quality and Part-Time Work in Australia'. *Labour and Industry* 15(3): 29–40.

—— and I. Campbell (1998) 'The Nature and Dimensions of Precarious Employment in Australia'. *Labour and Industry* 8(3): 5–21.

—— and J. Connell, eds. (2004) *International Perspectives on Temporary Agency Work*. London: Routledge.

Buroway, M. (1976) 'The Functions and Reproduction of Migrant Labor: Comparative Material from Southern Africa and the United States'. *American Journal of Sociology* 81: 1050–87.

—— (1979) *Manufacturing Consent: Changes in the Labor Process under Monopoly Capitalism*. Chicago: University of Chicago Press.

Burri, S. (2005) 'Working Time Adjustment Policies in the Netherlands'. *Working Time for Working Families: Europe and the United States*. Washington: Friedrich-Ebert-Stiftung, American University Washington College of Law.

—— (2006) 'Flexibility and Security, Working Time, and Work-Family Policies', in J. Fudge and R. Owens, eds., *Precarious Work, Women and the New Economy: The Challenge to Legal Norms*. Oxford: Hart Publishing, 305–28.

—— H. C. Opitz, and A. G. Veldman (2003) 'Work–Family Policies on Working Time Put into Practice: A Comparison of Dutch and German Case Law on Working Time Adjustment'. *International Journal of Comparative Labour Law and Industrial Relations* 19(3): 321–46.

BUSINESSEUROPE (2007) 'BUSINESSEUROPE Position Paper on the Green Paper "Modernising Labour Law to Meet the Challenges of the 21st Century".' At: <http://www.businesseurope.eu/DocShareNoFrame/docs/3/PMCLONFDJIOCA-KILGKOBBDLMPDB39DB1T19LI71KM/UNICE/docs/DLS/2007–00575-EN.pdf>.

Campbell, I. (2004) 'Casual Work and Casualisation: How Does Australia Compare?' *Labour and Industry* 15(2): 85–111.

Campbell, I. (2008) 'Australia: Institutional Changes and Workforce Fragmentation'. in S. Lee and F. Eyraud, eds., *Globalization, Flexibilization and Working Conditions in Asia and the Pacific*. Geneva: ILO, 115–52.

Cappelli, P., L. Bassi, H. C. Katz, D. Knoke, P. Osterman, and M. Useem (1997) *Change at Work*. New York: Oxford University Press.

Carens, J. H. (1987) 'Aliens and Citizens: The Case for Open Borders'. *The Review of Politics* 49(2, Spring): 251–73.

—— (2008) 'Immigration, Democracy and Citizenship'. Unpublished essay. At: <http://isites.harvard.edu/fs/docs/icb.topic162929.files/E_European_enlargement/Carens.pdf>.

Carle, E. (2004) 'Women, Anti-Fascism and Peace in Interwar France: Gabrielle Duchene's Itinerary'. *French History* 18(3): 291–314.

Carnoy, M. (2000) *Sustaining the New Economy: Work, Family and Community in the Information Age*. Cambridge, MA: Harvard University Press.

Cass, B. (1994) 'Citizenship, Work and Welfare: The Dilemma for Australian Women'. *Social Politics* 1(1): 106–24.

Castles, S. (2005) 'Nation and Empire: Hierarchies of Citizenship in the New Global Order'. *International Politics* 42: 203–24.

Catanzariti, J. and M. Byrnes (2005) 'Major Tribunal Decisions in 2005'. *Journal of Industrial Relations* 48(3): 357–68.

CESifo (Institute for Economic Research) (2002) 'Spotlight: Temporary Agency Employment in the European Union'. *CESifo Forum* 3/2002. Munich: CESifo, 47–8.

Chalmers, J., I. Campbell, and S. Charlesworth (2005) 'Part-time Work and Caring Responsibilities in Australia: Towards an Assessment of Job Quality'. *Labour and Industry* 15(3): 41–66.

Charnowitz, S. (1987) 'The Influence of International Labour Standards on the World Trading Regime: A Historical Overview'. *The International Labour Review* 126(5): 565–84.

—— (1995) 'Promoting Higher Labour Standards', in B. Roberts, ed., *New Forces in the World Economy*. Cambridge, MA: MIT Press, 402–26.

Charpentier, P., M. Lallement, F. Lefresne, and J. Loos-Baroin (2006) 'The French 35-Hour Week: A Decent Working Time Pattern? Lessons from Case Studies', in J.-Y. Boulin, M. Lallement, J. C. Messenger, and F. Michon, eds., *Decent Working Time: New Trends, New Issues*. Geneva: ILO, 181–208.

CIETT (2006) Executive Summary. *Position Paper: International Labour Conference, 95th Session 2006 Report V(1): The Employment Relationship*. Geneva.

Clarke, L. (1991) 'The Significance of Wage Forms: The Example of the British Construction Industry'. Bremen: 13th Annual Conference of the International Working Party on Labour Market Segmentation.

—— (1992) *Building Capitalism: Historical Change and the Labour Process in the Production of the Built Environment*. New York: Routledge.

Clarke, L. (2000) 'Disparities in Wage Relations and Social Reproduction', in L. Clarke, P. de Gijsel, and J. Janssen, eds., *The Dynamics of Wage Relations in the New Europe*. Boston: Kluwer Academic Publishers, 134–8.

Clauwaert, S. (2000) *Report 64: Survey of Legislation on Temporary Work*. Brussels: ETUI (European Trade Union Institute).

——W. Düvel, I. Schömann, and C. Wörgotter (2003) *Fundamental Social Rights in the European Union: Comparative Tables and Documents*. Brussels: ETUI.

Clayton, A. and R. Mitchell (1999) *Study on Employment Situations and Worker Protection in Australia: A Report to the International Labour Office*. Melbourne: The Centre for Employment and Labour Relations Law at the University of Melbourne.

Close, G. (1994) 'Definitions of Citizenship', in J. P. Gardner, ed., *Hallmarks of Citizenship: A Green Paper*. London: British Institute of International and Comparative Law, 3–10.

Clement, W. (1986) *The Struggle to Organize: Resistance in Canada's Fishery*. Toronto: McClelland & Stewart.

Clerc, J. M., ed. (1985) *Introduction to Working Conditions and Environment*. Geneva: ILO.

Cobble, D. S. (1994) 'Making Postindustrial Unionism Possible', in S. Friedman, R. Hurd, R. Oswald, and R. Seeber, eds., *Restoring the Promise of American Labor Law*. Ithaca, NY: Cornell University Press, 285–302.

Cole, G. D. H. (1963) *The Second International, 1889–1914 (A History of Socialist Thought: Volume III, Part II)*. London: Macmillan & Co. Ltd.

Commission for Labor Cooperation (2003) *The Rights of Nonstandard Workers: A North American Guide*. Washington: Secretariat of the Commission for Labor Co-Operation.

Conaghan, J. (2002) 'Women, Work and Family: A British Revolution?' in J. Conaghan, M. Fischl, and K. Klare, eds., *Labour Law in An Era of Globalization: Transformative Practices and Possibilities*. Oxford: Oxford University Press, 53–74.

Connell, R. W. (1987) *Gender and Power: Society, the Person and Sexual Politics*. Stanford, CA: Stanford University Press.

Cooney, S. (1999) 'Testing Times for the ILO: Institutional Reform for the New International Political Economy'. *Comparative Labor Law and Policy Journal* 20: 314–97.

Cordova, E. (1986) 'From Full-Time Wage Employment to Atypical Employment: A Major Shift in the Evolution of Labour Relations?' *International Labour Review* 125 (6): 641–57.

Cox, R. (1973) 'ILO: Limited Monarchy', in R. W. Cox and H. K. Jacobson, eds., *The Anatomy of Influence: Decision Making in International Organization*. New Haven: Yale University Press, 102–38.

——(1977) 'Labor and Hegemony'. *International Organization* 3(1): 385–424.

Cranford, C., J. Fudge, E. Tucker, and L. F. Vosko (2005) *Self-Employed Workers Organize: Law, Policy, and Unions*. Montreal and Kingston: McGill-Queen's University Press.

Creighton, B. (1994) 'The Forgotten Workers: Employment Security of Casual Employees and Independent Contractors', in R. McCallum, G. McCarry, and P. Ronfeldt, eds., *Employment Security*. Sydney: Federation Press, 51–78.

—— (1998) 'The ILO and the Protection of Fundamental Human Rights in Australia'. *Melbourne University Law Review* 22: 239–80.

Creutz, H. (1968) 'The ILO and Social Security for Foreign and Migrant Workers'. *International Labour Review* 97(4): 351–69.

Crompton, R., ed. (1999) *Restructuring Gender Relations and Employment: The Decline of the Male Breadwinner*. New York: Oxford University Press.

Crouch, C. (1993) *Industrial Relations and European State Traditions*. Oxford: Clarendon Press.

Curran, J. and R. Burrows (1986) 'The Sociology of Petit Capitalism: A Trend Report'. *Sociology* 20(2): 265–79.

Daguerre, A. and T. Larsen (2003) 'Policy Map EU—OMC on Social Inclusion'. WRAMSOC (Welfare Reform and Management of Societal Change) Working Paper.

Dale, A. (1991) 'Self-Employment and Entrepreneurship: Notes on Two Problematic Concepts', in R. Burrows, ed., *Deciphering the Enterprise Culture: Entrepreneurship, Petty Capitalism, and the Restructuring of Britain*. London and New York: Routledge, 35–52.

Daübler, W. (1999) 'Working People in Germany'. *Comparative Labor Law and Policy Journal* 21: 77–98.

Davidov, G. (2002) 'The Three Axes of Employment Relationships: A Characterization of Workers in Need of Protection'. *University of Toronto Law Journal* 52: 357–418.

—— (2004) 'Joint Employer Status in Triangular Employment Relationships'. *British Journal of Industrial Relations* 42(4): 727–46.

—— (2005) 'Who is a Worker?' *Industrial Law Journal* 34(1): 57–71.

—— and B. Langille, eds. (2006) *Boundaries and Frontiers of Labour Law: Goals and Means in the Regulation of Work*. Oxford: Hart Publishing.

Davies, P. (1999) 'Wage Employment and Self-Employment: A Common Law View'. *Reports to the 6th European Congress for Labour Law and Social Security*. Polish Section of the International Society for Labour Law and Social Security, 165–90.

—— and M. Freedland (2000a) 'Labour Markets, Welfare, and the Personal Scope of Employment Law'. *Oxford Review of Economic Policy* 16(1): 84–94.

———— (2000b) 'Employees, Workers, and the Autonomy of Labour Law', in H. Collins, P. Davies, and R. Rideout, eds., *Legal Regulation of the Employment Relation*. London: W. G. Hart Legal Workshop Series, Kluwer Law International, 267–86.

Deacon, B. (2001) 'International Organisations, the European Union and Global Social Policy', in R. Sykes, B. Palier, and P. Prior, eds., *Globalization and the European Welfare States: Challenges and Change*. Basingstoke: Palgrave, 59–77.

Deakin, S. (1998) 'The Evolution of the Contract of Employment 1900–1950: The Influence of the Welfare State', in N. Whiteside and R. Salais, eds., *Governance,*

Industry and Labour Markets in Britain and France: The Modernising State in the Mid-20th Century. London: Routledge, 212–30.

Deakin, S. (2000) 'Legal Origins of Wage Labour: The Evolution of the Contract of Employment from Industrialisation to the Welfare State', in L. Clarke, J. Janssen, and P. de Gijsel, eds., *The Dynamics of Wage Relations in the New Europe*. Boston: Kluwer Deventer, 32–44.

—— (2001) 'The Contract of Employment: A Study in Legal Evolution'. Cambridge: CBR Working Papers, University of Cambridge.

—— (2002) 'The Many Futures of the Contract of Employment', in J. Conaghan, M. Fischl, and K. Klare, eds., *Labour Law in an Era of Globalization: Transformative Practices and Possibilities*. Oxford: Oxford University Press, 117–81.

—— and F. Wilkinson (1989) *Labour Law, Social Security, and Economic Inequality*. London: The Institute of Employment Rights.

—— —— (1994) 'Rights vs. Efficiency? The Economic Case for Transnational Labour Standards'. *Industrial Law Journal* 23: 289–310.

Delanty, G. (1997) 'Models of Citizenship: Defining European Identity and Citizenship'. *Citizenship Studies* 1(3): 285–303.

Delevingne, M. (1934) 'The Pre-War History of International Labour Legislation', in J. T. Shotwell, ed., *The Origins of the International Labour Organization, Volume 1*. New York: Columbia University Press, 19–54.

Doeringer, P. B. and M. J. Piore (1971) *Internal Labor Markets and Manpower Analysis*. Lexington, MA: D. C. Health.

Doogan, K. (2005) 'Long-Term Employment and the Restructuring of the Labour Market in Europe'. *Time and Society* 14(1): 65–87.

Draper, H. and A. Lipow (1976) 'Marxist Women Versus Bourgeois Feminism', in R. Miliband and J. Saville, eds., *Socialist Register 1976* 13: 176–226.

DuBois, E. (1998) *Woman Suffrage and Women's Rights*. New York: New York University Press.

Duffy, A. and N. Pupo (1992) *Part-Time Paradox: Connecting Gender, Work and Family*. Toronto: McClelland and Stewart.

Dunnewijk, T. (2001) *Temporary Work Agencies in the Netherlands: Emergence and Perspective*. The Hague: CPB Netherlands Bureau for Economic Policy Analysis.

Eardley, T. and A. Corden (1996) *Self-Employed Earnings and Income Distribution: Problems of Measurement*. York: Social Policy Research Unit, University of York.

Ebbinghaus, B. and W. Eichhorst (2006) 'Employment Regulation and Labor Market Policy in Germany, 1991–2005'. IZA Discussion Paper No. 2405.

Economic Council of Canada (1990) *Good Jobs, Bad Jobs: Employment in the Service Economy*. Ottawa: Supply and Services Canada.

Edwards, R. (1979) *Contested Terrain: The Transformation of the Workplace in the Twentieth Century*. London: Heinemann.

EIRO (European Industrial Relations Observatory) (2002) *Economically Dependent Workers: Employment Law and Industrial Relations*. Paris: Eurofound.

Eklund, R. (2002) 'Temporary Employment Agencies in the Nordic Countries'. *Scandinavian Studies in Law* 43: 311–33.

Ellem, B., M. Baird, R. Cooper, and R. Lansbury (2005) '"WorkChoices": Myth-Making at Work'. *Journal of Australian Political Economy* 56: 13–31.

Ellis, E. (2005) *EU Anti-Discrimination Law*. Oxford and New York: Oxford University Press.

Elson, D. (1995) *Male-Bias in the Development Process*. Manchester: Manchester University Press.

Engblom, S. (2001) 'Equal Treatment of Employees and Self-Employed Workers'. *Journal of Comparative Labour Law and Industrial Relations* 17: 211–31.

England, G., I. Christie, and M. Christie (1998) *Employment Law in Canada*, 3rd edn. Toronto: Butterworths.

Esping-Andersen, G. (2000) Interview on Postindustrialism and the Future of the Welfare State. *Work, Employment & Society* 14(4): 757–69.

——(2002) 'A New Gender Contract', in G. Esping-Andersen, D. Gaille, A. Hemerijick, and J. Myles, eds., *Why We Need a New Welfare State*. Oxford: Oxford University Press, 68–95.

ETUC (European Trade Union Confederation) (2004) *Contribution on Behalf of the ETUC by Catelene Passchier, Confederal Secretary*. Brussels: ETUC, European Parliament.

——(2007) Position Adopted by the ETUC Executive Committee: Consultation of the European Social Partners on the EC's Green Paper COM (2006) 708 final Modernising and Strengthening Labour Law to Meet the Challenges of the 21st Century. Rome, 20–1 March.

EUROCIETT and UNI-Europa (2001) *Euro-CIETT/Uni-Europa Joint Declaration Objectives of the European Directive on Private Agency Work*. Brussels.

—— —— (2008) *Eurociett/UNI-Europa Joint Declaration on the Directive on Working Conditions for Temporary Agency Workers*. Brussels.

Evans, S., J. Goodman, and L. Hargreaves (1985) 'Unfair Dismissal Law and Employment Practice in the 1980s'. *Research Paper 53*. London: Department of Employment.

Expert Group on Flexicurity (2007) *Flexicurity Pathways: Expert Group on Flexicurity Interim Report*. Brussels: Stakeholder Conference on Flexicurity.

Everingham, C. (2002) 'Engendering Time: Gender Equity and Discourses of Workplace Flexibility'. *Time & Society* 11(2): 335–51.

Fagan, C. (2000) 'Men's Long Work Hours and Women's Short Work Hours: The Case of Britain'. *Working Time in Europe: Towards a European Working Time Policy*. Helsinki: Finnish EU Presidency Conference Report.

——(2001) 'Time, Money and the Gender Order: Work Orientations and Working Time Preferences in Britain'. *Gender, Work and Organization* 8(3): 239–66.

——and K. Ward (2003) 'Regulatory Convergence? Non-standard Work in the UK and the Netherlands', in S. Houseman and M. Osawa, eds., *Non-standard Work in Developed Economies: Causes and Consequences*. MI: WE UpJohn, 53–88.

Fagnani, J. and M.-T. Letablier (2004) 'Work and Family Life Balance: The Impact of the 35-Hour Laws in France'. *Work, Employment and Society* 18(3): 551–72.

———— (2006) 'The French 35-hour Working Law and the Work–Life Balance of Parents: Friends or Foes', in D. Perrons, C. Fagan, L. McDowell, K. Ray, and K. Ward, eds., *Gender Divisions and Working Time in the New Economy: Changing Patterns of Work, Care and Public Policy in Europe and North America.* Cheltenham: Edward Elgar, 79–90.

Fichtner, N. (2006) 'The Rise and Fall of the Country of Origin Principle in the EU's Services Directive: Uncovering the Principle's Premises and Potential Implications'. *Essays in Transnational Economic Law* 54.

Firebaugh, G. (2003) *The New Geography of Global Income Inequality.* Cambridge, MA: Harvard University Press.

Fix, M. and J. S. Passel (2002) 'The Scope and Impact of Welfare Reform's Immigrant Provisions'. *Assessing the New Federalism.* Discussion Paper. WA: The Urban Institute.

Ford, H. as interviewed by S. Crowther (1926) 'Henry Ford: Why I Favor Five Days' Work with Six Days' Pay'. *World's Work*: 613–16.

Forde, C. and G. Slater (2005) 'Agency Working in Britain: Character, Consequences and Regulation'. *British Journal of Industrial Relations* 43(2): 249–71.

Förster, M. F. (2000) 'Trends and Driving Factors in Income Distribution and Poverty in the OECD Area'. Labour Market and Social Policy Occasional Paper, No. 42. Paris: OECD, Social Policies Studies Division.

Fouarge, D. and C. Baaijens (2006) 'Labour Supply Preferences and Job Mobility of Dutch Employees', in J.-Y. Boulin, M. Lallement, J. C. Messenger, and F. Michon, eds., *Decent Working Time: New Trends, New Issues.* Geneva: ILO, 155–79.

Frager, R. A. and C. Patrias (2005) *Discounted Labour: Women Workers in Canada, 1870–1939.* Toronto: University of Toronto Press.

Frances, R. (1993) *The Politics of Work: Gender and Labour in Victoria 1880–1939.* Cambridge: Cambridge University Press.

——— L. Kealey, and J. Sangster (1996) 'Women and Wage Labour in Australia and Canada, 1880–1980'. *Labour History* 71 (Fall): 54–89.

Fraser, N. (1994) 'After the Family Wage'. *Political Theory* 22(4): 591–618.

——— (1997) *Justice Interruptus: Critical Reflections on the 'Postsocialist' Condition.* New York: Routledge.

——— and L. Gordon (1994) 'A Genealogy of Dependency: Tracing a Keyword of the US Welfare State'. *Signs* 19(2): 309–36.

Fredman, S. (1994) 'A Difference with Distinction: Pregnancy and Parenthood Reassessed'. *Law Quarterly Review* 110: 106–23.

——— (1997) *Women and the Law.* Oxford: Oxford University Press.

Freedland, M. (1995) 'The Role of the Contract of Employment in Modern Labour Law', in L. Betten, ed., *The Employment Contract in Transforming Labour Relations.* The Hague: Kluwer, 17–27.

Freedland, M. (1999) *Workers' Protection: United Kingdom National Study for the ILO.* Geneva: ILO.

—— (2003) *The Personal Employment Contract.* Oxford: Oxford University Press.

Frenette, M. (2002) 'Do the Falling Earnings of Immigrants Apply to Self-Employed Immigrants?' *Statistics Canada, Analytical Studies Branch.* Research Paper Series no. 195.

Fudge, J. (1991) *Labour Law's Little Sister: The Employment Standards Act and the Feminization of Labour.* Ottawa: Canadian Centre for Policy Alternatives.

—— (1997) *Precarious Work and Families.* Toronto: Centre for Research on Work and Society, York University.

—— (1999) 'New Wine into Old Bottles? Updating Legal Forms to Reflect Changing Employment Norms'. *University of British Columbia Law Review* 33(1): 129–52.

—— and B. Cossman, eds. (2002) *Privatization, Law, and the Challenge to Feminism.* Toronto: University of Toronto Press.

—— and L. F. Vosko (2001a) 'Gender, Segmentation and the Standard Employment Relationship in Canadian Labour Law and Policy'. *Economic and Industrial Democracy* 22(2): 271–310.

—— —— (2001b) 'By Whose Standards? Re-regulating the Canadian Labour Market'. *Economic and Industrial Democracy* 22(3): 327–56.

—— E. Tucker, and L. F. Vosko (2002) *The Legal Concept of Employment: Marginalizing Workers.* Ottawa: Law Commission of Canada.

—— —— —— (2003a) 'Employee or Independent Contractor? Charting the Legal Significance of the Distinction in Canada'. *Canadian Journal of Labour and Employment Law* 10(2): 193–230.

—— —— —— (2003b) 'Changing Boundaries of Employment: Developing a New Platform for Labour Law'. *Canadian Journal of Labour and Employment Law* 10(3): 361–98.

Gallie, D., M. White, Y. Cheng, and M. Tomlinson (1998) *Restructuring the Employment Relationship.* Oxford: Clarendon Press.

German Social Insurance (European Representation) (2007) *Joint Opinion of the German Social Insurance Umbrella Organizations on European Commission Green Paper Modernising Labour Law to Meet the Challenges of the 21st Century.* Brussels: German Social Insurance European Representation.

Gill, S. (1995) 'Globalization, Market Civilization, and Disciplinary Neoliberalism'. *Millennium: Journal of International Studies* 24(3): 399–423.

—— and D. Law (1988) *Global Political Economy: Perspectives, Problems and Policy.* Baltimore: Johns Hopkins Press.

Glenn, E. N. (2002) *Unequal Freedom: How Race and Gender Shaped American Citizenship and Labor.* Cambridge, MA, and London: Harvard University Press.

GMB (2007) *GMB Trade Union Response to EU Commission Green Paper—'Modernizing Labour Law to Meet the Challenges of the 21st Century' COM(2006) 708 Final.* London.

Goetschy, J. (1999) 'The European Employment Strategy: Genesis and Development'. *European Journal of Industrial Relations* 5(2): 117–37.

Golsch, K. (2003) 'Employment Flexibility in Spain and its Impact on Transitions to Adulthood'. *Work, Employment and Society* 17: 691–718.

Gonos, G. and H. Freeman (2005) 'Regulating the Employment Sharks: Reconceptualizing the Legal Status of the Commercial Temp Agency'. *Working USA* 8(3): 293–314.

Gordon, D. M., R. Edwards, and M. Reich (1982) *Segmented Work, Divided Workers.* Cambridge: Cambridge University Press.

Gordon, L. (1990) 'The New Feminist Scholarship on the Welfare State', in L. Gordon, ed., *Women, the State, and Welfare.* Madison: University of Wisconsin Press, 9–35.

Gottfried, H. (2009) 'The Making of Precarious Employment in Japan', in L. F. Vosko, M. MacDonald, and I. Campbell, eds., *Gender and the Contours of Precarious Employment.* London and New York: Routledge: 76–91.

Gray, A. (2004) *Unsocial Europe: Social Protection or Flexploitation?* London: Pluto Press.

Green, F. (2008) 'Temporary Work and Insecurity in Britain: A Problem Solved?' *Social Indicators Research* 88(1): 147–60.

Grunow, D., H. Hofmeister, and S. Buchholz (2006) 'Late 20th Century Persistence and Decline of the Female Homemaker in Germany and the United States.' *International Sociology* 21(1): 101–32.

Guest, D. (1985) *The Emergence of Social Security in Canada*, 2nd edn. Vancouver: UBC Press.

Guild, E. (1996) 'The Legal Framework of Citizenship of the European Union', in E. D. Cesarini and M. Fulbrook, eds., *Citizenship, Nationality and Migration in Europe.* London and New York: Routledge, 30–56.

Hall, M. (2008) 'Government and Social Partners Agree on Equal Treatment for Agency Workers in EU Directive'. EIROnline. At: <http://www.eurofound.europa.eu/eiro/2008/06/articles/uk0806039i.htm>.

Hall, R. (2006) 'Australian Industrial Relations in 2005: The WorkChoices Revolution'. *Journal of Industrial Relations* 48(3): 291–303.

Hall, S. and D. Held (1990) 'Citizens and Citizenship', in S. Hall and M. Jacques, eds., *New Times: The Changing Face of Politics in the 1990s.* London: Verso, 173–88.

Hammar, T., ed. (1985) *European Immigration Policy.* Cambridge: Cambridge University Press.

Hardason, Ó. and F. Romans (2005) 'Labour Market Latest Trends'. *4th Quarter 2004 Data.* EUROSTAT: Statistics in Focus, Population and Social Conditions.

Harvey, D. (1989) *The Condition of Postmodernity.* Oxford: Basil Blackwell.

—— (2006) *Spaces of Global Capitalism: Towards a Theory of Uneven Global Development.* New York: Verso.

Harvey, M. (1999) 'Economies of Time: A Framework for Analysing the Restructuring of Employment Relations', in A. Felstead and N. Jewson, eds., *Global Trends in Flexible Labour.* Basingstoke: Macmillan, 21–42.

Hasenau, M. (1991) 'ILO Standards on Migrant Workers: The Fundamentals of the UN Convention and their Genesis'. *International Migration Review* 25(4): 687–97.

Hassim, S. (2008) 'Global Constraints on Gender Equality in Care Work'. *Politics & Society* 36(3): 388–402.

Hepple, B. (1994) 'Equality: A Global Labour Standard', in W. Sengenberger and D. Campbell, eds., *International Labour Standards and Economic Interdependence.* Geneva: ILO, 123–33.

——(1997) 'New Approaches to International Labour Regulation'. *Industrial Law Journal* 26(4): 353–66.

Heron, C. (1989) *The Canadian Labour Movement: A Short History.* Toronto: James Lorimer.

Hilden, P. J. (1986) 'Women and the Labour Movement in France'. *The Historical Journal* 29(4): 809–32.

Hindess, B. (2000) 'Citizenship in the International Management of Populations'. *American Behavioral Scientist* 43(9): 1486–97.

Hirshmann, N. (1999) 'Difference as an Occasion for Rights: A Feminist Rethinking of Rights, Liberalism and Difference', in S. Hekman, ed., *Feminism, Identity, and Difference.* London: Frank Cass, 22–55.

Hochschild, A. (1997) *The Time Bind: When Work Becomes Home and Home Becomes Work.* New York: Henry Holt.

——(2000) 'Global Care Chains and Emotional Surplus Value', in W. Hutton and A. Giddens, eds., *On the Edge: Living with Global Capitalism.* London: Jonathan Cape, 130–46.

Hodgetts, J. E., W. McCloskey, R. Whitaker, and V. S. Wilson (1972) *The Biography of an Institution: The Civil Service Commission of Canada 1908–1967.* Montreal and Kingston: McGill-Queen's University Press.

Honeycutt, K. (1976) 'Clara Zetkin: A Socialist Approach to the Problem of Women's Oppression'. *Feminist Studies* 3(4): 131–44.

Howard, J. (2004) *A Stronger Economy, A Stronger Australia: The Howard Government Election 2004 Policy: Protecting and Supporting Independent Contractors.* Barton: The Liberal Party of Australia.

——(2005) 'Workplace Relations Reform: The Next Logical Step'. Address to the Sydney Institute. Sydney.

Howe, R. (1995) 'A Paradise for Working Men but Not Working Women: Women's Wagework and Protective Legislation in Australia, 1890–1914', in U. Wikander, A. Kessler-Harris, and J. Lewis, eds., *Protecting Women: Labour Legislation in Europe, United States and Australia, 1880–1920.* Urbana, IL: University of Illinois, 318–36.

Humphries, J. (1981) 'Protective Legislation, the Capitalist State, and Working Class Men: The Case of the 1842 Mines Regulation Act'. *Feminist Review* 7: 1–33.

Humphries, J. and J. Rubery (1984) 'The Reconstitution of the Supply Side of the Labour Market: The Relative Autonomy of Social Reproduction'. *Cambridge Journal of Economics* 8: 331–46.

Hunter, R. (1988) 'Women Workers and Federal Industrial Law: From Harvester to Comparable Worth'. *Australian Journal of Labour Law* 1: 147–71.

Hutchins, B. L. (E. L.) (1906) *Labour Laws for Women in Australia and New Zealand (Pamphlet)*. Adelphi, WC: The Women's Industrial Council.

—— (1907) *Labour Laws for Women in France*. Adelphi, WC: The Women's Industrial Council.

Hyde, A. (1998) 'Employment Law after the Death of Employment'. *University of Pennsylvania Journal of Labor and Employment Law* 1: 99–115.

—— (2000) *Classification of US Working People and its Impact on Worker Protection: A Report Submitted to the ILO*. Geneva: ILO.

Hyland, J. (2007) 'Britain: Unions Responsible for Harsh Conditions Facing Temporary Agency Workers'. World Socialist Web.

International Organization for Migration (2005) *World Migration 2005: Costs and Benefits of International Migration*. No. 882/22. Geneva: International Organization for Migration.

Isin, E. F. (2005) 'Engaging, Being, Political'. *Political Geography* 24(3): 373–87.

Jackson, A. (2006) 'Regulating Precarious Labour Markets: What Can We Learn from New European Models?' in Vosko, ed. (2006b), 277–98.

Jacobs, A. (1999) 'The Netherlands'. *Bulletin of Comparative Labour Relations* 36: 299–311.

—— (2005) 'The Netherlands: In the Tradition of Intersectoral Pacts'. *Bulletin of Comparative Labour Relations* 56: 89–116.

Jacobs, J. and K. Gerson (2004) *The Time Divide: Work, Family, and Gender Inequality*. Boston: Harvard.

Jacoby, S. M. (1985) *Employing Bureaucracy: Managers, Unions, and the Transformation of Work in American Industry, 1900–1945*. New York: Columbia University Press.

—— (1997) *Modern Manors: Welfare Capitalism since the New Deal*. Princeton: Princeton University Press.

Jeffery, M. (1995) 'The Commission Proposals on "Atypical Work": Back to the Drawing Board ... Again'. *Industrial Law Journal* 24(3): 296–9.

—— (1998) 'Not Really Going to Work? Of the Directive on Part-Time Work, "Atypical Work" and Attempts to Regulate It'. *Industrial Law Journal* 27(3): 193–213.

Jefferys, S. (2003) 'Critical Times for French Employment Regulation: The 35-Hour Week and the Challenge to Social Partnership', in J. Stanford and L. F. Vosko, eds., *Challenging the Market: The Struggle to Regulate Work and Income*. Montreal and Kingston: McGill-Queen's University Press, 346–64.

Jenson, J. (1989) 'Paradigms and Political Discourse: Protective Legislation in France and the United States before 1914'. *Canadian Journal of Political Science* 22 (2): 235–58.

Jessop, B. (1993) 'Towards a Schumpeterian Workfare State? Preliminary Remarks on Post-Fordist Political Economy'. *Studies in Political Economy* 40: 7–39.

—— (2002) 'Liberalism, Neoliberalism, and Urban Governance: A State-Theoretical Perspective'. *Antipode* 34(3): 452–72.

Jouhette, S. and F. Romans (2006) 'EU Labour Force Survey: Principal Results 2005'. *EUROSTAT, Population and Social Conditions: Statistics in Focus.* European Communities.

Junor, A. (1998) 'Permanent Part-Time Work: New Family-Friendly Standard or High Intensity Cheap Skills?' *Labour & Industry* 8(3): 77–96.

Kanter, R. M. (1993) 'Employability Security'. *Business & Society Review* 87: 11–14.

Kaplan, T. (1985) 'On the Socialist Origins of International Women's Day'. *Feminist Studies* 11(1): 163–71.

Kenner, J. (1999) 'The EC Employment Title and the "Third Way": Making Soft Law Work?' *The International Journal of Comparative Labour Law & Industrial Relations* 15(1): 33–60.

Kessler-Harris, A. (1982) *Out to Work: A History of Wage-Earning Women in the United States.* Oxford: Oxford University Press.

—— (1990) *A Woman's Wage: Historical Meanings and Social Consequences.* Lexington, MA: University Press of Kentucky.

—— (1995) 'The Paradox of Motherhood: Night Work Restrictions in the United States', in U. Wikander, A. Kessler-Harris, and J. Lewis, eds., *Protecting Women: Labour Legislation in Europe, United States and Australia, 1880–1920.* Urbana, IL: University of Illinois, 337–57.

—— (2001) *In Pursuit of Equity: Women, Men, and the Quest for Economic Citizenship in 20th-Century America.* New York: Oxford University Press.

——J. Lewis, and U. Wikander (1995) 'Introduction', in U. Wikander, J. Lewis, and A. Kessler-Harris, eds., *Protecting Women: Labour Legislation in Europe, United States and Australia, 1880–1920.* Urbana, Ill: University of Illinois, 1–28.

Kilpatrick, C. and M. Freedland (2004) 'How is EU Governance Transformative? Part-Time Work in the UK', in S. Sciarra, P. Davies, and M. Freedland, eds., *Employment Policy and the Regulation of Part-time Work in the EU: A Comparative Analysis.* Cambridge: Cambridge University Press, 299–357.

Kirton, J. J. and M. J. Trebilcock, eds. (2004) *Hard Choices, Soft Law: Voluntary Standards in Global Trade, Environment and Social Governance.* Aldershot: Ashgate.

Klammer, U., S. Keuzenkamp, I. Cebrián, C. Fagan, C. Klenner, and G. Moreno (2005) 'Working Time Options over the Life Course: Changing Social Security Structures'. Dublin: Eurofound.

Klaus, A. (1993) *Every Child a Lion: The Origins of Maternal and Infant Policy in the United States and France, 1890–1920.* Ithaca, NY: Cornell University Press.

Klem, M. C., M. F. McKiever, and W. J. Lear (1950) *Industrial Health and Medical Programs.* Washington: Federal Security Agency, Public Health Service, Division of Industrial Hygiene.

Kok, W. (2003) *Jobs, Jobs, Jobs: Creating More Employment in Europe*. Berlin: European Employment Task Force.

—— (2004) *Facing the Challenge: The Lisbon Strategy for Growth and Employment*. Luxembourg: Office for Official Publications of the European Communities.

Koven, S., and S. Michel (1990) 'Womanly Duties: Maternalist Politics and the Origins of Welfare States in France, Germany, Great Britain and the United States, 1880–1920'. *The American Historical Review* 95(4): 1076–108.

Krasas-Rogers, J. (2000) *Temps: The Many Faces of the Changing Workplace*. Ithaca, NY: Cornell University Press.

Kristeva, J. (1981) 'Women's Time'. *Signs* 7(1): 13–35.

Kuusisto, A. (2005) *Finland's Contribution to 'Temporary Agency Work in an Enlarged European Union'*. Brussels: EIRO.

Langille, B. (1997) 'Eight Ways to Think about International Labour Standards'. *Journal of World Trade* 31(4): 27–54.

—— (1999) 'The ILO and the New Economy: Recent Developments'. *International Journal of Comparative Labour Law & Industrial Relations* 15(3): 229–58.

—— (2002) 'Labour Policy in Canada: New Platform, New Paradigm'. *Canadian Public Policy* 28: 133–58.

Larner, W. (2000) 'Neoliberalism: Policy, Ideology, Governmentality'. *Studies in Political Economy* 63: 5–25.

Lawrence, F. (2007a) 'Misery at the Bottom of the Supermarket Supply Chain'. *The Guardian Online*, 15 Aug.

—— (2007b) 'Underpaid, Easy to Sack: UK's Second Class Workforce'. *The Guardian Online*, 24 Sept.

Lee, E. (1997) 'Globalization and Labour Standards: A Review of Issues'. *International Labour Review* 136(2): 173–89.

Lee, J. (1987) 'A Redivision of Labour: Victoria's Wages Boards in Action, 1896–1903'. *Historical Studies* 22: 352–72.

Leighton, P. (1986) 'Marginal Workers', in R. Lewis, ed., *Labour Law in Britain*. Oxford: Basil Blackwell.

Levin-Waldman, O. M. (2001) *The Case of Minimum Wage: Competing Policy Models*. Albany, NY: State University of New York Press.

Lewis, J. (1984) *Women in England 1870–1950: Sexual Divisions and Social Change*. Sussex, England: Wheatsheaf Books Ltd.

—— (1986a) 'The Working-Class Wife and Mother and State Intervention, 1870–1918', in J. Lewis, ed., *Labour and Love: Women's Experience of Home and Family, 1850–1940*. New York: Basil Blackwell Ltd., 99–120.

—— (1986b) 'Introduction: Reconstructing Women's Experience of Home and Family', in J. Lewis, ed., *Labour and Love: Women's Experience of Home and Family, 1850–1940*. New York: Basil Blackwell Ltd., 1–23.

—— (1992) 'Gender and the Development of Welfare Regimes'. *Journal of European Social Policy* 2(3): 159–73.

Lewis, J. (2001) 'The Decline of the Male Breadwinner Model: The Implications for Work and Care'. *Social Politics* 8(2): 152–70.

—— (2003) 'Economic Citizenship: A Comment'. *Social Politics* 10(2): 176–85.

—— and G. Astrom (1992) 'Equality, Difference, and State Welfare: Labor Market and Family Policies in Sweden'. *Feminist Studies* 18: 59–86.

—— and S. Giullari (2005) 'The Adult Worker Model Family, Gender Equality and Care: The Search for New Policy Principles and the Possibilities and Problems of a Capabilities Approach'. *Economy & Society* 34(1): 76–104.

—— T. Knijn, C. Martin, and I. Ostner (2008) 'Patterns of Development in Work/Family Reconciliation Policies for Parents in France, Germany, the Netherlands, and the UK in the 2000s'. *Social Politics* 15(3): 261–86.

—— and S. O. Rose (1995) 'Let England Blush: Protective Labor Legislation, 1820–1914', in U. Wikander, A. Kessler-Harris, and J. Lewis, eds., *Protecting Women: Labor Legislation in Europe, the United States, and Australia, 1880–1920*. Urbana, IL: University of Illinois Press, 91–124.

Lister, R. (1997) *Citizenship: Feminist Perspectives*. Basingstoke: Macmillan.

—— (2001) 'New Labour: A Study in Ambiguity from a Position of Ambivalence'. *Critical Social Policy* 21(4): 425–47.

—— (2007) 'Inclusive Citizenship: Realizing the Potential'. *Citizenship Studies* 11(1): 49–61.

Lokiec, P. (2004) 'The Framework of French Labour Law and Recent Trends in Regulation'. The Japan Institute for Labour Policy and Training, Comparative Labor Law Seminar. 9–10 Mar.

Lonnroth, J. (1991) 'The International Convention on the Rights of All Migrant Workers and Members of their Families in the Context of International Migration Policies: An Analysis of Ten Years of Negotiation'. *International Migration Review* 25 (4): 710–36.

—— (2000) *The European Employment Strategy, a Model of Open Co-ordination and the Role of the Social Partners*. Brussels: The Legal Dimension of the European Employment Strategy, 9–10 Oct.

Lorentsen, E. and E. Woolner (1950) *Fifty Years of Labour Legislation in Canada*. Canada: Department of Labour.

Lowe, G. (1980) 'Women, Work and the Office: The Feminization of Clerical Occupations in Canada, 1901–31'. *Canadian Journal of Sociology* 5: 354–65.

Lowell, B. L. (2001) 'Skilled Temporary and Permanent Immigrants in the United States'. *Population Research and Policy Review* 20(1): 33–58.

Lubin, C. R. and A. Winslow (1990) *Social Justice for Women: The International Labor Organization and Women*. Durham, NC: Duke University Press.

Luckhaus, L. (2000) 'Equal Treatment, Social Protection and Income Security for Women'. *International Labour Review* 139(2): 149–78.

Luxton, M. (1990) 'Two Hands for the Clock: Changing Patterns in the Gendered Division of Labour in the Home', in M. Luxton, H. Rosenberg, and S. Arat-Koc, eds., *Through the Kitchen Window: The Politics of Home and Family*. Toronto: Garamond Press, 39–55.

Luxton, M. and E. Reiter (1997) 'Double, Double, Toil and Trouble…Women's Experience of Work and Family', in P. Evans and G. Wekerle, eds., *Women and the Canadian Welfare State: Challenges and Change*. Toronto: University of Toronto Press, 197–245.

MacDonald, M., S. Phipps, and L. Lethbridge (2005) 'Taking its Toll: Implications of Paid and Unpaid Work Responsibilities for Women's Well-Being'. *Feminist Economics* 11(1): 63–94.

MacPherson, E. (1999) 'Collective Bargaining for Independent Contractors: Is the *Status of the Artist Act* a Mode for Other Industrial Sectors?' *Canadian Labour & Employment Law Journal* 7: 355–89.

McCallum, M. (1986) 'Keeping Women in their Place: The Minimum Wage in Canada, 1910–25'. *Labour/Le Travail* 17(Spring): 29–56.

McCallum, R. (1983) 'Protecting Infants: The French Campaign for Maternity Leaves, 1890s–1913'. *French Historical Studies* 13(1): 79–105.

—— (2005) 'Justice at Work: Industrial Citizenship and the Corporatisation of Australian Labour Law'. University of Sydney: Kingsley Laffer Memorial Lecture, 11 Apr.

—— (2006) 'Justice at Work: Industrial Citizenship and the Corporatization of Australian Labour Law'. *Journal of Industrial Relations* 48(2): 131–53.

McCann, D. (2008) *Regulating Flexible Work*. Oxford: Oxford University Press.

McKay, A. (2007) 'Why a Citizens' Basic Income? A Question of Gender Equality or Gender Bias'. *Work Employment and Society* 21(2): 337–48.

McLaughlin, E. (1995) 'Gender and Egalitarianism in the British Welfare State', in J. Humphries and J. Rubery, eds., *The Economics of Equal Opportunities*. Manchester: Equal Opportunities Commission, 291–312.

Mahaim, E. (1921) 'International Labour Law'. *International Labour Review* 1(3): 3–6.

—— (1934) 'The Historical and Social Importance of International Labor Legislation', in J. T. Shotwell, ed., *The Origins of the International Labor Organization*. New York: Columbia University Press, 3–18.

Mahon, R. (2002) 'Child Care: Toward What Kind of Social Europe?' *Social Politics* 9(3): 343–79.

Malone, C. (1998) 'Gendered Discourses and the Making of Protective Labour Legislation in England, 1830–1914'. *The Journal of British Studies* 37(2): 166–91.

Marín, E. (2006) 'The Employment Relationship: The Issue at the International Level', in G. Davidov and B. Langille, eds., *Boundaries and Frontiers of Labour Law*. Portland, OR: Hart Publishing, 339–54.

Marsden, D. (1999) 'Can the Right Labour Institutions Create Jobs?' *CentrePiece*.

—— (2004) 'The Network Economy and Models of the Employment Contract: Psychological, Economic, and Legal'. *British Journal of Industrial Relations* 42(2): 659–84.

Marshall, T. H. (1963) 'Citizenship and Social Class', in T. H. Marshall, ed., *Sociology at the Crossroads and Other Essays*. London: Heinemann, 67–127.

Meager, N. (1991) *Self-Employment in the United Kingdom*. Sussex: Institute of Manpower Studies.

Meehan, E. (1993) *Citizenship and the European Community*. London: Sage.

——(2000) 'Citizenship and the European Union'. ZEI Discussion Paper C63. At: <http://www.zei.de/download/zei_dp/dp_c63_meehan.pdf>.

Michon, F. (2005) *France's Contribution to 'Temporary Agency Work in an Enlarged European Union'*. Brussels: EIRO.

Middleton, J. (1996) 'Contingent Workers in a Changing Economy: Endure, Adapt or Organize?' *New York University Review of Law & Social Change* 22: 557–621.

Mishel, L., J. Bernstein, and H. Shierholz (2008) *The State of Working America 2008/ 2009*. Washington: The Economic Policy Institute.

Molyneux, M. (1985) 'Mobilization without Emancipation? Women's Interests, the State, and Revolution in Nicaragua'. *Feminist Studies* 11(2): 227–54.

Morris, L. (2002) *Managing Migration: Civic Stratification and Migrants' Rights*. London: Routledge.

Morse, D. A. (1969) 'Origins and Historical Development of the ILO: 1919–1948', in D. A. Morse, ed., *The Origin and Evolution of the ILO and its Role in the World Community*. New York: New York State School of Industrial and Labour, 3–34.

Mückenberger, U. (1989) 'Non-standard Forms of Employment in the Federal Republic of Germany: The Role and Effectiveness of the State', in G. Rogers and J. Rogers, eds., *Precarious Jobs in Labour Market Regulation: The Growth of Atypical Employment in Western Europe*. Geneva: International Institute for Labour Studies/ Free University of Brussels, 167–86.

——and S. Deakin (1989) 'From Deregulation to a European Floor of Rights: Labour Law, Flexibilisation and the European Single Market'. *Zeitschrift für ausländisches und internationales arbeits- und sozialRecht* 3(3): 157–206.

Muratore, L. (2004) 'Ministerial Circular Clarifies New Rules on Semi-Subordinate Work'. Brussels: EIRO.

Murray, J. (1999a) 'Social Justice for Women? The ILO's Convention on Part-Time Work'. *International Journal of Comparative Labour Law & Industrial Relations* 15(1): 3–19.

——(1999b) 'Normalising Temporary Work: The Proposed Directive on Fixed-Term Work'. *The Industrial Law Journal* 28(3): 269–81.

——(2001a) 'The International Regulation of Maternity: Still Waiting for the Reconciliation of Work and Family Life'. *The International Journal of Comparative Labour Law & Industrial Relations* 17(1): 25–46.

——(2001b) *Transnational Labour Regulation: The ILO and the EC Compared*. The Hague: Kluwer.

——(2001c) 'The Sound of One Hand Clapping? The "Ratcheting Labour Standards" Proposal and International Labour Law'. *Australian Journal of Labour Law* 14(3): 306–32.

Murray, J. (2001d) 'A New Phase in the Regulation of Multinational Enterprises: The Role of the OECD'. *Industrial Law Journal* 30(3): 255–70.

——(2005a) 'The AIRC's Test Case on Work and Family Provisions: The End of Dynamic Regulatory Change at the Federal Level?' *Australian Journal of Labour Law* 18: 325–43.

——(2005b) 'Work and Care: New Legal Mechanisms for Adaptation'. *Labour and Industry* 15(3): 67–87.

Mutari, E. and D. M. Figart (2000) 'The Social Implications of European Work Time Policies: Promoting Gender Equity?' in D. M. Figart and L. Golden, eds., *Working Time: International Trends, Theory, and Policy Perspectives*. London and New York: Routledge, 232–51.

—— ——(2004) 'Wages and Hours: Historical and Contemporary Linkages', in D. M. Figart, ed., *Living Wage Movements: Global Perspectives*. London: Routledge, 24–42.

Myles, J. (2002) 'A New Social Contract for the Elderly?' in G. Esping-Andersen, D. Gaille, A. Hemerijick, and J. Myles, eds., *Why We Need a New Welfare State*. Oxford: Oxford University Press, 130–72.

Neilsen, M. A. (Parliamentary Librarian) (2006) Bills Digest no. 19 2006–07. *Independent Contractors Bill 2006*. 4 Sept. At: <http://www.aph.gov.au/library/pubs/bd/2006–07/07bd019.htm#Contact>.

Nolan, P. (1983) 'The Firm and Labour Market Behaviour', in G. S. Bain, ed., *Industrial Relations in Britain*. Oxford: Blackwell, 291–310.

Nyland, C. and R. Castle (1999) 'The International Labour Organisation and the Australian Contribution to the International Labour Standards Debate'. *Journal of Industrial Relations* 41(3): 335–71.

Nystrom, B. (1999) 'Sweden', in R. G. Blainpain, ed., *Private Employment Agencies*. Kluwer: Bulletin of Comparative Labour Relations.

O'Connor, J. (2005) 'Employment-Anchored Social Policy, Gender Mainstreaming and the Open Method of Policy Coordination in the European Union'. *European Societies* 7(1): 27–52.

—— A. S. Orloff, and S. Shaver (1999) *States, Markets, Families: Gender, Liberalism and Social Policy in Australia, Canada, Great Britain and the United States*. Melbourne: Cambridge University Press.

Ocran, A. A. (1997) 'Across the Home/Work Divide: Homework in Garment Manufacture and the Failure of Employment Regulation', in S. B. Boyd, ed., *Challenging the Public/Private Divide: Feminism, Law, and Public Policy*. Toronto: University of Toronto Press, 144–67.

O'Donnell, A. (2004) '"Non-Standard" Workers in Australia: Counts and Controversies'. *Australian Journal of Labour Law* 17(1): 1–28.

OECD (Organisation for Economic Co-operation and Development) (1996) *Employment Outlook 1996*. Paris: OECD.

——(1998) 'Working Hours: Latest Trends and Policy Initiatives', in *Employment Outlook 1998*. Paris: OECD, 153–88.

OECD (2000) 'The Partial Renaissance of Self-Employment'. *Employment Outlook 2000*. Paris: OECD, 155–99.

—— (2002) 'Taking the Measure of Temporary Employment'. *Employment Outlook 2002*. Paris: OECD, 135–96.

—— (2005) *Employment Outlook 2005*. Paris: OECD.

—— (2008) *Employment Outlook 2008*. Paris: OECD.

O'Grady, J. (1991) 'Beyond the Wagner Act, What Then?' in D. Drache, ed., *Getting on Track*. Montreal and Kingston: McGill-Queen's University Press, 153–69.

O'Neill, S. (2008) 'Guide to the Federal Wage Safety Net'. Research Paper no. 13 2008–09. Parliament of Australia Parliamentary Library.

Ong, A. (2006) *Neoliberalism as Exception: Mutations in Citizenship and Sovereignty*. Durham: Duke University Press.

O'Reilly, J. (1994) *Banking on Flexibility: A Comparison of Flexible Employment in Retail Banking in Britain and France*. Brookfield: Avebury.

—— (1996) 'Theoretical Considerations in Cross-National Employment Research'. *Sociological Research Online* 1(1).

—— and C. Fagan, eds. (1998) *Part-Time Prospects: An International Comparison of Part-Time Work in Europe, North America and the Pacific Rim*. New York: Routledge.

—— and C. Spee (1998) 'The Future Regulation of Work and Welfare: Time for a Revised Social and Gender Contract?' *European Journal of Industrial Relations* 4(3): 259–81.

Orloff, A. S. (1993) 'Gender and the Social Rights of Citizenship: The Comparative Analysis of Gender Relations and Welfare States'. *American Sociological Review* 58(3): 303–28.

Ostner, I. and J. Lewis (1995) 'Gender and the Evolution of European Social Policies', in S. Liebfried and P. Pierson, eds., *European Social Policy*. Washington: Brookings, 159–93.

Owens, R. (2001) 'The "Long-Term or Permanent Casual": An Oxymoron or a "Well Enough Understood Australianism" in the Law?' *Australian Bulletin of Labour* 27(2): 118–36.

—— (2002) 'Decent Work for the Contingent Workforce in the New Economy'. *Australian Journal of Labour Law* 15(3): 209–34.

Parker, R. E. (1994) *Flesh Peddlers and Warm Bodies: The Temporary Help Industry and its Workers*. New Brunswick, NJ: Rutgers University Press.

Pateman, C. (1988) *The Sexual Contract*. Stanford, CA: Stanford University Press.

Pearce, D. (1990) 'Welfare is Not *for* Women: Why the War on Poverty Cannot Conquer the Feminization of Poverty', in L. Gordon, ed., *Women, the State, and Welfare*. Madison: University of Wisconsin Press, 265–79.

Pearson, R. (2004) 'The Social is Political: Towards the Re-politicization of Feminist Analysis of the Global Economy'. *International Feminist Journal of Politics* 6(4): 603–22.

Pedersen, S. (1993) *Family, Dependence, and the Origins of the Welfare State: Britain and France, 1914–1945*. Cambridge and New York: Cambridge University Press.

Perulli, A. (2003) *Economically Dependent / Quasi-Subordinate (Parasubordinate) Employment: Legal, Social and Economic Aspects*. Brussels: European Commission.

Perrons, D., C. Fagan, L. McDowell, K. Ray, and K. Ward (2006) *Gender Divisions and Working Time in the New Economy: Changing Patterns of Work, Care and Public Policy in Europe and North America*. Cheltenham: Edward Elgar.

Peters, M. (1999a) 'Neoliberalism', in *Encyclopaedia of Philosophy of Education*. Auckland. At: <http://www.ffst.hr/ENCYCLOPAEDIA/doku.php?id=neoliberalism#-neoliberalism>.

—— (1999b) 'Change of Family Policies in the Socio-cultural Context of European Societies'. *Comparative Social Research* 18: 135–60.

Pfau-Effinger, B. (1999) Change of Family Policies in the Socio-Cultural Context of European Societies. *Comparative Social Research* 18: 135–60.

Picchio, A. (1981) 'Social Reproduction and the Basic Structure of Labour Markets', in F. Wilkinson, ed., *The Dynamics of Labour Market Segmentation*. London: Academic Press, 193–209.

—— (1992) *Social Reproduction: The Political Economy of the Labour Market*. Cambridge: Cambridge University Press.

—— (1998) 'Wages as a Reflection of Socially Embedded Production and Reproduction Processes', in L. Clarke, P. de Gijsel, and J. Janssen, eds., *The Dynamics of Wage Relations in the New Europe*. Boston: Kluwer, 195–228.

—— (2000) 'The Reproduction of the Social Structure: Wages as a Reflection of Socially Embedded Production and Reproduction Processes', in L. Clarke, P. de Gijsel, and J. Janssen, eds., *The Dynamics of Wage Relations in the New Europe*. Boston: Kluwer, 195–214.

Pierson, R. R. (1990) 'Gender and the Unemployment Insurance Debates in Canada, 1934–1940'. *Labour/Le Travail* 25(Spring): 77–103.

Piore, M. (2002) 'The Reconfiguration of Work and Employment Relations in the United States at the Turn of the 21st Century', in P. Auer and B. Gazier, eds., *The Future of Work, Employment and Social Protection: The Dynamics of Change and the Protection of Workers*. Geneva: Proceedings of the France/ILO Symposium 2002, International Institute for Labour Studies, 171–89.

—— and C. F. Sable (1984) *The Second Industrial Divide: Possibilities for Prosperity*. New York: Basic Books.

Plantenga, J. (2002) 'Combining Work and Care in the Polder Model: An Assessment of the Dutch Part-Time Strategy'. *Critical Social Policy* 22(1): 53–71.

Pocock, B. (2005) 'The Impact of *The Workplace Relations Amendment (Work Choices) Bill 2005* (or *Work Choices*) on Australian Working Families'. Industrial Relations Victoria.

—— (2006) *The Labour Market Ate My Babies: Work, Children and a Sustainable Future*. Sydney: The Federation Press.

—— J. Buchanan, and I. Campbell (2004) *Securing Quality Employment: Policy Options for Casual and Part-Time Workers in Australia*. Adelaide: Chifley Research Centre.

Pocock, J. G. A. (1995) 'The Ideal of Citizenship since Classical Times', in R. Beiner, ed., *Theorizing Citizenship*. Albany, NY: State University of New York Press, 29–52.

Politakis, G. P. (2001) 'Night Work of Women in Industry'. *International Labour Review* 140(4): 403–28.

Polivka, A. (1996) 'Contingent and Alternative Work Arrangements, Defined'. *Monthly Labor Review* 110(10): 3–9.

——and T. Nardone (1989) 'On the Definition of "Contingent Work"'. *Monthly Labor Review* 112(12): 9–16.

Pollert, A. (1988) 'Dismantling Flexibility'. *Capital and Class* 34: 42–75.

Porter, A. (1993) 'Women and Income Security in the Post-War Period: The Case of Unemployment Insurance, 1945–62'. *Labour/Le Travail* 31: 111–44.

Probert, B. (1997) 'Gender and Choice: The Structure of Opportunity', in P. James, W. F. Veit, and S. Wright, eds., *Work of the Future: Global Perspectives*. St Leonards, NSW: Allen & Urwin, 181–97.

Procacci, G. and M. G. Rossilli (2003) 'Building Equality in the Policies of International Organizations', in C. Fauré, ed., *Political and Historical Encyclopedia of Women*. New York: Routledge, 503–22.

Ravn, A.-B. (1990) 'Social Democratic Debates on Protective Labour Legislation for Women during the Second International—The Danish Case'. Leuven: Tenth International Economic History Congress.

Rawling, M. (2007) 'The Regulation of Outwork and the Federal Takeover of Labour Law'. *Australian Journal of Labour Law* 20(2): 189–206.

Regent, S. (2003) 'The Open Method of Coordination: A New Supranational Form of Governance?' *European Law Journal* 9(2): 190–214.

Riley, J. (2007a) 'Regulating for Fair Dealing in Work Contracts: A New South Wales Approach'. *Industrial Law Journal* 36(1) March: 19–34.

——(2007b) 'Employees or Contractors? Engaging Staff Following Work Choices, and in the Light of the Proposed Independent Contractors Legislation'. University of New South Wales Faculty of Law Research Series, no. 57.

Robson, M. (1997) 'The Relative Earnings from Self and Paid Employment: A Time Series Analysis for the UK'. *Scottish Journal of Political Economy* 44(5): 502–18.

Rodgers, G. (1989) 'Precarious Work in Western Europe: The State of the Debate', in G. Rodgers and J. Rodgers, eds., *Precarious Jobs in Labour Market Regulation: The Growth of Atypical Employment in Western Europe*. Belgium: International Institute for Labour Studies, 1–16.

Roediger, D. R. and P. S. Foner (1989) *On Our Own Time: A History of American Labor and the Working Day*. London and New York: Verso.

Rose, N. (1996) 'Governing Advanced Liberal Democracies', in A. Barry, T. Osborne, and N. Rose, eds., *Foucault and Political Reason*. London: UCL Press, 37–64.

Rosenfeld, R. A. and G. E. Birkelund (1995) 'Women's Part-Time Work: A Cross-National Comparison'. *European Sociological Review* 11: 111–34.

Rousseau, D. M. (1995) *Psychological Contracts in Organizations: Understanding Written and Unwritten Agreements*. Thousand Oaks, CA: Sage Publications, Inc.

Rubery, J. (1989) 'Precarious Forms of Work in the United Kingdom', in G. Rodgers and J. Rodgers, eds., *Precarious Jobs in Labour Market Regulation: The Growth of Atypical Employment in Western Europe*. Belgium: International Institute for Labour Studies, 1–16.

—— (1998a) 'Part-Time Work: A Threat to Labour Standards?' in J. O'Reilly and C. Fagan, eds., *Part-Time Prospects: An International Comparison of Part-Time Work in Europe, North America and the Pacific Rim*. New York: Routledge, 137–55.

—— (1998b) *Women in the Labour Market: A Gender Equality Perspective*. Paris: OECD Directorate for Education, Employment, Labour & Social Affairs.

—— and C. Fagan (1994) 'Occupational Segregation: Plus ça Change . . . ?' in R. M. Lindley, ed., *Labour Market Structures and Prospects for Women*. Manchester: Equal Opportunities Commission (EOC), 29–42.

—— H. Figueiredo, M. Smith, D. Grimshaw, and C. Fagan (2004) 'The Ups and Downs of European Gender Equality Policy'. *International Relations Journal* 35(6): 603–28.

—— K. Ward, and D. Grimshaw (2005a) 'The Changing Employment Relationship and the Implications for Quality Part-Time Work'. *Labour & Industry* 15(3): 7–28.

—— —— —— (2006) 'Time, Work and Pay: Understanding the New Relationships', in J.-Y. Boulin, M. Lallement, J. C. Messenger and F. Michon, eds., *Decent Working Time: New Trends, New Issues*. Geneva: ILO, 123–51.

—— —— —— and H. Beynon (2005b) 'Working Time, Industrial Relations and the Employment Relationship'. *Time & Society* 14(1): 89–111.

Rupp, L. J. (1997) *Worlds of Women: The Making of an International Women's Movement*. Princeton: Princeton University Press.

Ruskin, N. and L. Smith (1998) 'The Role and Impact of International Labour Organisation Standards in the Australian Workplace'. *Journal of International Relations* 40: 314–25.

Sainsbury, D. (1996) *Gender, Equality, and Welfare States*. New York: Cambridge University Press.

—— (2006) 'Immigrants' Social Rights in Comparative Perspective: Welfare Regimes, Forms of Immigration and Immigration Policy Regimes'. *Journal of European Social Policy* 16(3): 229–44.

Sarina, T. and J. Riley (2006) 'Industrial Legislation in 2005'. *Journal of Industrial Relations* 48(3): 341–55.

—— —— (2007) 'Industrial Legislation in 2006'. *Journal of Industrial Relations* 49(3): 345–61.

Sassen, S., ed. (2002) *Global Networks, Linked Cities*. New York: Routledge.

—— (2005) 'New Global Classes: Implications for Politics', in A. Giddens and P. Diamond, eds., *The New Egalitarianism*. Cambridge: Polity, 143–53.

Sassen-Koob, S. (1978) 'The International Circulation of Resources and Development: The Case of Migrant Labor'. *Development & Change* 9(Fall): 509–45.

—— (1981) 'Towards a Conceptualization of Immigrant Labor'. *Social Problems* 29 (1): 65–85.

Sayer, L. C. (2005) 'Gender, Time and Inequality: Trends in Women's and Men's Paid Work, Unpaid Work and Free Time'. *Social Forces* 84(1): 285–303.

Scheele, A. (2002) 'Non-permanent Employment, Quality of Work and Industrial Relations'. Eurofound, EIRO. At: <http://www.eurofound.europa.eu/eiro/2002/02/study/tn0202101s.htm>.

Schellenberg, G. and G. S. Lowe (2001) 'What's a Good Job? The Importance of Employment Relationships'. CPRN Study no. W/05. Ottawa: Canadian Policy Research Networks Inc.

Schmid, G. (2006) 'Social Risk Management through Transitional Labour Markets?' *Socio-Economic Review* 4(1): 1–33.

Schömann, I., S. Clauwaert, and W. Düvel (2003) *Legal Analysis of the Implementation of the Fixed-Term Work Directive*. Brussels: European Trade Union Institute.

——R. Rogowski, and T. Kruppe (1998) *Labour Market Efficiency in the European Union: A Legal and Economic Evaluation of Employment Protection and Fixed-Term Contracts*. London: Routledge.

Sciarra, S. (2005) *The Evolution of Labour Law (1992–2003): General Report*. Luxembourg: Office for Official Publications of the European Communities.

Scott, J. W. (1988) 'Deconstructing Equality-Versus-Difference: Or, the Uses of Post-structuralist Theory for Feminism'. *Feminist Studies* 14(1): 32–50.

Ségol, B. (2004) 'Temporary Employment Agencies and the Services Directive'. UNI-EUROPA.

Sen, A. (2000) 'Work and Rights'. *International Labour Review* 139(2): 119–28.

Sengenberger, W. (1994) 'Labour Standards: An Institutional Framework for Restructuring and Development', in W. Sengenberger and D. Campbell, eds., *Creating Economic Opportunities: The Role of Labour Standards in Industrial Restructuring*. Geneva: IILS, 3–41.

——(2002) 'Globalization and Social Progress: The Role and Impact of International Labour Standards'. Conference Paper, Bonn.

——and D. Campbell, eds. (1994) *International Labour Standards and Economic Interdependence*. Geneva: ILO.

Sennett, R. (1998) *The Corrosion of Character: The Personal Consequences of Work in the New Capitalism*. New York: Norton.

Sharma, N. (2006) *Home Economics: Nationalism and the Making of 'Migrant Workers' in Canada*. Toronto: University of Toronto Press.

Shaver, S. (1992) *Focusing on Women: From Difference to Equality in the Australian Social Security System*. Canberra: Academy of Social Sciences Symposium.

Shklar, J. (1991) *American Citizenship: The Quest for Inclusion*. Cambridge, MA: Harvard University Press.

Sklar, K. K. (1988) 'The Greater Part of the Petitioners are Female: The Reduction of Women's Working Hours in the Paid Labor Force, 1840–1917', in G. Cross, ed., *Worktime and Industrialization: An International History*. Philadelphia: Temple University Press, 103–33.

Smith, M. P. (1999) 'The New High-Tech Braceros: Who is the Employer? What is the Problem?' in B. L. Lowell, ed., *Foreign Temporary Workers in America: Policies that Benefit America*. Westport: Quorum Press, 119–47.

Smith-Vidal, S. (1999) 'France'. *Bulletin of Comparative Labour Relations* 36: 245–54.

Social Platform (2005) 'The Services Directive, Services of General Interest (SGIs), and Social Services'. At: <http://www.socialplatform.org/module/FileLib/05–03ServicesDirective_SocialPlatform_Explanatorypaper_FinalEN.pdf>.

—— (2007) 'EC Green Paper on Labour Law Reforms—Soledar's Comments to the European Parliament'. Platform of European Social NGOs. At: <http://www.socialplatform.org/News.asp?news=13275>.

Soysal, Y. N. (1994) *Limits of Citizenship: Migrants and Postnational Membership in Europe*. Chicago: Chicago University Press.

Spruill-Wheeler, M. (1995) 'A Short History of the Woman Suffrage Movement in America', in M. Spruill-Wheeler, ed., *One Woman, One Vote: Rediscovering the Woman Suffrage Movement*. Troutdale, OR: New Sage, 9–20.

Staines, J. (2004) *From Pillar to Post: A Comparative Review of the Frameworks for Independent Workers in the Contemporary Performing Arts in Europe*. Brussels: IETM (Informal European Theatre Meeting).

Standing, G. (1989) 'Global Feminization through Flexible Labor'. *World Development* 17(7): 1077–95.

—— (1992) 'The Dynamics of European and American Labor Markets: Some Concluding Thoughts', in R. S. Belous, R. S. Hartley, and K. L. McClenahan, eds., *European and American Labor Markets: Different Models and Different Results*. Washington: National Planning Association, 112–16.

—— (1997) 'Globalization, Labour Flexibility and Insecurity: The Era of Market Regulation'. *European Journal of Industrial Relations* 3(1): 7–37.

—— (1999a) *Global Labour Flexibility: Seeking Distributive Justice*. Basingstoke Macmillan.

—— (1999b) 'Global Feminization through Flexible Labor: A Theme Revisited'. *World Development* 27(3): 583–602.

—— (2008a) 'The ILO: An Agency for Globalization?' *Development and Change* 39(3): 355–84.

—— (2008b) 'How Cash Transfers Promote the Case for Basic Income'. *Basic Income Studies: An International Journal of Basic Income Research* 3(1): 1–30.

Stanford, J. (2001) 'The Economic and Social Consequences of Fiscal Retrenchment in Canada in the 1990s'. *Review of Economic Performance & Social Progress* 1: 141–60.

—— and L. F. Vosko (2004) 'Challenging the Market: The Struggle to Regulate Work and Income (Introduction)', in J. Stanford and L. F. Vosko, eds., *Challenging the Market: The Struggle to Regulate Work and Income*. Montreal and Kingston: McGill-Queen's University Press, 3–32.

Stasiulis, D. K. and A. B. Bakan. (2005) *Negotiating Citizenship: Migrant Women in Canada and the Global System*. Toronto: University of Toronto Press.

Stewart, A. (1992) 'Atypical Employment and the Failure of Labour Law'. *Australian Bulletin of Labour* 18: 217–35.

—— (2002) 'Redefining Employment? Meeting the Challenge of Contract and Agency Labour'. *Australian Journal of Labour Law* 15(3): 235–76.

Stewart, M. L. (1989) *Women, Work and the French State: Labour Protection and Social Patriarchy, 1879–1919*. Montreal and Kingston: McGill-Queen's University Press.

Stone, K. V. W. (1995) 'Labor and the Global Economy: Four Approaches to Transnational Labor Regulation'. *Michigan Journal of International Law* 16: 987–1028.

—— (2001) 'The New Psychological Contract: Implications of the Changing Workplace for Labor and Employment Law'. *UCLA Law Review* 48(3): 519–662.

—— (2004) *From Widgets to Digits: Employment Regulation for the Changing Workplace*. Cambridge: Cambridge University Press.

Storrie, D. (2002) *Temporary Agency Work in the European Union*. Brussels: Office for Official Publications of the European Communities, Eurofound.

Strohmer, S. (2005) *Austria's Contribution to 'Temporary Agency Work in an Enlarged European Union'*. Brussels: EIRO.

Summers, C. (2000) 'Employment at Will in the United States: The Divine Right of Employers'. *University of Pennsylvania Journal of Labor and Employment Law* 3: 65–86.

Supiot, A. (2001) *Beyond Employment: Changes in Work and the Future of Labour Law in Europe*, trans. P. Meadows. Oxford: Oxford University Press.

—— M. Casas, J. de Munck, P. Hanau, A. Johansson, P. Meadows, E. Mingione, R. Salais, and P. van der Heijden (1999a) *Au-delà de l'emploi: Transformations du travail et devenir du droit du travail en Europe*. Rapport pour la Commission Europeénne. Paris: Flammarion.

—— —— P. Hanau, A. Johansson, P. Meadows, E. Mingione, R. Salais, and P. van der Heijden (1999b) 'A European Perspective on the Transformation of Work and the Future of Labor Law'. *Comparative Labor Law & Policy Journal* 20: 621–34.

Swepston, L. (1997) 'Supervision of ILO Standards'. *International Journal of Comparative Labour Law and Industrial Relations* 13(4): 327–44.

Swinnerton, K. A. and H. Wial (1995) 'Is Job Stability Declining in the US Economy?' *Industrial & Labor Relations Review* 48(2): 293–304.

Teeple, G. (1995) *Globalization and the Decline of Social Reform*. New Jersey: Humanities Press.

Tham, J. C. (2003) 'Legal Conceptions of Casual Employment', in P. Holland, ed., *The Proceedings of the 17th AIRAANZ Conference, Refereed Papers*. Melbourne: AIRAANZ (Association of Industrial Relations Academics of Australia and New Zealand).

—— (2004) 'The Scope of Australian Labour Law and the Regulatory Challenges Posed by Self and Casual Employment'. 2004 JILPT Comparative Labor Law Seminar, The Japan Institute for Labour Policy and Training.

Thomas, A. (1921) 'International Labour Organization: Its Origins, Development and Future'. *International Labour Review* 1(1): 5–22.

Thompson, E. P. (1967) 'Time, Work-Discipline and Industrial Capitalism'. *Past & Present* 38: 56–97.

Tilly, C. (1996) *Half a Job: Bad and Good Part-Time Jobs in a Changing Labor Market*. Philadelphia: Temple University Press.

Tiraboschi, M. and M. Del Conte (2004) 'Employment Contract: Disputes on Definition in the Changing Italian Labour Law'. Japan Institute for Labor Policy and

Training. At: <http://www.jil.go.jp/english/events_and_information/documents/clls04_delconte2.pdf>.

Toharia, L. and M. A. Malo (2000) 'The Spanish Experiment: Pros and Cons of the Flexibility at the Margin', in G. Esping-Andersen and M. Regini, eds., *Why Deregulate Labor Markets?* Oxford: Oxford University Press, 307–35.

Trubek, D. M. and J. Mosher (2001) 'New Governance, EU Employment Policy, and the European Social Model'. University of Wisconsin-Madison: Mountain or Molehill? A Critical Appraisal of the Commission White Paper on Governance, 10–12 May.

Trumper, R. and L. Wong (2007) 'Canada's Guest Workers: Racialized, Gendered, and Flexible', in S. Heir and B. Singh Bolaria, eds., *Race and Racism in 21st Century Canada*. Peterborough: Broadview, 151–73.

TUC (Trade Union Congress) UK (2006) 'European Parliament Plenary Vote on the Services Directive: Briefing for MEPs for EP Plenary Vote'. TUC, Feb.

—— (2007a) 'Agency Workers: Counting the Cost of Flexibility'. TUC, Equality and Employment Rights Department. At: <http://www.tuc.org.uk/extras/sectorreport.pdf>.

—— (2007b) 'Give Agency Workers Equal Rights from the First Say, says TUC'. At: <http://www.tuc.org.uk/equality/tuc-13938-f0.cfm>.

—— (2007c) 'Government Must End Discrimination against Temporary Workers and Crack Down on Rogue Recruitment Agencies, Says TUC'. At: <http://www.tuc.org.uk/equality/tuc-13841-f0.cfm>.

Tucker, E. (2005) '*Star* Wars: Newspaper Distribution Workers and the Possibilities and Limits of Collective Bargaining' in C. J. Cranford, J. Fudge, E. Tucker, and L. F. Vosko, eds., *Self-Employed Workers Organize*. Montreal and Kingston: McGill-Queen's University Press, 29–55.

UEAPME (European Association of Craft, Small and Medium-Sized Enterprises) (2007) 'UEAPME Position on the EC Green Paper "Modernising Labour Law to Meet the Challenges of the 21st Century"'. At: <www.ueapme.com/docs/pos_papers/2007/0703_pp_labour_law_green_paper_EN.pdf>.

UNICE (Union of Industrial and Employers' Confederations of Europe) (2002) UNICE Position Paper: Proposal for a Directive on Working Conditions for Temporary Workers (COM (2002) 149 final).

UNIEUROPA.(2008) 'A Step Forward for the Protection of Temporary Agency Workers in Europe'. 18 June. At: <http://www.union-network.org/unieuropan.nsf/EnByDate?OpenPage&Start40.2>.

Ursel, J. (1992) *Private Lives, Public Policy: 100 Years of State Intervention in the Family*. Toronto: Women's Press.

US Department of Labor (1999) *Futurework: Trends and Challenges for Work in the 21st Century*. Washington: US Department of Labour.

Vallée, G. (2005) *Towards Enhancing the Employment Conditions of Vulnerable Workers: A Public Policy Perspective*. Ottawa: Canadian Policy Research Networks.

van Voss, G. J. J. H. (1999) 'The "Tulip Model" and the New Legislation on Temporary Work in the Netherlands'. *International Journal of Comparative Labour Law and Industrial Relations* 15(4): 419–30.

Vogel, L. (1993) *Mothers on the Job: Maternity Policy in the US Workplace*. New Brunswick, NJ: Rutgers University Press.

Vosko, L. F. (1996) 'Irregular Workers, New Involuntary Social Exiles: Women and UI Reform', in J. Pulkingham and G. Ternowetsky, eds., *Remaking Canadian Social Policy: Social Security in the Late 1900s*. Toronto: Fernwood Publishing, 265–72.

—— (1997) 'Legitimizing the Triangular Employment Relationship: Emerging International Labour Standards from a Comparative Perspective'. *Comparative Labor Law & Policy Journal* 19: 43–78.

—— (1998) 'Regulating Precariousness? The Temporary Employment Relationship under the NAFTA and the EC Treaty'. *Relations Industrielles/Industrial Relations* 53 (1): 123–53.

—— (2000) *Temporary Work: The Gendered Rise of a Precarious Employment Relationship*. Toronto: University of Toronto Press.

—— (2002a) '"Decent Work": The Shifting Role of the ILO and the Struggle for Global Social Justice'. *Global Social Policy* 2(1): 1–25.

—— (2002b) 'Rethinking Feminization: Gendered Precariousness in the Canadian Labour Market and the Crisis in Social Reproduction'. Annual Robarts Lecture, John P. Robarts Centre for Canadian Studies. At: <http://www.genderwork.ca/modules/precarious/papers/vosko.2002.rethinking.pdf>.

—— (2003) 'Gender Differentiation and the Standard/Non-standard Employment Distinction: A Genealogy of Policy Intervention in Canada', in D. Juteau, ed., *Patterns and Processes of Social Differentiation: The Construction of Gender, Age, 'Race/Ethnicity' and Locality*. Toronto and Montreal: University of Toronto Press/University of Montreal Press, 25–80.

—— (2005) 'The Precarious Status of the Artist: Freelance Editors' Struggle for Collective Bargaining Rights', in C. J. Cranford, J. Fudge, E. Tucker, and L. F. Vosko, eds., *Self-Employed Workers Organize*. Montreal and Kingston: McGill-Queen's University Press, 136–70.

—— (2006a) 'Precarious Employment: Towards an Improved Understanding of Labour Market Insecurity', in Vosko, ed. (2006b), 3–39.

—— ed. (2006b) *Precarious Employment: Understanding Labour Market Insecurity in Canada*. Montreal and Kingston: McGill-Queen's University Press.

—— (2006c) 'Gender, Precarious Work and the International Labour Code: The Ghost in the Closet', in J. Fudge and R. Owens, eds., *Precarious Work, Women and the New Economy: The Challenge to Legal Norms*. Oxford: Hart Publishing, 53–75.

—— and L. Clark (2009) 'Gendered Precariousness and Social Reproduction in Canada', in L. F. Vosko, M. MacDonald, and I. Campbell, eds., *Gender and the Contours of Precarious Employment*. London and New York: Routledge, 26–42.

—— and N. Zukewich (2006) 'Precarious by Choice? Gender and Self-Employment', in Vosko, ed. (2006b), 67–89.

Vosko, L. F., N. Zukewich and C. Cranford (2003) 'Precarious Jobs: A New Typology of Employment', in *Perspectives on Labour and Income*. Ottawa: Statistics Canada.

Walby, S. (2000) 'Gender, Nations and States in a Global Era'. *Nations & Nationalisms* 6(4): 523–40.

Walker, J. A. (2008) 'Union Members in 2007: A Visual Essay'. *Monthly Labor Review*. Oct.: 28–39.

Wallace, J. (1983) 'Part-Time Work in Canada: Report of the Commission of Inquiry into Part-Time Work'. Ottawa: Labour Canada.

Walters, W. (2002) 'Deportation, Expulsion, and the International Police of Aliens'. *Citizenship Studies* 6(3): 265–92.

Waltman, J. (2000) *The Politics of Minimum Wage*. Chicago: University of Illinois Press.

Waring, P., M. Bray, and M. Barry (2006) *Evolving Employment Relations: Industry Studies from Australia*. Sydney: McGraw-Hill.

Watson, I. (2004) *Contented Casuals in Inferior Jobs? Reassessing Casual Employment in Australia*. Sydney: Australian Centre for Industrial Relations Research and Training.

Weiler, A. (2004) 'Annual Review of Working Conditions in the EU: 2003–2004'. Eurofound. At: <http://www.eurofound.europa.eu/ewco/reports/EU0406AR01/EU0406AR01.pdf>.

Weinkopf, C. (2006) 'A Changing Role for Temporary Agency Work in the German Employment Model?' *International Employment Relations Review* 12(1): 77–94.

Weir, A. (2005) 'The Global Universal Caregiver: Imagining Women's Liberation in the New Millennium'. *Constellations* 12(3): 308–30.

Weiss, M. (1999) 'The Framework Agreement on Fixed-Term Work: A German Point of View'. *International Journal of Comparative Labour Law & Industrial Relations* 15 (2): 97–104.

Whitworth, S. (1994) *Feminism and International Relations: Towards a Political Economy of Gender in Interstate and Non-governmental Institutions*. Basingstoke: Macmillan.

Wial, S. (1994) 'New Bargaining Structures for New Forms of Business Organization', in S. Friedman, R. W. Hurd, R. A. Oswald, and R. L. Seeber, eds., *Restoring the Promise of American Labor Law*. Ithaca, NY: ILR Press, 303–13.

Wikander, U. (1992) 'International Women's Congresses, 1878–1914: The Controversy over Equality and Special Labour Legislation', in M. L. Eduards, I. Elgqvist-Saltzman, E. Lundgren, C. Sjoblad, E. Sundin, and U. Wikander, eds., *Rethinking Change: Current Swedish Feminist Research*. Uppsala: Humanistisk-samhallsvetenskapliga forskningsradet, 11–36.

——(1995) 'Some Kept the Demand of Feminist Flags Waving: Debates at International Congresses on Protecting Women Workers', in U. Wikander, A. Kessler-Harris, and J. Lewis, eds., *Protecting Women: Labour Legislation in Europe, United States and Australia, 1880–1920*. Urbana, IL: University of Illinois, 29–62.

Wikander, U., A. Kessler-Harris, and J. Lewis, eds. (1995) *Protecting Women: Labor Legislation in Europe, the United States, and Australia, 1880–1920*. Urbana, IL: University of Illinois.

Williams, F. (1995) 'Race/Ethnicity, Gender, and Class in Welfare States: A Framework for Comparative Analysis'. *Social Politics* 2(2): 127–59.

Williams, R. (1983) *Keywords: A Vocabulary of Culture and Society*. Glasgow: Fontana Press.

Wimmer, A. and N. Glick Schiller (2002) 'Methodological Nationalism and Beyond: Nation-State Building, Migration and the Social Sciences'. *Global Networks* 2(4): 301–34.

Winchester, D. (2005) *United Kingdom's Contribution to 'Temporary Agency Work in an Enlarged European Union'*. Brussels: EIRO.

Wittig, M. (1980) 'The Straight Mind'. *Feminist Issues* 1(1): 103–11.

Women's Electoral Lobby Australia and National Pay Equity Coalition (2006) 'Submission to Australian Fair Pay Commission'. Women's Electoral Lobby Australia Inc.

Woolfson, C. and J. Sommers (2006) 'Labour Mobility in Construction: European Implications of the Laval un Partneri Dispute with Swedish Labour'. *European Journal of Industrial Relations* 12(1): 49–68.

Wroblewski, A. and C. Wallace (2006) 'Temporary Agency Work—National Reports: Austria'. Eurofound. At: <http://www.eurofound.europa.eu/pubdocs/2002/22/en/1/ef0222en.pdf>.

Yeatman, A. (1994) *Postmodern Revisionings of the Political*. New York and London: Routledge.

Yerkes, M. and J. Visser (2006) 'Women's Preferences or Delineated Policies? The Development of Part-Time Work in the Netherlands, Germany and the United Kingdom', in J.-Y. Boulin, M. Lallement, J. C. Messenger, and F. Michon, eds., *Decent Working Time: New Trends, New Issues*. Geneva: ILO, 235–61.

Zaal, I. (2005) *The Netherlands' Contribution to 'Temporary Agency Work in an Enlarged European Union'*. Brussels: EIRO.

Index

Index